THE BRITISH BOOK TRADE
From Caxton to the Present Day

Two views of Stationers' Hall from Almanacks *published by the Stationers' Company in 1781 and 1803. The Stationers' Company (see pp. 160 ff.) kept a register in which all books printed by members were entered before publication and the Copyright Act of 1842 enacted the statutory requirement to register at Stationers' Hall as a preliminary condition to an action for infringement of copyright. The Act of 1911 removed from the company the statutory responsibility it had exercised for some 350 years, but the register continues to provide a record of voluntary entries to assist in the proof of copyright, and 'Registered at Stationers' Hall' has replaced the once familiar words 'Entered at Stationers' Hall'*

Robin Myers

THE BRITISH
BOOK TRADE

From Caxton to the Present Day

*A Bibliographical Guide based on the Libraries of
the National Book League and St Bride Institute*

A GRAFTON BOOK
ANDRE DEUTSCH
in association with the National Book League

By the same author
A Dictionary of Literature in the English Language
Chaucer to 1940 (1970)

First published 1973 by
André Deutsch Limited
105 Great Russell Street London WC1

Printed in Great Britain by
Alden & Mowbray Ltd
at the Alden Press, Oxford

ISBN 0 233 96353 7

CONTENTS

LIST OF ILLUSTRATIONS

ACKNOWLEDGEMENTS

I am indebted to many for help and encouragement. The inadequacies, which remain my own, would have been greater but for those listed below. Above all I am grateful to James Moran who read the entire manuscript both in draft and final form, and whose optimism and willingness to discuss points helped to carry it to completion. Others who were generous of time and advice were:

James Barnes who drew on his store of knowledge of copyright history to assist me with section VIII. LAW RELATING TO THE BOOK TRADE;

Victor Bonham-Carter who read section I on AUTHORSHIP and gave valuable information particularly on 'The Society of Authors' and 'Public Lending Right';

Gavin Bridson who put the manuscript of his own bibliography at my disposal;

Eileen Colwell who read and commented on section VII. CHILDREN'S BOOKS;

Colin Franklin who gave help on section XII. PRIVATE PRESSES;

The late Frank Grunfeld who advised on X. PAPER FOR BOOKWORK;

Grace Hogarth who made suggestions on VII. CHILDREN'S BOOKS;

Ruari McLean who read sections IV, V and XI on BOOK DESIGN, BOOK ILLUSTRATION and THE PRINTING OF BOOKS twice and provided many references;

Bernard Middleton who read the draft of section II on BOOKBINDING and showed me early manuals and journals in his own collection that could not have been seen elsewhere;

James Mosley who gave specific help on section XI. THE PRINTING OF BOOKS and general advice and encouragement throughout the later stages of the work;

Winifred Myers who offered friendly comment on section IIIC. ANTI-QUARIAN BOOKSELLING;

Anne and Fernand G. Renier whose critical suggestions on section VII on CHILDREN'S BOOKS are incorporated, and who showed me items from their collection that I would not otherwise have seen;

C. H. Rolph who considered the draft of 'Censorship and Libel' in section VIII. LAW RELATING TO THE BOOK TRADE;

W. B. Stevenson who read sections III, VI and XIII on BOOKSELLING, HISTORY OF THE BOOK TRADE and PUBLISHING making his customary meticulous comments and who did the index;

Ben Weinreb whose critical acumen led to a reorganisation of section III. BOOKSELLING;

Berthold Wolpe, the last to be mentioned, but never the least, who gave an unstinting amount of time and thought to criticising sections V and XI on BOOK ILLUSTRATION and THE PRINTING OF BOOKS.

PREFACE

This book consists of a classified and annotated selection of works indicating the way in which the book trade evolved, with an historical bias which reflects that of the libraries on which it has been based. I took the invention of printing from movable type in Europe as a starting point, although trading in books goes back at least to the fifth century B.C. The contents are limited to organised commerce in books, excluding the non-commercial book world such as libraries and librarianship, which have been, in any case, adequately covered elsewhere, and other forms of printed communication – principally the vast field of newspapers and journalism.

As the work was chiefly intended for British booksellers, collectors, librarians, printers and publishers I thought that there would be no difficulty in keeping within the geographical and national bounds of Britain. But in bibliography one thing leads to another, and a too rigid adherence to self-imposed limits sometimes produces a false result. Compromise was inevitable; in describing British copyright, mention of international and American had to be made; in bookbinding, France has always overshadowed the rest of Europe including Britain; while printing history could not ignore Gutenberg. I drew my line here and there, and to others who would have drawn it at other points and argued with equal cogency for their decision, my distinctions will, at times, seem arbitrary. Journalism, mainly excluded, cannot be so in any account of censorship and libel; antiquarian bookselling spills over into the fields of uncommercial book collecting and even of descriptive bibliography. But if book collecting is admitted, why not, some will ask, autograph dealing and print-selling? Typography is included, so why not calligraphy, as showing the origin of letter forms? Why not stray (and it was hard not to), from book papers and papermaking, into the area of non-book papers, or from book-printing, into the cognate fields of jobbing, ephemeral printing and display work? Some limitations were imposed by lack of materials; no books exist on such relevant topics as sponsored publishing.

I made a choice on what may seem to be mutually exclusive grounds: titles were either well known and available, or they were key works in their day but not easily referred to outside the libraries from which I worked, mainly those of the National Book League and the St Bride

Institute. The N.B.L. collection consists of some 8,500 books and periodicals covering all aspects of the book trade. Its stock grew from a nucleus of some two hundred volumes donated in 1929 as the foundation of a reference library for dealing with queries about and by the trade. The St Bride Printing Library possesses a greater number of rarities and early books, more specifically on printing, but fewer on publishing and bookselling. Also consulted were the London College of Printing library of technical printing literature, and the special collection on bookselling and publishing, as well as the law library, of the London School of Economics.

Only works in book form are listed; periodical articles, with a few exceptions inadvertent or perverse, are not. I took this decision advisedly for a detailed guide to periodical literature would have bulked out a single volume work to unmanageable proportions. I realise the importance of periodical publications, often all there is, in technical and industrial areas where the scene changes rapidly, and in bibliographical studies. Therefore each section is appended by a list of relevant periodicals and trade journals which I hope will provide a fair guide to sources.

'Every system of classification is open to objections; but it is hoped that the one adopted will best facilitate reference to any book required.' Thus wrote Bigmore and Wyman in the *Dictionary of Printing* and I found that no laid-down scheme provided a complete solution, though several were tried. The Dewey and the Universal Decimal Classification are widely used and understood, but either would have entailed major reorganisation of material collected from the National Book League which uses a modified Bliss classification. Starting with this, I soon found that further modification was necessary in the working, since some sections of the library stock were telescoped while others were dispersed and absorbed here and there. Many titles would fit just as well into two or three places, and even whole sections overlapped at points. 'Preservation', for example, might be thought of as part of x. PAPER FOR BOOKWORK or of II. BOOKBINDING (I settled for BOOKBINDING where I could include leather preservation); publishing and bookselling were often one and the same until well into the nineteenth century. I placed entries where judgement seemed to dictate, discarding the idea of duplicating under different heads as this wastes space, and some readers find it more confusing than helpful. The way is signposted by an inordinate number of cross references, and divisional titles giving the contents of each section, while a comprehensive author-title index gives a final clue.

The main sections follow in alphabetical order, subsections in a progression dictated by the nature of the material, not identically arranged throughout, but on a similar pattern. Thus, book sections generally precede those of periodicals and or trade organisations, but in the case of section XI. THE PRINTING OF BOOKS it seemed better to place histories of trades unions immediately after the list of those organisations.

The bibliographical data for each entry consist of: author or editor, title, subtitle usually in full, first and latest revised edition or reprint of an early work, publisher wherever possible, place of publication other than London, date, mention of illustrations, bibliography, glossary of terms and other special features. Whenever they could be found, I have given the dates of birth and death of individuals, and of the founding of firms. Since many eluded my search, I had to decide between excluding all for the sake of symmetry or, as I have finally done, giving what I could though the results will seem haphazard. Comment on books listed is either brief summary or critical assessment except that, where the title is self-explanatory, and I had nothing worth while to add, there is none.

Reprint publishing of out-of-print standard works now accelerates so overwhelmingly that I should have been engaged in continual revision and the work indefinitely delayed, if I had tried to make a complete record of such reprints. Nevertheless, something may be useful, and thus I have given a random selection of those that came to my notice during the course of compilation and while the book was still in proof.

I believe the present work fills a gap. The published catalogues of the National Book League, St Bride's (both out of date on accessions and long out of print), the London School of Economics, and the relevant portions of the Manchester Public Library, together with the sections on book production in the various volumes of the *Cambridge Bibliography of English Literature*, offer full lists of books on the book trade, but no guidance on them. My work is a kind of bibliographical outline of the trade's history and workings, not a select library catalogue. Percy Freer's *Bibliography and Modern Book Production* was, I think, the only real parallel, but it covered different ground, is out of print and out of date, and was designed specifically as a textbook for South African library students.

The work took much longer to compile than was originally intended, and might have been indefinitely extended and improved. A halt had to be called at last, and I shall be grateful to users for suggestions and corrections towards a possible revised edition.

I conclude by quoting Bigmore and Wyman's apology:

'Had the compilers realised at the outset half that their task might demand of them, they would never have had the courage to attempt it; but they were stimulated by a belief in and experience of its usefulness, and their enthusiasm was sustained by the encouragement of those whose judgement they knew was entitled to respect.'

ROBIN MYERS
April 1972

AUTHORSHIP

(Excluding journalism, literary biography, authors' memoirs, and books on style.) (See also 'Copyright', pp. 203 ff, III. BOOKSELLING, and XIII. PUBLISHING.)

'*The Copying Press*' *illustration by Gustave Doré for the table of contents to Balzac's* Droll Stories (*actual size*)

1. Introduction

Authorship differs from other professions in being traditionally a spare-time occupation for which there is no regular training or apprenticeship. The profession of letters was either a hobby for gentlemen or needed a patron's support until the reading public grew large enough in the eighteenth century to take over the patron's role. The tradition of the amateur status of authors died hard and led to greater differences of outlook than generally exist between producer and supplier. The author felt strongly that he was the supplier of the raw material without which there would be no book trade. The publisher, on the other hand, at times felt that he was depending for his source of supply on a bunch of unpredictable amateurs without business principles. For which reason much of the history of authorship is the history of grievances.

Walter Besant, in *The Pen and the Book*, offered cynical advice on dealing with publishers:

Remember that a publisher is a man of business, who makes money by selling books. He is, therefore, moved by no enthusiasms for literature but simply by the consideration of what will pay. Meet him as one business man should meet another with the wholesome suspicion based on experience that he will 'best' you if he can.

The founding of the Society of Authors in 1884, and of the Publishers Association in 1895 have helped to put author–publisher relations on a more professional footing where each side can recognise that he has both rights and obligations. John Winton in his paper on 'Writing For Keeps' in *The Writer in the Market Place* writes as a satisfied supplier to the trade:

My publishers pay up on time, give me consistently good advice, and keep my books in print. Honestly, I don't think a writer can ask for more of his publishers than that. It is likely – more likely than not – that a writer and his publisher become personal friends . . . but I think a writer can save himself a lot of heartache if he remembers that his publisher is basically a man of business . . . And it works both ways. A writer is entitled to expect his publisher to pay his royalties due on time, to make a decent job of producing and publicising his book . . . but the publisher equally has the right to expect the writer to deliver his typescript on the day he said he would, to correct his proofs as he promised he would, and not knowingly submit material which is libellous or pirated from someone else.

2. History of Authorship (Chronological)

(See also under XIIIA. THE HISTORY OF PUBLISHING and VI. HISTORY OF THE BOOK TRADE, pp. 162ff.)

George Haven Putnam, AUTHORS AND THEIR PUBLIC IN ANCIENT TIMES: *A Sketch of Literary Conditions and of the Relations with the Public of Literary Producers, from the Earliest Times to the Fall of the Roman Empire,* 1st edition, 1893, 3rd edition, George Putnam's Sons, New York and London, Knickerbocker Press, 1923.

The author, founder of the American house of George Putnam's Sons, traces the beginnings of authorship in Greece, Alexandria, Rome, Constantinople and the Far East, 'the methods of the production and distribution of literature, and the nature of the relations between the authors and their readers' and discourses on book terminology in classical times.

George Haven Putnam, BOOKS AND THEIR MAKERS DURING THE MIDDLE AGES, George Putnam's Sons, 1896.

This covers some of the same ground.

Phoebe Sheavyn, THE LITERARY PROFESSION IN THE ELIZABETHAN AGE, English Series 1, Manchester, at the University Press, 1909.

This is an expanded version of papers originally published in *The Library.* The author deals with writers' relations with patrons, with official censors, with publishers, the theatre, authors and supplementary means of livelihood, personal relations among authors, authors and readers in the period 1558–1603.

H. S. Bennett, ENGLISH BOOKS AND READERS 1558–1603: *Being a Study in the History of the Book Trade in the Reign of Elizabeth I,* C.U.P., 1965.

Chapter 2, *Patronage,* is relevant to the subject of authorship history.

H. S. Bennett, ENGLISH BOOKS AND READERS 1603–1640: *Being a Study in the History of the Book Trade in the Reigns of James I and Charles I,* C.U.P., 1970.

This completes H. S. Bennett's study of printed books and readers from Caxton to the Civil War, a period when 'faith in the printed word spread rapidly and enthusiastically like a new religion' so that the early seventeenth century must be accounted 'a key-period in a past epoch' (Philip Edwards reviewing in *The Library*).

Percy Simpson, PROOF READING IN THE SIXTEENTH, SEVENTEENTH, AND EIGHTEENTH CENTURIES, O.U.P., 1935, new reprint, with a foreword by Harry Carter, 1970 (illustrated).

The author throws light on printer–author relations and the work finds a place here rather than under XI. THE PRINTING OF BOOKS. The book was the outcome of lectures on textual criticism to advanced students of the Oxford English school. The first two chapters appeared as papers in the *Oxford Bibliographical Society Proceedings*, 1927.

The reprint also includes the review by R. B. McKerrow of the original edition and critical notes on some passages of the book.

A. S. Collins, AUTHORSHIP IN THE DAYS OF JOHNSON: *Being a Study of the Relation between Author, Patron, Publisher and Public 1726–1780*, Robert Holden, 1927.

Much of the matter relates to copyright and to publishing and bookselling history seen from the author's angle. The theme is the decline of patronage and the growth of the reading public. Four chapters deal with author and bookseller (the effect of copyright security and the lapse of patronage, Grub Street, personal relations between author and bookseller, the advance from 1726–80), the copyright struggle (the 1710 act and the question of perpetual copyright), author and patron (the gradual decline of patronage), the growth of the public after 1750, James Lackington (see under III. BOOKSELLING, p. 62), popular reprints and the play-going public.

J. W. Saunders, THE PROFESSION OF ENGLISH LETTERS: *Studies in Social History*, Routledge & Kegan Paul, London, and University of Toronto Press, Toronto, 1964 (bibliography arranged by chapters).

The author's approach is sociological, tracing the evolution of the literary profession from Chaucer to the mass markets of the present age, the attitude of the major English writers to their public and their place in society. He is less concerned with trade matters than are Sheavyn and Collins, who deal with relations with publishers, finance, book production and the like.

G. H. & J. B. Putnam, AUTHORS AND PUBLISHERS, 1897.

Part 2 informs on authorship in the second half of the century (see under 'The Business Side of Authorship', p. 14 below).

Frederick H. Hitchcock, THE BUILDING OF A BOOK, 1906.

George W. Cable's article on *The Author*, Francis W. Halsey on *The*

Literary Adviser and Walter Littlefield on *Reviewing and Criticising* give insight into the state of authorship at the beginning of the century.

3. Authors on Authorship

I select:

ANONYMOUS (1840)

THE PERILS OF AUTHORSHIP: *An Enquiry into the Difficulties of Literature: Containing Copious Instructions for Publishing Books at the Slightest Possible Risk* ... by an old and popular author, 1840.

Together with:
THE AUTHOR'S ADVOCATE AND YOUNG PUBLISHER'S FRIEND, 1840.

An early and entertaining guide to authorship gives cynical warning: 'Reader! Art thou an author? If not, dost thou aspire to be an author? Have a care, should such be the case, what thou art about; for the difficulties of authorship are many.'

ARNOLD BENNETT (1867–1931)

Arnold Bennett, HOW TO BECOME AN AUTHOR: *A Practical Guide*, Literary Correspondence College, 1903 (list of proof marks).

Advice is offered on the formation of style, the writing of fiction and non-fiction and the business side of authorship.

Arnold Bennett, THE AUTHOR'S CRAFT, Hodder & Stoughton, 1915. This offers less specialist advice.

WALTER BESANT (1836–1901)

Walter Besant, AUTOBIOGRAPHY, Hutchinson, 1902.

This includes a chapter on the Society of Authors. (See under 'The Society of Authors', p. 18 below, for Besant's other writings on authorship.)

ISAAC D'ISRAELI (1776–1848)

Isaac D'Israeli, CALAMITIES OF AUTHORS: *Including Some Inquiries Respecting Their Moral and Literary Characters,* 2 vols., 1812.

Isaac D'Israeli, CURIOSITIES OF LITERATURE, *Consisting of Anecdotes, Characters, Sketches and Observations, Literary, Critical and Historical,* vols. 1 and 2, 1791–3, vol. 3, 1817.

Isaac D'Israeli, QUARRELS OF AUTHORS, *Or Some Memoirs of Our Literary History,* 3 vols., 1814.

These are the first works to describe in detail the plight of the professional writer.

ANTHONY C. DEANE

Anthony C. Deane, TIME REMEMBERED, Faber & Faber, 1945.

Reminiscences of authorship in the 1920s, and of the Society of Authors and the Authors' Club are contained in this personal memoir.

MICHAEL SADLEIR (1888–1957) (see p. 90 below)

Michael Sadleir, AUTHORS AND PUBLISHERS, Dent, 1932.

FRANK SWINNERTON (1884–   )

Frank Swinnerton, AUTHORS AND THE BOOKTRADE, Gerald Howe, 1932.

Personal reminiscence is mixed with information on the work of publishers' readers, literary agents, authors and advertising reviewers.

H. G. WELLS (1866–1946)

H. G. Wells, THE PROBLEM OF THE TROUBLESOME COLLABORATOR, privately printed, George Allen & Unwin, 1930.

A highly partisan account of the author's quarrel with H. P. Vowles.

H. G. Wells, SETTLEMENT OF THE TROUBLE BETWEEN MR. THRING AND MR. WELLS, *A Footnote to the Problem of the Troublesome Collaborator,* George Allen & Unwin, 1930.

Lord Gorell, ONE MAN, MANY PARTS, Odhams, 1956.

This describes the whole affair, a dramatic episode in the history of the Society of Authors and of authorship.

4. Literary Agents

Curtis Brown, CONTRACTS, Cassell, 1935.

Reminiscences of authors are interspersed with information on the work of the literary agent, though much less than could be hoped from one of the pioneers in that field who started his agency in 1905.

James Hepburn, THE AUTHOR'S EMPTY PURSE, *and the Rise of the Literary Agent*, O.U.P., 1968 (extensive bibliography on the condition of authorship).

This is brief yet exhaustive, describing the historical background, the precursors of the true agents, the early agents such as A. P. Watt, and the Pinker and Curtis Brown agency in America, and the 'complaining author today'.

Elisabeth Marbury, MY CRYSTAL BALL, Boni & Liveright, New York, 1923.

This is the memoir of 'the first notable agent on the American scene' (Hepburn).

The following contain chapters or sections on literary agents:

Walter Besant, THE PEN AND THE BOOK (see under 'Authorship Manuals', p. 10 below): chapter 2.

Charles Campbell, THE BUSINESS SIDE OF AUTHORSHIP (see under 'The Business Side of Authorship', p. 14 below).

William Heinemann, THE HARDSHIPS OF PUBLISHING (see under XIIIA. THE HISTORY OF PUBLISHING, p. 340).

The founder of the publishing house was a bitter adversary of literary agents.

Frederick H. Hitchcock, editor, THE BUILDING OF A BOOK (see under III. BOOKSELLING, p. 59).

Paul R. Reynolds contributes an article on *The Literary Agent*, in which he recommends several British publishing houses to American authors of his day.

Michael Sissons, *The Author and the Literary Agent* in THE WRITER IN THE MARKET PLACE (see under 'The Business Side of Authorship', p. 14 below).

Frank Swinnerton, AUTHORS AND THE BOOKTRADE (see under 'Authors on Authorship', p. 7 above).

Lists of Agents

Cassell's, DIRECTORY OF PUBLISHING (see under XIII. PUBLISHING, p. 370).

A. & C. Black, THE WRITERS' AND ARTISTS' YEARBOOK (see under 'Authorship Manuals', p. 10 below).

This contains a comprehensive list of agents and their specialities.

5. Authorship Manuals

A. *Historic Authorship Manuals (chronological)*

Saunders & Otley, THE AUTHOR'S PRINTING AND PUBLISHING ASSISTANT, *Comprising Explanations of the Process of Printing Preparation and Calculation of Manuscripts, Choice of Paper, Type, Binding, Illustrations, Publishing Advertising etc., with an Exemplification and Description of the Typographical Marks Used in the Correction of the Press,* 1st edition, 1839, 3rd edition, 1840.

Edward Bull, HINTS AND DIRECTIONS FOR AUTHORS IN WRITING AND PUBLISHING THEIR WORKS, Edward Bull, 1842.

This relates the early history of printing, offers rules for writing manuscripts (before the era of the typewriter), the best method of correcting or altering manuscripts, punctuation, remarks on the trade, advertising, easy rules for calculating how many pages of print a manuscript will make, how to correct proofs and the rapidity with which the work can be printed – here those accustomed to the marvels of the technological age are left gasping: 'If speed is particularly required, and if the author is living at a distance . . . and confides the correction of his proofs to his publishers, two or three volumes may at any time be got ready for delivery within a week or nine days. . . . The ordinary rate of print is about one octavo volume of three hundred pages and twenty-six lines in a page, in twelve days. At this rate, a novel, or any other light work in three volumes will be complete in thirty-six days. A pamphlet or short essay, bearing upon a political or any other topic of the day, may be printed and got ready for delivery within the space of twenty-four hours, at a trifling additional expense for nightwork, etc.'

G. H. & J. B. Putnam, AUTHORS AND PUBLISHERS (see under 'The Business Side of Authorship', p. 14 below).

Part 1 is, in effect, a manual of authorship.

Walter Besant, THE PEN AND THE BOOK, Thomas Burleigh, 1899.

This is a guide to writing, production costs, the choice of a publisher and copyright. A copy of the prospectus of the Society of Authors is appended.

B. *Modern Authorship Manuals*

Kathleen Betterton, TEACH YOURSELF TO WRITE, E.U.P., 1942.

This deals with different classes of writing such as historical fiction, detective fiction and writing for children, and, in a second part, the writer and the press, the writer and the publisher.
The *Teach Yourself* books are useful for exercises and bibliographies but they are fairly elementary.

A. & C. Black, THE WRITERS' AND ARTISTS' YEARBOOK: *a Directory for Writers, Artists, Playwrights, Writers for Film, Radio and Television, Photographers and Composers*, A. & C. Black, annual since 1907.

This essential reference work for practising authors lists British, American and Commonwealth journals, publishers, agencies and societies, news and press agencies, prizes and awards, special markets. A reference section includes information on copyright and subsidiary rights, indexing, translation, libel, income tax liability, typewriting services and much besides.

Frank Candlin, TEACH YOURSELF FREE-LANCE WRITING, E.U.P., 1951.

This has a chapter on copyright, libel, and markets, but is otherwise more concerned with journalism than book writing.

William Freeman, WRITING FOR PLEASURE AND PROFIT, E.U.P., 1959.

This too is more concerned with journalism.
    Several of the correspondence courses for aspiring writers, such as that of the London School of Journalism, produce booklets for the use of students on their courses which give business and literary advice.

THE LITERARY GENTLEMAN.

'The Literary Gentleman', from Punch's Valentines, *1842*

Michael Legate, DEAR AUTHOR ... *Letters from a Working Publisher to Authors, Prospective and Practised*, Pelham Books, 1972 (glossary of terms, index of subject matter).

Eighty-one very readable letters from a publisher of fiction to imagined authors covering commissions, contracts, royalties, rights, housestyle and such like. The author, who is editorial director of Corgi Books, writes more for the prospective than the practised author who will already know most of what is said.

Edward D. Seeber, A STYLE MANUAL FOR AUTHORS, Indiana University Press, Bloomington, 1965 (see also under 'The Preparation of Manuscripts and Correction of Proofs', below).

A surprising quantity of information is given in this booklet which explains and illustrates acceptable principles for the preparation of manuscripts, style, proof reading, etc. It also gives general suggestions on the number of copies needed, instruction on typography, mailing the manuscript, the type of paper to use, width of margin, the accepted practice in laying out preface, sub-titles, foreign words and phrases, footnotes, bibliographies, etc. Specimen pages are appended and the author is advised on presentation.

6. The Preparation of Manuscripts and Correction of Proofs

(See also under XI. THE PRINTING OF BOOKS, pp. 299f.)

British proof correcting marks are set out in almost every authorship manual and many of the works listed under 'Authorship Manuals' and elsewhere contain chapters on the preparation of manuscripts, details of recommended paper sizes, spacing, and so forth. The information given in Seeber (see above) is perhaps more useful to the inexperienced author than that contained in the pamphlets mentioned below but pamphlets are handier for quick reference.

British Standards 1219C: 1945, TABLE OF SYMBOLS FOR PRINTERS' AND CAMBRIDGE AUTHORS' PROOF CORRECTIONS.

Seventy-three marks recommended as standard British symbols are listed, together with codes of practice for the preparation of copy for the printer and four examples of different types of copy marked up and corrected on adjacent pages.

Among publishers who produce guides for their authors, I list, THE
CAMBRIDGE AUTHORS' AND PRINTERS' GUIDES. These include:

M. D. Anderson, BOOK INDEXING, 1971.
P. G. Burbidge, NOTES AND REFERENCES, 1952.
P. G. Burbidge, PRELIMS AND END-PAGES, 1963.
C. V. Carey, MAKING AN INDEX, 1951, 3rd edition, 1963.
Superseded by Anderson, *Book Indexing* (see above), but Carey's work is
better.
C. V. Carey, with an appendix by P. G. Burbidge, PUNCTUATION, 1957.
Brooke Crutchley, THE PREPARATION OF MANUSCRIPTS AND THE CORREC-
TION OF PROOFS, 1951, 2nd edition, 1964.
This lists fewer marks than the British Standard but quite enough to work
with. There is a useful introduction on make-up, illustrations and cross-
references.

McGraw-Hill, THE MCGRAW-HILL AUTHOR'S BOOK, 1955 (illustrated,
glossary).

This is much more substantial than the manuals put out by other publishers. Though it is intended as a guide to American publishing practice
it is just as useful for authors publishing in this country.

PERGAMON MANUAL FOR SCIENTIFIC TRANSLATORS, Pergamon Press,
Oxford, 1964.
This gives the Continental marks (pp. 34–8).

John Wiley, AUTHOR'S GUIDE FOR PREPARING MANUSCRIPT AND HANDLING
PROOF, John Wiley, New York, and Chapman & Hall, London, 1950,
3rd edition, revised, with an appendix on offset, 1960.

An author's introduction to production explains the author's part in
preparing manuscripts and illustrations for the publisher and for the
printer, how to check the engraver's proof, how to proof read and complete production.

7. The Business Side of Authorship: Royalties, Contracts, Rights

(See also under 'Authorship Manuals', pp. 10f. above; 'The Preparation
of Manuscripts', above, and 'Copyright' under VIII. LAW RELATING TO THE
BOOK TRADE, pp. 203ff.)

Publishers' memoirs and house histories give a great deal of information on the remuneration that authors received in the past. Some make wistful reading for the modern author, who learns that Lord Lytton was paid £20,000 by George Routledge for the right to publish eleven novels in the Routledge Railway Library, besides other sums nearly as vast when the enterprise proved successful (F. A. Mumby, *The House of Routledge*, see p. 347 below.)

Ray Astbury, editor, THE WRITER IN THE MARKET PLACE, Clive Bingley, 1969.

A conference in Liverpool in 1968 on the commercial situation of the writer today is the basis of this symposium by a bookseller, a publisher, a literary agent, a librarian and several authors.

Australian Society of Authors, A GUIDE TO BOOK CONTRACTS, Australian Society of Authors, Sydney, 1967.

This sets out the form of the book contract, and clear instructions regarding contractual obligations on illustrations, the delivery of the manuscript, copyright infringement, scale of royalties, subsidiary rights, option on future work, general legal formalities and much besides.

Charles Campbell, THE BUSINESS SIDE OF AUTHORSHIP (Boardman New Writers' Guides), Boardman, London and New York, 1965.

Writers are advised on selecting a market, literary agents, libel and copyright as well as on presentation of work.

Publishers Association, A GUIDE TO ROYALTY AGREEMENTS, prepared by the Agreements Committee of the Publishers Association, Publishers Association, 1959.

There are twenty-four sections each with examples and comments, appendixes on sales of translation rights, sheet sales, British publishers' traditional markets, 'fair dealing' and short passages.

G. H. & J. B. Putnam, AUTHORS AND PUBLISHERS, *A Manual of Suggestions for Beginners in Literature*, 7th edition, rewritten with additional material, George Putnam's Sons, New York and London, 1897.

The substantial first part of this work is entirely concerned with publishing agreements, royalties, the half-profit system, books published at the author's expense, copyright, authors' associations, and literary agents. Part 2 is an authorship manual.

James Spedding, PUBLISHERS AND AUTHORS, printed for the author, John Russell Smith, 1867.

Details of financial arrangements between publisher and author are followed by a postscript on publishers and bookbuyers.

G. Herbert Thring, THE MARKETING OF LITERARY PROPERTY, *With a Letter to the Author from Bernard Shaw on Book and Serial Rights,* Constable, 1933.

A clear account of copyright agreements, future book clauses, special clauses, serial rights, agents and much else still has some relevance, though times have changed.

8. Public Lending Right

With the demise of the circulating libraries, free lending has increased over the years until it has reached 6,000,000 volumes annually, and yet the author can no longer earn a living by book writing alone. P.L.R. was suggested as a means of remedying this unequal situation by granting British authors royalty payments on the use of their books in public libraries analogous with the performing rights on music and drama. The proposal was first put forward by the Society of Authors in 1951 but was long opposed by the Library Association largely on the grounds that it violated the principle of a free library service and was too difficult to administer. Various methods of financing the scheme were proposed but for many years none was found acceptable, until, in 1967, the Society of Authors, the Publishers Association and the Arts Council jointly suggested a plan in which the cost would be borne by the Government, thus leaving intact the principle of 'free' public libraries, and this has formed the basis of present negotiations culminating in a bill which it is hoped will shortly be put through Parliament.

Most of the writing on the subject of P.L.R. is to be found in the press – the *Bookseller* and *The Times* have printed letters from authors, publishers, and librarians, while *The Times Saturday Review* published an article on February 15, 1969. It has also been the subject of several debates in Parliament.

Arts Council of Great Britain, THE ARTS COUNCIL, 1968.

This leaflet summarises the plan which the Council prepared for the Minister of Education and Science.

Richard Findlater, editor, PUBLIC LENDING RIGHT: *A Matter of Justice,* André Deutsch and Penguin Books, 1971 (appendix gives Arts Council Proposals, 1967).

Lord Goodman, chairman of the Arts Council, introduces this symposium by ten eminent members of the world of books. Victor Bonham-Carter delineates the background to P.L.R., and Raymond Astbury the history of libraries since 1850; Richard Findlater gives some of the facts about *The Wages of Writing* while two authors, Angus Wilson and John Fowles, appeal against the authors' exploitation; Hilary Rubinstein puts the view of the literary agent, Jack Dove that of the public librarian and Peter du Sautoy that of the publisher; K. C. Harrison outlines the scheme operating in Scandinavia while Michael Freegard draws the parallel with musical performing rights.

A. P. Herbert, PUBLIC LENDING RIGHT, *A Preliminary Memorandum Humbly Submitted to the Society of Authors,* S.o.A., March 1960.

This includes a draft of a P.L.R. bill and five other appendices.

A. P. Herbert, LIBRARIES FREE-FOR-ALL ... *An Appeal to Parliament from Authors and Publishers,* Institute of Economic Affairs, 1962 (illustrated).

This booklet, published as Hobart Paper no. 19, proposed that public libraries be permitted to make an annual charge of 7s. 6d. per registered reader, the income to be used to improve the library service and to finance P.L.R.

Library Association, THE LIBRARY ASSOCIATION'S CASE AGAINST THE LIBRARIES (PUBLIC LENDING RIGHT) BILL, November 1960.

S.o.A., PUBLIC LENDING RIGHT, *A Short History,* Society of Authors bulletin no. 3, 1967 (see below).

S.o.A., YOUR POCKET BRIEF FOR P.L.R., Society of Authors, 1968.

This is a four-page summary of the P.L.R. proposals and arguments.

J. A. White, *Public Lending Right,* article in THE WRITER IN THE MARKET PLACE, see p. 14.

This analyses the Swedish, Danish and proposed British schemes and sets out the advantages and disadvantages of each.

9. The Society of Authors

The Society was founded by Sir Walter Besant in 1884 and aimed at furthering the establishment of international copyright, defining principles of agreements between authors and publishers, advising authors on 'good' publishers and advising young authors on the worth of their manuscripts. Some of these aims have been achieved; international copyright, for example, is now accepted as a principle; others were dropped as proving impracticable – it became an impossible task to advise young authors on the worth of their manuscripts, for example, a role that was gradually taken over by the literary agent. The distinction between 'good' and 'bad' publishers is no longer felt to apply in these more professional days, and instead the Society advises in general terms on the choice of a suitable publisher for a particular type of manuscript, and specifically on contracts and legal and other business matters connected with authorship. The Society has been instrumental in arousing interest in its proposed Public Lending Right (see above). It now incorporates separate associations for special classes of writer, the Children's Writers' Group, the Educational Writers' Group, the League of Dramatists, the Translators Association and the Radio Writers Association. It is responsible for administering seven writers awards, the Authors Contingency Fund and a Retirement Benefits Scheme.

THE AUTHOR, Journal of the Society, first published 1890, is now quarterly. This is the most comprehensive source of information about authorship as a profession.

Victor Bonham-Carter, EIGHTY YEARS AGO, *The Society of Authors 1884–1964*, S.o.A., 1964.

This short account of the foundation of the Society was written for the eightieth anniversary dinner in May 1964.

The Society issues the following series:

S.o.A., BULLETINS (written by S.o.A. staff and revised regularly)

1. TEACHERS AS AUTHORS, 1967.
2. TRANSLATORS AS AUTHORS, 1968.
3. PUBLIC LENDING RIGHT, *A Short History*, 1967.

QUICK GUIDES

1. COPYRIGHT, 1966.
2. THE PROTECTION OF TITLES, 1966.

B

3. PHOTOCOPYING AND THE LAW, with the Publishers Association, 1968.
4. INCOME TAX, revised edition 1968.
5. LIBEL, 1967.
6. YOUR COPYRIGHTS AFTER DEATH, 1972.

SURVEYS OF AUTHORSHIP

1. CRITICAL TIMES FOR AUTHORS, 1953.
2. **Richard Findlater,** WHAT ARE WRITERS WORTH?, 1963.
3. **Richard Findlater,** THE BOOK WRITERS, WHO ARE THEY?, 1966. This revealed that only some 16 per cent of all authors (of books) earn over £1,000 p.a. from writing.

The following are relevant to the Society's history:

George Bainton, editor, THE ART OF AUTHORSHIP, Bainton, 1891.

Bainton invited various well-known authors to contribute essays on the art and business of writing, without paying them a fee, and thus fell foul of the Society.

Walter Besant, THE LITERARY HANDMAID OF THE CHURCH, Glaisher, 1890.

This is an attack on the S.P.C.K. and other religious publishing houses.

Walter Besant, THE PEN AND THE BOOK, Burleigh, 1899.

The aim was to describe the 'literary life' in all its aspects, and incorporates much material from earlier S.o.A. booklists.

Walter Besant, AUTOBIOGRAPHY, Hutchinson, 1902.

This contains a chapter on S.o.A.

W. Morris Colles, LITERATURE AND THE PENSION FUND, Glaisher, 1892.

The author shows that the Civil List Pensions were distributed among civil servants and other unsuitable people rather than among those writers, artists and scholars which the Fund had been founded in order to help.

Edmund Gosse, THE GRIEVANCES BETWEEN AUTHORS AND PUBLISHERS, *Being the Report of the Conference of the Incorporated Society of Authors Held at Willis's Rooms in March 1887: with Additional Matter and Summary,* 1887.

This includes the following papers: *The Maintenance of Literary Property* by Walter Besant; *The Profession of Authorship* by Edmund Gosse; and an appendix by George Putnam on *Author–Publisher Relations* in the U.S. and a summary by Besant outlining the aims of the society.

D. Kilham Roberts, THE AUTHORS', PLAYWRIGHTS' AND COMPOSERS' HANDBOOK, annually 1935–40.

This is similar in aim and scope to the *Writers' and Artists' Year Book* (see p. 10) but written strictly from the author's point of view.

Trevor Russell-Cobb, PAYING THE PIPER: *The Theory and Practice of Industrial Patronage*, Queen Anne Press, 1968.

'The aim of this book is to encourage industry to support the arts'. Part 1 deals with the company as patron. One of the chapters of Part 2 is based on *What Are Writers Worth?* (see p. 18).

S. Squire Sprigge, THE COST OF PRODUCTION, 1890.

Sprigge was Secretary and later Chairman of the Society of Authors, and editor of the *Lancet* for many years.

S. Squire Sprigge, THE METHODS OF PUBLISHING, 1890.

This describes the methods of publishing then in vogue with the aim of emphasising the need to protect 'literary property'. An addenda by G. Herbert Thring was published for the Society, 1898.

G. Herbert Thring, THE MARKETING OF LITERARY PROPERTY (see under 'The Business Side of Authorship', p. 15 above).

10. Other Authors' Societies

ASSOCIATION OF BRITISH SCIENCE WRITERS

This aims to improve the standard of science writing and to help members in their work. Its activities include visits to research establishments and receptions for scientific authorities.

HE CRIME WRITERS' ASSOCIATION (founded 1953)

This Association holds monthly meetings in the National Book League. Its members are writers of literary and non-fiction works on crime.

THE CRITICS' CIRCLE (founded 1913)

This aims to promote the art of criticism and safeguard the professional interests of its members who are engaged in the writing or broadcasting of criticism of drama, music, films, ballet, television or radio. Membership is by invitation of its Council only.

P.E.N. INTERNATIONAL (founded 1921)

It aims to promote friendship and understanding between writers and to defend freedom of expression. The letters P.E.N. stand for Poets, Playwrights, Editors, Essayists, Novelists, but it is open to all writers of standing including translators. It is non-political and administers the P.E.N. Fund for Exiled Writers. The P.E.N. – UNESCO Translators' scheme promotes the translation of works by writers in the lesser known languages. It publishes P.E.N. NEWS, P.E.N. BULLETIN OF SELECTED BOOKS (bilingual French and English) and others.

THE ROMANTIC NOVELISTS' ASSOCIATION (founded 1960)

Aims to raise the prestige of romantic novelists. Membership is open to romantic and historical novelists. Its annual Major Award for the best romantic novel of the year is open to members and non-members.

THE SOCIETY OF AUTHORS (see above)

THE SOCIETY OF CIVIL SERVICE AUTHORS

The Society is open to all present and past civil servants. It advises aspiring authors but its activities are mainly social. It publishes a monthly CIVIL SERVICE JOURNAL.

THE WRITERS' GUILD (founded 1959)

This is a trade union open to film, radio and television script writers.

11. Literary Prizes and Awards

(See also under VII. CHILDREN'S BOOKS, pp. 190f.)

Lists of prizes for writers in English, as well as for translation, indexing and book illustration are to be found in:

A. & C. Black, THE WRITERS' AND ARTISTS' YEARBOOK (see under 'Authorship Manuals', p. 10 above).

Bowker, LITERARY AND LIBRARY PRIZES, 6th edition, revised and enlarged by Olga S. Weber, Bowker, New York and London, 1967.

This gives international, British and Canadian prizes, the American prizes being divided into categories such as juvenile, poetry, drama and library. In each case the conditions are given, together with a complete list of prizewinning authors, titles and publishers.

Cassell's DIRECTORY OF PUBLISHING (see under XIII. PUBLISHING, p. 370).

The National Book League Library keeps an index of literary and book trade prizes and awards, together with details of winners, which N.B.L. members can consult in the library.

SECTION II

BOOKBINDING

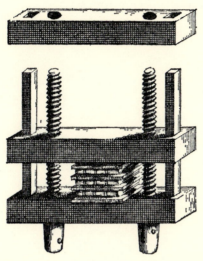

'*A Nipping Press*', *from Dudin,* L'Art du Relieur, *1772 (actual size)*
(*see p. 42*)

1. Introduction

Craft- or hand-binding is functional art and originated when the scroll manuscript was replaced by the codex form. From very early times the binding of a book served both as protection for the text and for decoration, as well as for identification of the contents, or, in the case of armorial bindings, of the owner. Leather was the most usual material employed as book covering often ornamented with blind-stamping, and later gold-tooling. In early periods bindings were sometimes jewelled and in the Renaissance period embroidered. Fine bindings are sometimes protected by a slip-case or box which is itself so beautifully decorated that occasionally this is protected by a further box. From the Renaissance period the edges of a book were gilded to present a smooth surface that would trap the dust and prevent it seeping into the pages of the book. Towards the end of the seventeenth century edges began to be marbled for the same purpose. This edging was also ornamental and during the Commonwealth period the purely decorative use of fore-edge painting came into being, a practice that was extended in the eighteenth and early nineteenth centuries.

The literature of bookbinding history dates from the end of the Victorian period with such scholars as Miss S. T. Prideaux, W. Y. Fletcher, E. P. Goldschmidt, W. H. J. Weale and Strickland Gibson. Others, notably Cyril Davenport, have been proved unreliable by later scholarship, yet their books have not yet been replaced by better work. Later writers include G. D. Hobson, and, in our day, H. M. Nixon and A. R. A. Hobson. Some practising craft-binders have also written key works on the technique of bookbinding – Zaehnsdorf in England, Léon Gruel in France and now, Roger Powell and Bernard Middleton. Some of the books on fine bindings are nearly as beautiful as the books they describe, and are themselves collected by bibliophiles.

In this section I have sometimes gone beyond the confines of the British book trade to include books on British collections of foreign bindings. Moreover, I have included a few foreign books on historical binding that are in the National Book League's library since it needs no linguist to make use of books in which text is subservient to illustration.

2. Bibliographies, General Histories, and Sale Catalogues of Fine Bindings and Important Collections

(See also the learned journals listed on pp. 103 f., which frequently contain monographs of early binders and bindings.)

J. R. Abbey, ENGLISH AND FRENCH BINDINGS, *From the Collection of J. R. Abbey,* Arts Council, 1949 (illustrated).

John Bagford, NOTES ON BOOKBINDING, edited by Cyril Davenport, Bibliographical Society, 1904.

Bagford was, according to Horne (see below) the first in England to attempt some methodical account of the art of bookbinding. He describes some of the works that are reproduced in Fletcher's volumes on book-bindings in the British Museum (see pp. 31 and 40).

Bodleian Library, GOLD TOOLED BOOKBINDINGS, Oxford, 1951.

Contains plates of gold tooling 1480–1774.

W. Brassington, A HISTORY OF THE ART OF BOOKBINDING, *With Some Account of the Books of the Ancients,* Elliot Stock, 1894 (illustrations include some coloured plates).

This is still a reliable work and the illustrations are of fine quality.

Joseph Cundall, editor, ON BOOKBINDING ANCIENT AND MODERN, 1881.

Contains a useful list of celebrated binders and patrons of bookbinding.

Edith Diehl, BOOKBINDING: *Its Background and Technique* (see p. 50).

David Diringer, THE HAND-PRODUCED BOOK, Hutchinson, 1953 (illustrated, bibliography).

Describes both the inside and the outside of books from the earliest systems of writing until the end of the manuscript period. It includes a description of the methods of covering manuscripts and scrolls.

E. P. Goldschmidt, GOTHIC AND RENAISSANCE BOOKBINDINGS, *Exemplified and Illustrated from the Author's Collection,* 2 vols., Ernest Benn, 1928, reprinted N. Israel, Amsterdam, 1970 (vol. 2 all plates).

Volume 1, contains an introduction, a catalogue raisonné, a synopsis of the collection, an index of binders' and booksellers' names, monastic binders and cyphers. This remains one of the most scholarly works on the subject.

John Harthan, BOOKBINDINGS, H.M.S.O. (Victoria and Albert Museum), 1st edition, 1950, 2nd edition revised, 1961 (illustrated, bibliography, glossary.)

An introduction on the development of bookbinding design is followed by plates illustrating seventy-two bindings from ninth-century Egypt to France in 1952. There is an appendix on bookbinding techniques with plates illustrating sewing, glueing, backing, lacing in boards, gold blocking and the use of a roll.

Hellmuth Helvig, HANDBUCH DER EINBANDKUNDE, 3 vols., Maximilien-Gesellschaft, Hamburg, 1953–55 (many plates.)

I include this although it is in German, since names, dates and illustrations are universally understood. Volume 1 covers the development, preservation and restoration of handbinding, its documentation and literature. Volume 2 lists bookbinders by country (France, Germany, Netherlands, England, Scandinavia, Italy, Spain and Hungary) and early binders from the sixteenth to the nineteenth centuries. Volume 3 is a register of names and places of European binders since 1850.

A. R. A. Hobson, THE LITERATURE OF BOOKBINDING (The Book no. 2), C.U.P. for the N.B.L., 1954.

A short introduction is followed by a bibliography of books on English, Scottish, Irish, Italian, French, Spanish, Flemish, German, American, Islamic bindings, general works and catalogues and an appendix on books in the National Book League on fine bindings and the binding craft and industry. This is still a useful bibliography although inevitably new books have come out since 1954 and the National Book League library has been considerably added to.

The following works by G. D. Hobson are all of importance:

G. D. Hobson, MAIOLI, CANEVARI AND OTHERS, Ernest Benn, 1926 (64 plates, 7 in colour, bibliography).

G. D. Hobson, THIRTY BINDINGS, First Edition Club, 1926.

This is a selection of the First Edition Club's seventh exhibition held at 25 Park Lane and includes French, Spanish and other bindings from the fifteenth century to 1773.

G. D. Hobson, BINDINGS IN CAMBRIDGE LIBRARIES, C.U.P., 1929 (illustrated).

G. D. Hobson, LES RELIURES A LA FANFARE, Chiswick Press, 1935 (illustrated).

The text is in French.

Robert Hoe, A LECTURE ON BOOKBINDING AS A FINE ART, *Delivered Before the Grolier Club, February 26, 1885,* Grolier Club, New York, 1886 (63 plates exemplify historic bindings in the author's collection).

This considers the early manuals and writers on bookbinding history.

Herbert P. Horne, THE BINDING OF BOOKS, 1st edition, Routledge, 1915, new edition, Kegan Paul, Trench & Trübner, 1927.

This has a preface on bookbinding literature followed by chapters on Italian, French and English bindings.

Ernst Kyriss, FESTSCHRIFT ERNST KYRISS, Max Hettler Verlag, Stuttgart, 1961.

Contains articles on bookbinding history by French, German, and English scholars written in these three languages.

Douglas Leighton, MODERN BOOKBINDING, *A Survey and a Prospect,* J. M. Dent, 1935 – one of the Dent Memorial Lectures (see pp. 154 f.).

Maggs Brothers, BOOKBINDINGS, *Historical and Decorative,* Maggs Bros., 1921.

Brander Matthews, BOOKBINDINGS OLD AND NEW, Bell, London, and Grolier Club, New York, 1896 (with plates and text illustrations).

This has chapters on bookbinding history and on commercial bookbinding.

William Matthews, MODERN BOOKBINDING PRACTICALLY CONSIDERED, *A Lecture Read Before the Grolier Club 1885,* Grolier Club, New York, 1889.

This describes the Aldine, Maioli, Grolier and other historic binding styles.

Wolfgang Mejer, BIBLIOGRAPHIE VON BUCHBINDEREI-LITERATUR, Heirsemann, Leipzig, Part 1, 1926, Part 2, 1933 (over 2,000 entries).

I select the following contributions to bookbinding scholarship by Howard M. Nixon:

H. M. Nixon, *Bookbinding Notes*, articles in the BOOK COLLECTOR, 1963.

H. M. Nixon, THE DEVELOPMENT OF CERTAIN STYLES OF BOOKBINDING, Private Libraries Association, 1963.

H. M. Nixon, BROXBOURNE LIBRARY, *Styles and Designs of Bookbindings from the 12th to the 20th Century*, Broxbourne Library and Maggs Bros., 1956 (illustrated).

There is a bibliographical description of each book and numerous coloured plates and text illustrations. Mr Nixon explains that 'the purpose of this book is to show what light the Broxbourne Library can throw on the history of taste and bookbinding . . . as many different styles of binding as possible have been chosen. . . . With but two or three exceptions, the bindings here reproduced are unpublished or have only appeared in book-sellers' or auction sale catalogues'.

H. M. Nixon, 12 BOOKS IN FINE BINDINGS FROM THE LIBRARY OF J. W. HELY-HUTCHINSON, Clarendon Press, Oxford, 1953.

H. M. Nixon, SIXTEENTH-CENTURY GOLD-TOOLED BOOKBINDINGS *in the Pierpont Morgan Library*, Pierpont Morgan Library, New York, 1971 (illustrated).

'Each of the seventy bindings discussed is given a full description and an illustration facing the text, and is made the subject of an essay on its owner and binder, and on related works from the same shop.' *Times Literary Supplement*, July 7, 1971.

Miss Prideaux's work is still regarded as authoritative. I include:

S. T. Prideaux, BIBLIOGRAPHY OF WORKS ON BOOKBINDING, privately printed, 1892.

S. T. Prideaux, AN HISTORICAL SKETCH OF BOOKBINDING, *With a Chapter on Early Stamped Bindings by E. Gordon Duff*, 1893 (extensive bibliography).

This is still a standard work but it is a pity that it is not illustrated.

S. T. Prideaux, BOOKBINDERS AND THEIR CRAFT, Zaehnsdorf, 1903.

S. T. Prideaux, MODERN BOOKBINDINGS, *Their Design and Decoration*, 1906 (illustrated).

S. T. Prideaux, VICTORIA AND ALBERT MUSEUM, *Notes on Printing and Bookbinding A Guide to the Exhibition of Tools and Materials Used in the Process,* H.M.S.O., 1921.

The illustrated sale catalogues of Bernard Quaritch include the following important collections of bindings:

Bernard Quaritch, A CATALOGUE OF FIFTEEN HUNDRED BOOKS, Quaritch, 1889.

Bernard Quaritch, A COLLECTION OF FACSIMILES FROM EXAMPLES OF HISTORIC OR ARTISTIC BOOKBINDING, Quaritch, 1889.

Bernard Quaritch, A CATALOGUE OF A PORTION OF THE LIBRARY OF CHARLES ISAAC ELTON AND MARY AUGUSTA ELTON, Quaritch, 1891.

Lists some important bindings.

Bernard Quaritch, A CATALOGUE OF ENGLISH AND FOREIGN BOOKBINDINGS OFFERED FOR SALE, Quaritch, 1921.

There are seventy-nine plates, some coloured, of English, French, Italian and mid-European bindings.

Sotheby & Co., THE COLLECTION OF BINDINGS OF J. R. ABBEY, 3 parts, Sotheby, 1965–67.

This illustrated sale catalogue of 2,243 items is a record of one of the most complete collections of bindings of all periods. These items, part only of Major Abbey's library, were sold at auction in three sales in June 1965, November 1966 and June 1967.

Studio, MODERN BOOKBINDINGS AND THEIR DESIGNERS, Studio, 1900.

One of the Studio special supplements (see also under IV. BOOK DESIGN AND PRODUCTION, p. 112). There are numerous colour and half-tone plates as well as text illustrations of binding styles of the Art Nouveau epoch.

Walter Art Gallery, HISTORY OF BOOKBINDING 525–1950 A.D., *An Exhibition Held at the Baltimore Museum of Art,* Baltimore, Maryland, 1957. A catalogue raisonné.

W. H. J. Weale, BOOKBINDINGS AND RUBBINGS OF BINDINGS, *In the Art Library, South Kensington Museum,* Eyre & Spottiswoode, 2 parts, 1894 and 1898.

There are chapters on bindings in eleven European countries with plates and illustrations of rubbings and an index from the libraries from which the illustrations have been drawn. A. R. A. Hobson considers this a much better work than *Early Stamped Bindings in the British Museum* completed after Weale's death by Laurence Taylor and published in 1922.

3. English Bookbinding (excluding Modern, Royal and Armorial)

G. Eliot Anstruther, THE BINDINGS OF TOMORROW, *A Record of the Work of the Guild of Women Binders and of the Hampstead Bindery*, Guild of Women Binders, 1902 (illustrated).

An introduction describes the Guild's work and the fifty coloured plates are described on an adjacent page.

H. Bailey, SHORT NOTICES ON THE BOOKBINDERS OF SALISBURY LIBRARY, Bell, 1881.

T. Julian Brown, THE STONYHURST GOSPEL OF ST. JOHN, *With a Technical Description of the Binding by Roger Powell and Peter Waters*, O.U.P. for the Roxburghe Club, 1970.

Cyril Davenport, ENGLISH EMBROIDERED BOOKBINDINGS, with an introduction by Alfred Pollard, Kegan Paul, Trench & Trübner, 1899 (illustrated).

Davenport's work has been superseded by later scholars, but no other work is given wholly to the embroidered bindings of the Renaissance period.

Seymour de Ricci, BRITISH AND MISCELLANEOUS SIGNED BINDINGS IN THE MORTIMER L. SCHIFF COLLECTION, 4 vols., John M. Schiff, New York, 1935 (mostly plates).

W. Y. Fletcher, ENGLISH BOOKBINDINGS IN THE BRITISH MUSEUM, *Illustrations of 63 Examples Selected on Account of Their Beauty and Historical Interest with Introduction and Description by W. Y. Fletcher*, Kegan Paul, Trench & Trübner, 1895.

The quality of the reproductions in this and the companion volume on foreign bindings (see p. 40) is very fine.

Strickland Gibson, EARLY OXFORD BINDINGS, Bibliographical Society, 1903. Contains fine plates of bindings and types of decoration.

Strickland Gibson, SOME NOTABLE BODLEIAN BINDINGS XII TO XVII CENTURIES, Clarendon Press, Oxford, 1901–04.

G. D. Hobson, ENGLISH BINDING BEFORE 1500, C.U.P., 1929.

This is the text of the Sandars' Lectures in Bibliography for 1927 and covers early bindings before 1300 and Gothic bindings 1450–1500.

G. D. Hobson, ENGLISH BINDINGS 1490–1940 IN THE LIBRARY OF J. R. ABBEY, privately printed at the Chiswick Press, 1940 (illustrated).

Describes bindings not reproduced elsewhere.

G. D. Hobson, BLIND STAMPED PANELS IN THE ENGLISH BOOK TRADE, *c.* 1485–1555, Bibliographical Society, 1944 (illustrations confined to a few text figures).

This, together with Oldham's works form a full study of the subject.

Eleanore Jamieson, ENGLISH EMBOSSED BINDINGS 1825–1850, O.U.P. for the Cambridge Bibliographical Society, 1972 (illustrated, bibliography).

Deals with the leather-covered papier maché stamped trade bindings used for gift books, annuals, etc. It is based on a F.L.A. thesis.

Neil R. Ker, FRAGMENTS OF MEDIAEVAL MANUSCRIPTS USED AS PASTE DOWNS IN OXFORD BINDINGS, *With a Survey of Oxford Bindings, c. 1515–1620,* Oxford Bibliographical Society, 1954.

Maggs Bros., BOOKBINDINGS OF GREAT BRITAIN 16TH TO THE 20TH CENTURY, Maggs Bros., 1957 and 1963 (many plates).

A sale catalogue of important bindings, many not recorded elsewhere.

H. M. Nixon, *English Bookbindings.* A regular series of articles in THE BOOK COLLECTOR (see p. 104).

Basil J. Oldham, ENGLISH BLIND-STAMPED BINDINGS, C.U.P., 1952 (illustrated, bibliography).

There are sixty-one plates and rubbings, a glossary of terms used in connection with blind stamped bindings, and a classification of rolls and ornaments. The subject of panel stamps is excluded as they are treated exhaustively by G. D. Hobson (see above).

Basil J. Oldham, BLIND PANELS OF ENGLISH BINDERS, C.U.P., 1958 (illustrated, bibliography).

The author, concerning himself with sixteenth-century English binders, has notes on individual panels such as acorn, animal, biblical, heraldic, religious, vertical, quadruple and triple panels. The first sixty-six plates reproduce rubbings of these. The rest are of tools not reproduced elsewhere and sources of some of the panel designs. The plates are not dated so that identification involves hunting through the text.

4. Individual English Bookbinders and Their Conditions of Work

General Works

Ellic Howe, A LIST OF LONDON BOOKBINDERS 1648–1815, Bibliographical Society, 1st edition, 1950, 2nd edition, 1963 (bibliography).

The introduction deals with the sources used in compilation and there is a seventeenth-century price list and a list of the directories consulted.

Ellic Howe and John Child, THE SOCIETY OF LONDON BOOKBINDERS 1780–1951, Sylvan Press, 1952.

There is an excellent introduction to the history of binding trade associations and social conditions.

Charles Ramsden, BOOKBINDERS OF THE UNITED KINGDOM OUTSIDE LONDON 1780–1840, Batsford, 1954 (illustrated).

An alphabetical list of English, Welsh, Scottish and Irish binders of the late eighteenth century, and a list of the directories consulted is appended.

Charles Ramsden, LONDON BOOKBINDERS 1780–1840, Batsford, 1956 (illustrated).

Has an invaluable introduction on trade associations and directories as well as stylistic developments in the period.

Works on Individual Binders

THOMAS BERTHELET (d. 1555)

Cyril Davenport, THOMAS BERTHELET: *Royal Printer and Bookbinder to Henry VIII*, Caxton Club, 1901.

H. M. Nixon has recently shown that Berthelet was not himself a practising binder; it was for long believed, erroneously it now appears, that he produced almost the first gilt tooled bindings in England.

JAMES BURN & CO. (established 1781)

Lionel S. Darley, BOOKBINDING THEN AND NOW, *A Survey of the First 178 Years of James Burn & Co.*, Faber & Faber, 1959 (illustrated, biliography).

Recounts one binding firm's history from 1781 to the end of the Second World War with plates of binding styles, a specimen of gold blocking and illustrations of presses and handbinding tools.

COBDEN-SANDERSON (see 'Doves Press', under XII. PRIVATE PRESSES, pp. 318 f.).

KITCAT (established 1798)

John Adams, THE HOUSE OF KITCAT, *A Story of Bookbinding 1798–1948*, privately printed G. & J. Kitcat, 1948 (illustrated).

A house history more concerned with personalities than techniques but containing interesting information relating to trade and social conditions.

EDGAR MANSFIELD (b. 1907)

Edgar Mansfield, MODERN DESIGN IN BOOKBINDING, *The Work of Edgar Mansfield Illustrated with an Introduction by H. M. Nixon*, Peter Owen, 1966.

Mr Nixon's introduction describes the development of Mansfield's binding art. There are biographical notes, seventy-six fine plates and text illustrations.

SAMUEL MEARNE (d. 1683)

Cyril Davenport, SAMUEL MEARNE AND HIS BINDINGS, reprinted from the *Proceedings of the Society of Antiquaries*, 1905.

This monograph has been superseded by later scholarship, but is still the only work in book form on Mearne. Ellic Howe (in *A List of London Bookbinders 1648–1815*, see p. 33 above) has pointed out that 'the post of

Royal Bookbinder was not necessarily held by a practising binder, and there is no evidence that Mearne ever bound a book himself'. Nevertheless, for want of a more accurate name, the bindings done while Mearne held office are still called Mearne bindings.

ROBERT RIVIERE (1808–82)

The firm of Riviere & Sons was absorbed by Bayntun's of Bath in 1939. By the end of the nineteenth century a hundred people were employed. The founder started bookbinding in Bath and later moved to London, where he bound for all the great collectors of the day, including the Queen and the Royal family. 'Taking into consideration the fact that he was entirely self-taught, his bindings are wonderful specimens of artistic taste, skill, and perseverance' (W. Y. Fletcher, *Dictionary of National Biography*). W. C. Hazlitt, in *Confessions of a Collector* (pp. 94–5) describes the founder thus: 'He was a capital old fellow, originally a bookseller at Bath. . . . He was ambidexter; for he executed a vast amount of modern binding for the trade, and was famous for his tree-marbled calf, which I have frequently watched in its various stages in his workshop. He was a trifle irritable at times. I had given him an Elizabethan tract to bind, and on inquiring after a reasonable interval it was not merely not done, but could not be found. I called two or three times, and Riviere at last exclaimed: "Damn the thing; what do you want for it?"—pulling out his cheque-book. I replied that I wanted nothing but my property, bound as ordered; and he was so far impressed by my composure that he said no more, and eventually brought the stray to light'.

Riviere & Sons, EXAMPLES OF MODERN BOOKBINDING, Quaritch, 1919.

5. Royal and Armorial Bookbindings

Babachelin-Deflorenne, LA SCIENCE DES ARMOIRES, *Avec Gravures dans la Texte*, Librairie des Bibliophiles, Paris, 1880.
A catalogue raisonné of armorial bearings used in bookbinding.

George F. Barwick, A BOOK BOUND FOR MARY QUEEN OF SCOTS . . . *The Geographie of Ptolemy, Printed at Rome 1490, With Notes on Other Books Bearing Queen Mary's Insignia*, Bibliographical Society Monograph, 1901.

Cyril Davenport, ROYAL ENGLISH BOOKBINDINGS, Seeley & Co., 1896 (illustrated, bibliography).

Covers royal bindings from 1100–1760 with excellent plates and text illustrations.

Cyril Davenport, ENGLISH HERALDIC BOOK-STAMPS FIGURED AND DESCRIBED, Constable, 1909 (illustrated, bibliography, index of arms).

Modern scholarship has revealed that a large proportion of the attributions are erroneous.

Grolier Club, THE CATALOGUE OF BOOKS FROM THE LIBRARIES OR COLLECTIONS OF THE CELEBRATED BIBLIOPHILES AND ILLUSTRIOUS PERSONS OF THE PAST, *With Arms or Devices upon the Bindings Exhibited at the Grolier Club in the Month of January, 1895,* Grolier Club, New York, 1895 (24 plates).

R. R. Holmes, SPECIMENS OF ROYAL FINE AND HISTORICAL BOOKBINDING, *Selected from the Royal Library, Windsor Castle,* Griggs, 1893.

There is an introduction and notes by Holmes, Librarian to Queen Victoria, and 152 magnificent plates with red and gold borders illustrating bindings of all styles and countries.

Reginald Arthur Rye and Muriel Sinton Quinn, HISTORICAL AND ARMORIAL BOOKBINDINGS, *Exhibited in the University Library, A Descriptive Catalogue,* University of London, 1937 (11 plates).

Alfred Wallis, EXAMPLES OF THE BOOKBINDERS' ART OF THE SIXTEENTH AND SEVENTEENTH CENTURIES, *Selected Chiefly from the Royal Continental Libraries,* With Descriptions and Introduction by Alfred Wallis, James Commin, Exeter, 1890 (illustrated).

6. French Bookbinding and Works in French

British Museum, BOOKBINDINGS FROM THE LIBRARY OF JEAN GROLIER, British Museum, 1965.

This is an illustrated catalogue of the loan exhibition held September 23 to October 31, 1965, and consists of an introduction and plates of 138 exhibits including eleven plates of distinctive binders' marks.

Gustave Brunet, ÉTUDES SUR LES RELIURES DES LIVRES ET SUR LES COLLECTIONS DES BIBLIOPHILES CÉLÈBRES, Moquet, Bordeaux, 1891.

Gustave Brunet, LA RELIURE ANCIENNE ET MODERNE, *Recueil de 116 Planches de Reliures Artistiques des XVIe, XVIIe, XVIIIe et XIXe Siècles ... Accompagnée d'une Table Explicative avec Notices Descriptives des 31 Reliures des Plus Remarquables,* Rouveyre et Blond, Paris, 1884 (116 lavish plates).

Seymour de Ricci, FRENCH SIGNED BINDINGS IN THE MORTIMER L. SCHIFF COLLECTION, John M. Schiff, New York, 1935, 3 vols., mainly of plates.

L. Dérome, LA RELIURE DE LUXE, LE LIVRE ET L'AMATEUR, Edouard Rouveyre, Paris, 1898 (illustrated).

W. Y. Fletcher, BOOKBINDINGS IN FRANCE, Seeley & Co., 1905 (8 colour plates and 31 text illustrations).

Léon Gruel, MANUEL, HISTORIQUE ET BIBLIOGRAPHIQUE DE L'AMATEUR DE RELIURES, Gruel & Engelmann, Paris, Part 1 1887, Part 2 1905 (illustrated with 69 colour plates, bibliography).

The magnificent plates of different styles of binding makes this history of bookbinding by a great French bookbinder, available to those who do not read French. The text is a study of the origin of book formats followed by a general historical introduction to bookbinding and an alphabetical annotated list of great Continental bindings and binders, providing all known information about them. The bibliography is classified and consists mainly of great rare books on binding in French although it includes a few English works in translation such as Arnett, Zaehnsdorf (see pp. 43 f.) and Dibdin's *Bibliographical Tour of France.*

Gumuchian, CATALOGUE DE RELIURES, *Du XVe au XIXe siècle en Vente à La Librairie Gumuchian et Cie.,* n.d.

A sumptuous sale catalogue illustrated with 125 plates of different styles of bindings, spines, ornaments, tools and filets, with annotations in English and French. The editors acknowledge the assistance of experts such as Léon Gruel, E. P. Goldschmidt, G. D. Hobson (qq.v.) and Dr Olivier.

National Book League, EXHIBITION OF CONTEMPORARY BOOKBINDINGS AND ILLUSTRATIONS, arranged by Pierre André and Lucie Weill-Guillardet, 1956 (7 plates).

Charles Ramsden, FRENCH BOOKBINDERS 1789–1848, Lund Humphries, 1950 (illustrated).

An introduction, followed by a sketch of French bookbinding between

An eighteenth-century bindery showing backing, sewing and ploughing, from Dudin, L'Art du Relieur, 1772 (see p. 42)

1789–1848, a bibliographical dictionary of binders under the towns where they were active, and an alphabetical index. The illustrations are of characteristic bindings by twenty-eight binders and two that are anonymous.

Octave Uzanne, LE RELIURE MODERN ARTISTIQUE ET FANTAISISTE, Edouard Rouveyre, Paris, 1887 (72 plates.)

7. Scottish Bookbinding

Most of the material on Scottish Bookbinding is to be found in the *Proceedings* of the Bibliographical Society and the Edinburgh Bibliographical Society, the *Aberdeen University Review* and *Scottish Notes and Queries.*

William Smith Mitchell, A HISTORY OF SCOTTISH BOOKBINDING 1432–1650, Oliver & Boyd, Edinburgh, 1955 (illustrated with 48 plates, bibliography, glossary).

M. J. Sommerlad, SCOTTISH WHEEL AND HERRINGBONE BINDINGS IN THE BODLEIAN LIBRARY, *An Illustrated Handlist,* Oxford Bibliographical Society, Oxford, 1967 (illustrated).

This is the first of the Oxford Bibliographical Society's *Occasional Publications.* A brief introduction is followed by a bibliographical description of the twenty-eight bindings listed, of which twenty-seven are illustrated.

8. Irish Bookbinding

Maurice Craig, IRISH BOOKBINDING 1600–1800, Cassell, 1954 (illustrated, bibliography).

Gives a list of noteworthy bindings with their locations and a list of published Irish bindings, illustrated by fifty-eight plates.

W. & G. Foyle, AN EXHIBITION OF IRISH BINDINGS FROM THE SEVENTEENTH TO THE TWENTIETH CENTURY, September 29 to October 29, 1954, Foyle, 1954 (illustrated).

9. American Bookbinding

I select the following which are in the library of the National Book League:

Henri René Dubois, AMERICAN BOOKBINDINGS IN THE LIBRARY OF HENRY WILLIAM POOR, George D. Smith, New York, 1903 (illustrated most magnificently in gold leaf and colours by Edward Bierstadt).

H. Lehmann-Haupt, editor, BOOKBINDING IN AMERICA, *Three Essays*, Southworth-Antheonsen Press, Portland, Maine, 1941, new edition 1967 (illustrated).

The first essay by H. D. French deals with early American handbinding; J. W. Rogers describes the rise of American edition binding; and the editor writes on the rebinding of old books.

C. Clement Samford and John M. Hemphill, II, BOOKBINDING IN COLONIAL VIRGINIA, Colonial Williamsburg, Williamsburg, Virginia, 1966 (illustrated, bibliography, classified as manuscript and printed sources).

10. Spanish Bookbinding

I select the following:

Francisco Hueso Rolland, EXPOSICION DE ENCUADERNACIONES ESPAÑO-LAS SIGLOS XII AL XIX, *Catalogo General Ilustrado*, Sociedad Española de Amigos Del Arte, Madrid, 1934 (61 plates of illustrations of particular styles, bibliography, list of exhibits).

Henry Thomas, EARLY SPANISH BOOKBINDINGS XI–XV CENTURIES, O.U.P. for the Bibliographical Society, 1939 (delivered in 1936) (bibliography, 100 plates with bibliographical descriptions).

11. Other Foreign Bookbinding

W. Y. Fletcher, FOREIGN BOOKBINDINGS IN THE BRITISH MUSEUM, *Illustrations of 63 Examples Selected on Account of Their Beauty or Historical*

Interest with Introduction and Descriptions by W. Y. Fletcher, Kegan Paul, Trench & Trübner, 1896.

This is a companion volume to *English Bookbindings in the British Museum* (see p. 31). It contains magnificent plates of many styles, periods and nationalities.

Ferdinand Geldner, BUCHEINBÄNDE AUS ELF JAHRHUNDERTEN, Bruckmann, Munich, 1958.

This covers bindings of all styles from the eleventh century to 1850 illustrated by 108 plates.

Ernst Kyriss, VERZIERTE GOTISCHE EINBÄNDE IM ALTEN DEUTSCHEN SPRACHGEBIET, 4 vols., Max Hettler Verlag, Stuttgart, 1953–58.

One of the great bookbinding scholars deals exhaustively with German blind stamped bindings of the early period.

12. Edition Binding (otherwise called Publishers' Cloth, Case Binding or Trade Binding) and Unsewn Binding

Until the beginning of the nineteenth century publishers issued their works unbound, as is still done in France to a considerable extent, and gentlemen had their books uniformly bound to their own specification. But with the coming of the Industrial Age and the increasing spread of literacy among the less wealthy, there grew a demand for cheaper books in serviceable bindings. The first trade bindings, in cloth, or half-bound in cloth and leather, were produced in about 1820. Later, paper over board, both gayer and cheaper, was also used. Trade or case binding differs from craft binding in that the book-covers are mass-produced separately as a case and then glued to the book, whereas in craft binding the book is laced onto boards and the boards and spine then covered with leather or cloth.

Unsewn or 'perfect' binding, a process whereby the separate leaves are glued into the back of the casing instead of first being sewn in sections, was introduced in 1836. Gutta percha or caoutchouc was used to fix the leaves to the casing. It was quite unsatisfactory for the purpose and the books thus bound fell to pieces in no time (see Middleton, *A History of English Craft Bookbinding Technique*, p. 30). But in the last thirty years the method has been so much improved that it can be used, not only for ephemeral paperbacks, but even for large art books.

John Carter, BINDING VARIANTS IN ENGLISH PUBLISHING 1820–1900 (Bibliographia Series, Bibliographical Studies in Book History and Book Structure no. 6, see pp. 95 f.), Constable, 1932 (16 collotype plates).

This is a companion volume to Sadleir (see below) and is followed by a bibliographical description of individual books within the period.

John Carter, PUBLISHERS' CLOTH 1820–1900, Constable, 1935.

An outline history.

John Carter, MORE BINDING VARIANTS, Constable, 1938.

Eleanore Jamieson, ENGLISH EMBOSSED BINDINGS 1825–1850 (see p. 32).

Douglas Leighton, CANVAS AND BOOKCLOTH, *An Essay in Beginnings*, reprinted for the Bibliographical Society, 1948.

The author, head of a well-known firm of trade binders, discusses fabric used in eighteenth-century and early nineteenth-century binding which made its appearance as early as 1771.

John Mason, EDITION CASE BINDING, Pitman, 1946 (illustrated).

A brief non-scholarly introduction to the subject.

Michael Sadleir, THE EVOLUTION OF PUBLISHERS' BINDING STYLES, 1770–1900 (Bibliographia Series, Bibliographical Studies in Book History and Book Structure no. 1, see pp. 95 f.), Constable, 1930 (illustrated).

This is the first of the studies of the development of publishers' cloth starting with the end of the period of 'bespoke' bookbinding.

13. Early Manuals (chronological)
(See also Hoe's *Lecture on Bookbinding as a Fine Art*, p. 28 above.)

Bookbinding manuals are much more difficult to locate than the early printing manuals and there are so far no modern reprints. Each successive writer builds on and plagiarises from his predecessors, as with printing manuals (q.v.).

Dudin, L'ART DU RELIEUR, *Doreur de Livres*, 1772 (16 plates of impositions, presses, styles of binding, tools and binders at work etc.).

The earliest work on the practice of bookbinding, a rare and beautiful book.

Thomas Martin, COMPLETE INSTRUCTOR IN ALL BRANCHES OF BOOK-BINDING is a reprint of a chapter in THE CIRCLE OF THE MECHANICAL ARTS, 1813.

N. Minshall, THE WHOLE ART OF BOOKBINDING, *Containing Valuable Recipes for Sprinkling, Marbling, Colouring,* Oswestry, 1811.

The first work in English on bookbinding. Neither St Bride nor the National Book League possesses a copy, although St Bride has a manuscript version *c.* 1815.

H. Parry, THE ART OF BOOKBINDING, 1818.

In neither the National Book League nor St Bride libraries.

G. Cowie, THE BOOKBINDER'S MANUAL: *Containing a Full Description of Leather and Vellum Binding: Also, Directions for Gilding of Paper and Book Edges: and Numerous Valuable Recipes for Sprinkling, Colouring, and Marbling: Together with a Scale of Bookbinders' Charges: a List of All the Book and Vellum Binders in London, etc.,* 1st edition, 1829.

The author points out that the book is not addressed to the experienced binder but 'there are many connected with the art, whose knowledge is but superficial; to these its pages may be considered highly important, as forming a regular system, and containing all that is really essential to enable them to execute their work with neatness and elegance'. Seven pages of bookbinders' names and addresses testify to a flourishing trade, while there were fifteen vellum binders, numerous tool makers, book clasp makers, gilders and five bookbinders' lodges in London.

John Andrews Arnett (or Hannett), BIBLIOPEGIA; *or, the Art of Book-binding, in All Its Branches,* illustrated with engravings, 1st edition, R. Groombridge *et al.,* 1835, 4th edition, enlarged, Simpkin Marshall, 1848, 6th and last edition, 1865 (illustrated, glossary).

St Bride possesses the first edition and the National Book League, the fourth of this once popular work. In his preface to the first edition the author defends his book: 'Difference of opinion will doubtless rise as to the propriety of making known the more difficult operations of the Art; but Science never lost by its general diffusion, and the clever workman will ever retain the elevated position which his taste, ingenuity, and attention entitle him to. With this view, the work is submitted to the Trade, and public generally, as a miscellany of *real practical utility,* and a record of the present state of the *Bibliopegic Art.*'

John Hannett (or Arnett), AN INQUIRY INTO THE NATURE AND FORM OF THE BOOKS OF THE ANCIENTS, *With a History of the Art of Bookbinding,* 1837.

Among the press opinions quoted in the advertisement leaf, the *Monthly Review* commented, '. . . To the Artist the work offers immediate and practical value, nor should any Bookbinder deny himself its possession: . . . The Author has employed a plain, unpretending, and sensible style of writing. The illustrations are curious and beautiful as well as numerous.'

James B. Nicholson, A MANUAL OF THE ART OF BOOKBINDING: *Containing Full Instruction in the Different Branches of Forwarding, Gilding and Finishing: also, the Art of Marbling Book-Edges and Paper. The Whole Designed for the Practical Workman, the Amateur, and the Book-collector,* Henry Carey Baird, Philadelphia, 1856 (illustrated, glossary).

The author admits that his work owes much to Arnett: 'The plan of the work is taken from Arnett's Bibliopegia . . . it was first intended merely to revise that production.' The author realised, however, that, 'the progress of the art of bookbinding has made nearly all the works written upon the subject obsolete; their descriptions no longer apply to the methods practised by the best workmen'. Mr Middleton, on the other hand, points out, in his *A History of English Craft Bookbinding Technique* (see p. 52) that an illustration of a backing machine on p. 174 differs 'very little from modern ones', and one must suppose that the craft of bookbinding has changed more in the 120 years since Nicholson published than it had in the previous half-century. Nicholson not only writes on the history and practice of binding but includes a section on restoring and gives such hints to collectors as the following:

'Never write your name upon the title page of a book.

Have your books cut as large as possible, so as to preserve the integrity of the margin.

Do not adopt one style of binding for all your books.

Let the bindings upon your books be characteristic of the contents.

Do not bind a newly printed book. It is liable to set off in the pressing.

Books are not intended for card racks or for receptacles for botanical specimens.

Saturate a rag with camphor and, when dry, occasionally wipe the dust from your books with it and you will not be annoyed with book worms.'

J. W. Zaehnsdorf, THE ART OF BOOKBINDING, Bell, 1st edition, 1880, 2nd edition, 1890 (illustrated, glossary).

A manual by one of the greatest craft-binders, the second edition greatly enlarged, with seven plates demonstrating historic binding styles. The

work is in three parts, the first comprising twenty-two chapters on forwarding, the second on finishing and the third on general information
mostly concerning repair and restoration.

Joseph Zaehnsdorf (1816–86), the father of the author of the above
work was the founder of the firm which produced some of the finest
binding in the nineteenth century; 'fine examples of his craftsmanship are
to be found in the libraries of all the great English collectors of the day'.
(W. Y. Fletcher, *Dictionary of National Biography*.)

14. Early Trade Journals

Clowes & Sons, THE BOOKBINDER, *An Illustrated Journal for Binders
Librarians and Lovers of Books*, 7 vols., 1888–94.

A mine of useful and diverting information, continued as THE BRITISH
BOOKMAKER after volume 3, but still nearly all of bookbinding interest.

THE BOOKBINDERS' TRADE CIRCULAR, 6 vols., October 1850–November
1877.

This was issued by the London Consolidated Society of Journeymen
Bookbinders, whose motto was 'United to support, but not combined to
injure'. It gives details of exhibitions, trade conditions and disputes,
early machinery including the first backing machine, and obituaries of
bookbinders in which we learn more about the disease that killed them
than the way in which they lived.

BOOKBINDING TRADES JOURNAL, collected in 3 vols., 1904–14.

This, the journal of the Bookbinders' and Machine Rulers' Consolidated
Union, ran from 1904 to 1914, edited by William Mellor, and gave technical information interspersed with literary titbits and illustrations.

THE BOOK FINISHER'S FRIENDLY JOURNAL, 1845–51.

Nicholson (see p. 44 above) drew some of his material from this.

15. Decorated Bookpapers Used in Bookbinding
(See also under X. PAPER FOR BOOKWORK, pp. 229 ff.)

The late Mrs Olga Hirsch was a lifelong collector of endpapers and
published a small catalogue of her collection which was incorporated in:

Albert Von Haemmerle in collaboration with Olga Hirsch, BUNT-PAPIER, *Herkommen Geschichte Techniken beziehangen zur Kunst,* Callwey, Munich, 1961 (many coloured plates).

Rosamund B. Loring, DECORATED BOOK PAPERS, *Being an Account of Their Design and Fashion,* 1st edition, 1940, 2nd edition, edited by Philip Hofer, C.U.P., 1952 (illustrated).

There is an introductory account of the life of Rosamund Loring (1889–1950) and her place in the study and making of decorated papers. The book describes Italian, Dutch, French, English and American book papers from 1730 and there is an appendix on the art of marbling, the preparation of paste papers and an alphabetical list of early makers of papers with locations.

16. Leather, Paper and Document Conservation (The use of Leather in Bookbinding, and Paper Deterioration)

Most craft-binders spend time on the restoration and repair of old books. Only leather is suitable for this work, although synthetic book coverings and specially treated canvasses have ousted leather from many types of commercial and library binding. The causes of paper deterioration and the decay of leather are thought very relevant to the binder's art.

Leather Decay

At the beginning of this century an attempt was made to find the causes of leather decay and to produce an 'acid-free' leather.

Library Association, LEATHER FOR LIBRARIES, Sound Leather Committee of the Library Association, 1905.

This consists of articles on the history of tanning and the reform movement to produce lasting leather, and specifications for the fittings of a small bindery.

P.I.R.A. (Printing Industry Research Association) (see under XI. THE PRINTING OF BOOKS, p. 305) THE CAUSES AND PREVENTION OF THE DECAY OF BOOKBINDING LEATHER, *Two Interim Reports of the Bookbinding*

Leather Committee, P.I.R.A. and the British Leather Manufacturers' Research Association, 1933 and 1936.

H. J. Plenderleith, THE PRESERVATION OF LEATHER BOOKBINDINGS, British Museum, 1946, revised 1947, several times reprinted (illustrated).

In a pamphlet the author discusses the P.I.R.A. research into the causes and prevention of decay, and includes the formula for the British Museum leather dressing.

H. J. Plenderleith, THE CONSERVATION OF ANTIQUITIES AND WORKS OF ART, O.U.P., 1956.

This is a basic reference work which derives from research in the British Museum laboratory and the earlier work of P.I.R.A. and the R.S.A. There are chapters on the treatment of animal skins, papyrus and paper.

Royal Society of Arts and the Worshipful Company of Leathersellers, REPORT OF THE COMMITTEE ON LEATHER FOR BOOKBINDING, edited by Viscount Cobham and Sir Henry Trueman Wood, Bell for the R.S.A., 1st edition, 1901, revised and enlarged, 1905 (illustrated).

This committee was set up as a result of the contretemps on the degeneration of leather in the late Victorian era which led to an attempt to apportion blame between the binder and the leather manufacturer. It started a movement to produce 'acid-free' leather but it was eventually found that whatever method of tanning was used, the acid in the air would, in time, rot leather.

Paper Durability, Conservation and Deterioration

The W. J. Barrow Research Laboratory of Richmond, Virginia, has carried out a long programme of research on paper durability. Publications include:

W. J. Barrow, THE BARROW METHOD, University of Virginia Press, 1954.

W. J. Barrow, MANUSCRIPTS AND DOCUMENTS, *Their Deterioration and Restoration*, University of Virginia Press, 1955.

W. J. Barrow and Leavis C. Sproull, PERMANENCE IN BOOK PAPERS: *Investigation of Deterioration in Modern Papers Suggests a Practical Basis for Remedy*, American Association for the Advancement of Science, 1959 (illustrated, tables).

This is reprinted from *Science*, April 1959.

Randolph W. Church, editor, THE MANUFACTURE AND TESTING OF DURABLE BOOK PAPERS *Based on the Investigations of W. J. Barrow*, Virginia State Library, Richmond, 1960 (tables, diagrams).

Barrow Research Laboratory, PERMANENCE/DURABILITY OF THE BOOK, *A Two Year Program*, Virginia State Library, Richmond, 1960 (illustrated).

Barrow Research Laboratory, TEST DATA OF NATURALLY AGED PAPER, Virginia State Library, Richmond, 1964 (illustrated, bibliography, tables).

Barrow Research Laboratory, SPRAY DEACIDIFICATION, Virginia State Library, Richmond, 1964 (illustrated, bibliography).

Barrow Research Laboratory, PERMANENCE/DURABILITY OF THE BOOK VI: *Spot Testing for Unstable Modern Book and Record Papers*, Virginia State Library, Richmond, 1969 (bibliography, tables).

W. Langwell, THE CONSERVATION OF BOOKS AND DOCUMENTS, Pitman, 1957 (bibliography).

This is a clear exposition of a technical subject. Mr Langwell has been working in this field for over thirty years and since the publication of the above has perfected the 'Postlip process' of cheap and simple lamination of documents with deacidifying tissue by a hot or cold method. This has passed all the tests subjected to it both by Mr Langwell himself and by the Barrow Research Laboratory.

Library Association, THE DURABILITY OF PAPER, *A Report of the Special Committee*, L.A., 1930.

This attempts to classify papers by raw material into groups as:

A. suited for permanence;
B. suited for relative permanence;
C. suited for general purposes where permanence is not essential;
D. paper for ephemeral productions.

The report urges the use of A and B for books, and the distinctive watermarking of the grade papers under licence of the Library Association or other recommended body.

P.I.R.A., DURABILITY OF PAPERMAKING, Stationers' Hall, 1931.

This is the P.I.R.A's report of tests on paper carried out according to the Library Association's specifications in the report listed above.

H. J. Plenderleith, THE CONSERVATION OF ANTIQUITIES AND WORKS OF ART (see p. 47 above).

17. Practical Bookbinding

(See also under 'Early Manuals', pp. 42 ff., and 'Leather, Paper and Document Conservation', pp. 46 ff.)

There used to be few books that described practical bookbinding, although some on the history of craft-binding, such as those by Bernard Middleton and Edith Diehl (see below) do in fact describe the processes involved.

Most of the works listed below are intended for the use of amateurs. There is only one work on trade binding in existence.

M. Bannister, A PICTORIAL MANUAL OF BOOKBINDING, Faber & Faber, 1965 (plates of machines, etc., glossary, bibliography).

Hans Bohse, Hans Eckhardt and Paul Weyl, DIE INDUSTRIELLE BUCHBINDEREN, FERTIGUNGSTECHNIK UND MASCHINENKUNDE, Fachbuchverlag, Leipzig, 1955 (242 illustrations).

Even for those who do not read German, the illustrations demonstrate the processes of case-binding very fully.

British Federation of Master Printers, PRINTING OFFICE PROCEDURE, B.F.M.P., 1969, 6 vols. (see also under XI. THE PRINTING OF BOOKS, p. 293).

Book 4 is mostly devoted to binding, both craft and case-binding, with a short paragraph on unsewn binding. There are informative text-figures on different types of folding, stitching and binding, plastic and wire binding, index cutting and machine ruling.

Eric Clough, BOOKBINDING FOR LIBRARIANS, A.A.L., 1957 (glossary).

Deals with library binderies, administration and expenditure of the day: dry but useful.

Douglas Cockerell, BOOKBINDING AND THE CARE OF BOOKS, *A Textbook for Bookbinders and Librarians*, 1st edition, 1901, 5th edition revised, Pitman, 1962 (illustrated).

C

Douglas Cockerell, NOTES ON BOOKBINDING, O.U.P., 1929 (illustrated).

Both these works by Cockerell have long been superseded, and are frowned on by the best craft-binders, but they continue to be tried favourites with amateurs. The name of Cockerell is a venerable one through his association with Cobden-Sanderson, and the Doves Press (see p. 318). His son's firm is virtually the last in this country to produce hand-marbled papers.

S. M. Cockerell, THE REPAIRING OF BOOKS, Sheppard Press, 1958 (illustrated, bibliography).

A. F. Collins, BOOKCRAFT FOR SENIORS, 1st edition, 1938, 4th edition revised, Dryad Press, 1959 (illustrated).

One of the Dryad Press booklists designed for teaching crafts in schools' The series is not well considered by professional binders since it over-simplifies and omits important points of technique.

S. D. Martin Cunha, CONSERVATION OF LIBRARY MATERIALS, *A Manual and Bibliography of the Care, Repair and Restoration of Library Materials,* Scarecrow Press, Metuchen, N.J., 1967.

Lionel S. Darley, INTRODUCTION TO BOOKBINDING, Faber, 1965 (illustrated, bibliography, glossary).

This describes the binder's tools, making a note-book, rebinding of old books, binding in leather and machine bookbinding.

Edith Diehl, BOOKBINDING: *Its Background and Technique,* 2 vols., Rinehart, New York and Toronto, 1946, reprinted Kennikat, 1967 (illustrated, bibliography, glossary of terms).

A standard work; vol. 1 traces the history, vol. 2 describes all the processes involved in craft binding.

Guido Gianni, IL LEGATORE DI LIBRI AD USO DEGLI ARTIGIANI E DEI DILETTANTI, Ulrice Hoepli, Milan, 1st edition, 1908, 5th edition enlarged, 1951 (latest edition, 152 illustrations and 50 plates of historical styles).

T. Harrison, THE BOOKBINDING CRAFT AND INDUSTRY, *An Outline of its History, Development and Technique,* 1st edition, 1908, 2nd edition, Pitman, 1930 (illustrated).

This small volume contains virtually nothing about early techniques, and historical design is dealt with very briefly. It is quite a useful introduction to commercial binding, however.

Paul N. Hasluck, BOOKBINDING, Cassell, 1930.

There are good illustrations of tools including marbling combs and a gilder's cushion.

Trevor Hickman, *Cloth Case Binding Repair and Repairing Books Bound in Leather*, article in PRIVATE LIBRARY, summer and autumn numbers,1966.

The author gives detailed descriptions of rebacking two cloth and two leather Victorian volumes. The article on cloth repair lists tools and materials that the amateur needs, that on leather repair gives the recipe for the British Museum leather dressing.

Carolyn Horton, CLEANING AND PRESERVING BINDINGS AND RELATED MATERIALS, Library Technology Program, American Library Association, Chicago, 1967 (illustrated, annotated bibliography).

This describes in simple terms and with the aid of excellent diagrams, each operation in repair and preservation. At the same time the author is at pains to point out which operations can be carried out by the amateur and which should be left to a trained binder.

THE LEIGHTON COURIER, 1938–39.

Six issues of the house organ of the Leighton-Straker Bookbinding Company, with much useful information on techniques and tools, historical and modern.

A. G. Martin, FINISHING PROCESSES IN PRINTING, Focal Press, 1972 (illustrated, bibliography).

The first full-scale book on trade binding, i.e. print finishing.

John Mason, LETTERPRESS BOOKBINDING, *Edition Case Binding, Stationery Binding, Loose-Leaf Book, Machine Ruling*, Pitman, 1933 (illustrated). Vol. 2 of *The Art and Practice of Printing* (see XIIIB. PRACTICAL PRINTING, p. 292).

This still useful work was reissued in separate parts under the editorship of John C. Tarr during 1946–7.

John Mason, BOOKBINDING, Warner, 1926.

John Mason, PRACTICAL COURSE IN BOOKCRAFT AND BOOKBINDING, Backus, 1947.

Bernard Middleton, A HISTORY OF ENGLISH CRAFT BOOKBINDING TECH-
NIQUE, Hafner, New York, 1963 (illustrated, 6 appendices).

The best book on the various processes of book construction through
the ages by the leading English book restorer, concludes with chapters
on restoration and equipment and appendices on the London bookbinding trade *c.* 1800, the growth of fine and wholesale binderies, and
the influence of the Arts and Crafts Movement on binding methods and
styles.

Bernard Middleton, THE RESTORATION OF LEATHER BINDINGS, Library
Technology Program, American Library Association, Chicago, 1972
(illustrated, bibliography).

Alex J. Philip, THE BUSINESS OF BOOKBINDING FOR LIBRARIANS, PUB-
LISHERS, STUDENTS, BINDERS AND THE GENERAL READER, 1st edition, 1912,
revised edition, 1934 (glossary of bookbinding terms and specimens of
book cloth then available).

Ivor Robinson, INTRODUCING BOOKBINDING, Batsford, 1968 (illustrated
bibliography).

An illustrated guide to craft binding, step by step, with appendixes on
standard British paper sizes, strawboard and millboard thicknesses, some
British and American terms compared, and suppliers of equipment, etc.

TENTH INTERNATIONAL CONGRESS OF MASTER PRINTERS, June 1960.

This contains a codification of all operations performed in the bookbinding
trade.

Laurence Town, BOOKBINDING BY HAND FOR STUDENTS AND CRAFTSMEN,
Faber & Faber, 1965 (bibliography, glossary, plates).

Alex J. Vaughn, MODERN BOOKBINDING, *A Treatise Covering both Letterpress and Stationery Branches of the Trade, with a Section on Finishing and Design,*
1st edition, Raithby Laurence, 1929, 4th edition, Charles Skilton, 1960.

Among the most important books on the practice of bookbinding.

George N. W. K. Whiley, PRODUCTION GUIDES (well illustrated).

These seven publicity booklets for the firm of George Whiley, makers of
blocking foil, give worthwhile information on blocking techniques, real
gold foil, research and development, gold blocking, design of blocks,
aluminium stamping foils and blocking techniques.

18. Current Trade Journals and Directories
(See also under XI. THE PRINTING OF BOOKS, p. 300 ff.)

Printing journals all contain material on the allied trades including binding. None is devoted exclusively to binding, though much is contained in:

THE PRINTING AND BINDING TRADES REVIEW, monthly, 1958–

Neither is there any current directory of binders alone. THE DIRECTORY OF PRINTERS' BOOKBINDERS' AND ALLIED TRADE SUPPLIERS, Charles Skilton, 1955–56, is still useful, though naturally often out of date.

THE DIRECTORY OF PAPERMAKING, PRINTING AND BINDING, 1950–67, is less comprehensive but more up to date.

19. Current Trade Associations and Societies
(See also under XI. THE PRINTING OF BOOKS, pp. 306 ff. for joint associations.)

BOOKBINDING AND ALLIED TRADES MANAGEMENT ASSOCIATION.

This is both a recreational and friendly society.

DESIGNER BOOKBINDERS (formerly the GUILD OF CONTEMPORARY BOOK-BINDERS) (founded 1955).

The foremost bookbinding society in Great Britain was renamed *Designer Bookbinders* in 1969 as being more in keeping with the times, and with the society's aim of promoting and exhibiting the art of the hand bound book and exerting a progressive influence on bookbinding design and technique. Its members are available as designers and consultants in industry, as lecturers and as specialist advisors and executants in book repair and restoration. Associate membership is open to historians, librarians, booksellers and others interested in fine bookbinding. Its forthcoming review, *D.B.*, *Designer Bookbinders Review*, will be available to members.

PRINTING AND KINDRED TRADES FEDERATION (see under XI. THE PRINTING OF BOOKS, p. 305).

BOOKSELLING

A. HISTORY OF NEW BOOKSELLING

(See also under IIIC. ANTIQUARIAN BOOKSELLING, AUCTIONEERING AND
COLLECTING, VI. THE HISTORY OF THE BOOK TRADE, IX. THE NET BOOK
AGREEMENT and XIIIA. THE HISTORY OF PUBLISHING.)

Illustration from W. Roberts, The Book-Hunter in London, *1895 (actual size)*
(see p. 89)

1. Introduction

By 1757 the two functions [of publisher and bookseller], were recognised as independent, but the business of booksellers was still held to be 'to purchase original copies from authors, to employ printers to print them, and publish and sell them in their shops. But their chief riches and profit is in the property of valuable copies'. Charles Knight mentioned that the greater number of City booksellers did not carry on the business of publisher pure and simple. They were factors of books for the London collectors and agents for the country booksellers (Plant, *The English Book Trade*, pp. 405–6).

Mr Sidney Hodgson recalls trade sales in his father's day, as late as the 1880s, before the Net Book Agreement clamped down on undercutting. The operation of such sales in which booksellers and publishers were involved in auctioneering is described by John Britton in his *Autobiography*, 1849:

A few of the large wholesale publishers of London are in the habit of making up, either annually or occasionally, what are called 'trade sales', when they prepare a catalogue of their large stock-books, and distribute it to a select number of retail dealers, who are invited to meet the publisher and his auctioneer at a certain tavern, where, after partaking of an early dinner, the trade auctioneer proceeds to dispose of the works named in the catalogue, to the parties present. The various lots comprise many copies of recently published works, and are offered and sold at rather less than the usual trade prices . . . with a moderate discount for cash. . . . The late Thomas Tegg . . . removed to Cheapside where he accumulated a large stock of books and established an evening auction. . . . Mr Hodgson, of Fleet Street, is at present the confidential and respected agent of the London publishers.

The flood of printed matter that pours from today's presses (an annual output of some 33,000 titles in this country alone) has forced booksellers to specialise more and more, for it is no longer possible for one man, or one establishment, to be omniscient.

Warren Snyder, in an article on retail bookselling in *The Building of a Book*, 1906, (see p. 59 below) says:

I recall a conversation I had two or three years ago with a man more than 70 years of age. He had started in his business life as a clerk in a bookstore and he said to me, 'There are no booksellers today like there were when I was in the book business. Then', he continued, 'a bookseller was thoroughly posted as to the contents of the books he had for sale, while now they know but little more about a book than its title.' I asked him if he ever stopped to compare the conditions under which the booksellers of today had to labor. I have read that in 1855 there were but 500 new books issued in the United States. In 1905, 50 years later, there were 7,500 new books launched on the market. This did not include 600 reprints. When there was an average of less than 10 new books published in a week, it was an easy task for an intelligent salesman to get a fair knowledge of the contents of everyone.

Specialisation in bookselling is largely a post-war feature. University bookselling was, for instance, seldom separately considered in pre-war days. Now that the number of universities and of full-time students proliferates, many new universities boast their own bookshops within their walls. Others specialise in technical, medical, foreign or children's books, and general booksellers have specialist departments or branches. In the last few years some have opened paperback shops.

2. General Histories of Bookselling
(Many also cover THE HISTORY OF PUBLISHING.)

Henry Curwen, A HISTORY OF BOOKSELLERS, THE OLD AND NEW, Chatto & Windus, 1873 (illustrated).

The author maintains that 'history is the essence of innumerable biographies' and exemplifies each facet that he describes by a particular firm; thus 'Classical and Educational Literature' is the sub-title of the chapter on *The Longman Family*, while *Chambers, Knight and Cassell* is subtitled 'Literature of the People', *Henry Colburn* is subtitled 'Three-Volume Novels and Light Literature', *Simpkin, Marshall and Co.* describes 'Collecting for the Country Trade', *Charles Edward Mudie*, 'The Lending Library', and *W. H. Smith and Son*, 'Railway Literature'. Hence this work is more a history of publishing than of bookselling.

ENCYCLOPAEDIA BRITANNICA, 10th and 11th editions.

An article on *Bookselling* by Joseph Shaylor describes the rise of the retail book trade on both sides of the Atlantic.

A. Growoll, THE PROFESSION OF BOOKSELLING: *A Handbook of Practical Hints for the Apprentice and Bookseller*, 2 vols., London and New York, 1893 and 1895 (illustrated).

This advises on trade catalogues, window-dressing, advertising, buying, moving and taking stock, circulating libraries and other practical matters that reveal much of bookselling practice on both sides of the Atlantic during the second half of the nineteenth century.

John Hampden, editor, THE BOOK WORLD, 1935 (see also under VI. HISTORY OF THE BOOK TRADE, p. 156).

This includes an article by J. G. Wilson on *Bookselling in London*, another by Basil Blackwell on *Provincial Bookselling*, and one by J. Ainslie Thin on *Second-hand Bookselling*.

John Hampden, editor, THE BOOK WORLD, 1957.

This contains articles on the trade in the 1940s and 1950s and includes *Bookselling in London and the Provinces, Wholesale Bookselling, Antiquarian and Secondhand*, one appendix on *Book Rings* and another on the *Book-sellers' Association*.

Frederick H. Hitchcock, editor, THE BUILDING OF A BOOK: *A Series of Practical Articles Written by Experts in the Various Departments of Book Making and Distributing*, Grafton Press, New York, 1906.

An introduction by Theodore L. de Vinne is followed by articles on *Selling at Wholesale* by Joseph Bray, *Selling at Retail* by Warren Snyder, *Selling by Subscription* by Charles S. Orcutt. The book also describes aspects of authorship, the rare book trade and printing, illustrating, binding, copyright and publicity.

Charles Knight, THE SHADOWS OF OLD BOOKSELLERS, 1865.

These lively, if unscholarly and unoriginal biographies of the eighteenth-century London publisher–booksellers are mainly derived from Boswell's *Life of Johnson* and Nichols's *Literary Anecdotes* (see p. 270).

Edward Marston, SKETCHES OF SOME BOOKSELLERS OF THE TIME OF DR. SAMUEL JOHNSON, 1902 (illustrated).

The author lifts whole phrases verbatim from Nichols's *Literary Anecdotes* (see p. 270).

Edward Marston, SKETCHES OF BOOKSELLERS OF OTHER DAYS, 1901 (illustrated).

This covers much the same ground as Knight and Roberts (see above and below), as well as including chapters on Samuel Richardson, Thomas Gent and James Lackington (qq.v.).

F. A. Mumby, PUBLISHING AND BOOKSELLING (see under VI. HISTORY OF THE BOOK TRADE, p. 157).

Marjorie Plant, THE ENGLISH BOOK TRADE (see under VI. HISTORY OF THE BOOK TRADE, p. 157).

Harold Raymond, PUBLISHING AND BOOKSELLING, Dent, 1938 (see p. 155).

William Roberts, THE EARLIER HISTORY OF BOOKSELLING, 1889.

This is much less good than the author's book on the rare book trade (see p. 89), and takes the reader for an unscholarly whisk through the centuries, from the dawn of bookselling in the seventh century to the eighteenth-century figures of Lintot, Dunton, Curll and others.

Joseph Shaylor, THE FASCINATION OF BOOKS: *With Other Papers on Books and Bookselling,* Simpkin, Marshall, 1912 (illustrated).

The author, described by F. A. Mumby as 'one of the most industrious chroniclers of the trade', sheds light on the Victorian bookselling scene, as well as including papers on *The Rise of the Christmas Annual, 19th Century Book Distributing,* and *Reprints and Their Readers.*

Alfred E. Stevens, THE RECOLLECTIONS OF A BOOKMAN, Witherby, 1933 (illustrated).

This autobiography, much concerned with the publishing firms of Heinemann and W. & R. Chambers, for whom the author worked for many years, is also informative about circulating libraries at the beginning of the twentieth century, when Stevens worked for Mudie's. One chapter is devoted to *Starting a Small Bookshop and Circulating Library.*

Sigfred Taubert, BIBLIOPOLA, *Pictures and Text about the Book Trade,* 2 vols., Dr Ernst Hausewedell, Hamburg, and Allen Lane, the Penguin Press, London, 1966 (lavishly illustrated).

Among the numerous aspects and personages dealt with are shop fronts, interiors, the bookseller, his assistants, the customer, the child, the book-buyer, the book-thief, the auctioneer and the antiquarian bookseller. The illustrations are fascinating, but the text, in German with stilted English and French translations, is disappointing for so ambitious a production.

3. Histories of Individual Bookshops and Memoirs of Booksellers

(See also under IIIC. ANTIQUARIAN BOOKSELLING, pp. 82 ff.)

Many histories of bookshops are slight pamphlets put out for propaganda purposes, and not considered worth including below.

BOWES & BOWES (see also under 'Macmillan' in XIIIA. THE HISTORY OF PUBLISHING, pp. 342 f.) (A bookshop first opened on this site 1588.)

George J. Gray, CAMBRIDGE BOOKSELLING AND THE OLDEST BOOKSHOP IN THE UNITED KINGDOM, Bowes & Bowes, Cambridge, 1925.

Robin Myers, *Bowes & Bowes Booksellers and Publishers,* article in the ANTIQUARIAN BOOKSELLERS JOURNAL, 1953.

ISAAC FORSYTH (1768–1859)

Isaac Forsyth MacAndrew, MEMOIR OF ISAAC FORSYTH *Bookseller in Elgin (1768–1859),* 1889.

HATCHARDS (established 1797)

James Laver, HATCHARDS OF PICCADILLY, 1797–1947, Hatchards, Piccadilly, 1947 (illustrated).

CHARLES HUMPHREYS (b. 1851)

THE LIFE OF CHARLES HUMPHREYS, *Bookseller of Paternoster Row, Streatham and Peckham Rye Told by Himself,* Wickliffe Press, n.d.

This is a pious autobiography by a bookseller member of the Salvation Army.

WILLIAM HUTTON (1723–1815)

William Hutton, THE LIFE OF WILLIAM HUTTON *Including a Particular Account of the Riots of Birmingham in 1791, to which is Subjoined the History of His Family,* published by his daughter, 1861, 2nd edition containing notices of his works, 1817.

The autobiography of the Birmingham topographer, bookseller, founder of a circulating library and owner of a paper warehouse, is described by Lowndes (see p. 101) as 'one of the most entertaining and instructive of mercantile autobiographies'.

JAMES LACKINGTON (1746–1815)

James Lackington made bookselling history by his speculations in the remainder trade. 'He determined to sell for cash at the lowest possible price and broke through the trade custom of destroying all but a few copies of remainders, and sold the whole stock at little profit. From buying books in small quantities he rose to purchasing entire libraries, and was able to set up a carriage and a country house at Merton. As soon as he had acquired a fortune he seems to have lost any love of books which he may have had' (*Dictionary of National Biography*).

James Lackington, MEMOIRS OF THE FIRST FORTY-FIVE YEARS OF THE LIFE OF JAMES LACKINGTON, *The Present Bookseller in Chiswell Street, Moorfields,* 1791.

This is a valuable source of information about bookselling in different parts of the country.

James Lackington, THE CONFESSIONS OF J. LACKINGTON, *Late Bookseller at the Temple of the Muses, in a Series of Letters to a Friend,* 1804.

This, written to make amends for his rogueries, is much less interesting than the *Memoirs.* (See also Paul Hollister, *The Author's Wallet,* p. 222 below.)

JOHN MENZIES (established 1833)

THE HOUSE OF MENZIES, John Menzies, 1958 (illustrated).

THE MILLERS

George Miller, LATER STRUGGLES IN THE JOURNEY OF LIFE: *or the After-noon of My Days . . . the Incidents and Every Day Occurrences of the Latter, and Most Unfortunate Part of the Real Life of a Country Bookseller,* Miller, Edinburgh, 1833.

Scots piety is mixed with detail of bookselling in Dunbar, Glasgow and Newcastle at the beginning of the nineteenth century.

W. J. Couper, THE MILLERS OF HADDINGTON, DUNBAR AND DUNFERMLINE: *A Record of Scottish Bookselling,* T. Fisher Unwin, 1914 (illustrated, biblio-

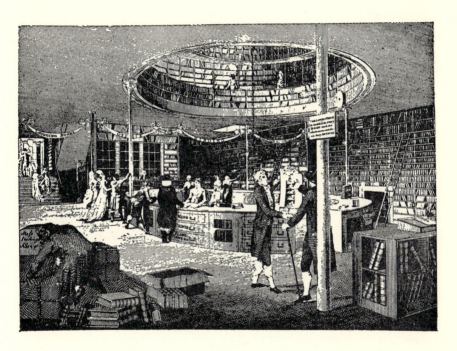

James Lackington's 'Temple of the Muses', the bookshop of an early remainder merchant
(see p. 62)

graphy of books written or edited by the Millers of Dunbar and Haddington, and of the East Lothian Press and the Dunfermline Press).

This is a full account of a Scottish bookselling family of the eighteenth
and nineteenth centuries.

HAROLD MONRO (1879–1932)

Joy Grant, HAROLD MONRO AND THE POETRY BOOKSHOP, Routledge &
Kegan Paul, 1967 (illustrated, bibliography).

This describes the Poetry Bookshop as a bookselling phenomenon and
propaganda for poetry, as well as giving an account of Harold Monro's
life and an evaluation of his own writings.

JOSEPH SHAYLOR

Joseph Shaylor, SIXTY YEARS A BOOKMAN, Selwyn & Blount, 1923.

In his autobiography, Joseph Shaylor writes on such aspects of bookselling
history as underselling and the Stationer's Company term catalogues.

W. H. SMITH (newsagent shop opened 1792)

Sir Herbert Maxwell, LIFE AND TIMES OF THE RIGHT HONOURABLE
WILLIAM HENRY SMITH, M.P., 2 vols., William Blackwood, Edinburgh and
London, 1893 (illustrated).

This biography of William Henry Smith the Second, is largely concerned
with his life as a public figure, although chapters 2 and 3 (pp. 44–98)
describe the establishment of railway bookstalls, production of railway
novels and the distribution of newspapers.

G. R. Pocklington, THE STORY OF W. H. SMITH, 1st edition, 1921, revised
edition by Gwen Clear, privately printed, 1949 (illustrated, appendix of
Events in the History of the Business).

JOHN SMITH & SON (GLASGOW) LTD. (established 1751)

A SHORT NOTE ON A LONG HISTORY, 1751–1925 (illustrated).

THOMAS TEGG (1776–1845)

This buccaneering remainder merchant has been described as 'a suitable
companion for James Lackington'. He bought up many of Scott's novels

on the cheap during the financial panic of 1826 (see 'Constable' under XIIIA. THE HISTORY OF PUBLISHING, p. 353), and sold them at a good profit; he said of himself, 'I was the broom that swept the booksellers' warehouses'.

A MEMOIR OF THE LATE THOMAS TEGG, *Abridged from His Autobiography by Permission of His Son, William Tegg*, privately printed, 1870.

JAMES THIN

[James Thin], REMINISCENCES OF BOOKSELLERS AND BOOKSELLING IN EDINBURGH IN THE TIME OF WILLIAM IV, privately printed, Oliver & Boyd, 1905 (illustrated).

WILLIAM WEST (1770–1854)

[William West], FIFTY YEARS RECOLLECTIONS OF AN OLD BOOKSELLER, Cork, 1835.

[William West], THREE HUNDRED AND FIFTY YEARS: *Retrospection of an Old Bookseller, Containing an Account of the Origin and Progress of Printing, Type Founding, and Engraving, in Their Various Branches*, Cork, 1830.

The author, an antiquary and bookseller, draws heavily on Nichols's *Literary Anecdotes* (see p. 270) but also gives stories not found elsewhere and information such as rules for drawing caricatures.

DAVID WYLLIE (established 1814)

A CENTURY OF BOOKSELLING 1814–1914, David Wyllie, 1914 (illustrated). Reprinted from the *Aberdeen Book Lover*, November 1914.

B. BOOKSELLING PRACTICE AND ORGANISATION

1. Introduction

Until the passing of the Industrial Training Act few thought of running training courses in shop-keeping and perhaps this partly explains the lack of books on bookselling practice and organisation. Following the vogue for business studies and in accordance with the Act, the Booksellers' Association has established a Charter Diploma in bookselling which devotes one-third of its course to bookshop management and practice (the remaining two-thirds go to elementary library studies, bibliography and English literature). There is nothing in the syllabus on special branches of bookselling which we may classify as general, antiquarian, university, paperback, library bookselling, bookstalls and wholesaling. Nor are there books on many of these aspects. It may be that textbooks will follow in the wake of the Diploma which is an attempt to raise the status of bookselling and attract the right kind of young people into a trade against which David Garnett (himself a one-time bookseller) warned: 'Above all, never be a bookseller; that is the worst of all; the hardest work and the worst paid.'

2. Manuals and Guides

Irene Babbidge, BEGINNING IN BOOKSELLING, André Deutsch, 1st edition, 1965, 2nd revised edition, 1971 (bibliography).

A slight but practical book, in three parts covering daily routine, orders and background information.

F. T. Bell and F. Seymour Smith, LIBRARY BOOKSELLING, André Deutsch, Grafton, 1966.

This is the joint work of a library supplier and a librarian and covers the Net Book Agreement and the Restrictive Practices Court (see also under IX. THE NET BOOK AGREEMENT, p. 225), the supply of books to universities, colleges and schools, the different views of authors and libraries in the Public Lending Right controversy (see also under I. AUTHORSHIP, pp. 15 ff.).

Timothy Dudley-Smith, CHRISTIAN LITERATURE AND THE CHURCH BOOKSTALL, Falcon Books, 1963.

Despite its deceptive title this is invaluable for all who wish to run a bookstall, Christian or otherwise. It describes how to start, run and build a bookstall, with advice on tables and bookstands. The appendixes consist of a form of application for a book agency, names and addresses of selected publishers, and of firms, services and organisations mentioned in the book.

Gerald Bartlett, editor, BETTER BOOKSELLING, Hutchinson, 1971.
This is a single volume reprint of the following pamphlets:

Erich Bailey, THE ECONOMICS OF BOOKSELLING, 1965 (bibliography).
Peter Stockham, UNIVERSITY BOOKSELLING, 1965 (bibliography).
Monique Fuchs, ACCOUNTING FOR BOOKSELLERS, 1965.
Gerald Bartlett, STOCK CONTROL IN BOOKSELLING, 1966.
Gerald Bartlett, BOOKSELLING BY MAIL, 1966.
R. G. Peacham, LIBRARY AND EDUCATIONAL SUPPLY IN BOOKSELLING, 1966.
John Hyams, CAREERS IN BOOKSELLING, 1968.
Leon Fontaine, CREATIVE BOOKSHOP STAFFING, 1968.
Charter Group Symposium, BOOKSHOP EQUIPMENT AND DESIGN, 1968.

Thomas Joy, THE TRUTH ABOUT BOOKSELLING, Pitman, 1952, revised edition, 1964.

The best of the very small number of reference books for aspiring or practising booksellers. It covers applications for inclusion in the *Directory of Booksellers*, the Library Licence scheme, the quantity bookbuying scheme, a glossary of trade terms and abbreviations, Book Tokens, Book Centre Ltd., established trade practice for allowances on net books, how to run a successful book sale and a list of important addresses. There are chapters on the Net Book Agreement, book trade charities and training for bookselling.

B. N. Langdon-Davies, THE PRACTICE OF BOOKSELLING, *With Some Opinions on Its Nature, Status and Future*, with a foreword by H. M. Wilson, Phoenix House, 1951.

This is still a standard work, though somewhat out of date in some respects and less practical than Joy (see above).

F. Seymour Smith, BIBLIOGRAPHY IN THE BOOKSHOP, André Deutsch, Grafton, 1st edition, 1964, 2nd revised edition, 1972.

Describes the service of the stock-holding booksellers, their method and technique. Mr Seymour Smith, a professional librarian who became W. H. Smith's bibliographer, was also the author of *An English Library* and *What Shall I Read Next?*

3. Surveys

Peter H. Mann and Jacqueline Burgoyne, BOOKS AND READERS, André Deutsch, 1969.

Peter H. Mann, BOOKSELLING: *An Occupational Survey*, University of Sheffield, Dept. of Sociological Studies, 1972.

Peter H. Mann, BOOKS: *Buyers and Borrowers*, André Deutsch, 1971.

4. Reference Works and Bibliographies

AMERICAN BOOKS IN PRINT (annual with 5-year cumulations), Bowker, New York and London.

There is a bi-monthly supplement, FORTHCOMING BOOKS. (For other basic American book trade bibliographies see in THE BOWKER ANNUAL *of Library and Book Trade Information* the section, *Some Basic Books for the Book Trade*, subsection, *Book Finding Tools*.)

BRITISH BOOKS IN PRINT: *The Reference Catalogue of Current Literature*, Whitaker (annual since 1957).

Records all British books *in print* at April each year, based on the weekly lists in the *Bookseller* (see p. 73), separately listed under author and title. It is preceded by a full list of publishers and their addresses, a list of British publishers' agents abroad, and an extensive book trade bibliography of the British book trade. It used to consist (1874–1932) of 135 publishers' catalogues bound in two volumes, until the increase in output made such an arrangement impracticable.

THE BRITISH NATIONAL BIBLIOGRAPHY (B.N.B.) (weekly since 1950, also quarterly, annual, and 5-year cumulations with classified index).

The new publications of the week are given under subject, together with an author and title index. It is compiled from the accessions of the Copyright Libraries Office, so that publication is frequently much in advance of notice in the B.N.B.

CHILDREN'S BOOKS IN PRINT (see under VII. CHILDREN'S BOOKS, p. 190).

CUMULATIVE BOOK INDEX (C.B.I.)., H. W. Wilson (monthly since 1928, except August, with frequent paperbound, annual, 2- and 5-year cumulations).

A world list of books in the English language, with author, title and subject entries. Special features are the identification of pseudonyms, and form lists of fiction (such as detective fiction).

CUMULATIVE BOOK LIST (C.B.L.), Whitaker (weekly since 1924, and cumulated quarterly, annually and 5-yearly).

This is a re-issue of the weekly list appearing in THE BOOKSELLER (see p. 73) incorporating the classified monthly list, CLASSIFIED LITERATURE. It lists new publications, where BOOKS IN PRINT lists those in print without regard to date of publication.

THE ENGLISH CATALOGUE OF BOOKS, Publishers' Circular (annual since 1801). It incorporated *The Catalogue of Books* (1801–36), *The London Catalogue of Books* (until 1835) and *The British Catalogue*.

Books issued in Britain are listed under author, title and subject. The earlier volumes, long out of print have been re-issued by the Kraus Reprint Corporation, New York. Despite deficiencies and inaccuracies, older issues of *The English Catalogue* give invaluable detail of nineteenth-century books.

HOW TO OBTAIN BRITISH BOOKS, *A Guide for Booksellers, Librarians and Other Professional Bookbuyers*, Publishers' Association, 1st edition, 1949, 7th edition, 1969.

Gives the names and addresses of British publishers, wholesalers, agents, etc., and information on how to order books, on the British Council, the Low-Priced Book Scheme, and much else.

INFORMATION ABOUT BRITISH BOOKS, *A Booklist for Booksellers, Librarians and Others Concerned with Sources of Information*, British Council, 1969.

This booklet contains information on how to find out about British books, and lists references for small, medium and large bookshops, lists books on bookselling and the names and addresses of British publishers.

PAPERBACKS IN PRINT, *A Reference Catalogue of Paperbacks in Print and on Sale in Great Britain*, Whitaker (since 1960 arranged under 50 main headings and including alphabetical author and title index, now quarterly as well as annual).

PUBLISHERS IN THE UNITED KINGDOM AND THEIR ADDRESSES, Whitaker (annual each February, since 1946).

Features of this list are the interleaving which allows changes of address to be inserted, and the appendix of publishers under *Standard Book Number*.

TECHNICAL AND SCIENTIFIC BOOKS IN PRINT, Whitaker (annual since 1965).

This records titles (excluding medicine) under 45 main headings and 300 sub-divisions.

5. Periodicals of Interest to Booksellers

THE BOOKSELLER, Whitaker (1858–).

This weekly journal of trade news, contains an alphabetical list of new books of the week (see *Books in Print* and C.B.L. above). Since 1924, the booklists have also been published quarterly and annually. Since 1970 it no longer contains monthly lists, which are replaced by a separate bi-monthly publication listing the previous and forthcoming month's books and called *Books of the Month and Books to Come*.

SMITH'S TRADE NEWS, W. H. Smith (1926–).

This weekly magazine contains news and feature articles on the book trade, with a special monthly feature on paperbacks, an annual children's book number in August, advertisements of businesses for sale or wanted, the week's bestsellers, etc. It covers the newspaper, magazine, stationery and toy trades as well as new bookselling.

T.L.S. (TIMES LITERARY SUPPLEMENT) (1902–).

This was originally a supplement of *The Times*, now a separately issued weekly of book reviews and articles on literary matters. It is important for librarians and teachers of literature, less so for new booksellers because its reviews appear too late for advance stock ordering.

6. Booksellers' Associations

(See also under ANTIQUARIAN BOOKSELLING, pp. 104 ff., and under XIII. PUBLISHING, pp. 371 f.)

THE BOOKSELLERS' ASSOCIATION OF GREAT BRITAIN AND IRELAND (founded 1895)

Until 1948, this was called *The Associated Booksellers of Great Britain and Ireland*. It comprises about 3,000 members organised into local branches. It operates the Book Token Scheme. It organises lecture courses in preparation for its Diploma in Bookselling. Those bookshops who employ staff with diplomas are members of the Charter Booksellers' Group.

Its publications include the B.A. LIST OF MEMBERS annually, the MARKET INDICATOR SERIES edited by G. R. Davies, and TRAINING FOR BOOKSELLING, 1968.

C. ANTIQUARIAN BOOKSELLING, AUCTIONEERING AND COLLECTING

No. 68. 5s.

'*To Be Sold by Auction*', *from a nineteenth-century wood-cut printers' specimen in the St Bride Printing Library (actual size)*

1. Introduction

The world of old books comprises the antiquarian and rare trade at the more costly, and the secondhand at the cheaper, end of the scale:

The lines of demarcation between 'rare books', 'old books', and 'secondhand books' have never been, and can never be, clearly defined. The same applies to most of those who deal in them; and the Antiquarian Booksellers' Association makes no distinction between a man who specialises in incunabula, another who deals only in Modern Firsts, a third who restricts himself to botany, and finally a general secondhand dealer, provided that his business is primarily in old books (John Carter, *A.B.C. for Book Collectors*).

The A.B.A. also includes the dealer in autograph letters and holograph material.

Big business organisation and methods have moved into the new bookseller's and auctioneer's worlds but have only affected a few antiquarian dealers. Indeed antiquarian bookselling can offer a livelihood to the individualist who likes to work more or less by himself and for himself, even sometimes combining part-time dealing (though this is not recognised by the A.B.A.) with another occupation unconnected with it.

The division between new and antiquarian bookselling is, like other divisions of the trade, of relatively recent date (see under 'History of New Bookselling', pp. 57 f.). There is still some overlap, for the specialist rare book dealer will stock important new books in his field. Some of the larger new booksellers, such as Heffer of Cambridge or Blackwell of Oxford have imposing rare book departments; or a firm of rare dealers such as Bernard Quaritch may run a department of new books. In general, however, the two now move in different spheres.

Unlike the new trade, the character of a rare book dealer's stock is affected by the exigencies of supply at least as much as by the desire to satisfy public demand. It is true that the rare or secondhand dealer does not have to contend with publishers and deadline dates as the new bookseller does, but he has other difficulties. He cannot always acquire desirable items, or only at a price that makes resale uncertain. He must therefore accept what is offered to him by private vendors or bid for them at auction. Then again, in order to get hold of a small number of wanted books, he may have to buy a whole library containing an overwhelming quantity of lesser grade stock which he may be too much of an optimist, or not have the heart, to jettison. The hunt for suitable stock is therefore a greater problem and requires more skill, than the selling of it.

The rare book dealer is in many ways more akin to the collector than he is to the new bookseller. The mastery of collations, condition and points that the antiquarian bookseller must command, ignores what is 'in print', and that is the entire concern of the new bookseller. This indifference to 'in print' can occasionally be carried to the point where an early edition of a work still available new is inadvertently sold as 'scarce'. Or, in the salerooms (where the bookseller cannot afford to be thus carried away if he hopes to prosper), a collector may be infected by the fun of the chase to the point where he bids more than the price in the publisher's current list.

The skills required for collecting and dealing are similar, but:

It is a fact that the professional bookdealer and the private collector although united by their love of books, are poles apart in their consideration of the end result. It can happen, however, that a bookdealer finds himself confronted with a group of books which awakens in him something of the collector's own passion and which he cannot therefore consider with the cold business sense that must generally govern his activity (Carla A. Marzoli, *Calligraphy 1535–1885*, Milan, 1962).

Value is not unimportant to the collector. But there are other considerations in his making a purchase: it fills a gap in his collection: it contains a particular reference that makes an otherwise worthless book valuable to him: it would be lost to him if he did not buy it there and then. For, as A. W. Pollard remarks in his article on 'Book Collecting' in the *Encyclopaedia Britannica*, 11th edition: 'To rescue good books from perishing is one of the main objects of book-collecting.'

The interests that unite bookseller and collector sometimes cause a collector to turn dealer. Or the twin motives of book love and the desire to make a capital investment may inspire a dealer to form a private collection, as did Dr A. S. W. Rosenbach of Philadelphia (see under VII. CHILDREN'S BOOKS, p. 180). Cynics maintain that such a collection generally consists of items that were bought for resale but which, for one reason or another, proved unsaleable.

Auctioneering is another world, little documented. The full history of Sotheby's, Hodgson's and Christie's is yet to be written. These great salerooms claim some of our most august rare book specialists. The separation of auctioneer from bookseller is a marked feature, though not exclusive to, the British book trade. In Holland, Germany and Switzerland sales are generally conducted by booksellers. The rare bookseller cannot depend on auction sales for the regular supply of stock (though they are a major source) as the new bookseller does on the publisher.

2. Auctions and Miscellaneous

Most of the literature on book auctions consists of articles in periodicals and chapters in books on collecting.

BOOK AUCTION RECORDS (see p. 103 below).

BOOK PRICES CURRENT (see p. 103 below, and 'Elliot Stock' under XIIIA. THE HISTORY OF PUBLISHING, p. 348).

Saleroom prices are misleading guides to rare book values for those ignorant of the factors that control them, but they provide a quick check for those who have no access to booksellers' catalogues, or lack the time to sift them.

Andrew Block, A SHORT HISTORY OF THE PRINCIPAL LONDON ANTIQUARIAN BOOKSELLERS AND BOOK AUCTIONEERS, Dennis Archer, 1933.

This reprint of the appendix to Block's *Book Collector's Vade Mecum* consists of brief notes on the lives and specialities of thirty-two leading booksellers of the day, mostly written anonymously by themselves, followed by notes on the Antiquarian Booksellers' Association and the *Clique* (see p. 103).

British Museum, LIST OF CATALOGUES OF ENGLISH BOOK SALES 1676–1900 *Now in the British Museum*, compiled by G. F. Barwick with an historical introduction by A. W. Pollard, 1915.

Richard Brown and Stanley Brett, THE LONDON BOOKSHOP: *Being Part One of a Pictorial Record of the Antiquarian Book Trade; Portraits and Premises with Prefatory Reminiscences by Percy Muir,* Private Libraries Association, 1971.

John Carter, A.B.C. FOR BOOK COLLECTORS (see p. 100) – entry on the practice of *Auctions* (pp. 27–30).

A. Growoll and Wilberforce Eames, THREE CENTURIES OF ENGLISH BOOKTRADE BIBLIOGRAPHY (see under VI. HISTORY OF THE BOOK TRADE, p. 163).

W. C. Hazlitt, THE BOOK COLLECTOR, 1904 (see p. 86).

The frontispiece drawn by H. M. Paget shows a book sale at Sotheby's (the original is still on view at 34 New Bond Street) with a guard giving a

'The Compleat Auctioneer', copper engraving by Sutton Nicholls, c. 1700

key to the twenty-nine leading booksellers and collectors of the day. Chapter 16 includes some history of book auctions.

Frederick H. Hitchcock, editor, THE BUILDING OF A BOOK, 1st edition, 1906 (see p. 59).

This contains a chapter on *Selling at Auctions* by John Anderson, and another on *Rare and Secondhand Books* by Charles E. Goodspeed.

A. R. A. Hobson, SOTHEBY & CO., privately printed, 1954.

Hodgson, ONE HUNDRED YEARS OF BOOK AUCTIONS 1807–1907, *A Brief Record of the Firm of Hodgson & Co.*, privately printed at the Chiswick Press, 1907.

T. Landau, ENCYCLOPAEDIA OF LIBRARIANSHIP, Bowes & Bowes, 3rd edition, 1966.

The article on *Auction Sales* (pp. 58–9) is followed by a short bibliography.

J. Lawler, BOOK AUCTIONS IN ENGLAND IN THE SEVENTEENTH CENTURY, 1676–1700, *With a Chronological List of the Book Auctions of the Period*, Elliott Stock, 1906.

This covers a short but important period in rare book history when the leading booksellers and publishers also travelled round the country as auctioneers, the most important of these dual personalities being William Cooper and Edward Millington.

E. Millicent Sowerby, RARE PEOPLE AND RARE BOOKS, Constable, 1967 (see also p. 90).

Miss Sowerby was Sotheby's first woman cataloguer from 1917 to 1923; she describes the personalities of the auction house in that period (chapters 5–11).

Archer Taylor, BOOK CATALOGUES: *Their Varieties and Uses*, Newberry Library, Chicago, Illinois, 1957.

This traces the evolution of book catalogues and their value as bibliographical tools under the heads of: the varieties of book catalogues, their uses, bibliographies of catalogues, a list of catalogues of private libraries and a checklist of books and articles cited. 'In using catalogues, and especially in using sale catalogues one must remember that many of them serve only a temporary purpose, for which they were hastily prepared . . .

one must therefore accept without loud complaint carelessness in citing, alphabetizing, and classifying titles, excessive brevity in citations, failures to provide cross references and indexes, and loosely defined categories'. Nowhere else has all this been so usefully pointed out.

The author, professor of German at the University of California, has written several other books on bibliographical subjects.

3. Memoirs and Biographies of Dealers and Collectors and Books on Book Collecting of Historical Interest

As with histories and biographies of other sections of the trade, some of the most important firms and collectors have no published annals, and some of the fullest works deal with by-ways of the trade; this makes the list below a haphazard affair.

Most of the discursive reminiscences of book collectors of the past have good things in them here and there; but a modern collector would not seek advice from them on information on how to proceed. Those below, examples of collecting taste and fashion of their day, belong to the history of collecting and thus are separated from recent books on method and practice which are to be found under the heading 'Modern Books on "Taste and Technique in Book-Collecting"', pp. 93 ff.

Memoirs and Biographies of Dealers and Collectors

JAMES BAIN LTD. (established 1808)

James S. Bain, A BOOKSELLER LOOKS BACK: *The Story of the Bains*, with an introduction by Hugh Walpole, Macmillan, 1940 (illustrated, bibliography of books on London).

This is less of a trade history than a biographical and topographical study. It starts with the birth of the first James Bain, 1794, and ends in 1937 and includes extracts from the diary of Louisa Bain and notebooks and poems by her son James. The firm has recently moved out of London, and is no longer connected with the Bain family.

WILLIAM BLADES (1824–90).

I select one work by the Caxton scholar (see also under XI. THE PRINTING OF BOOKS, pp. 273 f.) printer and collector whose important library formed the basis of the St Bride Printing Library (see also under XI. THE PRINTING OF BOOKS, pp. 309f.).

William Blades, THE ENEMIES OF BOOKS, *With a Preface by Richard Garnett,* Elliott Stock, 1896 (illustrated).

With plentiful anecdotes Blades enumerates the enemies of books as fire, water, gas and heat, dust and neglect, ignorance and bigotry, the book worm, other vermin, bookbinders who hack, wash, size and mend, collectors and servants and children.

SEYMOUR DE RICCI (1881–1944)

Seymour de Ricci, THE BOOK COLLECTOR'S GUIDE, Philadelphia, 1921.

Described by John Carter as 'an endlessly instructive work for the student of evolution in collecting taste', this lists the 2,500 books most sought by collectors of the day.

Seymour de Ricci, ENGLISH COLLECTORS OF BOOKS AND MANUSCRIPTS 1530–1930 *And Their Marks of Ownership,* C.U.P., 1930 (illustrated).

This is the text of the Sandars Lectures in Bibliography for 1929–30. The author was the first foreigner to deliver the Sandars lectures and after forty years the book still stands as a reliable work of reference. The fifteen lectures are devoted to such great collectors as Sir Robert Harley, Sir Thomas Phillipps and the Duke of Roxburghe.

THOMAS FROGNALL DIBDIN (1776–1847)

Though many despise Dibdin and few now read him, he has a place in the history of book collecting. John Carter, in *Taste and Technique in Book Collecting* describes him as 'the most prolific chronicler, anecdotist and publicist in the history of bibliophily. . . . His past serves to mark . . . the beginning of what we may call the pre-history of book-collecting as we know it today.' He has a place, among other reasons, for his reprints of Tudor and Stuart rarities for the Roxburghe Club (see p. 106) of which he was the first secretary. I select three works to show the collecting fashion of the time.

TYPOGRAPHICAL ANTIQUITIES *Or the History of Printing in England, Scotland and Ireland Containing Memoirs of Our Ancient Printers and a Register of the Books Printed by Them* . . . 4 vols., 1810 (illustrated) (see under XI. THE PRINTING OF BOOKS, p. 248).

THE LIBRARY COMPANION, *Or The Young Man's Guide and the Old Man's Comfort in the Choice of a Library*, 2 vols., 1824.

REMINISCENCES OF A LITERARY LIFE, 2 parts, 1836.

E. J. O'Dwyer, THOMAS FROGNALL DIBDIN, *Bibliographer and Bibliomaniac Extraordinary 1776–1847*, Private Libraries Association, 1967 (illustrated).

This is a useful, brief monograph, attractively produced, with a checklist of Dibdin's bibliographic works.

DEVAL & MUIR (see under 'Elkin Mathews' below).

DOBELL & SON (? –1972)

S. Bradbury, BERTRAM DOBELL, *Bookseller and Man of Letters*, Dobell, 1909.

A slim life of the firm's founder (1842–1914) with a bibliography of his works.

F. S. ELLIS (1830–1901)

George Smith and Frank Benger, THE OLDEST LONDON BOOKSHOP, *A History of Two Hundred Years*, Ellis, 1928, to which is appended a family correspondence of the eighteenth century (illustrated).

The earlier part of the book draws heavily on Boswell's *Life of Johnson* and Nichols's *Literary Anecdotes* (see p. 270). The latter part is of interest since it covers the reign of the great bookseller F. S. Ellis (1872–85) when the firm was agent for the British Museum and numbered most of the great collectors of the day among its clients. These included William Morris and Henry Huth whose monumental five-volume catalogue Ellis helped to compile with W. C. Hazlitt as advisory bibliographer.

W. Y. FLETCHER (1830–1913)

W. Y. Fletcher, ENGLISH BOOK COLLECTORS, Kegan Paul, Trench & Trübner, 1902 (illustrated, alphabetical list of 100 collectors from the fifteenth to the late nineteenth centuries).

WILLIAM CAREW HAZLITT (1834–1913)

The collector and bibliographer, grandson of the Romantic essayist, is described by John Carter in *Taste and Technique in Book Collecting* as represent-

REMINISCENCES

OF

A LITERARY LIFE;

BY THE REVEREND

THOS. FROGNALL DIBDIN, D.D.

" These are the Masters that teach without scolding and chastise without stripes "
RICHARD DE BURY.

LONDON:
JOHN MAJOR, 71, GREAT RUSSELL-STREET,
BLOOMSBURY.

MDCCCXXXVI.

The title page of T. F. *Dibdin's* Reminiscences of a Literary Life, *1836, showing the Stationers' Company's arms (see pp. 83 f.)*

ing 'the old school of collecting in its most finely crusted form'. He was for many years bibliographic adviser to the American collector Henry Huth (see under 'Ellis' above). I select the following from among his prolific writings on collecting:

W. C. Hazlitt, THE CONFESSIONS OF A COLLECTOR, Ward & Downey, 1897.

This memoir still yields useful information among its sixteen chapters. Anecdotes of the finds of collectors of the day and of booksellers such as F. S. Ellis (see above), the bookbinder Riviere (see p. 35) and of the changeable temper of the auction room, follow chapters on the collecting of china and coins.

W. C. Hazlitt, COLLECTIONS AND NOTES *with Supplements*, 1876–93.

This is considered by John Carter to be 'the first serious attempt to supplement Lowndes' (*Taste and Technique in Book Collecting*, see p. 94).

W. C. Hazlitt, THE BOOK COLLECTOR, *A General Survey of the Pursuit and of Those Who Have Engaged in It at Home and Abroad from the Earliest Period to the Present Time; With an Account of Public and Private Libraries and Anecdotes of Their Founders or Owners and Remarks on Bookbinding and on Special Copies of Books*, George Redway, 1904 (frontispiece of a book sale at Sotheby's).

This is the fruit of fifty years collecting, a history of bibliophily in sixteen chapters each summarised at the beginning, of which the author says 'it happened that I found myself the possessor of a considerable body of information, covering the entire field of book collecting in Great Britain and Ireland on the European continent, and incidently illustrating such cognate features as printing materials, binding and inscriptions on autographs some enhancing the interest of an already interesting item, others conferring on an otherwise valueless one a peculiar claim to notice'.

HOLBROOK JACKSON (1874–1948)

The one-time editor of the *New Age*, *T.P.'s Weekly* and other journals, Holbrook Jackson was an important bookman and collector. He wrote a great deal on collecting; I select the following:

THE ANATOMY OF BIBLIOMANIA, 2 vols., Soncino Press, 1930, and many times reprinted.

There are chapters on reading, books for study, libraries and the care of books, book thieves, bookbinding, book-hunting, 'the causes of bibliomania' and much else. The model which inspired it, Burton's *Anatomy of Melancholy*, makes for whimsy in a twentieth-century context, but there is much concrete bibliographical information among the whimsy.

THE FEAR OF BOOKS, Soncino Press, London, and Charles Scribner's Sons, New York, 1932.

The author considers that 'this book is complete in itself, but I like to think of it as part of its predecessor, *The Anatomy of Bibliomania*'. The first work described excessive book love, the sequel book hate, types of book haters, their causes and the fear engendered by pornography and seditious books.

MAGGS BROTHERS (established 1860)

Maggs, A CATALOGUE OF MAGGS CATALOGUES 1918–1968, Catalogue no. 918, Courier Press for Maggs Bros., Leamington Spa, 1969 (illustrated).

This gives details of some 700 important Maggs Catalogues, with a subject index appended. The introduction describes collections bought, the production of the catalogues and the firm's long association with the printer, Courier Press.

MARKS & CO. (1920–70)

Helen Hanff, 84 CHARING CROSS ROAD, André Deutsch, 1971.

Letters spanning twenty years, between Marks & Co., antiquarian booksellers in Charing Cross Road, and a New York journalist, provide amusement and insight into an aspect of the trade. The correspondence ended with the death of Frank Doel of Marks, followed by the closing of Marks & Co. in December 1970.

ELKIN MATHEWS (–1921)

P. H. Muir, MINDING MY OWN BUSINESS, Chatto & Windus, 1956, first published as a series of articles in the BOOK COLLECTOR.

The author tells of his association with the firm of Elkin Mathews (now called *Deval & Muir*), whose late director, A. W. Evans, did much through his catalogues to encourage a fashion in collecting eighteenth-century literature. It is also a personal account of how the author, John Carter, Graham Pollard and others have influenced collecting taste and extended the field of collecting in the last thirty years. For the firm's connection with John Lane, see above under XIIIA. THE HISTORY OF PUBLISHING, p. 335.

P. H. MUIR (see under 'Elkin Mathews' above)

A. E. NEWTON (d.1940)

An American collector whose books John Carter describes as beguiling; I select:

THE AMENITIES OF BOOK COLLECTING *And Kindred Affections*, Boston, 1918, John Lane, The Bodley Head, 1920 (illustrated).

This is a collection of essays on book collecting at home and abroad, on association books and first editions.

THE GREATEST BOOK IN THE WORLD *And Other Papers*, John Lane, The Bodley Head, 1928 (illustrated).

This includes chapters on colour-plate books, sporting books and Dickens's *Christmas Carol*.

THIS BOOK COLLECTING GAME, Routledge & Sons, 1930 (illustrated).

This deals with binding, the auction rooms and the format of the English novel among other topics.

GUISEPPE ORIOLI (1884–1943?)

G. Orioli, ADVENTURES OF A BOOKSELLER, privately printed, Florence, 1937, Chatto & Windus, 1938.

An entertaining and informative autobiography by the Italian bookseller who published D. H. Lawrence and dealt in rare books in London and Florence before and after the First World War. The privately printed edition contained passages that Orioli's London partner, Davis, objected to, and which were therefore suppressed in the trade edition.

SIR THOMAS PHILLIPPS (1792–1872)

Nicolas Barker, PORTRAIT OF AN OBSESSION, *The Life of Sir Thomas Phillipps, the World's Greatest Book Collector*, Constable, 1967 (illustrated).

This is an adaptation of the *Phillipps Studies* (see below) concentrating on the personality of this maniac collector and omitting some of the recondite bibliographical material.

E. Miller, PRINCE OF LIBRARIANS: *Antonio Panizzi*, André Deutsch, 1966.

This critical biography of Panizzi contains much about Phillipps and his love–hate relationship with the British Museum.

A. N. L. Munby, PHILLIPPS STUDIES, 5 vols., C.U.P., 1951–60 (illustrated).

Vol. 1: the catalogues of Phillipps's books;
Vol. 2: the family affairs of Phillipps, appendices on the will, discussion on James Orchard Halliwell (-Phillipps) and the mutilation of the Phillipps *Hamlet*;
Vols. 3 and 4: the formation of the Phillipps library and an account of the art collections, the then state of the trade, quarrels with the British Museum, and with Sir Frank Madden, Keeper of Manuscripts;
Vol 5: the dispersal (still continuing) of the library, and a general index to all five volumes.

BERNARD QUARITCH (1819–99).

The history of the firm has yet to be written. A fair picture of the life and activities of its founder, called the Napoleon of booksellers, can be found in the somewhat grudging entry in the *Dictionary of National Biography* which takes pains to point out that, 'he did not belong to the race of studious booksellers, for he had no wide acquaintance with books, except through the titles of those in current demand, and cared nothing for learning and literature in themselves'. A more sympathetic portrait is drawn by his daughter in:

A CATALOGUE OF BOOKS AND MANUSCRIPTS TO COMMEMORATE THE 100TH ANNIVERSARY OF THE FIRM OF BERNARD QUARITCH 1847–1947, *With a Portrait-Study of the Founder by His Daughter Charlotte Quaritch Wrentmore,* Quaritch, 1947 (illustrated).

B. Quaritch, CONTRIBUTIONS TOWARDS A DICTIONARY OF BOOK COLLECTORS, 14 parts, 1896–1914.

This contains some anecdotes of collectors not found elsewhere.

WILLIAM ROBERTS (1862–1940)

William Roberts, THE BOOK-HUNTER IN LONDON, *Historical and Other Studies of Collectors and Collecting,* Elliott Stock, 1895 (numerous illustrations, some of shops long passed out of existence).

This was the author's best book, for here he wrote with first-hand knowledge of the London trade drawing on his bookselling experience in book-hunting, auctions, bookstalls, booksellers, book thieves, knockouts and collectors (see also under IIIA. HISTORY OF NEW BOOKSELLING, p. 60 for Roberts, *Earlier History of Bookselling*).

A. S. W. ROSENBACH (1876–1953)

A. S. W. Rosenbach, BOOKS AND BIDDERS, *The Adventures of a Bibliophile*, Little, Brown, Boston, Mass., 1927 and George Allen & Unwin, London, 1928 (illustrated).

This is a reprint of nine articles that appeared in the *Saturday Evening Post* and *Atlantic Monthly* on literary forgeries, American children's books, old bibles, why America buys England's books and other collecting topics.

E. Millicent Sowerby, RARE PEOPLE AND RARE BOOKS, Constable, 1967.

Miss Sowerby worked for Rosenbach 1942–52 and part 3 of her book describes those years.

Edwin Wolf and John Fleming, ROSENBACH, *The Life of One of the Greatest Book Collectors*, Weidenfeld & Nicolson, 1960 (illustrated).

This is a full biography of the Philadelphia bookseller, (despite the title his fame rests on his position as a bookseller) who made history by the importance of the material he bought and sold. He also collected children's books and directed his staff to produce a catalogue for his collection. Edwin Wolf worked for Dr Rosenbach for many years.

MICHAEL SADLEIR (1888–1957) (see also pp. 7, 95, 353).

Michael Sadleir, novelist and director of Constable's was a collector and bibliographer to whom in the words of John Carter, 'the collecting of Victorian fiction owed not only momentum but direction and breadth. In his biography of Trollope, in his *Publishers' Binding Styles*, in his Studies of the fiction reprint series, even as early as his pioneer *Excursions in Victorian Bibliography*, 1922, there was revealed an acute perception of that fourth dimension in collecting technique: the publishing background of the books collected' (*Taste and Technique in Book Collecting*, q.v.).

Michael Sadleir, PASSAGES FROM THE AUTOBIOGRAPHY OF A BIBLIO-MANIAC, University of California Library, Los Angeles, 1962; a reprint of the introduction to:

Michael Sadleir, XIX CENTURY FICTION: *A Bibliographical Record Based on His Own Collection*, 2 vols., Constable, 1952.

This throws light on the motives and methods of a book collector.

CHARLES SAWYER

Charles J. Sawyer and F. J. Harvey Darton, ENGLISH BOOKS 1475–
1900, *A Signpost for Collectors with One Hundred Illustrations*, 2 vols., Sawyer,
London, and E. P. Dutton, New York, 1927.

Useful for a student of collecting taste; the authors were a bookseller
and a collector.

J. H. SLATER (b. 1854)

J. H. Slater, BOOK COLLECTING, *A Guide for Amateurs*, Swan Sonnenschein, 1892.

The author, remembered for *Engravings and Their Values* and for his
editing of *Book Prices Current* (see p. 103) wrote several, now superseded,
collecting guides, containing some information inaccessible elsewhere.
This one contains a list of the principal secondhand booksellers who
published catalogues with the dates of each firm's establishment. *Early
Editions of Some Popular Modern Authors*, 1894, was described by John
Carter and Graham Pollard (see below, p. 94) as a 'revolutionary primer'
of the new collecting fashion.

WALTER T. SPENCER (*c*. 1853/4–1936)

Walter T. Spencer, FORTY YEARS IN MY BOOK SHOP, Constable, 1923.

Edited with an introduction by Thomas Moult and probably written by
him in order to encourage interest in the collecting of Victorian literature
which the firm specialised in.

HENRY STEVENS (1819–86)

Wyman W. Parker, HENRY STEVENS OF VERMONT, *American Rare Book
Dealer in London 1845–1886*, N. Israel, Amsterdam, 1963 (illustrated,
bibliography of Stevens's publications).

This is an account of the man who made himself 'master of the trans-
atlantic rare book business' and whose successors, Henry Stevens, Son
& Stiles, were until recently the publishers of *Book Auction Records*
(see p. 103) and who still specialise in rare Americana. Stevens, besides
buying for the most important American libraries, filled gaps in Americana
in British libraries and bought over 100,000 volumes for the British
Museum. An ebullient individualist, he was 'as good a friend to scholarship and the library world in both countries as any bookseller in history'.
See also:

E. Miller, PRINCE OF LIBRARIANS, *Antonio Panizzi*, André Deutsch, 1966.

OCTAVE UZANNE (1852–1931)

Octave Uzanne, THE BOOK-HUNTER IN PARIS *With a Preface by Augustine Birrell*, Elliott Stock, 1893 (pen and ink sketches of book-hunting activities in Paris).

I select this volume of reminiscences containing 'a vast deal of heterogeneous information about these ancient stall-keepers, their ups and downs, and the buffets of fortune to which both they and their wares have been exposed'.

DR ROBERT WATT (1774–1819)

James Finlayson, AN ACCOUNT OF THE LIFE AND WORKS OF DR. ROBERT WATT *Author of the Bibliotheca Britannica*, 1897 (frontispiece portrait, appendix of dates and bibliography of Watt's works).

This is a brief biography of the pioneer bibliographer whose example inspired Lowndes to undertake the *Bibliographer's Manual* (see p. 101).

IOLO A. WILLIAMS (see under BIBLIOGRAPHIA SERIES pp. 95 f.)

Iolo A. Williams, SEVEN XVIIIth CENTURY BIBLIOGRAPHIES, Dulau, 1924.

Iolo A. Williams, THE ELEMENTS OF BOOK COLLECTING, Elkin Mathews & Marrot, 1927.

Iolo A. Williams, EARLY ENGLISH WATERCOLOURS, Constable, 1952.

This is perhaps more relevant to the art collector than the bookman.

JAMES WILSON (1850–1917)

Roger Burdett Wilson, OLD AND CURIOUS, *The History of James Wilson's Bookshop*, James Wilson, Birmingham, 1960 (illustrated).

The founder's grandson describes three generations of secondhand and antiquarian booksellers from the 1860s to the present. With notes on sources, letters from the eminent, and extracts from early catalogues.

General Works

John Hill Burton, THE BOOK-HUNTER, Blackwood, Edinburgh and London, 1862.

The second half of this discursive book describes book clubs, particularly the Roxburghe (see p. 106).

Cyril Davenport, BYWAYS AMONG ENGLISH BOOKS, Methuen, 1927 (illustrated).

This treats of collectors and collecting, printed and engraved books, binding, illustrating, miniature books, horn books, book stamps and bookplates. Appendixes list the books in which illustrations by the following artists will be found: George Baxter, H. K. Browne, George Cruikshank, Richard Doyle, John Leech and John Tenniel.

William Targ, CAROUSEL FOR BIBLIOPHILES: *A Treasury of Tales, Narratives, Songs, Epigrams and Sundry Curious Studies Relating to a Noble Theme,* with an introduction by William Targ, World Publishing Co., Cleveland and New York, 1955.

This is a selection of articles mainly by Englishmen on the theme of book collecting; writers include Holbrook Jackson, A. E. Newton, T. F. Dibdin, M. R. James, William Hazlitt, Ben Jonson and Joseph Addison.

4. Modern Books on 'Taste and Technique in Book Collecting' (with apologies to John Carter)

The private libraries of past times have mirrored the bookselling, and formed the collecting pattern of their day. The published catalogues of these libraries have come to be used by dealers and collectors as essential reference tools, though indiscriminate citation of them has been an abuse. After the First World War there was a new vogue in bibliophily and in the 1930s serious attention turned to the collecting of detective fiction, yellow backs, children's books, printed ephemera and the like; monuments were thereby built to the growth of the reading public and the history of literacy traced. Michael Sadleir's collection of nineteenth-century fiction, John Johnson's printed ephemera, Edgar Osborne's children's books and the Renier Collection of Children's Books and Equipment are supreme examples of the thematic kind of collecting that would have been beneath the notice of most of the gentleman collectors of the past (with the exception of a few Victorian collectors of ephemera).

Collectors such as Michael Sadleir and scholar-dealers such as John Carter, P. H. Muir and Graham Pollard have been propagandists for the new collecting fashion and it is largely through their efforts that minor literature is now recognised as a serious collector's objective. The revolution in taste has been further consolidated by the adaptation of the bibliographical apparatus worked out by such scholars as W. W. Greg, R. B. McKerrow and A. W. Pollard. John Carter and others have shown how bibliography can be applied to the practical business of dealing in and collecting modern or ephemeral books. Lastly they have added respectability to the newly established regime by showing it in its historical setting and chronicling the history of bibliophily.

John Carter, editor, NEW PATHS IN BOOK COLLECTING, *Essays by Various Hands,* with an introduction by John Carter, Constable, 1934.

There are key articles on: *Collecting Detective Fiction* by John Carter, *The Expansion of an Author Collection* by John T. Winterich, *Ignoring the Flag* by P. H. Muir, *English Book Illustration 1880–1900* by T. Balston, *American First Editions* by David A. Randall. John Carter comments: 'Collectors of yellow backs or music first editions or serial issues will hardly ignore the essays on those subjects by Michael Sadleir, C. B. Oldman and Graham Pollard in *New Paths in Book Collecting*' (*Taste and Technique in Book Collecting*, see below).

John Carter, editor, BOOK COLLECTING *Four Broadcast Talks* by R. W. Chapman, John Hayward, John Carter, Michael Sadleir, Bowes & Bowes, Cambridge, 1950.

This was a series of talks by bibliographers and members of the antiquarian book trade.

John Carter, BOOKS AND BOOK COLLECTING, Rupert Hart-Davis, 1956.

These essays on great book collectors, typographers, the collecting of detective fiction and the Wise forgeries, are reprinted from *The Colophon, Spectator, Bookseller* and other periodicals.

John Carter, TASTE AND TECHNIQUE IN BOOK COLLECTING, *A Study of Recent Developments in Great Britain and the United States,* 1st edition, C.U.P., 1948, 2nd edition with an epilogue, Private Libraries Association, 1970.

This is the text of the Sandars Lectures in Bibliography for 1947, the second edition containing notes and corrections as well as the Bibliographical Society presidential address for 1969. Although written over a quarter of a century ago most of what Mr Carter writes of collecting patterns, methods, tools, bookshops, rarity, condition and price trends, still stands. The first part of the book traces the evolution of book collecting from Roxburghe to the 1940s; the second deals with book-collecting methods in the post-war era. It could also be used as an annotated bibliography of books on collecting and bibliography.

R. L. Collison, BOOK COLLECTING, *An Introduction to Modern Methods of Literary and Bibliographical Detection,* Ernest Benn, 1957 (illustrated, bibliography).

This covers binding, proof-reading, watermarks, printing, title pages, advertisement leaves, endpapers, forgeries, publishing and bookselling, the care of books, and other matters. There are appendixes on general bibliography, landmarks in the history of book production and a very useful who's who in book collecting.

P. H. Muir, BOOK COLLECTING AS A HOBBY: *In a Series of Letters to Everyman,* Cassell, 1947.

P. H. Muir, BOOK COLLECTING, *More Letters to Everyman,* Cassell, 1949 – a sequel.

These are elementary primers of the new fashion of book collecting which have had considerable influence.

P. H. Muir, editor, TALKS ON BOOK COLLECTING *Delivered Under the Authority of the Antiquarian Booksellers Association* by P. H. Muir, E. P. Goldschmidt, Simon Nowell-Smith, John Carter, H. M. Nixon, I. Kyrle-Fletcher and Ernest Weil, Cassell, 1952 (illustrated).

This is the text of a course delivered in the National Book League during the winter of 1948–49 which initiated young booksellers to certain accepted trade theories and practices. Talks covered the language of book collecting, fashions in book collecting, bookbinders and milestones in book collecting and showed how bibliographical theory could be applied in practice.

Michael Sadleir, A READER'S GUIDE TO BOOK COLLECTING, C.U.P. for the N.B.L., 1947.

This, even though out of date, provides a useful list classified under 'first books for the beginner', a mixed batch of reading, books for book collectors, a few bibliographies of individual writers, and book prices.

Michael Sadleir, editor, BIBLIOGRAPHIA, *Studies in Book History and Book Structure 1750–1900,* Constable, London, and Bowker, New York, 1930–36.

This excellent series, long out-of-print and pioneer studies in their day, consists of ten volumes:

Michael Sadleir, THE EVOLUTION OF PUBLISHERS' BINDING STYLES, 1770–1900 (see under II. BOOKBINDING, p. 42).

Guy Chapman, A BIBLIOGRAPHY OF WILLIAM BECKFORD OF FONTHILL, 1930.

R. W. Chapman, CANCELS, *with Eleven Facsimiles in Collotype,* 1930 (illustrated).

Greville Worthington, A BIBLIOGRAPHY OF THE WAVERLEY NOVELS, 1931 (illustrated).

P. H. Muir, POINTS 1874–1930, *Being Extracts From a Bibliographer's Note Book,* 1931.

John Carter, BINDING VARIANTS IN ENGLISH PUBLISHING 1820–1900, (illustrated) (see under II. BOOKBINDING, p. 42).

Iolo A. Williams, POINTS IN EIGHTEENTH-CENTURY VERSE, *A Bibliographer's and Collector's Scrapbook,* 1934 (illustrated).

P. H. Muir, POINTS: *Second Series 1886–1934,* 1934.

I. R. Brussel, ANGLO-AMERICAN FIRST EDITIONS 1826–1900: *East to West Describing First Editions of English Authors Whose Works Were Published in America Before Their Publication in England,* 1935.

I. R. Brussel, ANGLO-AMERICAN FIRST EDITIONS: *West to East 1826–1900 Describing First Editions of American Authors Whose Books Were Published in England Before Their Publication in America,* 1936.

5. Pioneer and Key Studies in Bibliography

Critical bibliography, the comparative and historical study of the make-up of books, is applicable to all who deal in or collect rare books, although it is largely outside the scope of the present Guide. Among pioneer bibliographers A. W. Pollard (1859–1944) was the doyen and, together with others mentioned below, a founder member of the Bibliographical Society. He made a major contribution to Shakespearean scholarship with:

SHAKESPEARE'S FOLIOS AND QUARTOS: *A Study in the Bibliography of Shakespeare's Plays 1594–1685,* Methuen, 1909;

SHAKESPEARE'S FIGHT WITH THE PIRATES *And the Problems of the Trans-
mission of His Text*, Alexander Moring, 1917; and
SHAKESPEARE'S HAND IN THE PLAY OF SIR THOMAS MORE, C.U.P., 1923.

The bibliographical principles demonstrated in these works were
further developed by W. W. Greg (1875–1959) and R. B. McKerrow
(1872–1940) (see pp. 98 and 99). R. W. Chapman (1881–1959) (see
BIBLIOGRAPHIA SERIES p. 96 above) applied these principles to the study
of eighteenth-century texts and John Carter, Graham Pollard and Michael
Sadleir (qq.v.) to the nineteenth.

Theodore Besterman, THE BEGINNINGS OF SYSTEMATIC BIBLIOGRAPHY,
O.U.P., 1935 (illustrated, bibliography).

Part 1 of this work is a history up to the seventeenth century of systematic
bibliography defined by Greg (see below) as the enumeration and classification of books; Part 2 lists bibliographies printed to the end of the sixteenth
century.

Bibliographical Society, THE BIBLIOGRAPHICAL SOCIETY 1892–1942,
Studies in Retrospect, 1945.

Ten outstanding articles by major scholars including W. W. Greg, E. P.
Goldschmidt, Michael Sadleir and F. P. Wilson. Sir Frank Francis outlines
the Society's achievements in *Sketch of the First Fifty Years of the Society*. A
list of members 1892–1942 and another of the Bibliographical Society's
publications 1892–1945 is appended. This, moreover, together with
George Watson Cole, *Index to Bibliographical Papers 1877–1932*, University
of Chicago Press for the Bibliographical Society of America, 1933, gives
a nearly complete index to bibliographical studies in that pioneer period.

Fredson Bowers, PRINCIPLES OF BIBLIOGRAPHICAL DESCRIPTION, Princeton University Press, Princeton, N.J., and Clarendon Press, Oxford, 1949.

Professor Bowers's work is a development of McKerrow's (see p. 99)
and assumes a knowledge of the earlier scholar's work. He says, 'the
methods of descriptive bibliography seem to have evolved from a triple
purpose; 1, to furnish a detailed analytical record of the physical characteristics of a book which would simultaneously serve as a trustworthy
source of identification . . . 2, to provide an analytical investigation and
an ordered arrangement of these physical facts which would serve as the
prerequisite for textual criticism of the books described; 3, to approach
both literary and printing or publishing history through the investigation
and recording of appropriate details in a related series of books'.

Fredson Bowers, BIBLIOGRAPHY AND TEXTUAL CRITICISM, Clarendon Press, Oxford, 1964.

This is the text of the Lyell lectures for 1959 in which Professor Bowers relates bibliography and textual criticism, whereas McKerrow (see below) is concerned with the physical make-up of the book.

James Duff Brown (1862–1914), A MANUAL OF PRACTICAL BIBLIOGRAPHY, Routledge, London, and Dutton, New York, 1906.

The author was a founder member of the Bibliographical Society and inventor of Brown's system of library classification (a good system, though seldom now used). This manual was 'compiled for the use of students of elementary practical bibliography who are interested in book description. It makes no pretence to satisfy the needs of the book-hunter or the person interested in historical typography or ancient manuscripts'. It was superseded by McKerrow's more detailed work (see below).

Arundell Esdaile, A STUDENT'S MANUAL OF BIBLIOGRAPHY, 1st edition 1931, revised Roy Stokes, George Allen & Unwin and the Library Association, 1954.

This was based on a series of lectures to library students. A reading list divided into two parts is appended to each chapter. 'Those who quail before McKerrow's admittedly formidable array of technicalities can secure a pass degree with Arundell Esdaile's excellent and rather less exacting manual' (J. Carter, *Taste and Technique in Book Collecting*, see p. 94 above). It will probably be superseded by Padwick (see below).

David Foxon, THE TECHNIQUE OF BIBLIOGRAPHY (The Book no. 6), C.U.P. for the N.B.L., 1955.

An introduction defines bibliography and is followed by an annotated list of books on bibliography, collecting and allied subjects.

Philip Gaskell, A NEW INTRODUCTION TO BIBLIOGRAPHY, Clarendon Press, Oxford 1972.

This is intended as a successor to McKerrow (see below), establishing bibliographical practice for the later era of machine printing, where McKerrow had done so for the era of hand printing.

W. W. Greg, THE COLLECTED PAPERS OF SIR WALTER GREG, edited by J. C. Maxwell, O.U.P., 1966.

The editor selects twenty-eight of the thirty-seven papers which Sir Walter Greg left to be collected. These include, *The Function of Bibliography in*

Literary Criticism Illustrated in a Study of the Text of King Lear; What is Bibliography?; The Present Position of Bibliography; An Elizabethan Printer and His Copy. These give some idea of the scope and calibre of this great scholar's work (see also VI. HISTORY OF THE BOOK TRADE, p. 161).

T. H. Horne, AN INTRODUCTION TO THE STUDY OF BIBLIOGRAPHY *To Which Is Prefixed a Memoir of the Public Libraries of the Ancients*, Cadell & Davies, 1814 (illustrated, bibliography).

Horne is to English critical bibliography what Watt and Lowndes are to enumerative bibliography, and this is the first work of its kind.

R. B. McKerrow, AN INTRODUCTION TO BIBLIOGRAPHY FOR LITERARY STUDENTS, Clarendon Press, Oxford, 1927, and many times reprinted.

John Carter describes this as 'that classic exposition of general principles which immediately became and is likely to remain the standard work on its subject' (*A.B.C. for Book Collectors*, see p. 100 below). In 1948 he considered it 'the indispensable basic manual in matters of fact, the classic authority in matters of judgement . . . bibliographers disagree with him at their peril on questions of principle' (*Taste and Technique in Book Collecting*, see p. 94 above).

E. W. Padwick, BIBLIOGRAPHICAL METHOD, *An Introductory Survey*, J. Clarke, 1969.

This is a manual intended for library students and it may well supersede Esdaile (see above). It is easier to use than McKerrow (and more up to date). The matter is dealt with chronologically and includes methods of bibliographical approach to modern texts, which McKerrow does not.

M. J. Pearce, A WORK BOOK OF ANALYTICAL AND DESCRIPTIVE BIBLIOGRAPHY, Clive Bingley, 1970.

An attempt is made to reduce Fredson Bowers, *Principles of Bibliographical Description* (see above) to an easily understood basic set of rules, with examples and exercises, designed to give students a basic knowledge of the layout and of formula construction required for a bibliographical description of a printed book of any period.

Roy Stokes, THE FUNCTION OF BIBLIOGRAPHY, André Deutsch, 1969.

Traces the development of bibliographical technique from Blades.

Archer Taylor, THE BIBLIOGRAPHICAL HISTORY OF ANONYMA AND PSEUDONYMA, University of Chicago Press, Chicago, Ill., 1951, and C.U.P., London, 1952.

D. Williamson, BIBLIOGRAPHY: *Historical, Analytical and Descriptive,* Clive Bingley, 1967.

This explains Bowers's theories in simple terms.

6. Reference Works

So many collectors, so many reference works: it goes without saying that the following brief list gives select examples of major reference works, those relating to specialist fields may be found under V. BOOK ILLUSTRATION, XI. THE PRINTING OF BOOKS, and XII. PRIVATE PRESSES. John Carter in his lecture on 'Tools and Terminology' (in *Taste and Technique . . .*) says that 'specialists are often able to rely on such comprehensive works in their field as Darlow and Moule's great catalogue of Bibles, or the Schwerdt catalogue of Hunting, Hawking and Shooting; Mr George Arent's tobacco collection or M. André Simon's Bibliotheca Bacchica . . .'. Those given below, seemingly oddly assorted, are those that every bookseller be he specialist or general dealer, will refer to. All thematic bibliographies are omitted.

John Carter, A.B.C. FOR BOOK COLLECTORS, Rupert Hart-Davis, 1st edition, 1952, 5th edition, 1972.

A guide to 'such words and phrases, commonly used in book-collecting, as would be likely to puzzle an educated reader faced for the first time by a bookseller's or an auctioneer's catalogue' (Preface to first edition). It has become an established authority, referred to and quoted by experienced collectors and members of the trade.

David Foxon, ENGLISH BIBLIOGRAPHICAL SOURCES 1720–40, Archive Press, 1972.

Follows on chronologically from G.K.W., S.T.C. and Wing (qq.v.).

GESAMTKATALOG DER WIEGENDRUCKE, Leipzig, 1925 continuing (cited as G.K.D.W. or G.K.W.).

This gives the location of all copies of incunabula where fewer than ten are believed to exist.

L. F. T. Hain, REPERTORIUM BIBLIOGRAPHICUM AD ANNUM 1500, Stuttgart, 4 vols., 1826–38, and **C. A. Copinger,** SUPPLEMENT TO HAIN, 3 vols., 1895–1902.

A reprint of this catalogue of incunabula was published in Milan, 1948.

S. Halkett and J. Laing, DICTIONARY OF ANONYMOUS AND PSEUDONYMOUS ENGLISH LITERATURE, with supplements edited by others, 8 vols., Oliver & Boyd, 1882–1950.

A further supplement is being prepared by the British Museum Bibliographical Information Service and is soon to be published. It is an indispensable reference work for collectors and dealers since so many works before the nineteenth century were published anonymously.

L. M. Harrod, THE LIBRARIANS' GLOSSARY AND REFERENCE BOOK *Of Terms Used in Librarianship and the Book Crafts*, André Deutsch, 1st edition, 1938, 3rd edition revised, 1971.

Equally useful to the librarian, for whom it is intended, as to the bookseller or collector, this exhaustive glossary of book terms might, in its latest enlarged edition, be compared to John Carter, *A.B.C. for Book Collectors* (see above) for handy reference. The difference is that John Carter's work is more limited in scope but each entry is in the form of an essay whereas Harrod gives brief dictionary definitions.

Menno Hertzberger, DICTIONARY FOR THE ANTIQUARIAN BOOK TRADE *in French, English, German, Swedish, Danish, Italian, Spanish and Dutch*, International League of Antiquarian Booksellers, Paris, 1956.

The main body of the dictionary is in language order as listed above. French is the key language for the 1,225 entries. The compiler apologises: 'no one is more conscious than the undersigned that this dictionary is far from complete'. Despite its inadequacies, it is the best polyglot trade dictionary that there is.

W. T. Lowndes, THE BIBLIOGRAPHER'S MANUAL OF ENGLISH LITERATURE, George Bell, 1834, revised H. G. Bohn, 11 vols. in 4, 1858–64.

Lowndes was inspired by the achievement of Watt's *Bibliotheca Britannica* to attempt this pioneer enumerative bibliography; 'he was the first and last man to attempt singlehanded a bibliographical manual for the whole of English literature'. It still contains a certain amount of information which cannot easily be found elsewhere – 'it was of great value in 1834 and not contemptible today' (John Carter, *Taste and Technique in Book Collecting*).

A. W. Pollard and G. R. Redgrave, compilers, with others, A SHORT TITLE CATALOGUE OF BOOKS PRINTED IN ENGLAND, SCOTLAND AND IRELAND AND OF ENGLISH BOOKS PRINTED ABROAD 1475–1640, Bibliographical Society, 1926 (generally cited as S.T.C.). A new edition is in preparation.

Robert Watts, BIBLIOTHECA BRITANNICA; *Or a General Index to British and Foreign Literature,* 4 vols., Edinburgh, 1824.

A monumental work for its day, which inspired Lowndes (see p. 101) and is succeeded in our days by the S.T.C. and Wing (qq.v.).

Donald Wing, compiler, A SHORT TITLE CATALOGUE OF BOOKS PRINTED IN ENGLAND, SCOTLAND, IRELAND, WALES AND BRITISH AMERICA, *And of English Books Printed in Other Countries 1641–1700,* Columbia University Press for the Index Society, 3 vols., New York and London, 1945–51 (generally cited as Wing).

This is a sequel to S.T.C. (see above) but lists only the holdings of selected libraries in Great Britain and the U.S.A. Many of the listed libraries have more than doubled their holdings in the twenty-five years since the information was gathered (see also *The English Catalogue of Books,* p. 72).

7. Directories of Antiquarian Bookselling

The Clique, ANNUAL DIRECTORY OF BOOKSELLERS IN THE BRITISH ISLES, *Specialising in Antiquarian and Out-of-print Books,* Clique, 1st edition, 1969, 2nd edition, 1971.

Gerald Coe, THE BOOK COLLECTOR'S DIRECTORY, Wilbarston, 1st edition, 1967, Pilgrim Publications, 3rd edition, 1970.

Gerald Coe, THE COMPLETE BOOKSELLER'S DIRECTORY, Wilbarston, 1966– .

This was first issued as *The Small Bookseller's Directory.*

DEALERS IN BOOKS, The Sheppard Press (biennial in ¦intention, but there are gaps, latest edition, 1972).

This lists dealers in secondhand and antiquarian books in the British Isles, alphabetically, geographically and by speciality. It is prefixed by useful information on current reference books, periodicals, abbreviations

commonly used in booksellers' catalogues, book sizes, supplies and services, etc.

A. P. Wales, editor, WORLD DIRECTORY OF BOOKSELLERS, *An International Guide to Booksellers*, Wales, 1970.

The booksellers are listed under country, with address, telephone number, type of business. Occasionally out-of-date information is given, but on the whole this is a valuable directory.

8. Trade Periodicals and Serial Publications

BOOK AUCTION RECORDS, Stevens, Son & Stiles, 1903–68, Dawson 1969– . (generally cited as B.A.R.).

This lists book auction prices in London and New York.

BOOK COLLECTING AND LIBRARY MONTHLY, 1968– .

Not strictly a trade periodical, though mainly of interest to the trade, it contains short articles on bibliographical subjects, wants and books for sale and lists the previous month's London auction room prices.

THE BOOK MARKET.

This contains advertisements and lists of secondhand and antiquarian books for sale by dealers, and it is supplied only to them.

BOOK PRICES CURRENT, 1887–1956, first edited by J. H. Slater (see p. 91).

This also recorded auction prices.

THE CLIQUE, 1890– .

This incorporates *The Book Dealers' Weekly* and *The Book Trade Journal*. It is supplied only to booksellers and contains advertisements and lists of books wanted by dealers in the secondhand and antiquarian trade.

9. Bibliographical and Book Collecting Journals

(All these are of major importance to collectors and bibliographers.)

BIBLIOGRAPHICAL NOTES AND QUERIES, Elkin Mathews, 1935–39.

THE BOOK COLLECTOR, 1952– , quarterly.

This contains scholarly articles on bibliographical subjects and general information of interest to antiquarian booksellers, collectors and librarians.

THE BOOK COLLECTOR'S QUARTERLY, edited by Desmond Flower and A. J. A. Symons, Cassell, 1930–37.

THE BOOKWORM, *A Treasury of Old Literature*, 6 vols., Elliot Stock, 1888–93.

THE COLOPHON, *A Book Collector's Quarterly*, Pynson Printers, New York, continued as THE NEW COLOPHON, 1st series, 1930–35, and NEW COLOPHON, *A Quarterly for Bookmen*, 1935–40.

THE LIBRARY, *Proceedings of the Bibliographical Society*, 1889 – , quarterly.

The Bibliographical Society's special monographs and dictionaries of the book trade are mentioned under VI. HISTORY OF THE BOOK TRADE, pp. 164 ff.

NOTES AND QUERIES, Clarendon Press, Oxford, 1849– , monthly.

This includes articles on many literary, scholarly and bibliographical points.

PAPERS OF THE BIBLIOGRAPHICAL SOCIETY OF AMERICA, 1906– , quarterly.

THE PRIVATE LIBRARY, 1957 – , annual.

PROCEEDINGS OF THE OXFORD BIBLIOGRAPHICAL SOCIETY, 1922– , annual.

STUDIES IN BIBLIOGRAPHY, *Papers of the Bibliographical Society of the University of Virginia*, 1948– , annual.

TRANSACTIONS OF THE CAMBRIDGE BIBLIOGRAPHICAL SOCIETY, 1949– , annual.

10. Trade Associations

ANTIQUARIAN BOOKSELLERS' ASSOCIATION (founded 1906)

Membership is open to any bookseller dealing mainly in out-of-print books, who has been trading for five years. It aims to promote the sale of antiquarian and rare books, to improve the trade's status, promote honourable business conduct, help members in need, and act as a body in matters where individual action would be ineffectual. A.B.A. MISCELLANY, 1964, a twice-yearly magazine issued to members, of reports, articles and matters of interest to the trade. It succeeds the *Newsletter*.

THE SOCIETY OF ANTIQUARIAN BOOKSELLERS' EMPLOYEES (The Bibliomites) (founded 1951)

Its aims are social, educational and benevolent. Membership is open to all employed in the Antiquarian Book Trade. It issues a magazine, BIBLIO-NOTES.

11. Bibliographical and Book Collecting Societies

BIBLIOGRAPHICAL SOCIETY LONDON (founded 1892)

Its journal, THE LIBRARY, originally issued jointly with the Library Association, contains valuable articles and bibliographies on subjects not published in book form. It also issues many important monographs and works of reference, including the various Dictionaries of Printers and Printing (see under VI. HISTORY OF THE BOOK TRADE, pp. 164 ff.), and the SHORT TITLE CATALOGUE (see p. 102).

BIBLIOGRAPHICAL SOCIETY OF AMERICA (founded 1904)

It publishes quarterly PAPERS OF THE BIBLIOGRAPHICAL SOCIETY and monographs including G. W. Cole, INDEX TO BIBLIOGRAPHICAL PAPERS, published by the Bibliographical Society and the Library Association, London, 1877–1932 (see p. 97).

BIBLIOGRAPHICAL SOCIETY OF THE UNIVERSITY OF VIRGINIA (founded 1950)

Its publications include annual STUDIES IN BIBLIOGRAPHY and occasional monographs.

CAMBRIDGE BIBLIOGRAPHICAL SOCIETY (founded 1949)

It publishes annual PROCEEDINGS and occasional monographs.

EDINBURGH BIBLIOGRAPHICAL SOCIETY (founded 1890)
It publishes TRANSACTIONS and occasional monographs.

FIRST EDITIONS CLUB (1922–1931)
This was founded by A. J. A. Symons.

INTERNATIONAL BIBLIOPHILE ASSOCIATION (Association International nationale de Bibliophilie) (founded 1963)

OXFORD BIBLIOGRAPHICAL SOCIETY (founded 1922)
It publishes annual PROCEEDINGS and occasional monographs.

PRIVATE LIBRARIES ASSOCIATION (P.L.A.) (founded 1957)

A society of book collectors and of private printers, which publishes a quarterly, THE PRIVATE LIBRARY, as well as the annual PRIVATE PRESS BOOKS and monographs and reprints of books on collecting and bibliography.

ROXBURGHE CLUB (founded 1812)

This was the first and remains the greatest of the book clubs, founded to commemorate the dispersal of the library of the third Duke of Roxburghe (1740–1804). Membership was limited to twenty-four bibliophiles, T. F. Dibdin (see p. 83 f.) being the first secretary. Each member is expected to present and pay for a limited edition of a volume of some rarity once in his career.

BOOK DESIGN AND PRODUCTION

(See also under II. BOOKBINDING, V. BOOK ILLUSTRATION, XI. THE PRINTING
OF BOOKS and XII. PRIVATE PRESSES.)

Initial letter B, from a manuscript life of St Birinus of the twelfth century, from W. A. Chatto
A Treatise on Wood-Engraving *1839 (actual size) (see p. 123)*

1. Introduction

The book designer is the architect who plans the physical structure. As a functional artist he has to bear in mind the use his production is going to be put to, as well as its cost within that context. He is equally concerned with aesthetic considerations though not in the abstract. His choice of typeface, for example, must depend on its legibility, the kind of reader the book aims at, and therefore the economic selling price, and his choice is dependent on the practical point of the range of types and processes a particular printer can offer. Every part of the book is the designer's province, not only layout of the main body of the text, but also binding, illustrations and ornament. The jacket, too, is nowadays considered an important selling feature.

Before the war less was planned in the publisher's production department and more in the printer's office. Indeed book design as a course of study in schools of art is a post-war development; formerly those who wished to use their art in the service of the world of books had to choose between courses in illustration or typography. It goes without saying that book design and typographical design come together at many points and contemporary typographers such as Stanley Morison, Jan Tschichold and Berthold Wolpe have preferred to call themselves book designers and have perhaps spent more of their lives planning book layouts than designing typefaces.

The history of book design is the history of the evolution from scroll to page, from manuscript to printed book and is thus part of *Historical Bibliography* (see under VI. HISTORY OF THE BOOK TRADE, pp. 153 ff.). The high standard of post-war British book design is due in part to an increasing awareness of the importance of good design in all spheres, but also to the lasting influence of the Private Press Movement (see p. 313). Such men as Sir Francis Meynell, Stanley Morison and Oliver Simon did much to bring its ideals into the world of commercial publishing and to make that world aware of the importance of good book design and a high standard of production. In the past, we are told, printers printed without reference to visual impact of legibility. Indeed books may not have been planned with paper and pencil in the publisher's or printer's office as they are today, but it is hard to believe that such extraordinary felicity of type and page design as the old printers generally achieved could have come about entirely by chance.

2. History of Book Design
(See also under V. BOOK ILLUSTRATION, pp. 119 ff.)

Seán Jennett, THE MAKING OF BOOKS (see p. 251).
Part 2 is devoted to *The Design of Books*.

Richard de la Mare, A PUBLISHER ON BOOK PRODUCTION, Dent, 1936
see also p. 155).

John Lewis and John Brinkley, GRAPHIC DESIGN, *With Special Reference to Lettering, Typography and Illustration*, Routledge & Kegan Paul, 1954 (extensively illustrated, bibliography).

This surveys letter forms and alphabets, the effects of the Italian Renaissance on thought and design, type and lettering design 1500–1800, commercial printing and the influence of Victorian typefaces, the Gothic Revival, Art Nouveau and the work of some outstanding contemporary designers and illustrators.

John Lewis, ANATOMY OF PRINTING, *The Influences of Art and History on Its Design*, Faber & Faber, 1971 (illustrated).

This is a detailed analysis of the various factors in art and history that have affected the design of the printed page from Gutenberg to computerised typesetting and the web-fed multi-colour offset press.

John Lewis, THE TWENTIETH CENTURY BOOK, *Design and Illustration*, Studio, 1967 (illustrated).

This is an important work, part history, part anthology, on the type, illustration, layout, format, binding and book jacket of the twentieth-century book.

Ruari McLean, MODERN BOOK DESIGN FROM WILLIAM MORRIS TO THE PRESENT DAY, Faber & Faber, 1958 (illustrated).

Mr McLean reviews the period in which the work of typography, design and illustration was beginning to be co-ordinated.

Ruari McLean, VICTORIAN BOOK DESIGN, *And Colour Printing*, Faber & Faber, 1963 (illustrated).

The introduction sketches the background, and later chapters describe the work of Whittingham and Pickering, Baxter and Charles Knight, children's books up to 1850, early lithography and Owen Jones, yellow backs, Vizetelly, Evans, colour printing from wood, publishers' binding styles and other aspects of Victorian book design.

3. Bibliographies and Exhibition Catalogues

(See also under VI. HISTORY OF THE BOOK TRADE for general bibliographies of the trade and the catalogues of special libraries which have sections on book design and production.)

Percy Freer, BIBLIOGRAPHY AND MODERN BOOK PRODUCTION (see p. 155).

A section is given to books on production and design.

Robin Myers, A HANDLIST OF BOOKS AND PERIODICALS ON BRITISH BOOK DESIGN SINCE THE WAR, *To Accompany the Galley Club Exhibition of Book Design 1945–66 Selected by Will Carter*, Galley Club, 1967.

This lists books and periodicals under the headings of General Book Design, Textbooks and Children's Books, Individual Publishing Houses and Designers, Private Presses, Illustration, Binding Styles, Book Jackets.

N.B.L., EXHIBITION CATALOGUES ON BRITISH BOOK DESIGN AND INTERNATIONAL BOOK DESIGN 1944–71, National Book League (16 catalogues published 1945–72).

These are the records, sometimes annotated and illustrated, of the annual exhibitions on book design and production that have been held at the National Book League since the end of the war. They are extensively reviewed in the T.L.S., and reviews and catalogues together provide a record of the fashion and progress in post-war book production. Three selectors are nominated each year to choose the books and edit the catalogue and these have included Harry Carter, John Carter, Will Carter, Douglas Cleverdon, Ruari McLean, Sir Francis Meynell, Stanley Morison, Beatrice Warde, Hugh Williamson and Berthold Wolpe.

Hugh Williamson, BOOK TYPOGRAPHY, *A Handlist for Book Designers*, (The Book no. 1), C.U.P. for the N.B.L., 1955.

This includes books on design and on typography preceded by an introduction.

4. Illustrated Reviews of Book Design and Production
(alphabetical under title)

THE ANNUAL OF DESIGN AND ART DIRECTION, Studio Vista, 1964– .

This is the record of the annual exhibition of the Design and Art Directors' Association.

THE ART OF THE BOOK, edited by **Bernard Newdigate,** Studio, 1938.

This illustrates book production and type design 1900–38 in England, America, Holland, Germany and France. There is an index of designers, printers, presses and papermakers and various insets supplied by different presses.

THE ART OF THE BOOK, *Some Records of Work Carried Out in Europe and U.S.A. 1939–50*, edited by **Charles Ede,** Studio, 1951.

This is a sequel to the above, describing and illustrating the various facets of book production from type design to binding.

DESIGNERS IN BRITAIN, *A Biennial Pictorial Review of Industrial and Commercial Design*, 1947– .

The first three volumes were edited by Peter Ray and published by Alan Wingate, subsequent volumes were edited by Herbert Spencer and published by André Deutsch. Sponsored by the Society of Industrial Artists, they include sections on illustration, book design and book jackets.

MODERN PUBLICITY, 1965/66 and 1966/67 edited by **Ella Moody,** 1968/69 and 1969/70 edited by **Felix Gluck,** Studio Vista.

This reviews among other areas, typefaces and book jackets.

SEVENTEEN GRAPHIC DESIGNERS, Balding & Mansell, 1963 (illustrated).

This illustrates the work of seventeen contemporary British designers and gives samples of book pages.

5. Handbooks on Book Design
(See also under V. BOOK ILLUSTRATION and XI. THE PRINTING OF BOOKS.)

I select the following, including one or two typographical works that are intended for the designer's rather than the printer's use:

THE BULL-FIGHT OF GAZUL.

Once more, once more!—in dust and gore to ruin must thou reel!—
In vain, in vain thou tearest the sand with furious heel—
In vain, in vain, thou noble beast!—I see, I see thee stagger,
Now keen and cold thy neck must hold the stern Alcaydé's dagger!

They have slipped a noose around his feet, six horses are brought in,
And away they drag Harpado with a loud and joyful din.
Now stoop thee, lady, from thy stand, and the ring of price bestow
Upon Gazul of Algava, that hath laid Harpado low.

Tailpiece of 'The Bullfight of Gazul,' from Ancient Spanish Ballads, *translated by J. G. Lockhart, with ornamental borders and vignettes by Owen Jones, 1842 (actual size)*

E

John R. Biggs, THE USE OF TYPE, *The Practice of Typography*, Blandford, 1954 (illustrated, bibliography, glossary).

There are sections on choice of type, spacing, making and lettering a layout, equipment, colour, paper and press work. The author is mainly concerned with book work but he includes sections on advertising and business printing.

Christopher Bradshaw, DESIGN (Facts of Print Series), Studio Vista, 1964 (illustrated, glossary).

The author contends that: 'All fields of graphic design for print are involved. Newspaper design say, or book design, has no unique visual or psychological rules to function under ... and therefore what appears from the pages following ought to be equally relevant to all works of printing.' The author describes the relation of designer to customer, the materials and machines used, the function of design and production demands.

Geoffrey Dowding, FACTORS IN THE CHOICE OF TYPEFACES, Wace, 1957 (illustrated).

Geoffrey Dowding, FINER POINTS IN THE SPACING AND ARRANGEMENT OF TYPE, Wace, 1st edition, 1954, 3rd edition revised, 1966 (illustrated, bibliography).

This was originally a series of lectures at the London College of Printing and 'describes those details of setting which seem so often to be ignored or forgotten'. It is divided into two parts, the first deals with the setting of text matter and the second of display matter.

Ken Garland, GRAPHICS HANDBOOK, Studio Vista, 1966.

Michael Hutchins, TYPOGRAPHICS, *A Designer's Handbook of Printing Techniques*, Studio Vista, London, and Reinhold, New York, 1969.

Printing processes, type, paper and binding are explained in design terms.

Marshall Lee, BOOK MAKING, *An Illustrated Guide to Design and Production*, Bowker, New York, 1965 (illustrated, glossary, bibliography).

This is a comprehensive manual in American terminology.

John Lewis, A HANDBOOK OF TYPE AND ILLUSTRATION, *With Notes on Certain Graphic Processes and the Production of Illustrated Books*, Faber & Faber, 1956 (illustrated).

The first part of this work discusses illustration techniques, the second, typography, printing processes, binding design and book jackets.

John Lewis, TYPOGRAPHY: BASIC PRINCIPLES, *Influences and Trends Since the Nineteenth Century*, Studio Vista, 1963 (illustrated, glossary).

An historical first chapter is followed by an appraisal of present-day trends, and a description of the mechanics of typography.

Leslie G. Luker, BEGINNER'S GUIDE TO DESIGN IN PRINTING, Adana, 1961 (illustrated, glossary, classification of typefaces).

This is chiefly intended for the owners of Adana machines, with advice on how to deal with an order that is too big for the Adana printer. It is not primarily concerned with book-printing work but the sections dealing with type selection, the use of rules, initials and borders, and an appraisal of the principles of design are relevant to book work.

Keith Murgatroyd, MODERN GRAPHICS, Studio Vista, 1969.

Raymond Roberts, TYPOGRAPHICAL DESIGN, Ernest Benn, 1966 (illustrated, bibliography).

The author briefly describes type families, twentieth-century letter forms, reproduction processes, symmetry and asymmetry, layout, the similarities and differences between book and advertising typography in a designer's terms.

Herbert Spencer, DESIGN IN BUSINESS PRINTING, Sylvan Press, 1952 (illustrated, bibliography).

In describing the printing of catalogues, handbooks and brochures, the author is writing about printing whose primary purpose is to inform and 'publicity printing which seeks first, by its design, to interest and then, by its message, to persuade'. Mr Spencer covers such matters as symmetrical and asymmetrical layout, paper and type, the paragraph, footnotes and the design of the book including – a matter of controversy among designers – whether type should run across, up or down the spine.

Vincent Steer, PRINTING DESIGN AND LAYOUT, *The Manual for Printers, Typographers and all Designers and Users of Printing and Advertising*, with a foreword by Beatrice Warde, Virtue & Co., 1st edition, 1934, 4th edition, 1951 (illustrations of nearly 500 typefaces, and a series of 48 type circulation charts, glossary, bibliography).

This is a type designer's vade-mecum.

John Charles Tarr, HOW TO PLAN PRINT, Crosby Lockwood, 1st edition, 1938, 2nd edition revised, 1949 (illustrated, bibliography).

This covers type selection, reproductive services, the principles of design and decoration, book typography, layout and the preparation of copy including a table of untrimmed paper sizes.

Joseph Thorp, editor, DESIGN IN MODERN PRINTING, *The Year Book of the Design Industry Association 1927–1928*, Ernest Benn, 1938 (illustrated).

This is an unusual yearbook in the form of letters to a nephew describing the work of the Design and Industries Association and considering contemporary book and poster design with illustrations of menus, labels, booklets, posters, title pages, book pages and memorial tablets. There is a chapter on the work of Harold Curwen, the Doves Press Bible, Edward Johnston, Francis Meynell and the legibility of typefaces.

Hugh Williamson, METHODS OF BOOK DESIGN, *The Practice of an Industrial Craft*, O.U.P., 1st edition, 1956, 2nd edition revised, 1966 (illustrated, bibliographies both at chapter ends and at the end of the book).

More a guide to book production than design, despite its title. It is not a manual of design, nor does it discuss philosophies of design, such as asymmetry versus symmetry, roman versus sans serif type, but describes each phase and process of book production. Appendixes give type measurements, a table of typeface popularity and colour analysis and synthesis. It is the only work entirely devoted to design in *book* printing.

6. Book Jackets

Trade publishers nowadays often give more attention to the design of a jacket than they do to that of the binding of a book. Nevertheless there is still only one book entirely given to the subject.

Frederick Day, *Book Jackets and their Treatment,* article in BOOK DESIGN AND PRODUCTION, no. 2, 1959, pp. 20–4.

B. S. Biro, *Technique of the Book Jacket,* article in BOOK DESIGN AND PRODUCTION, Autumn 1963, pp. 156–9.

Charles Rosner, THE GROWTH OF THE BOOK JACKET, Sylvan Press, 1954 (illustrated).

Kurt Weidermann, BOOK JACKETS AND RECORD SLEEVES, Thames & Hudson, and André Deutsch, 1969 (illustrated, index of designers, publishers and manufacturers).

The text is tri-lingual, consisting of an introduction to the 290 pages of illustration. The book is part of a series of international surveys on modern commercial design. 'Each book', we are told, 'is planned so that it can be used as a practical manual.'

7. Important Series

FACTS OF PRINT, edited by **James Moran,** Studio Vista.

Seven books were issued in this series.

STUDIO PAPERBACKS, edited by **John Lewis,** Studio Vista (all illustrated).

A series of practical instruction books, twenty-eight have so far been issued, covering aspects of design and industrial art.

8. Periodicals

Most of the periodicals described under XI. THE PRINTING OF BOOKS, p. 300 ff., contain articles on design.

THE DESIGNER (1944–).

This is the monthly journal of the Society of Industrial Artists and Designers (see below).

DESIGN AND INDUSTRIES ASSOCIATION YEAR BOOK AND MEMBERSHIP LIST (1916–).

The annual of the Design and Industries Association (see below), issued free to members.

GRAPHIS (1944–).

This annual edited by **Walter Herdeg** and printed in English, French and German contains sections on book jackets, paperbacks and other kinds of print design.

9. Societies and Trade Associations

THE DESIGN AND INDUSTRIES ASSOCIATION (founded 1916)

DOUBLE CROWN CLUB (see p. 167)

THE GALLEY CLUB

An association of book production staff who meet socially and to discuss matters of professional concern.

THE PUBLISHERS ASSOCIATION, BOOK PRODUCTION MANAGERS' GROUP

SOCIETY OF INDUSTRIAL ARTISTS (see under V. BOOK ILLUSTRATION, p. 149)

SECTION V

BOOK ILLUSTRATION

(See also under IIIC. ANTIQUARIAN BOOKSELLING, AUCTIONEERING AND COLLECTING, IV. BOOK DESIGN, VII. CHILDREN'S BOOKS and XI. THE PRINTING OF BOOKS.)

Initial letter P, showing a wood-engraver at work with his lamp and globe, drawn by R. W. Buss, from W. A. Chatto, A Treatise on Wood-Engraving, *1839 (actual size) see p. 123*

1. Introduction

Works on book illustration are difficult to separate from those on book design since the artist's and book designer's work overlaps at many points. This used to be less so. The pictorial type of illustration, a set piece reproduced on a separate plate, is familiar to us in contemporary editions of nineteenth- and early twentieth-century novels, both adult and juvenile. We connect Dickens's characters with the Cruikshank illustrations, Leech's Jorrocks with Surtees's, Sherlock Holmes is the man that Sidney Paget portrayed, Alice the girl drawn by Tenniel. Where are the modern counterparts? Even in the area of children's books, though classic book illustration is still sometimes to be met, text and illustration now generally merge; and in technical and educational books, which provide book illustrators with most of their work today, diagrams and text figures are integrated with typographic layout.

The techniques of illustration and the processes of reproduction have changed as much as, or more than, the style. Most art work was engraved by hand until photographic methods became current, and the engraver was no more than a skilled craftsman. The work was then often coloured by hand by artisan colourists until the progress of colour printing made this unnecessary. The reproduction wood-engraver, the copper or steel engraver, was rarely executing his own creations; a notable exception was William Blake who, as a trained engraver, preferred to carry out his own designs.

The revival of wood-engraving in modern times has made it both an art and a craft; but in other illustration techniques, the artist is divorced from the technical execution. It is small wonder that the artist may find it beyond his powers to grasp the technicalities of the new processes, since printing science develops as fast as, or faster than the technologist himself can follow it. Yet it is essential for the artist to realise the limitations of the medium he is designing for. Otherwise it may be his fault and not the printer's if an artistic gem is ruined in the reproduction because of the illustrator's ignorance of what print can do, or from indifference to the extra cost involved in adding one or two extra printings in order to achieve the exact colours of his original painting. How simple life must have been for the manuscript or incunable illuminator who was able to execute his own *mise en page*.

2. General Histories and Bibliographies

David Bland, ILLUSTRATION OF BOOKS, Faber & Faber, 1st edition, 1951, latest edition revised, 1969 (illustrated, bibliography, glossary of technical terms).

This work is mainly devoted to book illustration after the arrival of printing. It is in two parts, the first gives the history of book illustration from the beginning to the present day, and includes a chapter on children's books. The second describes the processes of illustration and their application in clear, non-technical terms. The new edition contains nineteen new plates, an extended bibliography, a revised chapter on nineteenth-century illustration and an updated chapter on the twentieth century.

David Bland, A BIBLIOGRAPHY OF BOOK ILLUSTRATION, (The Book no. 4), C.U.P. for the N.B.L., 1955.

David Bland, A HISTORY OF BOOK ILLUSTRATION, Faber & Faber, 1st edition, 1958, revised edition, 1969 (illustrated, extensive bibliography).

This forms a very good introduction to its subject but, covering so wide a field, it is necessarily superficial. The bibliography lists books in French, German, Italian, and the Scandinavian languages but does not include monographs on individual works or illustrators.

Henri Bouchot, THE PRINTED BOOK, *Its History, Illustration and Adornment from the Days of Gutenberg to the Present Time,* translated and enlarged by Edward C. Bigmore with 118 illustrations of facsimiles, of early typography, printers' marks, copies of books, illustrations, and special bindings, Grevel, 1887.

This work covers type, paper, ink, bookbinding and libraries but concentrates most attention on the illustration and adornment of books. The author says, 'the book appealing in its present form to a special public interested more in artistic than in purely typographical topics, our attention has been more particularly given to illustrators, designers, engravers, etchers and so forth. Such graphic embellishment seemed to us of more weight than the manufacture of paper . . . the technical aspect of the subject has been very briefly dealt with in a separate chapter'. The scope of this still important book is from 1462 to the late nineteenth century.

T. M. MacRobert, FINE ILLUSTRATION, *In Western European Printed Books,* H.M.S.O., 1969 (illustrated, bibliography).

This provides an excellent scholarly introduction to the subject.

3. Histories of Wood-Cut and Wood-Engraving

Thomas Balston, ENGLISH WOOD-ENGRAVING 1900–1950, Art and Technics, 1951 (bibliography, illustrated).

This gives examples of work by sixty-seven modern wood-engravers.

John R. Biggs, WOOD-CUTS, WOOD-ENGRAVINGS, LINOCUTS AND PRINTS BY RELATED METHODS OF RELIEF PRINT MAKING, Blandford Press, 1958 (206 illustrations, bibliography).

This simple manual of instruction describes the techniques of woodcutting, wood-engraving and so forth, with a list of suppliers and equipment appended.

Douglas Percy Bliss, A HISTORY OF WOOD-ENGRAVING, with 120 illustrations, introduction by Campbell Dodgson, J. M. Dent, London, and Dutton, New York, 1928 (bibliography).

This and the earlier work of Chatto (see below) form the standard histories of wood-engraving by a well-known practitioner of the art.

Noel Brooke, WOODCUTS AND WOOD ENGRAVINGS, Print Collector's Club, 1926.

A most useful essay is followed by magnificent illustrations in collotype.

W. A. Chatto, A TREATISE ON WOOD-ENGRAVING *Historical and Practical with Upwards of 400 Illustrations Engraved on Wood by John Jackson*, 1st edition, 1839, 2nd edition with an additional chapter by Henry G. Bohn, Chatto & Windus, 1861, reprinted Gale Research Co., Detroit, 1969.

This still important work describes engraving in antiquity including stamps on Babylonian bricks and Roman seals and brasses; the progress of wood-engraving from playing cards from wood blocks, block books, and the invention of typography; wood-engravings in connection with the press, Caxton, map printing, the decline of block books, Dürer and Chiaroscuro; the further progress and decline of wood-engraving, its revival in the eighteenth century. The work concludes with a chapter on contemporary artists, Evans, Richard Doyle, Jewitt, Vizetelly and others.

THE FLEURON (see also under XI. THE PRINTING OF BOOKS, p. 301), nos. 1–4, 1927–30, contains important articles by Eric Gill, Paul Nash,

Robert Gibbings, A. F. Johnson and others, illustrated by some of the best wood-cuts of the period.

Herbert Furst, THE MODERN WOOD-CUT *A Study of the Evolution of the Craft,* with a chapter on the practice of xylography by W. Thomas Snaith with over 216 illustrations, John Lane, The Bodley Head, 1924.

This is the standard work on wood-cuts, comparable to Bliss and Chatto (see above).

Herbert Furst, editor, THE WOODCUT, annual, 1927–   .

Edward Hodnett, ENGLISH WOOD-CUTS 1480–1535 (Bibliographical Society Illustrated Monograph no. 22), 1935, reprinted with addenda 1971 (illustrated, bibliography).

The core of the work is a catalogue of cuts, covering all the books containing cuts printed by Caxton, Wynkyn de Worde, Richard Pynson and minor printers, preceded by an introduction, and followed by a bibliography of illustrated books and an index of cuts by sizes.

Kenneth Lindley, THE WOODBLOCK ENGRAVERS, David & Charles, Newton Abbot, 1970 (illustrated, bibliography).

The author 'examines the course of trade engraving from its emergence among the jobbing printers and printers of chapbooks of the eighteenth century to its virtual demise in the face of photographic blockmaking'. Most of the illustrations are reproduced for the first time.

George E. Mackley, WOOD ENGRAVING, The National Magazine Company, 1948 (illustrated).

A manual by one of the greatest living masters of the craft of wood-engraving.

National Book League, WOOD-ENGRAVING IN MODERN ENGLISH BOOKS, The Catalogue of an Exhibition arranged by Thomas Balston, October 1949 (illustrated).

An introduction is followed by a chronological list of the ten modern illustrators exhibiting.

Imre Reiner, WOOD-CUT/WOOD-ENGRAVING, *A Contribution to the History of the Arts,* 1947.

A seventeen-page introduction is followed by ninety-one pages of plates, 1414–1945.

Malcolm C. Salaman, THE NEW WOOD-CUT, Studio Special Spring Number, edited by Geoffrey Holme, 1930 (illustrated).

This covers not only Great Britain but France, Hungary, Germany, Italy, Spain, Austria, Russia, Poland, Czechoslovakia, Sweden and Norway, Holland, Canada, Japan and the United States. There is an index of illustrations arranged alphabetically under artists.

George E. Woodberry, A HISTORY OF WOOD-ENGRAVING, Sampson Low, Marston, 1883, reprinted Gale Research Co., 1969 (illustrated, bibliography).

This is chiefly useful for the bibliography of works in English, French, German and Italian.

4. Studies of Individual Wood-Engravers and Wood-Cut Artists

THE FLEURON (see p. 123 above) contained valuable articles on several important illustrators, not much written on elsewhere.

THOMAS BEWICK (1753–1828).

'Bewick's work as publisher and engraver falls into three classes: books published by him, alone or together with others, decorated with his own woodcuts or those prepared under his supervision; other men's books with his woodcuts; and the vast mass of "single-cuts", invoice headings, broadsides, race-cards and so forth, their nature and extent briefly outlined on the title-page to Hugo's *Bewick Collector* and which, with much matter of doubtful attribution, form a large part of that remarkable catalogue' (S. Roscoe, *Thomas Bewick*, see below).

I select the following works, by and on, Bewick:

Thomas Bewick, A MEMOIR OF THOMAS BEWICK, *Written by Himself with Wood-Engravings*, edited by Austin Dobson, 1887.

This has been, up to now, the definitive edition, no longer easily accessible. Iain Bain is working on a new edition, which will include the 'scandalous reminiscences' that Dobson refrained from restoring to the text bowdlerised by Bewick's daughter, Jane.

Thomas Bewick, A MEMOIR, etc., Cresset Press, 1961.

This is a slightly abridged version of Austin Dobson's edition, collected with the British Museum's manuscript but omitting some of the rambling homilies.

Austin Dobson, THOMAS BEWICK AND HIS PUPILS, Chatto & Windus, 1889 (first published in the *New York Magazine*, 1881–82, illustrated).

The first nine chapters cover Bewick's life and work; the last four deal with his pupils including Charlton Nesbit, Luke Clennell, William Harvey and John Jackson.

Thomas Hugo, THE BEWICK COLLECTOR, *A Descriptive Catalogue of the Work of Thomas and John Bewick*, Reeve, 1866, with a supplement, 1868.

This monumental illustrated checklist, with an appendix of portraits, autographs, works of pupils, etc., 'the whole described from the original' is still a major work of reference despite the inaccuracies and wrong attributions brought to light by Sydney Roscoe and other later scholars.

Selwyn Image, THOMAS BEWICK, Print Collector's Club, 1932.

This consists of an illuminating essay and seventeen fine reproductions in collotype.

S. Roscoe, THOMAS BEWICK, *A Bibliography Raisonné of Editions of the General History of Quadrupeds, the History of British Birds and the Fables of Aesop, Issued in his Lifetime,* O.U.P., 1953.

This supplements, and in many cases corrects, Hugo's *Bewick Collector* (see above).

Reynolds Stone, WOOD-ENGRAVINGS OF THOMAS BEWICK, Rupert Hart-Davis, 1953.

A biographical introduction which quotes extensively from Bewick's autobiography and distinguishes his work from that of his many pupils, is followed by 336 Bewick cuts and fifteen by his pupils reproduced in collotype.

Montague Weekly, THOMAS BEWICK, O.U.P., 1953 (illustrated).

This is an historical study of Bewick based on *A Memoir* (see above) and on Bewick letters unavailable to earlier biographers. The author 'avoids losing himself in the jungle of Bewick bibliography' mapped out by Roscoe and others.

EDWARD GORDON CRAIG (1872–1966)

Edward Gordon Craig, WOODCUTS AND SOME WORDS, J. M. Dent, 1924 (illustrated).

Partly autobiographical, partly technical, this fascinating work is illustrated with reproductions of some of the author's finest wood-cuts.

THE DALZIEL BROTHERS (George 1815–1902, Edward 1817–1905)

THE BROTHERS DALZIEL, *A Record of Fifty Years Work in Conjunction with Many of the Most Distinguished Artists of the Period 1840–1890*, Methuen, 1901 (illustrated).

This self-laudatory and unscholarly book is mostly based on unverified memoirs, but it is quite amusing.

EDMUND EVANS (1826–1905)

Ruari McLean, editor, REMINISCENCES OF EDMUND EVANS, *Wood-Engraver and Colour Printer 1826–1905*, Clarendon Press, Oxford, 1967 (illustrated, checklist and informative introduction by Ruari McLean).

JOHN FARLEIGH

John Farleigh, GRAVEN IMAGE, *An Autobiographical Textbook*, Macmillan, 1940 (illustrated).

The author describes his work for private presses, book jackets, the illustrations for G. B. Shaw's *Black Girl in Search of God* and he includes letters between himself and Shaw. He explains the technique of wood-engraving and describes the various stages in illustrating a book.

ROBERT GIBBINGS (see also the 'Golden Cockerel Press' under XII. PRIVATE PRESSES, pp. 321 f., for Gibbings's work there).

Patience Empson, editor, THE WOOD-ENGRAVINGS OF ROBERT GIBBINGS, *With Some Recollections of the Artist,* J. M. Dent, 1959 (illustrated, bibliography, list of art galleries, museums and libraries holding Robert Gibbings's engravings).

An introduction by Thomas Balston evaluates Gibbings's place in the revival of wood-engraving and speaks of his work at the Golden Cockerel (see p. 321). This is followed by some recollections by Robert Gibbings and over 300 pages of illustrations.

A. Mary Kirkus, ROBERT GIBBINGS, *A Bibliography*, edited by Patience Empson and John Harris with a chronological checklist and notes on the Golden Cockerel Press, J. M. Dent, 1962 (illustrated).

This is a *catalogue raisonné* of books illustrated, printed or published by Gibbings, and a checklist of critical work by him. This is followed by notes on some of the devices used by the Press, a description of its printing methods and biographical notes.

JOAN HASSALL (b. 1906)

Ruari McLean, editor, THE WOOD-ENGRAVING OF JOAN HASSALL, O.U.P., 1960 (illustrated).

Reproductions of engraved illustrations showing the scope of Miss Hassall's work are preceded by an excellent introduction by Ruari McLean.

ORLANDO JEWITT

Harry Carter, ORLANDO JEWITT, O.U.P., 1962 (illustrated).

This is an admirable monograph on the wood-engraver who specialises in Gothic architecture.

GWEN RAVERAT (1885–1958)

Reynolds Stone, editor, THE WOOD-ENGRAVINGS OF GWEN RAVERAT, Faber & Faber, 1959 (110 illustrations).

The introduction is the comment of one wood-engraver on the technique used by another, which, 'for both hard and soft woods was the same. She used the normal wood-engraver's tools, graver, scooper, and so on, on the end of the grain. She did not use the wood-engraver's knife on the plank as the soft-wood entries might suggest'. The illustrations represent nearly all the artist's wood-engravings and have for the most part been printed from the original blocks.

ERIC RAVILIOUS (1903–42)

THE WOOD ENGRAVINGS OF ERIC RAVILIOUS, Lion & Unicorn Press, forthcoming.

R. Harling, NOTES ON THE WOOD-ENGRAVINGS OF ERIC RAVILIOUS, Faber & Faber for the Shenval Press, 1946 (illustrated).

REYNOLDS STONE (b. 1909)

Myfanwy Piper, REYNOLDS STONE, Art and Technics, 1951 (illustrated).

A thirty-four-page introduction is followed by sixty-two pages of illustration of Reynolds Stone's work including that done for the National
Book League, the Rampant Lions Press and the Elkin Mathews's book
labels (qq.v.).

5. Studies of Individual Illustrators (excluding Wood-Cut Artists and Wood-Engravers)

(See also under VII. CHILDREN'S BOOKS, pp. 192 ff.)

FRANCESCO BARTOLOZZI (1727–1815)

Andrew W. Tuer, BARTOLOZZI AND HIS WORKS, 2 vols., 1881 (illustrated).

A biographical sketch of Bartolozzi, is followed by a description of his
methods of engraving, and a catalogue of 2,000 of his prints. Tuer also
describes and illustrates the works of Angelica Kauffman, the Boydells
and others whose work was engraved by Bartolozzi. There are chapters
on the hobby of print collecting, Bartolozzi's pupils, and a list of stipple
engravers of the Bartolozzi school.

AUBREY BEARDSLEY (1872–98)

I select:

Brigid Brophy, BLACK AND WHITE, *A Portrait of Aubrey Beardsley*,
Jonathan Cape, 1968 (illustrated, bibliography).

A useful brief study concentrating over-much, perhaps, on the erotic and
pornographic elements in Beardsley.

Brian Reade, BEARDSLEY, Studio Vista, 1967 (illustrated).

In the introduction Sir John Rothenstein evaluates the importance of
Beardsley who 'developed an almost mesmeric power of making his
work credible – even though the laws of gravity, anatomy, perspective
and the like are so frequently disregarded ... even today he is difficult
precisely to place in the hierarchy of modern artists. ... He is a very
minor figure, yet in many of his drawings there is something formidable
... appropriate to a more magisterial figure'. The introduction is followed
by a critical biography, and a guide to the 286 pages of plates.

Aymer Vallance, A BOOK OF FIFTY DRAWINGS BY AUBREY BEARDSLEY, Leonard Smithers, 1897.

Aymer Vallance, A SECOND BOOK OF FIFTY DRAWINGS BY AUBREY BEARDSLEY, Leonard Smithers, 1899.

Stanley Weintraub, BEARDSLEY, *A Biography*, W. H. Allen, 1967.

WILLIAM BLAKE (1757–1827)

Blake was both a skilled craftsman and a most unusual and novel painter whose influence on later book illustrators is still felt. He invented a new process of engraving on copper which he used for reproducing some of his own work.

I select:

Laurence Binyon, THE DRAWINGS AND ENGRAVINGS OF WILLIAM BLAKE, Studio, 1922 (introduction, profusely illustrated).

Anthony Blunt, THE ART OF WILLIAM BLAKE, O.U.P., 1959 (illustrated).

Mr Blunt shows the development of Blake's art, his relation to his contemporaries and the sources of his style.

John Wingfield Digby, SYMBOL AND IMAGE IN WILLIAM BLAKE, Clarendon Press, Oxford, 1957 (illustrated, bibliography of the illuminated books).

This book is based on three lectures on the meaning of Blake's art illustrated by the newly found picture at Arlington Court and *The Gates of Paradise*, with reference to nearly sixty other designs and paintings by Blake, all of which are reproduced here. There is a list of the principal public collections of Blake, and of the books he illustrated.

Geoffrey Keynes, WILLIAM BLAKE'S ENGRAVINGS, Faber & Faber, 1950 (introduction by Geoffrey Keynes, 118 pages of plates, 25 wood-cuts of Thornton's *Virgil* and numerous line engravings).

Geoffrey Keynes and Edwin Wolf, WILLIAM BLAKE'S ILLUMINATED BOOKS, Grolier Club, New York, 1953 (illustrated).

This is part of the Grolier Club's bibliography of William Blake, 1921, with a preface on Blake's methods of working.

H. K. BROWNE (PHIZ) (1815–82)

David Croal Thomson, LIFE AND LABOURS OF HABLOT KNIGHT BROWNE: '*Phiz*', Chapman & Hall, 1884 (illustrated, list of books illustrated by 'Phiz').

Negligible as biography, but useful for the illustrations and bibliography.

JOHN BUCKLAND-WRIGHT (1897–1954)

Anthony Reid, A CHECK-LIST OF THE BOOK ILLUSTRATION OF JOHN BUCKLAND-WRIGHT, *Together with a Personal Memoir*, Private Libraries Association, Pinner, 1968 (illustrated, bibliography).

This is a study with a list of illustrations and a checklist of Buckland-Wright's published and unpublished work, and of his dust-wrapper designs.

RANDOLPH CALDECOTT (1846–86)

Henry Blackburn, RANDOLPH CALDECOTT, *A Personal Memoir of His Early Art Career*, Sampson Low, Marston, 1886 (172 illustrations in the text).

This is still the standard work on the nineteenth-century comic artist whose work was engraved and printed by Edmund Evans (see p. 127). There is a list of Caldecott's picture books.

WALTER CRANE (1845–1915)

Walter Crane, AN ARTIST'S REMINISCENCES, Methuen, 2nd edition, 1907 (extensively illustrated).

Few artists have left so informative an autobiography as Walter Crane who was involved in the Pre-Raphaelite and Arts and Crafts Movements and knew all the members of these circles.

Gertrude C. E. Massé, A BIBLIOGRAPHY OF THE FIRST EDITIONS OF BOOKS ILLUSTRATED BY WALTER CRANE, *With a Preface by Heywood Sumner and a Frontispiece after G. E. Watts*, Chelsea Publishing Co., 1923.

This work is incomplete and stands in need of revision and correction.

GEORGE CRUIKSHANK (1792–1828)

I select:

Albert M. Cohn, GEORGE CRUICKSHANK, *A Bibliographical Catalogue of the Printed Works Illustrated by George Cruikshank*, Longmans, 1914.

'*The Librarian's Nightmare*', *a vignette by George Cruikshank from J. Bateman,* The Orchi-
daceae of Mexico and Guatemala, *1837 (actual size). The book is an elephant folio of outsize
dimensions and weightiness, and will not fit on any library shelf. Truly a librarian's
nightmare, Cruikshank's joke can only be fully appreciated in the original where the tiny vignette
floats in an ocean of margin, as do the rest of the illustrations and text, thus rendering
its vast format ludicrous*

Albert M. Cohn, GEORGE CRUIKSHANK, *A Catalogue Raisonné of the Work Executed During the Years 1806–1877*, with collations, notes, approximate values (long out of date), facsimiles and illustrations, Bookman's Journal, 1924 (illustrated).

This and the preceding work form the definitive bibliography of George Cruikshank. The second work has separate sections on printed books, etchings, lithographs, wood-cuts, lottery puffs, and books and articles relating to George Cruikshank.

Ruari McLean, GEORGE CRUIKSHANK, *His Life and Work as a Book Illustrator*, Art and Technics, 1948 (illustrated).

Richard A. Vogler, THE INIMITABLE GEORGE CRUIKSHANK, University of Louisville Libraries, Kentucky, 1948 (illustrated, extensive bibliography).

This annotated exhibition catalogue is indispensable for the study of Cruikshank's work today.

GUSTAVE DOR (1832–83)

This French arti tachieved great success in his lifetime, as an illustrator in London.

Louis Dezé, GUSTAVE DORÉ, *Bibliographie et Catalogue complet de l'Œuvre*, Paris, 1930.

Millicent Rose, GUSTAVE DORÉ, Pleiade Books, 1946.

CLAUD LOVAT FRASER (1890–1921)

SIXTY-THREE UNPUBLISHED DESIGNS BY C. LOVAT FRASER, First Editions Club, 1923 (introduction by Holbrook Jackson).

Gerard Hopkins, *The Sketchbooks of C. L. Fraser*, article in ALPHABET AND IMAGE, vol. 7, 1948 (illustrated in colour).

Holbrook Jackson, *Claud Lovat Fraser: Illustrator*, article in THE FLEURON, vol. 1, 1923.

Haldane Macfall, THE BOOK OF LOVAT, J. M. Dent, 1923.

Christopher Millard, THE PRINTED WORK OF CLAUD LOVAT FRASER, Henry Danielson, 1923 (illustrated).

This is a bibliography of 743 items.

JAMES GILLRAY (1756–1815)

Arts Council, JAMES GILLRAY, 1967.

The illustrated catalogue of an exhibition.

Draper Hill, JAMES GILLRAY, Phaidon, 1965 (illustrated).

The standard modern biography.

STEPHEN GOODEN

Campbell Dodgson, AN ICONOGRAPHY OF STEPHEN GOODEN, Elkin Mathews, 1944 (illustrated).

This handsome volume of engravings (mostly done on copper with a burin) by the engraver of the Nonesuch Press Bible (see under XIII. PUBLISHING, pp. 344 f.) is preceded by a preface and introduction by Campbell Dodgson.

KATE GREENAWAY (see under VII. CHILDREN'S BOOKS, p. 194).

WILLIAM HOGARTH (1697–1764)

Although William Hogarth was not a book illustrator, his techniques and the type of narrative art that he developed were a major influence on painters and illustrators throughout the nineteenth century. For this reason I include him. I select as relevant here:

Austin Dobson, WILLIAM HOGARTH, Sampson Low, Marston, 1891 (illustrated, bibliography of books and pamphlets relating to Hogarth, a catalogue of prints by him and a catalogue of his paintings).

ARTHUR BOYD HOUGHTON (1836–1875)

Laurence Housman, ARTHUR BOYD HOUGHTON, Kegan Paul, Trench & Trübner, 1895 (illustrated).

A sympathetic short essay and excellent reproductions.

LYNTON LAMB (b. 1907)

Lynton Lamb, DRAWING FOR ILLUSTRATION, O.U.P., 1962 (illustrated, glossary, bibliography).

This is an artist's personal account of the technical processes involved in illustrating books. The first chapters are critical and historical, later chapters explain terms and agreements, the relation between publisher, printer and illustrator, and describe the various methods of reproduction.

EDWARD LEAR (1812–88)

Edward Lear is chiefly remembered for his nonsense songs and illustrations of them, but his work as a natural history artist is equally important, and he therefore finds a place here.

I select:

Vivien Noakes, EDWARD LEAR, *The Life of a Wanderer*, Collins, 1968 (illustrated, bibliography).

This excellent biography contains a chronological table, a full bibliography of the works published in Lear's lifetime, those published posthumously (both classified), books about Lear and background for further reading.

PAUL NASH (1899–1946)

David Bland wrote: 'Nash, who is better known as a painter than an illustrator, had been caught up in the revival of wood-engraving in the twenties and had been one of the few to recognise the possibility of the wood-cut' (*A History of Book Illustration*, see p. 122 above).

Rigby Graham, A NOTE ON THE BOOK ILLUSTRATIONS OF PAUL NASH, Brewhouse Press, Wymondham, 1965.

This is an illustrated bibliography.

THOMAS ROWLANDSON (1756–1827)

Edward C. J. Wolf, ROWLANDSON AND HIS ILLUSTRATIONS OF EIGHTEENTH CENTURY LITERATURE, Munksgaard, Copenhagen, 1945 (illustrated, bibliographies at chapter ends).

The author describes caricature in England before Rowlandson, the events of his life, his connection with eighteenth-century prose, verse and drama, and his caricatures of literary men.

E. H. SHEPARD (see under VII. CHILDREN'S BOOKS, p. 194)

JAMES MCNEILL WHISTLER (1834–1903)

Whistler cannot be omitted, although he was a magazine rather than a book illustrator.

Campbell Dodgson, THE ETCHINGS OF JAMES MCNEILL WHISTLER, Studio, 1923 (extensively illustrated, mainly from *Once a Week*).

This includes a complete list of the extant etchings.

REX WHISTLER (1905–44)

Laurence Whistler, REX WHISTLER, *His Life and His Drawings*, Art and Technics, 1948 (illustrated).

Laurence Whistler and Ronald Fuller, THE WORK OF REX WHISTLER, Batsford, 1960 (illustrated).

This is the definitive catalogue of his work, by his brother, superbly illustrated.

6. The Illustration of Early Books

E. P. Goldschmidt, THE PRINTED BOOK OF THE RENAISSANCE, *Three Lectures on Type, Illustration and Ornament*, C.U.P., 1950 (illustrated).

A. W. Pollard, EARLY ILLUSTRATED BOOKS, *A History of the Decoration and Illustration of Books in the Fifteenth and Sixteenth Centuries*, Kegan Paul, Trench & Trübner, 1893 (illustrated).

This is still the most scholarly introduction to its subject and covers the decoration and illustration of the printed book in Germany, Italy, France, Holland, Spain and England.

A. W. Pollard, FINE BOOKS, Methuen, 1912 (illustrated, classified bibliography).

This covers the printing as well as the illustration of fine books, collecting and collectors (qq.v.), block books and the illustration of early German, Dutch, Italian, French and Spanish books, English wood-cut and engraved illustration and late foreign illustrated books.

7. Nineteenth-Century Book Illustration (excluding Wood-cut and Wood-Engraving)

(See also under 'Twentieth-Century Book Illustration', below, for some illustrators working in both centuries.)

Walter Crane, OF THE DECORATIVE ILLUSTRATION OF BOOKS OLD AND NEW, Bell, 1901, new edition, 1972 (illustrated).

This book originated in three lectures which Crane gave to the Society of Arts in 1889 on: the evolution of illuminated manuscripts, the transition after the invention of printing, the decline of illustration in the sixteenth century and its modern revival, the revival of printing as an art in Crane's time; and general principles of designing book ornaments and illustration with a consideration of arrangement, spacing and treatment.

John Harvey, VICTORIAN NOVELISTS AND THEIR ILLUSTRATORS, Sidgwick & Jackson, 1970 (illustrated).

Philip James, ENGLISH BOOK ILLUSTRATION 1800–1900, King Penguin, 1947 (text illustrations, 10 pages of plates some coloured, bibliography).

This is an excellent brief introduction to nineteenth-century book illustration with four pages of notes on technical processes, explained in simple terms.

Ruari McLean, VICTORIAN BOOK DESIGN *And Colour Printing* (see under IV. BOOK DESIGN AND PRODUCTION, p. 110).

Forrest Reid, ILLUSTRATORS OF THE SIXTIES, Faber & Faber, 1928 (illustrated).
An important work.

Malcolm C. Salaman, BRITISH BOOK ILLUSTRATION YESTERDAY AND TODAY, edited by Geoffrey Holme with a commentary by Malcolm C. Salaman, Studio, 1923 (134 pages of plates, many coloured).

A list of artists is followed by a forty-page introduction on book illustration in the nineteenth century, and the Art Nouveau period as far as the end of the First World War.

E. E. D. Sketchley, BOOK ILLUSTRATION OF TODAY, *Appreciation of the Work of Living English Illustrators*, with lists of their books and an introduction by A. E. Pollard, Kegan Paul, Trench & Trübner, 1903 (illustrated).

This is still an important book with chapters on, and bibliographies of, decorative books, open air illustrations, character illustrations, children's book illustrators and an index of late nineteenth-century artists.

R. Margaret Slythe, THE ART OF ILLUSTRATION 1750–1900, Library Association, 1970 (illustrated, select bibliography, index of names).

Written as a thesis for the Fellowship of the Library Association, this book is based on Lord Clark's collection at Saltwood Castle, and is thus more limited than its title suggests; it covers little new ground.

James Thorpe, ENGLISH ILLUSTRATION, *The Nineties*, Faber & Faber, 1935 (illustrated).

This is more concerned with periodical than with book illustration but the two naturally overlap. A chapter devoted to *Some Illustrated Books* gives lists of the books illustrated during this period by Walter Crane, Arthur Rackham and Hugh Thomson.

Gleeson White, ENGLISH ILLUSTRATION, *The Sixties 1855–70*, Constable, 1897, reprinted Kingsmead Bookshop, 1970.

This covers magazine as well as book illustration, with examples of the work of such artists as Ford Madox Brown, Sir J. E. Millais, Rossetti and Whistler.

8. Twentieth-Century Book Illustration (excluding Wood-Cut and Wood-Engraving)
(See also under 'Nineteenth-Century Book Illustration', above for some illustrators working in both centuries.)

F. J. Harvey Darton, MODERN BOOK ILLUSTRATION IN GREAT BRITAIN AND AMERICA, Special Winter Number of *The Studio*, edited by C. Geoffrey Holme, Studio, 1931 (illustrated).

Harvey Darton's informative introduction on the work of early twentieth-century illustrators is followed by an index of illustrators and numerous text illustrations and plates, some in colour.

Eleanor Garvey, THE ARTIST AND THE BOOK 1860–1960, *In Western Europe and the United States*, Museum of Fine Arts, Boston, 1961 (bibliography, illustrated).

This is an illustrated *catalogue raisonné* of an exhibition held in the Boston Museum of Fine Arts in 1960. Philip Hofer explains in his introduction, 'the year 1860 was chosen as a point of departure not only because exactly one hundred years could be encompassed but also because this date was about the moment when the invention of photography by Daguerre and Fox-Talbot (in 1839) was beginning to be applied successfully to *reproduction* in the graphic arts'. There is an index of authors and publishers and each entry (listed alphabetically) gives the artists' dates, brief biographical and critical notes, and a bibliographical description of each exhibition entry. Children's illustrators are excluded as belonging to a special category of artists. There is a geographical index which shows France in the lead with 182 illustrators and England in fourth place with twenty-six.

Bob Gill and John Lewis, ILLUSTRATION, *Aspects and Directions,* Studio Vista, 1964 (illustrated).

The authors consider the influences on the work of the modern illustrator, and present a lively survey of the best of contemporary illustration taken from the pages of European and American books, periodicals and newspapers.

R. P. Gossop, BOOK ILLUSTRATION, *A Review of the Art as It Is Today,* J. M. Dent, 1937.

This is the seventh of the important series of Dent Memorial lectures on aspects of the book trade. It is a survey of book illustration in the 1930s, its technical developments, uses, costs and art training, with a foreword by Hugh Dent.

Robin Jacques, ILLUSTRATORS AT WORK, Studio Vista, 1963 (illustrated).

Mr Jacques, himself a well-known illustrator, discusses 'the illustrative tradition' of Bewick and others, describes processes of reproduction, gives a symposium of illustrators' drawings, and an account by some of the artists themselves of their chosen methods of work. It includes biographical detail and line portraits of artists, some of which is not easily found elsewhere.

John Lewis, THE TWENTIETH CENTURY BOOK (see under IV. BOOK DESIGN AND PRODUCTION, p. 110).

Ruari McLean, MODERN BOOK DESIGN (see under IV. BOOK DESIGN AND PRODUCTION, p. 110).

National Book League, BRITISH BOOK ILLUSTRATION 1935–45, C.U.P. for the N.B.L., 1946 (illustrated).

This is a catalogue of an exhibition, with an introduction by Philip James.

9. Colour-Plate Books, Studies of Colour Printing and Colour Printers

I select the following, omitting all thematic bibliographies of illustration as being beyond the scope of the present Guide:

J. R. Abbey, SCENERY OF GREAT BRITAIN AND IRELAND IN AQUATINT AND LITHOGRAPHY 1770–1860, *From the Library of J. R. Abbey, A Bibliographical Catalogue,* privately printed at the Curwen Press, 1952 (illustrated).

J. R. Abbey, LIFE IN ENGLAND IN AQUATINT AND LITHOGRAPHY 1770–1860, *Architecture, Drawing Books, Art Collections, Magazines, Navy and Army, Panoramas etc.,* Curwen Press, 1953 (illustrated).

J. R. Abbey, TRAVEL IN AQUATINT AND LITHOGRAPHY 1770–1860, 2 vols., Maggs, 1956/7 (illustrated).

Volume 1 covers the world, Europe and Africa, volume 2 covers Asia, Oceana, Antarctica, and America. These four sumptuous works are the *catalogues raisonnés* of Major Abbey's monumental collection. The notes, especially those in *Travel,* by Michael Olivier, contain much research and information on printing processes and publishing procedures, not available elsewhere. The collection, bought by Mr Paul Mellon, will shortly be housed in a library to be specially built at Yale.

G. A. Audsley, THE ART OF CHROMOLITHOGRAPHY, *Popularly Explained and Illustrated by 44 plates Showing Separate Impressions of All the Stones Employed; and All the Progressive Printings in Combination from the List Cover to the Finished Picture,* Fisher Unwin, 1883.

This is one of the several works showing the separate impressions which went to make up a nineteenth-century commercial colour print by chromolithography.

R. M. Burch, COLOUR PRINTING AND COLOUR PRINTERS, *With a Chapter on Modern Processes by W. Gamble,* Pitman, 1910 (illustrated).

This was the first book to attempt a complete history of colour printing from the fifteenth to the early twentieth centuries.

C. T. Courtney Lewis, THE STORY OF PICTURE PRINTING IN ENGLAND, *During the Nineteenth Century or Forty Years of Wood and Stone,* Sampson Low, 1928 (many illustrations in colour, others in black and white).

An excellent account of the colour printers of the nineteenth century and their processes, containing much information not to be found elsewhere, but unfortunately not giving references for the facts quoted. Much of Courtney Lewis's information came from conversations, either with the printers themselves or their relatives, speaking or writing from memory, which, without documentary corroboration, must be treated with reserve.

C. T. Courtney Lewis, GEORGE BAXTER COLOUR PRINTER, *His Life and Work A Manual for Collectors*, Sampson Low, Marston, 1908 (black and white illustrations).

This describes Baxter's life and career, explains his importance in colour printing, and the complication of the licences granted by him. There are hints to collectors and chapters on the catalogues of the various kinds of Baxter prints.

C. T. Courtney Lewis, GEORGE BAXTER THE PICTURE PRINTER, Sampson Low, 1924 (extensively illustrated in colour and black and white).

This was Courtney Lewis's final and definitive work on Baxter, produced in a limited edition, and includes a catalogue of all his prints.

Martin Hardie, ENGLISH COLOURED BOOKS, Methuen, 1906 (illustrated in colour and black and white).

Most of the information in this work is also to be found in Courtney Lewis and Burch (see above) but Martin Hardie writes better than either and has a wider knowledge and appreciation of art.

Jane Lewine, BIBLIOGRAPHY OF EIGHTEENTH CENTURY ART AND ILLUS-TRATED BOOKS, *Being a Guide to Collectors of Illustrated Books in English and French of the Period*, Sampson Low, Marston, 1898 (35 illustrations).

This work is still useful although it has been superseded by the Abbey Catalogues (see above) and others. The author explains that 'bibliography . . . may now be almost regarded as having entered the domain of science . . . Of books with embellishments, now so much in vogue, and so deservedly coverted by the intelligent amateur, the record is almost barren. To supply this long outstanding want has been my primary motive'. The entries are alphabetical under author or subject followed by title, details of format, number of plates in many cases and price.

S. T. Prideaux, AQUATINT ENGRAVING: chapter on *The History of Book Illustration*, Duckworth, 1909, reprinted Foyle, 1968 (illustrated, bibliography).

This is still a standard work covering the history of processes, the development of colour printing, Ackermann, aquatint in foreign travel,

English typography, sport and natural history, caricature and costume. There are appendixes on books published before 1830 with aquatint plates, biographical notes of engravers whose names appear on the plates and of artists, and an alphabetical list of engravers with the books illustrated by them.

R. V. Tooley, ENGLISH BOOKS WITH COLOURED PLATES 1790–1860, *A Bibliographical Account of the Most Important Books Illustrated by English Artists in Colour Aquatint and Colour Lithography*, Batsford, 1st edition, 1935, 2nd edition, 1954.

This provides a guide to fashion as reflected by rare book prices, with collations of those considered important in the bookseller's world, but it is of very little use to the historian of book illustration.

10. Early Manuals of Engraving (chronological)

William Faithorne, THE ART OF GRAVING AND ETCHING, *Wherein is Expressed the True Way of Graving in Copper . . . to Which Is Added, the Way of Printing Copper-Plates, and How to Work the Press*, 2nd edition, 1702 (illustrated with plates of tools and techniques).

T. Hodson, THE CABINET OF THE ARTS, *Or a Complete System of Etching, Engraving, etc.*, 1803–06.

C. Hullmandel, THE ART OF DRAWING ON STONE, 1824.

C. F. Partington, THE ENGRAVERS' COMPLETE GUIDE, *Comprising the Theory and Practice of Engraving with Its Modern Improvements, in Steel Plates, Lithography, etc.*, c. 1825.

Part of *The Mechanics' Gallery of Science and Art*. Every process is briefly but meticulously described.

T. H. Fielding, THE ART OF ENGRAVING, *With Various Modes of Operation Under the Following Different Divisions: Etching, Soft-ground Etching, Line Engraving, Chalk and Stipple, Aquatint, Mezzotint, Lithography, Wood Engraving, Medallic Engraving, Electrography and Photography*, 1st edition, 1841, 2nd edition, 1844.

S. T. Davenport, ON PRINTS AND THEIR PRODUCTION, 1869.

Philip Gilbert Hamerton, DRAWING AND ENGRAVING; *A Brief Exposition of Technical Principles and Practice*, 1892.

H. W. Singer and W. Strang, ETCHING, ENGRAVING AND OTHER METHODS OF PRINTING PICTURES, 1897.

This is a key work.

W. H. Ward, THE PRINTING ARTS; *A Description of the Methods Now In Use, More Particularly with Regard to Illustration*, 1900.

11. Studies of Illustration Techniques and Processes of Reproduction (excluding Wood-Cut and Wood-Engraving)
(See also under XI. THE PRINTING OF BOOKS, pp. 292 ff., and under 'Early Manuals of Engraving', above)

The following selected works describe reproduction processes as they relate to book illustration, bearing in mind that there is no technique that is confined to the reproduction of illustrations.

Grant Arnold, LITHOGRAPHY, *And How To Do It*, Dover, New York, 1941 (illustrated).

The author explains that he 'actively practised lithography over a period of ten years as artist, printer and instructor, and has introduced over 600 artists, educators and students to the craft. . . . The purpose of this volume is to set forth the elements of lithography step by step, and to demonstrate the principles particularly suited to the needs of the artist'. An appendix gives a list of the materials needed for auto-lithography.

John R. Biggs, ILLUSTRATION AND REPRODUCTION, Blandford Press, 1950 (illustrated).

This illustrates the different states of reproduction and is intended to teach the graphic artist what he can expect machines to be able to do with his work. The views of artists such as Bawden, Buckland-Wright (see below), Faith Jacques, Ronald Searle and Nigel Lambourne are included.

Henry Blackburn, THE ART OF ILLUSTRATION, W. H. Allen, 1894 (95 illustrations).

Despite its early date, this is still very useful for its descriptions of the various older methods of book illustration; useful too are the chapters on author, illustrator, and publisher, and the list of blockmakers working at the end of the nineteenth century. The quality and reproduction of the illustrations is excellent.

Felix Brunner, A HANDBOOK OF GRAPHIC REPRODUCTION PROCESSES, *A Technical Guide Including the Print-Making Processes for Art Collectors and Dealers, Librarians, Booksellers, Publishers, Artists, Graphic Designers and the Printing Trade*, Tiranti, 1962.

The text is in English, French and German. The German original is translated into very stilted English. For example the author contends that his work 'contains a complete and systematic identifying procedure with magnifications which permit identification of a printing process on a basis of a reproduction . . . separate chapters deal with the evolution and uses of each technique. . . . There is a special chapter devoted to the dangers of forgeries'.

John Buckland-Wright, ETCHING AND ENGRAVING, *Techniques and the Modern Trend*, Studio Vista, 1953 (illustrated).

John Buckland-Wright describes the theory and technique of the following processes: line engraving, drypoint, mezzotint, stipple, etching, soft ground, aquatint, sugar aquatint, relief prints and deep etch, combined processes, intaglio, wood-cut and lino-cut, wood-engraving, wood block and lino printing. In fact all the processes of illustration are described in sufficient detail to be recognised within the compass of one medium-sized book.

Harold Curwen, PROCESSES OF GRAPHIC REPRODUCTION IN PRINTING, Faber & Faber, 1st edition, 1934, 4th edition revised, 1966 (illustrated, bibliography).

This classic work describes the processes of intaglio, stencilling, lithography and photographic reproduction, photogravure and collotype.

Cyril Davenport, MEZZOTINTS, Methuen, 1904 (illustrated, annotated bibliography).

This describes what mezzotints are and the processes used from the mid-seventeenth century when mezzotint was first invented to the late nineteenth century.

Henri Delaborde, ENGRAVING, WITH ORIGIN, PROCESSES AND HISTORY, translated by R. A. M. Stevenson, with an additional chapter on English engraving by William Walker, Cassell, 1886 (illustrated).

This is still a standard work, and deals chronologically with xylography, playing cards, intaglio, etching in the Low Countries, seventeenth-century line-engraving, etc. A chronological table of English engravers is appended.

Thomas E. Griffits, THE RUDIMENTS OF LITHOGRAPHY, Faber & Faber, 1956 (illustrated).

The author describes auto-lithography, commercial lithography, the colour range of printing inks, the technique of lithographic artists as well as discussing equipment, press work, register marks, paper and imposition, shading mediums and textures, and the combining of photolitho and drawn colour work. He is also the author of *The Technique of Colour Printing by Lithography*, 1944, and *Colour Printing*, 1948.

Philip Gilbert Hamerton, THE GRAPHIC ARTS, *A Treatise on the Varieties of Drawing, Painting, and Engraving in Comparison with Each Other and with Nature*, Seeley, Jackson & Halliday, 1882 (illustrated).

This is still a standard work, covering more than book illustration. There are chapters on drawing, wash drawing, charcoal, oil monochrome, etc., as well as on such processes as wood-engraving, etching and drypoint, line engraving, aquatint and mezzotint, and lithography.

Jules Heller, PRINT MAKING TODAY, *An Introduction to the Graphic Arts*, Pitman, 1959 (illustrated, bibliography).

This is 'a book that tells what fine prints are, what they were, and how to make them'. Each part contains a visual survey of the work of past and present masters; an illustrated technical section explains the procedures step by step, and a special work shop section describes printing problems.

Arthur M. Hind, A HISTORY OF ENGRAVING AND ETCHING, *From the Fifteenth Century to the Year 1914*, Constable, 1st edition, 1918, 3rd edition revised, 1923, Dover reprint, New York, 1970 (illustrated, bibliography).

This is the standard history of engraving (Delaborde explains technique where Hind describes the historical events). Appendixes include a list of engravers classified by country, a classified bibliography of works used, an index of engravers and a bibliography of works on them, a list of engravers by name, by monogram, by marks, by dates, by subject or locality, and a list of their principal works.

Arthur M. Hind, The British Museum, A GUIDE TO THE PROCESSES AND
SCHOOLS OF ENGRAVING, *With Notes on Some of the Most Important Masters,*
2nd edition, 1923.

This reprint of the first chapter of Hind's *A History of Engraving and
Etching* (see above), gives clear descriptions of the three forms of print
namely relief, intaglio and surface. It describes wood-cut and wood-
engraving, also other forms of intaglio such as etching and lithography.
There are notes on some of the most important masters of illustration,
descriptions and illustrations of such tools as the scraper, the graver, the
burnisher, the etching needle, the mezzotint rocker and the roulette used
in stipple.

James Shirley Hodson, AN HISTORICAL AND PRACTICAL GUIDE TO ART
ILLUSTRATION, *In Connection with Books, Periodicals, and General Decoration
with Numerous Specimens of the Various Methods,* 1885 (illustrated).

The author gives leisurely explanations of various methods of illustration
such as line engraving, stipple wood-engraving, chromo-litho, zinco-
graphy, aquatint, photolitho and photogravure. He also gives biographical
details of artists and engravers, some not easily found elsewhere.

John Lewis, A HANDBOOK OF TYPE AND ILLUSTRATION, *With Notes on
Certain Graphic Processes and the Production of Illustrated Books,* Faber &
Faber, 1956 (illustrated).

Mr Lewis describes the reproduction of drawings by letterpress and
offset, direct and photographic methods of reproduction. Methods of
illustration shown include colour lino-cuts, wood-engravings and
coloured wood-cuts, line copper engravings and coloured etchings, relief
etchings and coloured lithographs. There is also a list of paper sizes,
imposition details, materials and costs. The book deals with other facets
of production such as binding and typography.

John Lewis and Edwin Smith, THE GRAPHIC REPRODUCTION OF PHOTO-
GRAPHY AND WORKS OF ART, Cowell, 1969 (illustrated).

This is not strictly a book about book illustration. It explains the techni
calities of graphic reproduction, the old processes such as etchings, wood-
engraving, mezzotint and lithograph as well as the modern photographic
processes much more clearly than they are described elsewhere. It also
outlines the preparation of copy for book illustration.

Joseph and Elizabeth Robins Pennell, LITHOGRAPHY AND LITHOGRA-

PHERS, *Some Chapters in the History of Art, with Technical Remarks and Suggestions and with Many Illustrations*, 1898.

This cumbersome volume describes Senefelder's invention and lithography in France and England.

W. P. Robins, ETCHING CRAFT, *A Guide for Students and Collectors*, with a foreword by Martin Hardie, Bookman's Journal and Print Collector, 1922 (illustrated, extensive bibliography).

'The collector will welcome Mr. Robins's exceedingly lucid account of how etchings are produced . . . but is likely to prize the volume most for the valuable brief notes which it contains about all the leading etchers from the days of Rembrandt to our own time' (*Daily Telegraph* review, February 1923).

Malcolm C. Salaman, THE OLD ENGRAVERS OF ENGLAND, *In Their Relation to Contemporary Life and Art (1540–1800)*, Cassell, 1906 (illustrated, bibliography).

This is a work for collectors and social historians. It traces the art of copper-plate engraving, including line-engravers, mezzotint and stipple.

Michael Twyman, LITHOGRAPHY *1800–1850, The Techniques of Drawing on Stone in England and France and their Application in Works of Topography*, O.U.P., 1970 (158 plates, bibliographies of literature on the history and techniques 1801–20, and of sources of the early history and techniques of lithography).

This describes lithography as an artist's medium and is not concerned with commercial lithography as used in modern book printing (see also under XI. THE PRINTING OF BOOKS, p. 253, for Twyman, *Printing 1770–1970*).

Peter Weaver, THE TECHNIQUE OF LITHOGRAPHY, Batsford, 1964 (illustrated).

This primer concentrates on technique rather than aesthetics with sections on equipment, preparation, paper and ink and a glossary.

12. Reference Works and Important Series
(For Periodicals, see under XI. THE PRINTING OF BOOKS, pp. 300 ff.).

Walter Amstutz, editor, WHO'S WHO IN GRAPHIC ART, *An Illustrated Book of Reference to the World's Leading Graphic Designers, Illustrators,*

Typographers and Cartoonists, Amstutz & Herdeg, Zurich, 1962 (illustrated' useful bibliography).

The artists are listed alphabetically under country with entries in English, French and German. There is a list of artists' societies, and an index by name, by country, and by special field. As with all such works of reference the editor's choice sometimes appears arbitrary and can surprise by omissions, but this does not invalidate the extreme usefulness of the work. Each entry is accompanied by a photograph of each artist and by specimens of his work.

Hilary and Mary Evans, SOURCES OF ILLUSTRATION 1500–1900, Adams & Dart, 1971 (illustrated).

This is a practical reference work for those engaged in picture research, and includes a detailed description of all the illustration processes, with a guide to public collections and commercial picture libraries in Britain, France, Germany and the U.S.A. The many illustrations demonstrate the variety of material available.

Graham Reynolds, editor, ENGLISH MASTERS OF BLACK AND WHITE, Art & Technics, 1948–1950.

This series of monographs comprises the following artists (see also under 'Studies of Individual Wood-Engravers', pp. 125 ff.):

R. Harling, EDWARD BAWDEN;
Graham Reynolds, THOMAS BEWICK;
Ruari McLean, GEORGE CRUIKSHANK;
Daria Hambourg, RICHARD DOYLE;
D. P. Whiteley, GEORGE DU MAURIER;
Jonathan Mayne, BARNETT FREEDMAN;
June Rose, JOHN LEECH;
James Thorpe, PHIL MAY;
James Thorpe, E. J. SULLIVAN;
Frances Sarzano, SIR JOHN TENNIEL;
Laurence Whistler, REX WHISTLER.

SOCIETY OF INDUSTRIAL ARTISTS YEARBOOK

This intermittent list of members of the S.I.A. gives address, telephone number, and speciality. There is an index classified under fields of practice, including general illustration, technical illustration, lettering and calligraphy, typography and cartoons.

STUDIO SPECIAL NUMBERS

During the 1920s and 1930s the Studio Magazine produced special numbers in book form on aspects of the book, which are mentioned under the relevant sections of this Guide. Many of them relate to book illustration.

13. Professional Societies

SOCIETY OF INDUSTRIAL ARTISTS AND DESIGNERS, 7 Woburn Square, W.C.1. (founded 1930)

This was the first society of industrial designers in the world, and membership is open to engineering designers, graphic artists, illustrators and designers concerned with all branches of visual communication. Its aims are to maintain standards of performance and professional conduct and to supply members of the profession with information about it. There are four classes of membership, Fellowship, Membership, Associateship and Licentiateship. It publishes, intermittently, a yearbook.

SOCIETY OF LITHOGRAPHIC ARTISTS, DESIGNERS, ENGRAVERS AND PROCESS WORKERS, 54 Doughty Street, London, W.C.1

This is a printing trade union.

SECTION VI

HISTORY OF THE BOOK TRADE

'Securing a Friend in the Press', from Punch, *1842 (actual size)*

1. Introduction

There was scarcely any division of ... the branches of the Book Trade until very modern times [wrote Charles Knight in *Shadows of Old Booksellers*, 1865 (see p. 59 above)] the dealers in old books, the publisher of new books, the book-printers, the printers of journals, and even the book auctioneers and printsellers, held a common place in the registers of that ancient company which had existence before the introduction of printing, that of the 'Stationers or Textwriters' who wrote and sold all sorts of books then in use. The division of employment amongst all those connected with paper and print ... was of very slow growth.

The present section of this Guide comprises those works that deal with the history of the whole trade; for which reason most relate to the sixteenth to eighteenth centuries before the 'division of employment', that Knight speaks of, had taken place. Elsewhere an attempt has been made to deal with books according to divisions into printing, binding, publishing, bookselling and so forth, divisions that are at times somewhat arbitrary.

2. General Histories, Bibliographies and Reference Works

Ray Astbury, BIBLIOGRAPHY AND BOOK PRODUCTION, Pergamon Press, Oxford, 1967.

In the preface the author says: 'The object of this book is ... to serve as introduction to current problems and trends in bibliographical organization and the book trade, with an outline of the main methods of book production, ... and to point the interrelationships between various aspects of publishing, bookselling, printing, and bibliography.' It covers the structure of the publishing trade today, copyright, book production, the information explosion and bibliographies.

Norman E. Binns, AN INTRODUCTION TO HISTORICAL BIBLIOGRAPHY, L.A., 1st edition, 1953, 2nd edition, 1962 (illustrated, bibliographies and L.A. examination papers at chapter ends).

This is a textbook for Library Association students, a clear, concise review of handwriting and early writing materials, the history of papermaking, block books and the inventions of printing, the history of printing throughout Western Europe, private presses in England, the United States and Canada, typography and type founders illustration processes, bookbinding history, publishing and bookselling, collectors and collecting, copyright and the development of book trade bibliography.

Basil Blackwell, THE WORLD OF BOOKS, *A Panorama*, J. M. Dent, 1932 (foreword by Hugh Dent).

This is the first of the Dent Memorial Lectures, in which Basil Blackwell considers the role of the good bookman, the publisher, the printer, the papermaker, the binder and the bookseller and other members of the world of books.

CAMBRIDGE BIBLIOGRAPHY OF ENGLISH LITERATURE, edited by **F. W. Bateson,** 5 vols., C.U.P., 1939–40, revised edition, edited George Watson, 1969 continuing.

Sections in each volume on *Book Production and Distribution, Regulation of the Book Trade, Book Collecting, Booksellers* and *Publishers* form a full bibliography of book trade literature, compiled for the *Cambridge History of English Literature* by A. W. Pollard and revised and enlarged for the new edition by James Mosley, librarian of the St Bride Printing Library (q.v.).

DENT MEMORIAL LECTURES

'The framework of our book world is the genius of individuals; we lesser men fill in the structure, so long as individual genius is allowed scope, our little world will stand.'

In 1930 Hugh Dent provided a fund in memory of his father, J. M. Dent, for an annual lecture on some aspect of book production, 'designed to be helpful to all of us who seek to win our living in the perilous realm of letters' (Basil Blackwell). The lectures were discontinued at the outbreak of war and never renewed as it was felt to be an anticlimax to follow in the steps of the distinguished bookmen who gave the original lectures covering all the major aspects of the book world. The fund was combined with a grant from the G.L.C. in 1959 to provide a £100 travelling bursary for a student of the London College of Printing, awarded on the basis of a successful essay on the subject of the student's course of study. The recently inaugurated *Beatrice Warde Memorial Lectures* will fulfil a similar function to the pre-war Dent lectures.

Basil Blackwell, THE WORLD OF BOOKS, 1931 (see above).

Michael Sadleir, AUTHORS AND PUBLISHERS, 1932 (see also under I. AUTHORSHIP, p. 7).

John Johnson, THE PRINTER: HIS CUSTOMERS AND HIS MEN, 1933 (see under XI. THE PRINTING OF BOOKS, p. 251).

R. H. Clapperton, PAPER AND ITS RELATIONSHIP TO BOOKS, 1934 (see under X. PAPER FOR BOOKWORK, p. 230).

Douglas Leighton, MODERN BOOKBINDING, 1935 (see under II. BOOKBINDING, p. 28).

Richard de la Mare, A PUBLISHER ON BOOK PRODUCTION, 1936 (see under IV. BOOK DESIGN AND PRODUCTION, pp. 110 and XIII. PUBLISHING, p. 330).

R. P. Gossop, BOOK ILLUSTRATION, 1937 (see under V. BOOK ILLUSTRATON, p. 139).

Harold Raymond, PUBLISHING AND BOOKSELLING, 1938 (see also p. 60).

Frank Swinnerton, THE REVIEWING AND CRITICISM OF BOOKS, 1939.

David Diringer, THE HAND-PRODUCED BOOK, Hutchinson, 1953 (illustrated, bibliography).

This describes book production from earliest times to the end of the manuscript period in the later Middle Ages.

Desmond Flower, *Printing and Publishing,* in Cassell's ENCYCLOPAEDIA OF LITERATURE, 1963.

This provides an introduction to the study of printing, typography, the gradual separation of the trade, and modern developments.

Percy Freer, BIBLIOGRAPHY AND MODERN BOOK PRODUCTION, *Notes and Sources for Student Librarians, Printers, Booksellers, Stationers, Book-Collectors,* Witwatersrand University Press, Johannesburg, 1954.

In some ways similar in scope to the present Guide, this concentrates on technical aspects rather than on the history and practice of bookselling and publishing. It aims to be a textbook for South African library students with examination questions appended.

Geoffrey Ashall Glaister, GLOSSARY OF THE BOOK, *Terms Used in Paper-Making, Printing, Bookbinding and Publishing with Notes on Illuminated Manuscripts, Bibliophiles, Private Presses and Printing Societies,* George Allen & Unwin, 1960 (illustrated).

This indispensable encyclopaedia of every aspect of books and the book trade is at present being revised. There are appendixes on some type specimens, Latin place names as used in imprints of early printed books, the contemporary private press, proof correction symbols, and a short (sic) reading list.

John Hampden, editor, THE BOOK WORLD, Nelson, 1935.

John Hampden, THE BOOK WORLD TODAY, *A New Survey of the Making and Distribution of Books in Britain,* with an introduction by Sir Stanley Unwin, George Allen & Unwin, 1957.

Articles include those on authorship, the literary agent, educational publishing, book production, bookselling new and antiquarian, British books overseas, the National Book League.

Horace Hart, BIBLIOTHECA TYPOGRAPHICA IN USUM EORUM LIBROS AMANT: *A List of Books about Books,* The Printing House of Leo Hart, Rochester, New York, 1933, reprinted Gryphon Books, Ann Arbor, 1971.

'The list began as a guide for a young man who was interested in printing, and who wanted to know what books he ought to buy, and not to buy, yet awhile. It has been made up from the books that he has been able to see for himself, in the half dozen libraries easiest to consult.' Similar in scope to the present work, but more personal and idiosyncratic, it is divided into sections on the letters of the alphabet, paper and paper-making, manuscripts and illumination, printers and printing, bookbinding, publishing and bookselling, bibliography, book collecting and periodicals, each with a brief note or quotation from the book in question.

Joseph Hill, THE BOOK MAKERS OF OLD BIRMINGHAM: *Authors, Printers and Booksellers,* Shakespeare Press for Cornish Brothers, Birmingham, 1907 (illustrated).

This includes some known names, principally Baskerville, Caslon and William Hutton (qq.v.), as well as descriptions of little-known bookshops, printers and newspapers which give a picture of the provincial book trade in the eighteenth century.

London School of Economics, A CLASSIFIED CATALOGUE OF WORKS ON PUBLISHING AND BOOKSELLING, *in the British Library of Political and Economic Science,* 1st edition, 1936, latest edition, 1961.

This collection concentrates on books on the economics of and conditions of work in publishing in this country and abroad.

Manchester Public Library, THE MANCHESTER REFERENCE LIBRARY SUBJECT CATALOGUE, *Section 655, Printing, Part 11, Type and Typesetting, Printing Processes, Publishing and Bookselling, Copyright,* edited by G. E. Haslam, Manchester Libraries Committee, 1963.

This includes much that is technical on printing, publishing and bookselling in seventeen countries besides the United Kingdom. It gives the Library UDC number of each book listed.

F. A. Mumby, PUBLISHING AND BOOKSELLING, *A History from the Earliest Times to the Present Day,* |Jonathan Cape, new edition revised, 1956 (with an extensive bibliography by W. H. Peet, brought up to date by F. A. Mumby).

This work, first published in 1930 (without a bibliography) as *The Romance of Bookselling,* is being further revised and brought up to date by Ian Norrie. It is a mine of information, much of it based on personal knowledge.

N.B.L., BOOKS ABOUT BOOKS, *A Catalogue of the Library of the National Book League,* C.U.P. for the N.B.L., 1st edition, 1933, 5th edition enlarged and revised, 1955.

(See *Preface* for a history and scope of this collection.) The present work, based on the National Book League Library, follows its system of classification.

Marjorie Plant, THE ENGLISH BOOK TRADE, *An Economic History of the Making and Sale of Books,* George Allen & Unwin, 1st edition, 1939, 2nd edition revised, 1965 (illustrated, chapter by chapter bibliography and list of authors cited).

A key work on the economic and legal aspects of book trade history, describing the structure of the industry, conditions of employment and trade unions, terms, cost, copyright and the different processes of printing, and the Net Book Agreement (see pp. 221 ff.).

A DECREE

Concerning OF *Printing* &c.

Starre-Chamber,

CONCERNING

PRINTING,

*Made the eleuenth day of July.
last past.* 1637.

¶ Imprinted at London by *Robert Barker,*
Printer to the Kings moſt Excellent
Maieſtie: And by the Aſſignes
of *Iohn Bill.* 1637.

Title page of the Decree Concerning Printing *which imposed severe penalties on unlicensed and
seditious printers, and which was one of the last measures carried out by the Star Chamber
before its abolition in 1641*

Harold Raymond, PUBLISHING AND BOOKSELLING, *A Survey of Post-War Developments and Present-Day Problems,* J. M. Dent, 1938.

This, the eighth of the Dent Memorial Lectures (see pp. 154 f.), deals with the controversial subject of distribution of books, also book clubs, paperbacks (then just beginning), and the achievements of the then National Book Council in promoting books.

St Bride Foundation, A CATALOGUE OF THE TECHNICAL REFERENCE LIBRARY OF WORKS ON PRINTING AND THE ALLIED ARTS, St Bride, 1919.

The record of what was, even fifty years ago, one of the most comprehensive and valuable collections of works on the book trade, it is, unfortunately, unclassified. Books on printing naturally predominate since St Bride's was, until 1922, an institute of printing (see under XI. THE PRINTING OF BOOKS, p. 309) which, with growth, broke away to become the London College of Printing. After that date evening lectures, organised by the Librarian, were held on aspects of printing and allied subjects.

St Bride Foundation, A CATALOGUE OF THE PERIODICALS RELATING TO PRINTING AND ALLIED SUBJECTS *In the Technical Library of the Saint Bride Institute,* with an introduction by Ellic Howe, 1951.

F. D. Sanders, editor, BRITISH BOOK TRADE ORGANISATION: *A Report on the Work of the Joint Committee,* with an introduction by Stanley (later Sir Stanley) Unwin, George Allen & Unwin, 1939.

This describes the structure and organisation of the book trade in the twentieth century. Sections on getting and fulfilling orders, distribution and trade organisation and practices, are followed by seventeen appendixes on such matters as co-operative advertising, library licence, exhibitions.

Leslie Stephen and Sidney Lee, DICTIONARY OF NATIONAL BIOGRAPHY, Smith Elder, 22 vols., 1908; O.U.P., 8 supplementary vols., 1901–69.

An invaluable source of biographical information for historians of the book trade. 'An informal revision of many articles' is contained in the *Errata Notes* of the *Bulletin* of the Institute of Historical Research, 1923– (see Winchell, *Guide to Reference Works,* Chicago, 8th edition, 1968).

Mary C. Turner, editor, THE BOOKMAN'S GLOSSARY, 1st edition, 1925, 4th edition, revised and enlarged, Bowker, New York, 1961 (originally a serial in the *Publishers' Weekly,* 1924).

The 3rd edition was edited by a committee of the staff of Bowker including F. G. Melcher, Jacob Blanck and Anne J. Richter. Appendixes include book trade terms, proof marks, and select reading list.

Whitaker, BRITISH BOOKS IN PRINT, (see also under III BOOKSELLING (p. 71).

The main body of the work is preceded by a very useful book trade bibliography.

3. The Stationers' Company

To separate the Stationers' Company from the rest of the trade's history during the sixteenth and seventeenth centuries may be thought to make an artificial, if not an absurd, distinction. But it makes the present Guide easier to use. From 1557 until the expiry of the Licensing Act (1695), the Stationers' Company so dominated the book world that growth of a provincial trade was stunted and the London trade had little existence outside the Company's control. Today it is one of the few City Livery Companies to admit to membership only those who have trade connections. It therefore continues to exert considerable influence. It has been the rallying point, in recent years, of a number of trade activities, including the launching of the Institute of Printing (see under XI. THE PRINTING OF BOOKS, p. 305). Its annual lectures are also important. Cyprian Blagden (see below), considers the reasons for its waning power in the nineteenth century:

The Company has remained . . . uncommitted to any branch of the trade; but it has not, on the strength of this, become a Chamber to which all branches might look for guidance and settlement of differences. It was during the nineteenth century that the Stationers' Company 'retired' from the book trade. . . . This has been followed by a general retirement of the book trade from the vicinity of St Paul's; and the fires of the end of December 1940 hastened this centrifugal movement.

The Bibliographical Society, particularly during the early years of the present century edited and published much material from the Company's archives. The work of such pioneer scholars as Edward Arber, E. Gordon Duff, H. R. Plomer, Alfred Pollard, R. B. McKerrow and more recently, W. W. Greg, appeared in the Society's Proceedings (from 1920 called *The Library*) and also produced a series of early trade dictionaries, separately listed below. Their researches laid the foundation on which later trade historians could build. Greg and Boswell in *Records . . . 1576–1602* (see below) explain the haphazard nature of the source material: 'Since these are the records kept by the clerk in the spacious but unmethodical days of Elizabeth, I need hardly say that the decrees and ordinances contain all sorts of matters that one would never dream of looking for, and at the same time omit many that one thought one had a right to expect.'

Edward Arber, A TRANSCRIPT OF THE REGISTERS OF THE COMPANY OF STATIONERS IN LONDON, 1554–1640, 5 vols. (1875–94, privately printed).

Edward Arber, A LIST, BASED ON THE REGISTERS OF THE STATIONERS' COMPANY, *Of 837 London Publishers between 1553 and 1640*, Birmingham, 1890.

These, and the other source books listed below, have lengthy and illuminating introductions, giving the background to the documents published.

Cyprian Blagden, THE STATIONERS' COMPANY, *A History, 1403–1959*, George Allen & Unwin, 1960 (illustrated, bibliography).

Not only does this tell a coherent story, but it is valuable for dealing in detail with what has been little covered elsewhere, namely the period 1660–1810 and the last 150 years of waning power.

W. W. Greg, A COMPANION TO ARBER, *Being a Calendar of Documents in Edward Arber's Transcript . . . with Text and Calendar of Supplementary Documents*, O.U.P., 1967.

This supplements Arber's work for the reigns of James I and Charles I, each document being preceded by explanatory, critical and historical notes. The first section, covering Licensers for the press, was prepared for publication after Greg's death by Cyprian Blagden and I. G. Philip.

W. W. Greg, LICENSERS FOR THE PRESS TO 1640, Oxford Bibliographical Society, 1962.

This is a biographical index based mainly on Arber's Transcript, published after Greg's death. (On the manuscript Greg had written, 'This has been carefully checked and revised and may be printed as it stands.')

W. W. Greg and E. Boswell, RECORDS OF THE STATIONERS' COMPANY, 1576–1602, *From Register B*, Bibliographical Society, 1930 (illustrated).

This fills the gap that Arber was forced to leave in his Transcript since the Court of the Stationers' Company of his day refused permission to publish sections of the B Register. The introduction includes sections on the election of Liverymen, Masters and Wardens, master printers, apprentices and others.

William A. Jackson, editor, RECORDS OF THE STATIONERS' COMPANY 1602–1640, Bibliographical Society, 1957.

This follows on from Greg and Boswell (see above).

Graham Pollard, *The Early Constitution of the Stationers' Company*, article in THE LIBRARY, 4th Series, vol. 18, no. 3, December 1937.

Leona Rostenberg, LITERARY, POLITICAL, SCIENTIFIC, RELIGIOUS, AND LEGAL PUBLISHING, PRINTING AND BOOKSELLING IN ENGLAND, 1551–1700, 2 vols., Burth Franklin, New York, 1965 (illustrated).

This is a study of the publications, careers and influence of twelve members of the Stationers' Company: Thomas Wight, Thomas Thorpe, Nathaniel Butter, Nicholas Bourne, Job Bellamy, William Dugard, Michael Sparke, Livewell Chapman, John Martyn, Robert Scott, Robert Stephens, Richard and Anne Baldwin.

4. The History of the Book Trade 1450–1775

The organisation of the trade did not change very much from the invention of printing until the end of the eighteenth century in that there was little of 'division of employment'. By the end of the period the power of the Stationers' Company was waning, copyright was legally acknowledged, and the trade was beginning to split into its modern components, so that its later history is to be found under the appropriate sections of this Guide.

H. G. Aldis, THE BOOK TRADE 1557–1626, C.U.P., 1909 (bibliography).

This reprint of Aldis's article in the *Cambridge History of English Literature,* volume 4, describes the Star Chamber Decree regarding the licensing of literature, copyright, John Day, book fairs, prices and the trade in Cambridge, Oxford and Scotland.

H. S. Bennett, ENGLISH BOOKS AND READERS 1475 TO 1557: *Being a Study in the History of the Book Trade from Caxton to the Incorporation of the Stationers' Company,* C.U.P., 1952 (bibliography).

Caxton and his literary heritage are evaluated and literacy in the period reviewed together with the regulations of the book trade, patronage, the demand for books, translations and translators, printers and printing. Appendixes give a handlist of publications by Wynkyn de Worde, 1492–1535, and a trial list of translations into English printed between 1475–1560.

H. S. Bennett, ENGLISH BOOKS AND READERS 1558–1603, *Being a Study in the History of the Book Trade in the Reign of Elizabeth I,* C.U.P., 1965 (bibliography).

In the sequel, H. S. Bennett covers the same ground, but for the later period, as well as giving an account of the total output of books and pamphlets of the period, examining the relations between authors and readers and the part played by the book trade in the intellectual life of the age.

E. Gordon Duff, THE PRINTERS, STATIONERS AND BOOKBINDERS OF WESTMINSTER AND LONDON FROM 1476 TO 1535, C.U.P., 1906 (illustrated).

The text of the eight Sandars lectures for the Lent term 1899 and May term 1904. Four concern the printers of the period (also separately published by Aberdeen University Press, 1899), three relate to the stationers and one to the bookbinders.

E. Gordon Duff, ENGLISH PROVINCIAL PRINTERS, STATIONERS AND BOOKBINDERS TO 1557, C.U.P., 1912 (illustrated and contains bibliography).

The book trade in Oxford, Cambridge, St Albans, York, Hereford, Tavistock, Abingdon, Ipswich, Worcester, Canterbury, Exeter, Winchester and Greenwich is here considered. An appendix lists books printed by provincial printers or for provincial stationers.

W. W. Greg, SOME ASPECTS AND PROBLEMS OF LONDON PUBLISHING BETWEEN 1550 AND 1650, O.U.P., 1956.

The text of the Lyell lectures for 1955, contains a prefatory letter to Professor F. P. Wilson on how the subject came into being. These six outstanding lectures deal with the Stationers' records, licensing for the press, 'Entrance' (i.e. entrance of the copy of a book in the Stationers' Register) and copyright, imprints and patents and their interpretation. Of 'Entrance', Greg says, 'I believe that Alfred Pollard was the first critic to realize that entrance of a copy in the Stationers' Register might be used, not as a step towards publication, but to block the way to unauthorised printing, and to suggest that plays were sometimes actually entered with this purpose.'

A. Growoll and Wilberforce Eames, THREE CENTURIES OF ENGLISH BOOKTRADE BIBLIOGRAPHY, 1st published 1903, The Holland Press, 1964.

This consists of chapters by A. Growoll on the beginnings of book trade bibliography since the introduction of printing, the 'term' catalogues, Stationers' Company lists, early book trade journals, eighteenth- and nineteenth-century book trade bibliography. It is followed by a list of catalogues, trade journals and bibliographies, 1595–1902, compiled by Wilberforce Eames.

Rudolf Hirsch, PRINTING, BOOKSELLING AND READING 1450–1550, Otto Harrassowitz, Wiesbaden, 1967 (illustrated).

This is based on the trade in Germany whose conditions at this early date were similar to those in this country. Mr Hirsch deals in general terms with the transition from script to print, printing, the cost of production, cost and management, bookselling, protection restraint and politics, national and local characteristics of the book trade and finally, printing and reading.

Graham Pollard, editor, THE EARLIEST DIRECTORY OF THE BOOK TRADE BY JOHN PENDRED (1785), Bibliographical Society, 1955 (illustrated, appendix of source material).

This reprint of *The London and Country Printers', Booksellers', and Stationers' Vade Mecum* lists printers, founders, plate makers, stationers, binders, booksellers, goldbeaters, and newspapers, preceded by a textual, biographical and critical introduction.

R. M. Wiles, SERIAL PUBLICATION IN ENGLAND BEFORE 1750 (see under XIII. PUBLISHING, p. 330).

5. Dictionaries of the Book Trade

E. Gordon Duff, A CENTURY OF THE ENGLISH BOOK TRADE: *Short Notices of All Printers, Stationers, Book-binders, and Others Connected with It from the Issue of the First Dated Book in 1457 to the Incorporation of the Company of Stationers in 1557,* Bibliographical Society, 1905 (bibliography).

An historical survey of the period is followed by a list of the principal books quoted, short biographical notes on the printers, etc., of the period, an index of London signs before 1558, as well as a chronological index of foreign places, printers and stationers.

E. Gordon Duff, ENGLISH PROVINCIAL PRINTERS, STATIONERS AND BOOKBINDERS TO 1557, C.U.P., 1912 (illustrated, contains bibliography).

George J. Gray, THE EARLIER CAMBRIDGE STATIONERS AND BOOKBINDERS AND THE FIRST CAMBRIDGE PRINTER, O.U.P. for the Bibliographical Society, 1904 (Illustrated Monograph no. 13).

The work is divided into two parts, the first includes a summary of the position of stationers and binders in the university with appendixes listing prices of writing, binding and repairing, sales of book *cautions* (books deposited as pledges by students). The second part lists sixteenth-century printers and gives the regulations concerning booksellers, bookbinders, and stationers of the university of 1583. Illustrations include examples of Godfrey's and Speerincks's bindings, rolls and stamps used by Siberch (the first Cambridge printer) and by Godfrey.

W. H. Hodson, BOOKSELLERS, PUBLISHERS AND STATIONERS DIRECTORY, 1855 (see Graham Pollard, below).

R. B. McKerrow, A DICTIONARY OF THE PRINTERS AND BOOKSELLERS AT WORK IN ENGLAND, SCOTLAND AND IRELAND FROM 1557 TO 1640, Bibliographical Society, 1910.

An introduction surveys the state of the trade and regulations relating thereto.

H. R. Plomer, A DICTIONARY OF THE BOOKSELLERS AND PRINTERS WHO WERE AT WORK IN . . . 1641–1667, Bibliographical Society, 1907.

This fills the gap between the Stationers' Registers and the Term Catalogues of Arber (see under 'Stationers' Company', p. 161 above), and gives the imprint showing place, biographical detail and description of the character of the trade carried on, preceded, as with the above mentioned works, by a background history of the trade during the period.

H. R. Plomer, with the help of **H. G. Aldis, E. R. McDix, G. J. Gray and R. B. McKerrow,** edited by **Arundell Esdaile,** A DICTIONARY OF THE PRINTERS AND BOOKSELLERS . . . 1668 TO 1725, O.U.P. for the Bibliographical Society, 1922.

This covers an important period of trade history marked by the expiry of the Licensing Act in 1695, the imposing of paper and pamphlet duties which caused many English books to be printed abroad at cheaper rates, the Copyright Act of 1709 and the establishment of provincial presses.

H. R. Plomer, G. H. Bushnell and E. R. McDix, A DICTIONARY OF THE PRINTERS AND BOOKSELLERS . . . 1727 TO 1775, O.U.P. for the Bibliographical Society, 1932.

The last of the Bibliographical Society's dictionaries includes quotations from authorities such as Timperley (see p. 288).

Graham Pollard, HODSON'S BOOKSELLERS, PUBLISHERS AND STATIONERS DIRECTORY 1855, *A Facsimile of the Copy in the Bodleian Library, Oxford,* Oxford Bibliographical Society occasional Publication no. 7, Bodleian Library, Oxford, 1972.

An introduction by Graham Pollard gives some of the hitherto unpublished information on the London sharebook system and the gradual separation of publishing from wholesaling that Mr Pollard first imparted in the Sandars Lectures in Bibliography in 1959.

Ernest James Worman, ALIEN MEMBERS OF THE BOOK-TRADE DURING THE TUDOR PERIOD: *Being an Index of Those Whose Names Occur in the Returns of Aliens, Letters of Denization, and Other Documents by the Huguenot Society,* Bibliographical Society, 1906.

6. Wills of the Old Printers, Booksellers and Bookbinders

The Bibliographical Society's volumes of abstracts of the wills of early members of the trade 'throw light on the customs' as on the organisation and early equipment of printers, binders and booksellers.

CAMBRIDGE

George J. Gray and William Mortlock Palmer, ABSTRACTS FROM THE WILLS AND TESTAMENTARY DOCUMENTS OF PRINTERS, BINDERS AND STATIONERS OF CAMBRIDGE, FROM 1504 TO 1699, Bibliographical Society, 1915.

In a letter to Henry Aldis, January 19, 1916, Gray says: 'I am rather proud of the book and hope it will do credit to our remarkable Cambridge School of Bibliography. I have traced *where* the University printers printed, and can now take back to the sixteenth century the occupancy of no. 1 Trinity Street as a bookseller's shop. Mr Bowes was very pleased when I communicated this fact to him...' (see also under III. BOOKSELLING, p. 61).

LONDON

H. R. Plomer, ABSTRACTS FROM THE WILLS OF ENGLISH PRINTERS AND STATIONERS FROM 1492 TO 1630, Bibliographical Society, 1903.

'The object kept in view in this compilation has been to illustrate, as far as possible, the history of printing and bookselling, and the plan followed has been to give the date of the making of the will, the place of burial, the bequests, the names of the executors, overseers and witnesses, and the date upon which the will was proved. . . . The more important bequests, such as those left to the Stationers' Company, or which serve to throw light on the customs of the printing and bookselling trades, have been given in the words used by the testators. . . . The bulk of these wills are those of booksellers. Nor is this surprising. In the first place, the booksellers greatly outnumbered the printers. In the second place, while in the early days of the art of printing, the printers were men of good social position . . . the growth of the monopolies and the fierce trade competition quickly altered this state of things. . . .' (Introduction).

OXFORD

Strickland Gibson, ABSTRACTS FROM THE WILLS AND TESTAMENTARY DOCUMENTS OF BINDERS, PRINTERS AND STATIONERS OF OXFORD, FROM 1493 TO 1638, Bibliographical Society, 1907.

7. Book Trade Organisations

BOOK TRADE BENEVOLENT SOCIETY (founded 1968)

This has replaced the old-established Book Trade Provident Institution and administers funds for the relief of elderly members of the book trade or those who are otherwise in need. It maintains homes at the Booksellers' Retreat for retired members of all branches of the trade.

DOUBLE CROWN CLUB (founded 1924)

This dining club, tacitly limited to men, was founded by Oliver Simon, Hubert Foss and Holbrook Jackson. Members include distinguished printers, typographers, designers, publishers and bibliophiles. Dinners were held at various London restaurants and are now generally held at Kettners where papers are read and discussed. The menu for each dinner is specially designed.

NATIONAL BOOK LEAGUE

Founded 1924 as the National Book Council, this became the National Book League 1944 and works for the wider use of books. While it receives support from all branches of the book trade it is independent of any of them, and is therefore able to speak to bodies which would perhaps suspect a commercial purpose in those more directly involved in the sale of books. Its members range from private individuals interested in books and reading who make use of its club facilities, to schools, libraries and members of the book trade, both corporate and private. Its Book Production Library forms the basis of the present Guide, and its attached Book Information Bureau answers some 45,000 queries a year on book matters. It organises book exhibitions throughout the country and issues booklists and readers' guides. Its quarterly journal is BOOKS.

THE SETTE OF ODD VOLUMES (founded by Bernard Quaritch, 1878)

Forty-two (originally twenty-one) authors, booksellers, publishers, collectors and literary men dine together six times a year when one of the number reads a paper. Publications called *opuscula* are produced at the expense of individual members and limited to 133 copies. These comprise papers previously delivered at meetings, reprints of rare works or original publications. By 1963 there were 120 *opuscula*. Members are designated by humorous or antiquarian titles.

THE SOCIETY OF BOOKMEN (founded 1921)

Founded by Hugh Walpole, the Society consists of 100 distinguished members of the world of books and letters, who are invited to take up membership. Its aims are to promote the use of books and to discuss and initiate developments for the good of the book trade. The Society of Bookmen, led by Hugh Walpole and the late Sir Stanley Unwin, initiated the idea of an organisation that took shape as the National Book Council (see above).

WORSHIPFUL COMPANY OF STATIONERS AND NEWSPAPER MAKERS (see also 'Stationers' Company', frontispiece and pp. 160 ff. above).

Founded as a guild as early as 1403, it was granted a royal charter 1557. In 1933 it amalgamated with the Newspaper Makers. Until the early years of the present century it was necessary to register books at Stationers' Hall for copyright protection. Its present-day activities include the binding of apprentices in the printing and allied trades, the provision of pensions and the maintenance of its own school. Its school is now partly maintained by the Local Authority since, following the 1944 Education Act, it became voluntary aided; it therefore continues to have a board of governors, some of whom are nominated by the Company.

CHILDREN'S BOOKS

Newbery's shop in St Paul's Churchyard (actual size)
(see p. 344)

1. Introduction

Broadly I define a children's book as one written for the entertainment or instruction of a child up to the teens. Books about the writing, illustrating, history, collecting and selection of children's books abound, whereas, for some reason, very little has been published on other specialist types of writing. In the last decades children's books and children's reading have been increasingly the subject of special study and most general publishers now have a children's editor to deal entirely with the publication of children's books and the public library service trains special children's librarians.

2. Biographies of Children's Writers

Gillian Avery, NINETEENTH CENTURY CHILDREN'S BOOKS, Hodder & Stoughton, 1965.

Particularly useful is the appendix of 120 biographical references to authors before 1900.

BODLEY HEAD MONOGRAPHS

This series, under the general editorship of Kathleen Lines, comprises standard biographies by well-known children's writers and librarians as follows:

LOUISA M. ALCOTT

Cornelia Meigs, LOUISA M. ALCOTT AND THE AMERICAN FAMILY STORY, 1970.

J. M. BARRIE

Roger Lancelyn Green, J. M. BARRIE, 1968.

LUCY BOSTON

Jasper Rose, LUCY BOSTON, 1965.

LEWIS CARROLL

Roger Lancelyn Green, LEWIS CARROLL, 1960.

WALTER DE LA MARE

Leonard Clark, WALTER DE LA MARE, 1960.

MRS EWING

Gillian Avery, MRS EWING, 1961.

ELEANOR FARJEON

Eileen Colwell, ELEANOR FARJEON, 1961.

KENNETH GRAHAME

Eleanor Graham, KENNETH GRAHAME, 1963.

RUDYARD KIPLING

Rosemary Sutcliff, RUDYARD KIPLING, 1960.

ANDREW LANG

Roger Lancelyn Green, ANDREW LANG, 1962.

C. S. LEWIS

Roger Lancelyn Green, C. S. LEWIS, 1969.

HUGH LOFTING

Edward Blishen, HUGH LOFTING, 1968.

JOHN MASEFIELD

Margery Fisher, JOHN MASEFIELD, 1963.

MRS MOLESWORTH

Roger Lancelyn Green, MRS MOLESWORTH, 1961.

E. NESBIT
Anthea Bell, E. NESBIT, 1960.

BEATRIX POTTER
Marcus Crouch, BEATRIX POTTER, 1969

HOWARD PYLE
Elizabeth Nesbitt, HOWARD PYLE, 1966.

ARTHUR RANSOME
Hugh Shelley, ARTHUR RANSOME, 1960.

RUTH SAWYER
Virginia Haviland, RUTH SAWYER, 1965.

R. L. STEVENSON
Dennis Butts, R. L. STEVENSON, 1966.

NOEL STREATFEILD
Barbara Ker Wilson, NOEL STREATFEILD, 1961.

ROSEMARY SUTCLIFF
Margaret Meek, ROSEMARY SUTCLIFF, 1962.

GEOFFREY TREASE
Margaret Meek, GEOFFREY TREASE, 1960.

HENRY TREECE
Margery Fisher, HENRY TREECE, 1969.

Bodley Head are now reissuing the monographs in groups of three as follows:

ARTHUR RANSOME, RUDYARD KIPLING AND WALTER DE LA MARE, 1968;
HUGH LOFTING, GEOFFREY TREASE AND J. M. BARRIE, 1968;
LEWIS CARROLL, E. NESBIT AND HOWARD PYLE, 1968;
HENRY TREECE, C. S. LEWIS AND BEATRIX POTTER, 1969.

Brian Doyle, WHO'S WHO OF BOYS WRITERS AND ILLUSTRATORS, Hugh Evelyn, 1964.

This is a duplicated list of some 750 boys' authors and 200 artists with biographical and bibliographical information on them.

Brian Doyle, WHO'S WHO OF CHILDREN'S LITERATURE, Hugh Evelyn, 1968 (illustrated, bibliography).

This consists of biographical and bibliographical information on 400 authors and artists, British, American and continental, arranged in two alphabetical lists. Despite its deficiencies, it fills a real gap.

Alec Ellis, HOW TO FIND OUT ABOUT CHILDREN'S LITERATURE (see under 'Reference Works', p. 188 below).

Pages 86–8 have further studies of individual authors.

Muriel Fuller, editor, MORE JUNIOR AUTHORS, H. W. Wilson, New York, 1963.

This is a companion volume to the foregoing, of 268 entries.

S. J. Kunitz and H. Haycraft, editors, THE JUNIOR BOOK OF AUTHORS, H. W. Wilson, New York, 1st edition, 1934, 2nd edition, 1951.

This comprises 289 autobiographical sketches of authors and illustrators, mainly American.

3. General Histories
(See also under 'Collecting Early Children's Books' pp. 178 ff. below.)

F. J. Harvey Darton, CHILDREN'S BOOKS IN ENGLAND: *Five Centuries of Social Life*, C.U.P., 1st edition, 1932, 2nd edition, with an introduction by Kathleen Lines, 1958 (illustrated, bibliography).

The second edition contains an additional annotated bibliography of books of general and specific interest published since 1932. Kathleen Lines says: 'It is probably safe to say that Darton will never be supplanted. . . . Throughout his scholarly, yet at the same time humanly revealing account of the development of children's literature beginning with the chapbook versions of medieval romances and covering, with remarkably few omissions, all important writing for children up to the appearance of

Alice and *The Jungle Books*, the reader has confidence in the author's handling of a massive amount of material.'

Alec Ellis, A HISTORY OF CHILDREN'S READING AND LITERATURE, Pergamon Press, Oxford, 1968 (illustrated, bibliography).

Mr Ellis covers the period 1740–1965, with chapters on the books themselves, the educational background and the libraries in existence. The needs of the modern library student are well catered for by the author, who is a lecturer in librarianship. His approach consequently contrasts with that of Harvey Darton and Percy Muir. Illustrations include a schedule of lesson books for the scholars reproduced from the minutes for 1847 of the Committee of Council on education, and the title page of *Bootle Public Library Catalogue of Books for the Young*, 1901.

E. M. Field, THE CHILD AND HIS BOOKS: *Some Account of the History and Progress of Children's Literature in England*, Wells Gardner, Darton & Co., London, 1891 (illustrated).

Harvey Darton (see above) cites Mrs Field as the only author before him to treat the subject with any completeness. Less scholarly than his own work and less professional than Mrs Thwaite (see below) it is, nevertheless, informed and informative. Mrs Field traces the history of children's literature from pre-Conquest books that she surmises a child might have seen to the developments of her own day. Side-heads make for easy use and quotations at the head of each chapter provide a further guide to contents.

Cornelia Meigs, Anne Thaxter Eaton, Elizabeth Nesbitt and Ruth Hill Viguers, A CRITICAL HISTORY OF CHILDREN'S LITERATURE: *A Survey of Children's Books in English from the Earliest Times to the Present, Prepared in Four Parts under the Editorship of Cornelia Meigs. Decorations by Vera Bock. Introduction by Dr Henry Steele Commager*, The Macmillan Co., New York, 1953 (extensive bibliographies at chapter ends).

This is a definitive history of children's literature, and includes work on American children's literature.

Montrose J. Moses, CHILDREN'S BOOKS AND READING, Mitchell Kennerley, New York, 1907.

Besides giving a historical survey of English and continental children's books, one section deals with the classification of children's books and book selection under the title of *The Library and the Book*. An appendix gives a classified list of children's books with a select background bibliography. It is not noticeably American in slant.

Percy Muir, ENGLISH CHILDREN'S BOOKS, 1600–1900, Batsford, 1954 (illustrated, bibliographies at the end of each chapter).

This is a well-documented volume by a bookseller and writer on book collecting.

M. F. Thwaite, FROM PRIMER TO PLEASURE: *An Introduction to the History of Children's Books in England from the Invention of Printing to 1900 with a Chapter on Some Developments Abroad,* Library Association, 1963 (illustrated, bibliography).

Covering much the same ground as Harvey Darton (see above), this is intended 'as an introduction to more scholarly and detailed histories of literature for boys and girls'. It is informative rather than critical. Appended is a chronological table of the more important works mentioned in the text from 1479–1900 and a full, but selected, bibliography of the works consulted by the author listed chapter by chapter in a further appendix.

John Rowe Townsend, WRITTEN FOR CHILDREN: *An Outline of English Children's Literature,* Garnett Miller, 1965 (illustrated, bibliography of books on children's literature).

This is a readable short history up to the late 1950s excluding picture books.

4. Particular Aspects and Periods

Frank Eyre, TWENTIETH CENTURY CHILDREN'S BOOKS, Longmans, Green for the British Council, 1952 (23 illustrations, bibliography, list of Carnegie Award winners).

Four chapters cover the history of children's books, books with pictures, the in-between books and fiction for children.

Beulah Folmsbee, HISTORY OF THE HORN BOOK, Horn Book, Boston, Massachusetts, 1942, reprinted 1965 (illustrated, bibliography).

An excellent brief outline, more accessible for students than Tuer (see below).

See also under 'Choosing Books for Children' pp. 183 ff. below:

Roger Green, TELLERS OF TALES; **P. Hazard,** BOOKS, CHILDREN AND MEN; and under 'Reference Works' below: **Alec Ellis,** HOW TO FIND OUT ABOUT CHILDREN'S LITERATURE; **Gollard and Thompson,** BIOGRAPHIES FOR CHILDREN.

Bettina Hurlimann, THREE CENTURIES OF CHILDREN'S BOOKS IN EUROPE, translated and edited by Brian Alderson, O.U.P., 1967 (illustrated, bibliography).
This is intended as an informal introduction to a neglected field of study. It is a personal survey of the subject, based on the author's own collection and seems at times, therefore, somewhat random and arbitrary. Moreover, being intended for a non-English readership, it sometimes labours what is obvious to us and curtails what we find less familiar. The bibliography is divided country by country with occasional annotations and there is a list of biographies of children's writers.

Bettina Hurlimann, PICTURE-BOOK WORLD, translated and edited by Brian Alderson, O.U.P., 1968 (illustrated, bibliography).
This is intended as a supplement to *Three Centuries of Children's Books in Europe* (above). It is an anthology of modern picture books for children from twenty-four countries with a bio-bibliographical supplement by Elisabeth Waldmann, sources of further reading and sources of information.

Alice Jordan, FROM ROLLO TO TOM SAWYER AND OTHER PAPERS, Horn Book, Boston, Massachusetts, 1948.
This is a useful monograph of twelve chapters on nineteenth-century American children's books.

P. M. Pickard, I COULD A TALE UNFOLD; *Violence, Horror and Sensationalism in Stories for Children,* Tavistock Publications, 1961 (glossary of mythology, bibliography).
Besides tracing the history of children's literature from the beginnings to the comic, the author surveys children's reading and viewing habits (see also under 'Choosing Books for Children', p. 184 below).

William Sloane, CHILDREN'S BOOKS IN ENGLAND AND AMERICA IN THE SEVENTEENTH CENTURY: *A History and a Checklist, together with the Young Christian's Library, the First Printed Calalogue of Books for Children,* King's Crown Press, Columbia University, New York, 1955.
The history of English and American children's books with notes is followed by a chronological checklist of children's books; and *The Young*

Christian's Library, a facsimile of the pamphlet in the Bodleian Library (see also under 'Collecting Early Children's Books', below). The author defines a children's book as 'what was written to interest children of the day'; he dismisses Harvey Darton's definition 'printed works printed ostensibly to give children spontaneous pleasure' and therefore excludes adult classics later produced as children's books such as the *Pilgrim's Progress*.

Andrew W. Tuer, HISTORY OF THE HORN BOOKS, *With 300 illustrations*, 1st edition 2 vols., The Leadenhall Press, 1896, 2nd edition 1 vol., 1897, 1st edition reprinted Blom, New York, 1968.

This is still the definitive work on the subject of early alphabet boards. The first edition contains specimens of seven horn books in pockets at the beginning of each volume. The second, one-volume edition contains three, one of oak, one of card and one of ivory. The 'Contents' summarises each chapter for easy reference.

E. S. Turner, BOYS WILL BE BOYS, Michael Joseph, 1948 (illustrated).

This is the history, racily told by a journalist, of comics and boys' stories.

5. Collecting Early Children's Books – Anthologies, Catalogues of Collections, Bibliographies

F. W. Bateson, editor, THE CAMBRIDGE BIBLIOGRAPHY OF ENGLISH LITERATURE, C.U.P., 1940, 4 vols., and Supplement, 1957, new edition edited by George Watson, 5 vols. 1969 continuing.

Contains bibliographies of children's literature, 600–1900, and critical works, compiled and edited by Harvey Darton (see p. 174).

CATCHPENNY PRINTS, *163 Popular Engravings from the 18th Century*, originally published, Bowles & Carver, n.d., Dover Reprint, New York, 1970.

Leonard de Vries, FLOWERS OF DELIGHT CULLED BY LEONARD DE VRIES FROM THE OSBORNE COLLECTION OF EARLY CHILDREN'S BOOKS: *An Agreeable Garland of Prose and Poetry for the Instruction and Amusement of Little Masters and Misses and Their Distinguished Parents. Embellished with 750 Elegant Woodcuts and Engravings on Wood and Copper of which Upwards of 125 are Neatly Coloured, Selected with the Greatest Care for Juvenile Minds 1765–1830*, Dobson, 1965.

It concludes with a note on the Osborne Collection (see p. 196) by Henry C. Campbell, the chief librarian of Toronto Public Library, an anthologist's apology by the compiler telling the story of how his interest in early children's books stemmed from a search for juvenile books on scientific experiments in Amsterdam Children's Library in 1957. Notes on the original books give bibliographical details including page sizes in centimetres, notes on some writers, illustrators and publishers reprinted from the Osborne Catalogue and a list of books on early children's books in Britain and America.

Leonard de Vries, editor, AN ANTHOLOGY FROM VICTORIAN BOOKS AND PERIODICALS IN THE COLLECTION OF ANNE AND FERNAND RENIER, with an introduction by M. F. Thwaite, Arthur Barker, 1967.

This is an engaging volume but not well enough documented, bibliographical notes only give page sizes in centimetres where historical detail would be more useful. M. F. Thwaite's introduction is lively and informative, but the book is a minor tribute to a monumental collection (see p. 196) and this is the first book on it.

Gumuchian & Cie, LES LIVRES DE L'ENFANCE DU XVe AU XIXe SIECLE, *Preface de Paul Gavault,* 2 vols., the second containing plates, 1930, Holland Press Reprint, 1 vol. (with a small selection of the plates), 1967.

This monumental bibliography of children's books contains a handlist of works on children's books, besides the 6,251 entries with bibliographical notes, a table of books printed by the Newberys and their associates, and of those printed in the United States.

Hammersmith Public Library, EARLY CHILDREN'S BOOKS, *A Catalogue of the Collection in the London Borough of Hammersmith Public Libraries* (cyclostyled), 1965.

Charles F. Heartman, AMERICAN PRIMERS, INDIAN PRIMERS, ROYAL PRIMERS AND 37 OTHER TYPES OF NON-NEW ENGLAND PRIMERS, ISSUED PRIOR TO 1830: *A Bibliographical Checklist Embellished with 26 cuts, with an Introduction and Indexes,* Harry B. Weiss, New Jersey, 1935.

National Book League, CHILDREN'S BOOKS OF YESTERDAY, *A Catalogue of an Exhibition Held at 7 Albemarle Street, London, During 1946,* compiled by Percy H. Muir with a foreword by John Masefield, C.U.P. for the N.B.L., 1946, reissued Singing Tree Press, Detroit, Mich., 1971.

Drawn from the collection formed by F. R. Russell and sold to the National Magazine Company, it contains 1,001 items, annotated and classified with an introduction to each section.

Edgar Osborne, EARLY CHILDREN'S BOOKS, 1566–1910, *A Catalogue Prepared at the Boys and Girls House (Toronto)* by Judith St John, with an introduction by Edgar Osborne, Toronto Public Library, Canadian 1st edition, 1958, 2nd edition with additions, 1966 (illustrated).

This is the catalogue of 3,000 items in the Osborne Collection (see p. 196). The preface explains its scope. Edgar Osborne's introduction recounts how the collection developed and gives his reasons for the bequest. Appendixes consist of a chronological list of editions, 1566–1799: a list of illustrators and engravers, some with annotations: and an annotated list of publishers, booksellers and printers. The second edition includes a selected list of recent editions 1542–1910, and the Lillian H. Smith Collection, 1911–63 (illustrated), a list of donors from Toronto, the rest of Canada, Great Britain and the United States.

Barbara Quinnan, FABLES FROM INCUNABULA TO MODERN PICTURE BOOKS: *A Selective Bibliography*, Library of Congress, Washington, 1966.

This is divided into sections on Indian and Related Fables: Aesop; La Fontaine; and Krylov.

Anne and Fernand Renier, WHAT THE CHILDREN LIKE, *A Selection of Children's Books, Toys and Games From the Renier Collection, Exhibited at the Victoria & Albert Museum*, December 1970–February 1971.

This catalogue of 178 items is annotated by Irene Whalley and Anne Hobbs (see also p. 196 below).

S. Roscoe, NEWBERY, CARNAN, POWER: *A Provisional Checklist of Books for the Entertainment, Instruction and Education of Children and Young People, Issued under the Imprints of John Newbery and His Family in the Period 1742–1802.*

This duplicated list is prefaced by biographical notes and a list of collectors and collections.

A. S. W. Rosenbach, EARLY AMERICAN CHILDREN'S BOOKS, WITH BIBLIO-GRAPHICAL DESCRIPTIONS OF THE BOOKS IN HIS PRIVATE COLLECTION, Southworth Press, Portland, Maine, 1933.

This lists 816 items chronologically, 1682–1836, with full bibliographical data, and biographical notes on the authors and 104 facsimiles, some in colour. An introduction by Dr Rosenbach gives the history of the collection and comments on trends, authors and publishers (see also p. 90 above).

William Targ, editor, THE BIBLIOPHILE IN THE NURSERY: *A Bookman's Treasury of Collectors' Lore on Old and Rare Children's Books*, World Publishing Co., Cleveland and New York, 1957 (illustrated).

The bibliophile and collector has only fairly recently realised the riches of this field; this book consists for the most part of selections from the works of authorities on their subjects and also includes specially commissioned articles by Elisabeth Ball on *Cries of London*, by C. Walker Barrett on *Little Women*, by Irvin Kerlan on *Collecting Contemporary Books for Children*. There is unfortunately no index.

A. W. Tuer, PAGES AND PICTURES FROM FORGOTTEN CHILDREN'S BOOKS BROUGHT TOGETHER AND INTRODUCED TO THE READER, The Leadenhall Press, 1898–99, reprinted Dover Publications, New York, 1971.

This is an illustrated, quick guide to the children's books of the first decades of the nineteenth century.

6. Chapbooks
(See also 'Catnach Press' under XI. THE PRINTING OF BOOKS, p. 272.)

'Chapmen', Harvey Darton tells us in *Children's Books in England* (see below), 'of the tribe of Autolycus, were the travelling salesmen who, but for a few gypsy vans, have now practically vanished from the face of England. When print grew cheap, news-sheets, ballads, broadsheets and inexpensive books were popular wares in the pedlar's packs.' Chapbooks, crude and ephemeral productions, the predecessors of the paperback on the one hand and the comic on the other, flourished from the seventeenth to the nineteenth centuries before the era of universal education and cheap books. They were, in effect, broadsides folded twice, paper-covered penny pamphlets of ballads, folk-tales, romances, jokes, riddles and sermons generally illustrated with crude wood-cuts. Many were designed for child readers. Leslie Shepard is of the opinion that, 'the popularity of so many ballads, fairy tales and romances in modern times owes as much to chapbooks and broadsides as to the memories of old nurses and songmen'. Chapbooks have a part in the history of the book trade as in the rise of literacy, the development of printing and the history of children's books.

John Ashton, CHAP-BOOKS OF THE EIGHTEENTH CENTURY, London, 1882, reprinted Blom, New York, 1967.

PUZZLECAP'S

AMUSING

RIDDLE BOOK.

A Cock.

For vigilance and courage true,
I've no superior—equals few :
Bold and alert I meet the foe,
In all engagements valour show ;
And if he proves too proud to yield,
One falls before we quit the field.

MOTHER HUBBARD

AND

HER DOG.

Old Mother Hubbard is merrily laughing,
At her droll Dog smoking and quaffing.

Devonport: Printed by S. & J. KEYS.

The title pages of two nineteenth-century chapbooks for children (actual size)
(see p. 181 f.)

Robert Hays Cunningham, AMUSING PROSE CHAPBOOKS CHIEFLY OF THE LAST CENTURY, London and Glasgow, 1889.

F. J. Harvey Darton, CHILDREN'S BOOKS IN ENGLAND: *Five Centuries of Social Life*, C.U.P., 1st edition, 1932, 2nd edition, 1958 (see chapter 5: *The Pedlar's Pack*; *The Running Stationers*).

G. L. Gomme and H. B. Wheatley, CHAP-BOOKS AND FOLK-LORE TRACTS, 5 vols., 1885.

James O. Halliwell-Phillips, A CATALOGUE OF CHAP-BOOKS, GARLANDS, AND POPULAR HISTORIES, 1849.

William Harvey, SCOTTISH CHAPBOOK LITERATURE, Paisley, 1903.

Victor E. Neuburg, CHAPBOOKS: *A Bibliography of References to English and American Chapbook Literature of the Eighteenth and Nineteenth Centuries*, Vine Press, 1964.

Victor E. Neuburg, THE PENNY HISTORIES, *A Study of Chapbooks for Young Readers over Two Centuries*, O.U.P., 1968.

Leslie Shepard, JOHN PITTS, *Ballad Printer of Seven Dials, London, 1765–1844, with a Short Account of His Predecessors in the Ballad and Chapbook Trade*, P.L.A., 1969 (illustrated).

C. Welsh and W. H. Tillinghast, A CATALOGUE OF ENGLISH AND AMERICAN CHAPBOOKS AND BROADSIDES IN HARVARD COLLEGE LIBRARY, Harvard University Press, Cambridge, Mass. 1905, reprinted, Singing Tree Press, Detroit, Mich., 1968.

Harry B. Weiss, A BOOK ABOUT CHAPBOOKS: *The People's Literature of Bygone Times*, 1942, reprinted with notes on the illustrations and an addendum to the bibliography by Folklore Associates, Hatboro, Pennsylvania, 1969.

7. Choosing Books for Children

May Lamberton Becker, CHOOSING BOOKS FOR CHILDREN, O.U.P., 1937 (booklists at chapter ends, some illustrated).

This is a pioneer work long superseded as a practical guide to book selection.

Annis Duff, BEQUEST OF WINGS: *A Family's Pleasure with Books,* Viking, New York, 1944.

Annis Duff, LONGER FLIGHT: *A Family Grows Up with Books,* Viking, New York, 1955.

The subtitles are self-explanatory. Mrs Duff's books, derived from reading with her own children, are useful, though written for an American readership.

Anne Thaxter Eaton, TREASURE FOR THE TAKING, revised edition, Viking, New York, 1957.

This gives comment on 585 titles classified in sixty-four categories of which the last is *About Books and Reading*: in this section ten books are by American authors including Mrs Eaton's own work.

Sara Innis Fenwick, editor, A CRITICAL APPROACH TO CHILDREN'S LITERATURE, University of Chicago Press, Chicago and London, 1967.

This consists of twelve papers originally published in the *Library Quarterly*, 1967, ranging from *Children's Reading and Adult's Values* to *The Critic and Children's Literature*, and given at the 31st annual conference of the graduate Library School of the University of Chicago. See also under 'General Histories', p. 175, above: **Montrose J. Moses,** CHILDREN'S BOOKS AND READING; **Cornelia Meigs,** A CRITICAL HISTORY OF CHILDREN'S LITERATURE. See also under 'Particular Aspects and Periods', p. 176 f., above: **P. M. Pickard,** I COULD A TALE UNFOLD; **Bettina Hurlimann,** PICTURE-BOOK WORLD. See also under 'Reference Works', pp. 189 f., below: **N.B.L.,** BOOKS, THE TEACHER AND THE CHILD; **Ruth Hill Viguers,** MARGIN FOR SURPRISE.

Margery Fisher, INTENT UPON READING: *A Critical Appraisal of Modern Fiction for Children,* Brockhampton, 1961 (illustrated and containing annotated, classified bibliographies at chapter ends), revised edition 1964 (containing two chapters on recent development).

This is a major contribution to its field which began as an attempt to guide the reading of the author's own children. There are extracts from the books commented on.

Roger Green, TELLERS OF TALES: *Children's Books and Their Authors from 1800–1964,* 1st edition, 1946, rewritten and revised, Edmund Ward, 1965.

This is both an historical and a critical treatment of the subject. It is illustrated, contains bibliographical notes, a list of authorities, another of children's authors and their works, a chronological list of children's books and of the Carnegie and Kate Greenaway awards.

Paul Hazard, BOOKS, CHILDREN AND MEN, translated from the French LES LIVRES, LES ENFANTS ET LES HOMMES, by Margaret Mitchell, Horn Book, Boston, Mass., 1944.

This classic work deals, both historically and critically, with European and American children's books as well as juvenile versions of adult books.

Nancy Larrick, A PARENT'S GUIDE TO CHILDREN'S READING: *For Parents of Pre-School and Elementary School Boys and Girls,* Doubleday, New York, 1958.

This is an illustrated list of favourite books for children classified according to age level and of books and films about children's reading.

Nancy Larrick, A TEACHER'S GUIDE TO CHILDREN'S BOOKS, Charles Merrill, Columbus, Ohio, 1960 (illustrated).

This is a sequel to *A Parents' Guide,* in four parts giving practical examples throughout. Part 1 'describes the interests of children at various grade levels and the books that meet their needs'. Part 2 discusses ways of arousing children's interest in good literature. Part 3 'evaluates classroom activities and appraises the wealth of books now available'; it includes a chapter on how a book is made. Part 4 consists of two annotated booklists of favourite children's books published in recent years, and of books on children's books (mostly American) and American book clubs.

Naomi Lewis, BEST CHILDREN'S BOOKS OF 1963, Hamish Hamilton, 1964; ... 1964, published 1965; ... 1965, published 1966; and ... 1966, published 1967.

Miss Lewis's annotated selections are classified in sixteen categories.

Kathleen Lines, FOUR TO FOURTEEN, C.U.P. for the N.B.L., 1st edition, 1949, 2nd edition, 1956 (illustrated).

This is still useful.

Evelyn Rose Robinson, READINGS ABOUT CHILDREN'S LITERATURE, David Mackay Company, New York, 1966.

These articles, some reprinted from other sources, are by leading specialists in their fields (mainly American). The book is divided into nine parts such as *Selection, History and Trend, Illustration, Fiction,* and *Non-fiction.*

Lillian H. Smith (see also under 'Collecting Early Children's Books', p. 180, above), THE UNRELUCTANT YEARS: *A Critical Approach to Children's Literature*, A.L.A., Chicago, Ill., 1953 (contains bibliographies at chapter ends).

This is an important work by a collector of early children's books.

Geoffrey Trease, TALES OUT OF SCHOOL: *A Survey of Children's Fiction*, William Heinemann, 1st edition, 1959, 2nd edition, 1964 (illustrated, bibliography).

This was hailed as the first critical survey of children's literature.

Geoffrey Trease, ENJOYING BOOKS, Phoenix House, 1951 (illustrated, bibliography of suggested titles, and a key to pronunciation).

This was written to help children choose their own books.

Dorothy Neal White, ABOUT BOOKS FOR CHILDREN, O.U.P., 1946 (bibliography).

This is a guide to picture books, fairy stories, realistic tales, books on arts and crafts and so on.

Dorothy Neal White, BOOKS BEFORE FIVE, O.U.P. for the New Zealand Council for Educational Research, 1954.

This is a record in diary form of the response made to books by the author's own daughter between the ages of two and five.

Among organisations which produce regular lists and guides to children's book exhibitions are:

Kent Education Committee's Catalogues of recommended books and publications for secondary schools (1951–   );

the Library Association, Youth Libraries Group;

the National Book League (with some twenty printed or duplicated lists on special aspects of books for children currently in print);

the School Library Association;

Toronto Public Libraries, Youth Libraries Group.

8. Periodicals (that review children's books and articles on children's literature)

AUSTRALIAN BOOK REVIEW, Hyde Park Press, Adelaide, Australia (1963–   ).

This contains articles and lists of recent books.

BOOKBIRD, *News Bulletin of the International Board on Books for Young People* (see p. 197) (1958–).

This quarterly has articles, lists of prizewinning books, news from national sections, and recommendations for translation.

BOOKS FOR YOUR CHILDREN, edited by **Anne Wood,** Anne and Barrie Wood (December 1965–).

This quarterly has articles on children's books and educational problems of the younger age groups and lists the books to be used in the B.B.C.'s *Story Time.*

CHILDREN'S BOOK NEWS, Children's Book Centre (1965–) (issued as NEW BOOKS, 1964).

Reviews new books.

GROWING POINT: *Regular Review of Books for the Growing Families of the English Reading World, and for Parents, Teachers, Librarians and Other Guardians,* edited and published by **Margery Fisher,** Northampton, (1962–).

This is issued nine times a year and contains critical reviews mostly written by the editor as well as special articles such as *Special Review* featuring one outstanding title, *An Old Favourite* reviewing a new edition of a classic. An annual index to titles, authors, illustrators, translators, is separately issued.

THE GUARDIAN

This daily newspaper now publishes regular features on children's books.

THE HORN BOOK MAGAZINE, Horn Book, Boston, Mass. (1924–).

This is currently edited by Mrs Ruth Hill Viguers. It is a 'magazine of criticism with international interest' issued six times a year.

IFLA NEWS (1962–). Journal of the International Federation of Library Associations (quarterly).

JUNIOR BOOKSHELF: *A Review of Children's Books* (1936–).

This comes out six times a year, and contains articles and unsigned reviews, a quarterly section on foreign books and an annual index separately printed.

THE SCHOOL LIBRARIAN, *And School Library Review* (1937–   ).

This is the journal of the School Library Association (see p. 197) and contains signed articles and reviews.

THE TIMES LITERARY SUPPLEMENT (1902–   ).

This has supplements on children's books, spring and autumn.

Y.L.G. NEWS

The journal of the Library Association Youth Libraries Group comes out three times a year.

9. Reference Works

Marcus Crouch, BOOKS ABOUT CHILDREN'S LITERATURE, Library Association, 1st edition, 1963, revised edition, 1968.

This is based on the Woodfield Collection of Children's Books housed in the Department of Librarianship, Manchester College of Commerce, which is for the use of Library Association members. It is categorised as History of Children's Literature, Criticism and Biography, Illustration, Authorship. The biography section comprises half the book.

J. A. Cutforth and S. H. Battersby, CHILDREN AND BOOKS, Basil Blackwell, Oxford, 1962 (illustrated).

This is 'a book about using books; it is not a book about running a library' (in infant and junior schools). It suggests ways of getting children to use books for stimulus and information. It contains appendixes on helping children to look things up and on sources of information and help (see also Geoffrey Trease, *Enjoying Books*, p. 186 above, which also deals with this aspect).

Alec Ellis, HOW TO FIND OUT ABOUT CHILDREN'S LITERATURE, Pergamon Press, Oxford, 1st edition, 1966, 2nd edition, 1968.

This is about books on children's literature. There are seventeen chapters on such aspects as: *National Organizations and Collections: Periodical Articles*: and *A History of Children's Literature to 1900*.

Keith S. Gollard and R. W. Thompson, editors, BIOGRAPHIES FOR CHILDREN: *A Select List,* 1st 3 editions, Dagenham Public Libraries, 1960, 1961, 1963; 4th edition, London Borough of Havering Libraries, Romford, Essex, 1967.

This lists the whereabouts of biographies for children with an index of authors (see also John Rowe Townsend, *Written for Children,* p. 176 above; Gumuchian & Cie, *Les Livres de L'Enfance,* p. 179 above).

Virginia Haviland, editor, CHILDREN'S LITERATURE: *A Guide to Reference Sources,* Library of Congress, Washington, 1966 (illustrated).

This is an exhaustive survey of the material, its 1,073 numbered items are annotated and classified within eight principal sections. It is the result of several years' activity begun soon after the Children's Book Section was established in the Library of Congress, 1963. It consists of books, articles and pamphlets on all aspects of children's literature, history, criticism, writing and illustrating for children, bibliography, etc. It concludes with a directory of associations and agencies.

Antony Kamm and Boswell Taylor, BOOKS AND THE TEACHER: *How Educational Publishing Affects Teachers and Librarians: A Handbook on the Choice, Requisition and Use of Books,* University of London Press, 1966.

This was written to meet the needs of teachers and librarians. It explains the distinction between net and non-net books, lists sources of help, gives a glossary of printing and book trade terminology. The reference section lists book clubs, booksellers with large stocks of secondhand books, library equipment suppliers, important dates in the history of books and printing, proofmarks and common typefaces arranged in families.

Muriel Lock, REFERENCE MATERIAL FOR YOUNG PEOPLE (The Reader's Guide Series), Clive Bingley, 1967.

This is a guide to the selection of non-fiction which fills a gap. It is arranged under *Encyclopedias and Dictionaries; The World Scene and Current Affairs* (which includes how-to-do-it books and those on hobbies and trades); *The World of Nature* which includes books on great scientists and on the sciences and natural history; *The World of Man; History and Geography* and *Career Books* and others.

National Book League, BOOKS, THE TEACHER AND THE CHILD: *A Bibliographical Tool Prepared by the Association of Teachers in Colleges and Departments of Education and the National Book League,* 1961.

'This book was primarily intended for young teachers starting their careers. . . . Bibliographical sources were suggested to help keep up to date with new publications.' It is divided into sections on *Librarians and the Art of Reading*; *Textbooks*; *Book Reviews*.

Anne Pellowski, THE WORLD OF CHILDREN'S LITERATURE, Bowker, New York and London, 1968.

This major reference work is the outcome of a questionnaire sent out to thirty countries (twenty-four replied) by the International Board on Books for Young People (I.B.B.Y.) (see p. 197) and the International Youth Library (I.Y.L.). Sections are geographical, each with an introduction, and 4,495 items in all, are listed. They comprise monographs, series and multi-volume works as well as periodical articles relating to library work with children, the history and criticism of children's literature, children's reading interests and allied subjects such as folklore. National bibliographies of children's books are included as well as special exhibitions, lists of recommended books, anthologies and biographical dictionaries – but not single author studies.

Ruth Hill Viguers, MARGIN FOR SURPRISE: *About Books, Children and Librarians*, Constable Young Books, 1966.

Written from the point of view of the American librarian. Its bibliography of recommended books is commented on in the text.

Whitaker, CHILDREN'S BOOKS IN PRINT (1969).

This is an annual catalogue of the children's books in print in Great Britain in January of each year, classified under a system indicating reading ability and age interest.

10. Children's Book Awards and Prizes
(See also under 1. AUTHORSHIP, p. 21)

Unlike the awards given for adult books, children's book awards do help to sell more copies. Children's librarians, teachers and booksellers, if not the general public, use the awards as a guide to selection. Many of the books mentioned under other subsections have lists of the awards and winners.

There are now so many national and international children's book awards that only a selection can be mentioned. They include:

THE CALDECOTT MEDAL (1938–)

Presented by the American Frederic G. Melcher for the best illustrated book for children.

THE CARNEGIE MEDAL (1958–)

This was started by the Library Association for an outstanding book for children by a British subject, published in the United Kingdom during the previous year (amended to allow Commonwealth writers, 1968).

THE ELEANOR FARJEON AWARD (1965–)

This is awarded by the Children's Book Circle (see p. 196) to a librarian, teacher, author, artist, publisher, reviewer, television producer or any other person considered to be doing outstanding work for children's books.

THE GUARDIAN AWARD FOR CHILDREN'S FICTION (1967–)

The *Guardian* awards an annual prize of a hundred guineas for the best novel for children by a British or Commonwealth writer.

THE HANS CHRISTIAN ANDERSEN MEDALS (1956–)

These are conferred by the International Board on Books for Young People (see p. 197) on a living author who is judged to have made a lasting contribution to juvenile literature. An author's complete works are taken into consideration. Since 1966 a second medal has been awarded to a living illustrator of children's books. The national section in Britain is incorporated in the National Book League.

THE KATE GREENAWAY MEDAL (1957–)

This is the Library Association's award for the illustration of a children's book by a British artist.

THE NEWBERY MEDAL (1921–)

Offered by Frederic G. Melcher as an incentive for better quality in children's books, given annually to the author of the most distinguished contribution to American literature for children published during the preceding year.

Books on Individual Awards

Lee Kingman, NEWBERY AND CALDECOTT MEDAL BOOKS, 1956–65, vol. 3, Horn Book, Boston, Mass., 1965.

This includes *Picture Books Today* by Norma R. Fryatt.

Library Association, CHOSEN FOR CHILDREN: *An Account of the Books Which Have Been Awarded the Library Association Carnegie Medal, 1936–57,* L.A., 1957 (illustrated).

This contains extracts from the winning books and biographical notes on the authors.

Bertha Mahony Miller and Elinor Whitney Field, NEWBERY MEDAL BOOKS, 1922–55, *With Their Authors' Acceptance Papers and Related Material Chiefly from the Horn Book Magazines,* vol. 1, Horn Book, Boston, Mass., 1955.

This gives biographical notes on the medallists and extracts from the prize-winning books.

Bertha Mahony Miller and Elinor Whitney Field, CALDECOTT MEDAL BOOKS, 1938–57, vol. 2, Horn Book, Boston, Mass., 1957.

This includes *What Is a Picture Book?* by Esther Averill.

Irene Smith, A HISTORY OF THE NEWBERY AND CALDECOTT MEDALS, The Viking Press, New York, 1957.

This contains an appendix of award books and the runners up for each of the two medals.

11. The Illustration of Children's Books

(See also under V. BOOK ILLUSTRATION, pp. 121 ff., 'Collecting Early Children's Books', and 'Children's Book Awards', above.)

Bertha E. Mahony, Louise Payson Latimer and Beulah Folmsbee, ILLUSTRATORS OF CHILDREN'S BOOKS, 1744–1945, Horn Book, Boston, Mass., 1947 (illustrated, bibliography).

Part 1 deals with history and development in twelve articles by different experts; Part 2 contains biographies of living illustrators; Part 3, bibliographies compiled by Louise Payson Latimer; and Part 4, the appendix, contains sources, notes and references and a list of artists represented by illustrations. Side heads help quick reference.

Charles Morris, THE ILLUSTRATION OF CHILDREN'S BOOKS, Library Association Pamphlet no. 16, 1957 and 1965 (bibliography).

This is very handy for quick reference.

John Ryder, ARTISTS OF A CERTAIN LINE: *A Selection of Illustrators of Children's Books*, The Bodley Head, 1960 (illustrated, index of 42 artists and a list of their illustrations, their addresses and their speciality).

The introduction is followed by biographical notes and a postscript giving information on eleven more artists.

Janet Adam Smith, CHILDREN'S ILLUSTRATED BOOKS, (Britain in Pictures Series), Collins, 1948 (illustrated).

Andrew W. Tuer, 1000 QUAINT CUTS FROM BOOKS OF OTHER DAYS: *Including Amusing Illustrations from Children's Story Books, Fables, Chapbooks* . . . , 1886.

This collection of some 1,100 woodcuts from blocks of the early nineteenth century, includes early chapbook blocks (see under 'Chapbooks', pp. 181 f.).

Ruth Hill Viguers, Marcia Dalphin and Bertha Mahony Miller, compilers, ILLUSTRATORS OF CHILDREN'S BOOKS, 1946–1956, *A Supplement to Illustrators of Children's Books, 1744–1945*, Horn Book, Boston, Mass., 1958.

An introduction by Bertha Mahony Miller is followed by three parts: Part 1, three articles by authorities on eleven years of illustration in children's books; Part 2, brief biographies of the illustrators by Ruth Hill Viguers; Part 3, a bibliography of the illustrators and their work by Marcia Dalphin.

Studies of Individual Illustrators (see also under V. BOOK ILLUSTRATION)

EDWARD ARDIZZONE (b. 1900)

THE YOUNG ARDIZZONE, *An Autobiographical Fragment*, Studio Vista, 1970 (illustrated).

KATE GREENAWAY (1846–1901)

Edward Ernest, editor, THE KATE GREENAWAY TREASURY, *With an Introduction by Ruth Hill Viguers,* Collins, 1968 (bibliography of Kate Greenaway's writings).

This anthology of the illustrations and writings of Kate Greenaway is preceded by a biographical sketch by M. H. Spielmann and G. S. Layard, and a selection of letters to and from John Ruskin.

M. H. Spielmann and G. S. Layard, KATE GREENAWAY, A. & C. Black, 1905 (illustrated).

EDWARD LEAR (see under V. BOOK ILLUSTRATION, p. 135)

BEATRIX POTTER (1866–1943) (see also under 'Major Collections of Children's Books', p. 195 below).

Margaret Lane, THE TALE OF BEATRIX POTTER, Warne, 1st edition, 1946, 2nd edition revised and enlarged, 1968 (illustrated, bibliography of Beatrix Potter's works).

This is the definitive biography.

Leslie Linder, THE HISTORY OF THE WRITINGS OF THE ART OF BEATRIX POTTER, Warne, 1971 (illustrated in colour and black and white).

Anne Carroll Moore, THE ART OF BEATRIX POTTER, Warne, 1st edition, 1955, 2nd edition, 1956 (extensively illustrated in colour and black and white).

National Book League, BEATRIX POTTER 1866–1943, *Centenary Catalogue 1966,* N.B.L., 1966 (illustrated, introduction by Leslie Linder).

National Book League and the Trustees of the Linder Collection, THE LINDER COLLECTION *Of the Work and Drawings of Beatrix Potter,* N.B.L., 1971 (illustrated in colour and black and white) (see under 'Major Collections of Children's Books', p. 195 below).

E. H. SHEPARD (b. 1879)

E. H. Shepard, DRAWN FROM MEMORY, Methuen, 1957.

E. H. Shepard, DRAWN FROM LIFE, Methuen, 1961 (autobiography with illustrations in the text).

12. Writing for Children and the Work of Children's Editors

(See also under 1. AUTHORSHIP, pp. 10 ff.)

Jean Poindexter Colby, WRITING, ILLUSTRATING AND EDITING CHILDREN'S BOOKS, Hastings House, New York, 1967 (bibliography).

This, though American, is one of the few useful books on the work of the children's editor. Part 1 gives practical advice on contracts, royalties and special rights; Part 2 explains editorial and production requirements, the steps in producing a picture book and printing methods; Part 3 describes the different editorial departments and their functions, aspects of children's book publishing, The Children's Book Council and the requirements of a children's book editor.

13. Major Collections of Children's Books

Birmingham Public Library: 2,000 items, eighteenth century to the present.

British Museum: *Court Bookshop Collection* of 900 eighteenth- and nineteenth-century items donated by H. M. Lyon.

Hammersmith Public Library: some 1,100 items, mainly nineteenth century.

Harrogate Public Library: some 1,200 books, eighteenth century to twentieth century.

International Youth Library, Munich, founded 1948, closely associated with the International Board on Books for Young People (see p. 197) and sponsored by them.

The Linder Collection of the Works and Drawings of Beatrix Potter. This comprises over 300 original drawings and illustrations, as well as the first editions of Beatrix Potter's books, presented by the Trustees of the Linder Collection in July 1970, and housed in the Library of the National Book League, together with a specially commissioned portrait of Beatrix Potter by Delmar Banner.

Maidstone Public Library: over 1,000 items, eighteenth and nineteenth centuries.

National Book League: *Reference Collection of Current Children's Books*: A permanent exhibition of children's books published during the previous twelve months.

The Osborne Collection of Early Children's Books, 1566–1910: now in the Boys and Girls House, Toronto Public Library. The collection was supplemented by the *Lillian B. Smith Collection of Books Published since 1911* (see also under 'Collecting Early Children's Books', p. 180, above).

Preston Public Library: *The Spencer Collection* (over 100 items) of children's books, 1725–1914 presented to the library in 1948.

Renier Collection of Children's Books: assembled by Anne and Fernand Renier, over a period of fourteen years, it comprises more than 40,000 items, books, games, school equipment, etc. It is among the world's larger collections of children's books. It was donated to the Victoria and Albert Museum, South Kensington in 1970 and is being transferred to the Museum over a period of years (see also under 'Collecting Early Children's Books, p. 180 above). 'It is intended to provide material on such subjects as the history of education, social customs, moral and religious instruction, changes in taste, behaviour and fashion and developments in book production and illustration. The collection has been built up as an interrelated and coherent whole and the donor has been constantly aware that the ephemera of today become the treasured rarities of tomorrow.'

St Bride Institute: collection of Newbery books and chapbooks.

Unesco: a reference library of more than 100,000 volumes arranged by country with a small lending library for children. It is also an information and exhibition centre and has children's paintings and picture books.

Victoria and Albert Museum: collection of some 5,000 early children's books which includes between 1,500 and 2,000 items in the *Guy Little Collection*, donated by the collector in 1953 (see also 'Renier Collection' above).

14. Children's Book Organisations

CHILDREN'S BOOK CIRCLE (founded 1962)

An organisation of children's book editors, representing all the leading publishers of children's books. The *Eleanor Farjeon Award* (see p. 191) for distinguished services to children's literature is given by this organisation.

THE CHILDREN'S WRITERS' GROUP (founded 1963)

A group formed within the Society of Authors in order to improve standards of writing for children.

INTERNATIONAL BOARD ON BOOKS FOR YOUNG PEOPLE (founded 1953)

The first international body to concern itself exclusively with children's literature. It publishes a quarterly, BOOKBIRD (see also under 'Periodicals', p. 187 above) and instituted the biennial *Hans Christian Andersen Award*, 1956 (see also under 'Children's Book Awards', p. 191 above and 'International Youth Library', p. 195).

THE JOINT COMMITTEE ON BOOKS FOR CHILDREN (founded 1966)

The National Book League deals with information on all aspects of children's literature for this body which grew out of conferences organised by the North-West Polytechnic School of Librarianship. There are representatives from bookselling, publishing, education and librarianship.

NATIONAL BOOK LEAGUE (founded 1944)

The National Book League advises on school libraries, organises exhibitions of children's books, administers the British branch of the *Hans Christian Andersen Award* (see p. 191) and puts out many lists of children's books. For its other activities see under VI. HISTORY OF THE BOOK TRADE, pp. 167 f.

SCHOOL LIBRARY ASSOCIATION (founded 1937)

Regional and local branches hold meetings and issue booklists to members. Subject panels draw up booklists in conjunction with other organisations. Its journal is THE SCHOOL LIBRARIAN AND SCHOOL LIBRARY REVIEW (see also under 'Choosing Books for Children, p. 186; and 'Periodicals', p. 188). Since 1958 the Library Association and School Library Association have been jointly concerned in organising the Certificate for Teacher Librarians.

LAW RELATING TO THE BOOK TRADE

(See also under I. AUTHORSHIP, pp. 13–19, 'Stationers' Company' in VI.
HISTORY OF THE BOOK TRADE, pp. 160 ff., and IX. THE NET BOOK AGREE-
MENT, pp. 219 ff.)

Illustration from W. Roberts, The Book-Hunter in London, *1895 (actual size)*
(see p. 89)

1. Introduction

(Mainly on 'Copyright' – see also under section on 'Censorship' below.)

The government early realised that the invention of printing was a powerful weapon in the hands of the seditious, the treasonous or the heretical. The Stationers' Company turned matters to their own advantage by assuming the role of crown watchdogs and after the granting of the charter of incorporation in 1557, only Company members, or those holding a special patent, might print books for sale in England, while only the universities of Oxford and Cambridge were allowed to set up a printing press outside London. Copyright was thus a matter of state security, its infringement a security risk rather than theft.

The conception of authors' rights was first recognised by the Queen Anne Statute of 1709, petitioned for by the booksellers, in an attempt to stop literary piracy. It was 'an Act for the Encouragement of Learning, by vesting the copies of printed books in the authors or purchasers of such copies'. It also ruled that copies were to be deposited in the royal library and those of the universities of Oxford and Cambridge and two in Scotland. Though it was pretty ineffectual both in putting a stop to piracy and in enforcing the legal deposit of books in libraries, the statute laid down important principles.

Throughout the eighteenth century the booksellers strove to establish their claim to perpetual copyright based on common law until a test case of 1774 dashed their hopes. In the nineteenth century Serjeant Talfourd took up the cause on behalf, not of the booksellers, but of the authors. He failed, in 1837, to get the term of copyright extended from twenty-eight to sixty years, but five years later a bill was passed which increased copyright to forty-two years, or seven years after the author's death, whichever was the longer.

He obtained a number of petitions . . . one which he thought too richly studded with jests to be presented to the House of Commons, yet its wit embodies too much wisdom to allow of its exclusion from this place. . . .

The Humble Petition of the Undersigned Thomas Hood: '. . . The fruits of another's brains ought no more to be cast amongst the public than a Christian woman's apples or a Jewess's oranges. . . . That, whereas in other cases, long possession is held to affirm a right to property, it is inconsistent, and unjust that a mere lapse of 28, or any other term of years, should deprive an author at once of principal and interest in his own literary fund. To be robbed by Time is a sorry encouragement to write for Futurity. . . . That a man's hair should belong to his head, so his head should belong to his heirs – whereas, on the contrary, your petitioner has ascertained, by nice calculations, that one of his principal copyrights will expire on the same day that his own son comes of age.

The very law of nature protests against an unnatural law that compels an author to write for anybody's posterity than his own' (Purday, see p. 208 below).

The Act of 1911 made copyright part of a deceased author's property, to be bequeathed with his more tangible goods; the term was increased to fifty years after an author's death, or, in the case of posthumous works, to fifty years after publication. Moreover, it introduced a new principle, which was further developed in the 1956 Act, that of 'fair dealing . . . for the purposes of private study, research etc.'; this was to apply to reading and reciting extracts from a published work, and the printing of short passages of copyright material in a book composed of mainly non-copyright matter that was designed expressly for use in schools.

In the last thirty years subsidiary rights such as those for paperbacks, film and translation, have often proved to be more valuable literary properties than the original copyright of a book. These, the 1956 Act legislated to protect, and included a provision for 'the reproduction by libraries of articles for private study'.

We now await legislation on a newly established right, that on books loaned from public libraries (see 'Public Lending Right' under I. AUTHOR-SHIP, pp. 15 ff.).

In the nineteenth century overseas piracy of British books became common. After independence the Americans pirated our authors without scruple. Oscar Wilde complained:

. . . I found but poor consolation for my journey in the fact that the boys who infest the cars and sell everything that one can eat – or should not eat – were selling editions of my poems vilely printed on a kind of grey blotting paper, for the low price of ten cents. Calling these boys on one side I told them that though poets like to be popular they desire to be paid, and selling editions of my poems without giving me a profit is dealing a blow at literature which must have a disastrous effect on poetical aspirants. The invariable reply that they made was that they themselves made a profit out of the transaction and that was all they cared about (*Impressions of America*, 1883).

Some American authors and publishers such as George Putnam realised that the lack of copyright could act both ways, but it was not until 1891 that enlightened self-interest won the day, and the United States first entered into an international copyright agreement.

On the continent too, many publishers pirated English books in order to undercut the British publishers supplying the home market. Charles Manby Smith (see p. 287) purported to find well-paid work as a compositor in a Paris printing office in 1826 when he might have starved for want of employment in London:

... After the novel of 'Woodstock' was completed, came Cooper's 'Last of the Mohicans', and then a pocket edition of the works of Lord Byron, which was followed by other popular works, pirated from English authors and proprietors as fast as they made their appearance. The want of an international law of copyright was the occasion of our prosperity; and the question of printer's piracy, though it was not very profoundly discussed amongst us, was, whenever alluded to, invariably settled on the principle that, 'whatever is, is right'.

Most of the major powers, but not the United States, were signatories to the Berne Convention, ratified in 1886. A new law, the Universal Copyright Convention of 1952 reduced the term of copyright laid down by Berne and merely demanded general provision for 'adequate and effective protection of the rights of authors and other copyright proprietors'. The Berne signatories, and most of the Latin American republics, together with the United States signed U.C.C., the U.S.S.R. remaining an outstanding exception.

The Stockholm Act of the Berne Union of 1967, introduced a protocol allowing developing countries to reprint gratis, works that were to be used for any educational purpose. Many consider that if this is ratified it will undermine the principle of international literary property that has been so long establishing, and will extend an invitation to pirates.

2. Copyright

Gerald Abrahams, THE LAW FOR WRITERS AND JOURNALISTS, Herbert Jenkins, 1958 (tables of statutes and cases, invaluable brief bibliography of legal sources).

Describes those parts of the law which the author needs to know about, either for his protection or for use in his writing.

Guy Aldous, Douglas Falconer and William Aldous, THE LAW OF PATENTS (see under Tyrell, p. 209 below).

R. E. Barker, THE REVISED BERNE CONVENTION: *The Stockholm Act, 1967; A Review with an Article by Article Summary,* Publishers' Association, 1967.

J. J. Barnes, AUTHORS, PUBLISHERS AND POLITICIANS: *The Quest for Anglo-American Copyright, 1815–54,* forthcoming.

Footnotes form a virtual bibliography.

Augustine Birrell, THE LAW AND HISTORY OF COPYRIGHT IN BOOKS, Cassell, 1899.

Now merely of historical interest, these seven lectures still provide a well-written account of the origin of copyright, the Stationers' Company, the struggle for perpetual copyright and the Queen Anne Act of 1709, with a review of the enactments of the eighteenth and nineteenth centuries.

A. &. C. Black, THE WRITERS' AND ARTISTS' YEARBOOK, annual.

This contains the following articles on law relating to authors:

F. E. & E. P. Skone James, *Copyright*, pp. 324–8:

F. E. & E. P. Skone James, *U.S. Copyright*, pp. 338–41:

F. E. & E. P. Skone James, *The Florence Agreement*, pp. 341–2:

E. P. Skone James, *Subsidiary Rights*, pp. 342–5.

James Evans, *Libel*, pp. 359–64.

T. A. Blanco-White, INDUSTRIAL PROPERTY AND COPYRIGHT, Stevens, 1962.

This combines three small booklets on copyright, patents and the law of unfair competition, to provide a simple explanation of the law in these fields.

T. A. Blanco-White and Robin Jacob, PATENTS TRADE MARKS, COPYRIGHT AND INDUSTRIAL DESIGN, Sweet & Maxwell, Concise College Texts, 1970 (table of cases).

This updates and enlarges Blanco-White's earlier work, and is divided into four parts, the last being devoted to copyright as being one type of industrial design.

Henry G. Bohn, THE QUESTION OF UNRECIPROCATED FOREIGN COPYRIGHT IN GREAT BRITAIN . . . 1851.

This is, in effect, the account of a protest meeting called to consider whether foreign authors should enjoy copyright protection in England.

R. R. Bowker, COPYRIGHT: *Its Law and Its Literature*, Low, Marston, Searle and Rivington, New York, 1886 (bibliography by Thorvald Solberg).

R. R. Bowker, COPYRIGHT, ITS HISTORY AND ITS LAW, Houghton Mifflin, Boston and New York, 1912.

This and the above were the standard works on American copyright for their time.

Peter Burke, A TREATISE ON THE LAW OF COPYRIGHT, J. Richards, 1842.

Good and reliable for its time.

Henry C. Carey, LETTERS ON INTERNATIONAL COPYRIGHT, Hurd and Houghton, Philadelphia, Pa., 1st edition, 1853, 2nd edition (which includes fresh commentary), 1868.

A key work of its day.

P. F. Carter-Ruck, E. P. and F. E. Skone James, COPYRIGHT, *Modern Law and Practice*, Faber & Faber, 1965.

Kenneth Diplock comments in a foreword: 'This is how legal textbooks should be written; intelligible to the non-lawyer whose business or vocation is intimately affected by a particular branch of law, comprehensive for the general lawyer . . . and a reference book for the specialist lawyer with an opinion to write'.

Aubert Clark, THE MOVEMENT FOR INTERNATIONAL COPYRIGHT IN 19TH CENTURY AMERICA, Catholic University of America Press, Washington, 1960.

A convenient book based on secondary sources.

W. A. Copinger and F. E. Skone James, COPYRIGHT: *Including International Copyright with the Statutes and Orders Relating Them to Forms and Precedents*, Sweet & Maxwell, 1st edition by W. A. Copinger, 1870, 10th edition, 1965.

This constantly revised work is the standard book on copyright.

D. H. Mervyn Davies, THE COPYRIGHT ACT 1956, Sweet & Maxwell, 1957 (tables of cases and statutes and comparative tables showing whether the provisions of the Copyright Acts of 1911 and 1956 are parallel).

This edition of the Copyright Act, 1956, by a leading lawyer is preceded by an introduction defining copyright and explaining the operation of the present Act. It is perhaps easier to use than Skone James as it relates to the 1956 Act because it is more circumscribed.

J. P. Eddy and E. Roydhouse, BUTTERWORTH'S ANNOTATED LEGISLATION SERVICE, (Statutes Supplement no. 100), Butterworth, 1957.

The first six parts of this follow the arrangement of the sections of the Copyright Act, 1956, then there follows a review of the Act's transitional provisions and summaries of the law in other countries.

K. Ewart, COPYRIGHT, C.U.P., 1952, and many times reprinted as a Cambridge Authors' and Printers' Guide, no. 5.

This outlines in eighteen concise pages British and International copyright practice.

FEDERATION OF MASTER PRINTERS' ANNUAL.

A section on printer's law, pages 609–55, reviews contracts, factory regulations, designs and trade marks, as well as those aspects of censorship and libel that concern the printer.

R. A. Fisher, A DIGEST OF THE REPRINTED CASES . . . 1756–1870, S. Whitney and Co., San Francisco, Calif., 1871.

A section on copyright summarises all the cases in this period.

James Fraser, A HANDY-BOOK OF PATENT AND COPYRIGHT LAW, S. Low, 1860.
The standard work for its time.

N. N. Gidwani, editor, COPYRIGHT, LEGALISED PIRACY? Indian Committee for Cultural Freedom, New Delhi, 1968.

India's view of the Stockholm Protocol for developing countries set forth in a series of papers by British and Indian writers and economists with an appendix giving the Stockholm Act, 1967, and the protocol regarding developing countries. The editor, in his introduction, maintains: 'It will be less honest for India to claim to be a developing country in the matter of book production . . . the free use of foreign copyright material is no substitute for a bold programme of enlisting and encouraging Indian scholars and writers to produce the books we need.'

Frederick R. Goff, THE FIRST DECADE OF THE FEDERAL ACT OF COPYRIGHT, 1790–1800, Library of Congress, Washington, 1951.

A reliable work on an important decade in the history of American copyright.

Charles Montgomery Gray, COPYHOLD, EQUITY AND THE COMMON LAW, (Harvard Historical Monograph, no. 53), Harvard University Press, Cambridge, Mass., 1963 (table of cases, bibliography).

This is very much a book for legal historians providing a case study of sixteenth-century jurisprudence and reconstructing the first stage of a body of law concerning copyhold.

R. C. Barrington Kenyon, THE HISTORY OF THE LEGAL DEPOSIT OF BOOKS *Throughout the British Empire*, Library Association, 1938 (preface by Sir Frederic Kenyon, table of cases, index of statues, bibliography).

Much of this has been made irrelevant to modern copyright by the provisions of the 1956 Act and now by the Stockholm Act, but it was an important work in its day.

Stephen P. Ladas, THE INTERNATIONAL PROTECTION OF LITERARY AND ARTISTIC PROPERTY, 2 vols., The Macmillan Co., New York, 1938.

The best of its sort for the periods covered.

W. J. Leaper, COPYRIGHT AND PERFORMING RIGHTS, Stevens & Sons, 1957.

This aspect of copyright has increasing relevance to books with the proposed provision in the Copyright Act for a public lending right on books analogous with Performing Rights (see also 'Public Lending Right' under I. AUTHORSHIP, pp. 15 ff.).

J. J. Lowndes, AN HISTORICAL SKETCH OF THE LAW OF COPYRIGHT, Saunders and Benning, 1840.

This gives the background to Serjeant Talfourd's bill of 1847, which extended the period of copyright.

E. J. McGillivray, editor, COPYRIGHT CASES, annual, Publishers Association, 1907–49.

These reports of copyright cases in the British and American courts form the basis of copyright case law.

Sir Frank Mackinnon, NOTES ON THE HISTORY OF COPYRIGHT, with paragraphs on *International Copyright* and on *The Copyright Act of 1956* by Kenneth Ewart being Appendix 2 of *The Oxford Companion to English Literature*, 4th edition revised, 1967.

An extremely clear outline history of copyright in England from the invention of printing to the present day, with important acts and test cases described.

Robert Maugham, A TREATISE ON THE LAWS OF LITERARY PROPERTY, 1828.

A reliable work for its period.

Margaret Nicholson, A MANUAL OF AMERICAN COPYRIGHT PRACTICE *For Writers, Publishers, and Agents*, O.U.P., New York, 1st edition, 1945, 2nd edition revised, 1956 (select bibliography, appendixes giving the Universal and Berne Copyright Conventions, and the copyright law in the United States).

This is the United States equivalent of Copinger and Skone James on British copyright, namely a reference compendium of copyright law and procedure.

Simon Nowell-Smith, INTERNATIONAL COPYRIGHT LAW *and the Publishers in the Reign of Queen Victoria*, Clarendon Press, Oxford, 1968 (illustrated).

The author, in these Lyell lectures for 1965–66 reviews the confusions in British statute and case law before the Berne Convention of 1887, and the first International Copyright Act of 1891. The lecturer's main concern is with the practical effects of developing legislation on the techniques of publishing and printing, with special reference to colonial problems, hitherto little explored.

Lyman Ray Patterson, COPYRIGHT, *In Historical Perspective*, Vanderbilt University Press, Nashville, Tenn., 1968 (bibliography, table of cases).

The story of copyright developments in the United States from the sixteenth century to the present day is told with clarity, if with some over-simplification.

Charles H. Purday, editor, COPYRIGHT, *A Sketch of Its Rise and Progress . . . with Suggestions on the Statutory Requirements for the Disposal and Security of a Copyright . . .* , Reeves and Turner, 1877.

An interesting work for its period which gives in full Hood's petition to be submitted with Serjeant Talfourd's evidence to Parliament for amendment of the Copyright Act.

George Haven Putnam, INTERNATIONAL COPYRIGHT *Considered in Some of Its Relations to Ethics and Political Economy*, George Putnam's Sons, New York, 1879.

This address delivered before the New York Free-Trade Club, 1878, traces the history of international copyright and concludes: 'We may, I trust, be able, at no very distant period, to look back upon, as exploded fallacies of an antiquated barbarism, the beliefs that the material prosperity of a community can be assured by surrounding it with Chinese walls of restrictions to prevent it from purchasing in exchange for its own products its neighbors' goods ... and appropriating its neighbors' books' (see also under 'American Publishers and Publishing', p. 359).

Charles Reade, THE EIGHTH COMMANDMENT, Trübner and Co., 1860.

The novelist argues cogently in favour of international copyright.

Thorvald Solberg, COPYRIGHT IN CONGRESS 1789–1904, Government Printing Office, Washington, 1905.

A standard history of American copyright.

Thorvald Solberg, COPYRIGHT IN CANADA AND NEWFOUNDLAND, Government Printing Office, Washington, 1903.

Thomas Tyrell, THE LAW OF PATENTS, 1st edition, 1884, 11th edition, revised by Guy Aldous, Douglas Falconer and William Aldous, Sweet & Maxwell, 1965.

The definitive study of patents.

R. F. Whale, PROTOCOL REGARDING THE DEVELOPING COUNTRIES, *The Stockholm Act of the Berne Copyright Union, British Copyright Union*, British Copyright Council, 1968.

This examines the protocol clause by clause and concludes: 'The Protocol is not the issue of a reasoned and constructively balanced consideration of all the elements in the situation but of misunderstanding and political expediency.'

R. F. Whale, COMMENT ON COPYRIGHT, British Copyright Council, 1969 (foreword by Sir Alan Herbert).

R. F. Whale, COPYRIGHT, 1971.

A survey of the theory of authors' rights, details of the Copyright Act, 1956, international copyright rules, the American system and recent legislation is given in terms designed for the non-specialist who needs to have a working knowledge of copyright law. This describes the gradual transmutation of the right to make copies into an authors' right and explains the position of Britain, France, Germany and the U.S.A. in interpreting that right. The author proposes the creation of the permanent consultative

H

'*The Lawyer*', *from* Punch, *1842*

committee of Intellectual Property to deal with the increasingly urgent task of advising on the problems of photo-copying, computer input, broadcast relays, etc.

As Sir Alan Herbert puts it: 'The author's "right" is most easily described as an intangible property right. Precisely because that property is intangible it is easily filched by the ignorant or unscrupulous; confiscated by a careless legislative Act, or never called into existence, as in the case of the proposed Public Lending Right; yet it is by virtue of his copyright that an author is enabled to pursue his profession and to give to the world the literary . . . works which are the basis of our civilisation.'

3. Censorship and Libel

During the first three centuries of printing, suppression of subversion was the motive for censorship more than denunciation of indecency and pornography. 'By the mid seventeenth century journalism, a new element in English letters, had come into existence and from then on the government's energies were directed more to the restraint of their activities than to the restriction of the book trade' (*Oxford Companion to English Literature*). We have generally omitted the literature of journalism from this guide but in the case of censorship its history is bound up with that of the book trade. When the Licensing Laws expired in 1695 and were seen to have failed as an effective restraint, the government tried an economic measure. The Stamp Act of 1712 which taxed paper, was not repealed until the mid-nineteenth century. The result, however, was not quite as expected; the number of publications of all kinds, not only seditious ones, was reduced by it.

The eighteenth and early nineteenth centuries were also a battleground for those who feared revolution and supported censorship against those who clamoured for free speech, a campaign that is too tangled to describe here.

Political censorship gradually metamorphosed into guardianship of public morals, obscenity being a religious matter, often called blasphemy. It was a charge of blasphemy that was brought against Shelley for his *Queen Mab*. The power of obscene literature 'to deprave and corrupt' found legal expression in Lord Campbell's Obscenity Law of 1853. Gradually a belief developed thereafter that the writer of integrity should be entirely unshackled. Oscar Wilde, disastrously for himself, was the first to maintain unashamedly: 'There is no such thing as a moral or an immoral book. Books are well written, or badly written' (*Trials*, see p. 215 below).

His contention found final recognition in the Obscene Publications Act of 1958, when 'literary merit' was officially allowed as a defence against a charge of obscenity.

The later history of censorship is a theatrical rather than a book trade matter. For over a hundred years the Lord Chamberlain's office included the duty of dramatic censor. This was abolished in 1968.

The law of libel, as distinct from obscene libel, affords protection from defamation of character and is not intended as a method of exercising political or moral control. On occasions, book writers and publishers are prosecuted for libel, but the press is more generally wary of this law than the book world is.

4. The Law of Obscene Libel or Obscenity (or Pornography)

Arts Council, THE OBSCENITY LAWS, *A Report of the Working Party Set Up by a Conference Convened by the Chairman of the Arts Council of Great Britain,* André Deutsch, 1969, foreword by John Montgomerie.

'Formulated more than 102 years ago, the obscenity law enforces an arbitrary, obsolete and largely irrelevant definition of obscenity.' The Working Party set up in 1968 to study the existing law, as modified by the 1959 Chatterley case which allowed the defence of literary merit outweighing obscenity, recommended that the obscenity law be repealed outright. This book includes the working party's report in full, the draft of a recommended bill, summaries of discussion with forty-two distinguished people, and the documents of laws affecting obscenity in Denmark.

Paul Blanshard, THE RIGHT TO READ, Beacon Press, Boston, Mass., 1955 (extensive bibliography).

Written by a lawyer in racy, non-legal language, this deals with censorship against sedition and on moral grounds. Its bibliography provides a reading list for those who wish to pursue the subject of American censorship.

John Chandos, editor, 'TO DEPRAVE AND CORRUPT . . .' *Original Studies in the Nature and Definition of 'Obscenity',* Souvenir Press, 1962.

A collection of studies by leading lawyers and authors in England and America.

Alec Craig, THE BANNED BOOKS OF ENGLAND, AND OTHER COUNTRIES; *A Study of the Conception of Literary Obscenity*, George Allen & Unwin, 1st edition, 1937, 2nd edition, 1962 (bibliography, foreword by E. M. Forster).

The author reviews literary obscenity in law and practice and concludes that 'there is a roughly discernible class of worthless and pernicious writing which can usefully be designated by the term "pornography". The lines of distinction are not, however, clear cut between this class and harmless, and even beneficial, eroticism, or between it and true literature'.

Alec Craig, ABOVE ALL LIBERTIES, George Allen & Unwin, 1942 (bibliography).

This describes the law in relation to certain historic writers and publishers such as Edmund Curll and Havelock Ellis, and discusses the problem of pornography.

Alec Craig, editor, The Society of Labour Lawyers and the Progressive League, MEMORANDA OF EVIDENCE SUBMITTED TO THE SELECT COMMITTEE OF THE HOUSE OF COMMONS ON OBSCENE PUBLICATIONS, The Progressive League, 1958.

Robert B. Downs, editor, THE FIRST FREEDOM, American Library Association, Chicago, 1960.

This symposium is a mine of information on the obscenity laws in the United States.

James Anson Farrar, BOOKS CONDEMNED TO BE BURNT, Elliot Stock, 1892.

The book collector's view is given here: 'There is another sort of attraction that belongs to all forbidden fruit in books which some public authority has condemned to the flames. And seeing that to collect something is a large part of the secret of human happiness, it occurred to me that a variety of the happiness that is sought in book collecting might be found in making a collection of books of this sort.'

Richard Findlater, BANNED! *A Review of Theatrical Censorship in Britain*, McGibbon & Kee, 1967 (bibliography).

This is a history of theatrical censorship and the Lord Chamberlain's office, whose function as theatrical censor was abolished in 1968.

Anne Lyon Haight, BANNED BOOKS: *Information Notes on Some Books Banned for Various Reasons at Various Times and in Various Places,* 1st edition, Bowker, New York, 1935, 2nd edition, revised and enlarged, 1955.

This consists of a kind of bibliography of banned books through the ages, listed chronologically, under author, with chronological notes of their case history as banned books.

Morris L. Ernst, in his introduction, claims that this book makes a major contribution to freedom for books.

Laurence Hanson, GOVERNMENT AND THE PRESS 1695–1763, O.U.P., 1936 (extensive bibliography of primary sources and later works).

This scholarly monograph describes the relationship between government and newspaper press from the expiration of the Licensing Act to the publication of Wilkes's *North Briton,* no. 45, which led to the prosecution for libel of editor, printer and publisher.

H.M.S.O., CHILDREN AND YOUNG PERSONS (HARMFUL PUBLICATIONS) ACT, H.M.S.O., 1955.

This was originally passed for a limited term, and made permanent by the Expiring Laws Act, 1969.

H.M.S.O., OBSCENE PUBLICATIONS ACT, 1959, H.M.S.O., 1959. MINUTES OF EVIDENCE TAKEN BEFORE THE SELECT COMMITTEE ON THE OBSCENE PUBLICATIONS BILL *And Appendices in Session 1956–57,* H.M.S.O., 1958.

This allowed literary merit as a defence and made way for the test case of the Penguin publication of *Lady Chatterley's Lover.*

H.M.S.O., OBSCENE PUBLICATIONS ACT, 1964, H.M.S.O., 1964.

This stopped up the loophole in the 1958 Act allowing the display of obscene articles in shops. It strengthened the law preventing the publication for gain of obscene matter and the publication of things intended for the production of obscene matter.

D. H. Lawrence, PORNOGRAPHY AND OBSCENITY, Criterion Miscellany no. 5, Faber & Faber, 1929.

In this much quoted essay Lawrence campaigned in the defence of so-called pornography on moral grounds for 'What is pornography to one man is the laughter of genius to another'.

H. Montgomery Hyde, A HISTORY OF PORNOGRAPHY, William Heinemann, 1964 (bibliography, appendix on the *Fanny Hill* case).

The author attempts to define pornography, traces the changing social attitudes to it through the ages, and includes a chapter on 'publishers, censorship and the law'.

H. Montgomery Hyde, editor, THE TRIALS OF OSCAR WILDE, *Regina (Wilde) v. Queensbury: Regina v. Wilde and Taylor,* William Hodge, 1948 (illustrated).

This verbatim report of the Wilde trials with an explanatory introduction by H. Montgomery Hyde is a valuable document in the history of obscene libel. In the first trial, Wilde was cross-examined on the subject of the alleged obscenity of the theme of his novel *Dorian Gray.* He maintained: 'there is no such thing as a moral or an immoral book. Books are well written, or badly written.' 'That expresses your view?' 'My view on art, yes.' 'Then, I take it, that no matter how immoral a book may be, if it is well written, it is, in your opinion, a good book?' 'Yes, if it were well written so as to produce a sense of beauty, which is the highest sense of which a human being can be capable. If it were badly written, it would produce a sense of disgust.' Wilde, sadly for him, was speaking sixty years before the defence of literary merit was established.

Olympia Press, L'AFFAIRE LOLITA, *Défense de l'Ecrivain,* Olympia Press, Paris, 1957.

A defence by the publishers of Nabokov's *Lolita* on the grounds that '. . . Nous voulons d'autre part révéler les dangers de la censure morale qui s'exerce encore en nos jours sur la chose écrite et sur l'œuvre d'art . . .'

O.C.E.L., CENSORSHIP AND THE LAW OF THE PRESS, being Appendix I of *The Oxford Companion to English Literature,* 4th edition revised, 1967.

This gives a concise, factual and detailed history of the control of the press and of dramatic performances, with a description of the present law of the press and drama regarding censorship and libel.

Charles Rembar, THE END OF OBSCENITY, *The Trials of Lady Chatterley, Tropic of Cancer and Fanny Hill,* André Deutsch, 1969 (foreword by Norman Mailer).

The author defended these four books against the charge of obscenity in the United States Supreme Court, and here recounts his fight for a revolutionary reform of the obscenity laws in the United States.

C. H. Rolph, editor, DOES PORNOGRAPHY MATTER? Routledge & Kegan Paul, 1961.

Contributions by Lord Birkett, Sir Herbert Read, Geoffrey Gorer, Dr Soper and others, are summed up by the editor who concludes that the question of pornography should be regarded as a social rather than a personal problem.

C. H. Rolph, BOOKS IN THE DOCK, André Deutsch, 1969 (foreword by John Mortimer).

This surveys the swift development of literary frankness and gives critical consideration to the proposals for the reform of the law on obscenity and pornography. A final summary reflects on the question of the value of privacy and its relation to personal dignity.

C. H. Rolph, editor, THE TRIAL OF LADY CHATTERLEY, *Regina v. Penguin Books Limited,* Penguin Books, 1961 (illustrated).

An introduction explains the circumstances surrounding this test case which did more than any other to change legal and social attitudes to obscenity by introducing, for the first time, the idea of literary merit outweighing obscenity, which swayed the judgment which must otherwise have gone against Penguin Books. The publishers had carefully timed their publication in order to provide a test case.

Norman St John-Stevas, OBSCENITY AND THE LAW, Secker & Warburg, 1956 (introduction by Sir Alan Herbert, bibliography, list of statutes, reported cases and banned books, appendix of obscene publications Bill, 1955).

This traces the history of obscenity from early classical times to the twentieth century, with a concluding chapter on authors' rights, the corruption of youth through books and the role of the law in such cases.

Alan V. Schwartz and Morris L. Ernst, THE SEARCH FOR THE OBSCENE MILESTONES OF THE LAW SERIES, with an introduction by Philip Sharp, Macmillan, 1964.

This describes the skirmishes and battles between the censorious and the unshockable.

5. The Law of Libel or Defamation

P. F. Carter-Ruck and Oswald S. Hickson, THE LAW OF LIBEL AND SLANDER, Faber & Faber, 1953.

Joseph Dean, HATRED, RIDICULE OR CONTEMPT, *A Book of Libel Cases*, Pan, 1953 (bibliography).

An introduction defining libel is followed by an account of a variety of English libel cases from 1828–1938.

Morris L. Ernst and Alexander Lindey, HOLD YOUR TONGUE! *Adventures in Libel and Slander*, introduction by A. P. Herbert, Methuen, 1936.

'The book is written by lawyers, but for laymen. They have learning, but they deal with life.'

J. C. C. Gatley, LIBEL AND SLANDER, Common Law Library no. 8, 1st edition, Sweet & Maxwell, 1924, 6th edition revised by R. L. Lewis and P. S. C. Lewis, 1967.

This is the definitive work on libel and slander.

H.M.S.O., REPORT OF THE COMMITTEE ON THE LAW OF DEFAMATION, H.M.S.O., 1948.

H.M.S.O., DEFAMATION ACT, 1952, H.M.S.O., 1952.

Michael Rubinstein, editor, WICKED, WICKED LIBELS, Routledge & Kegan Paul, 1972.

Articles by lawers, publishers and editors concerned with the workings of the Law of Libel. They write in a lively fashion and with many scholarly references.

THE NET BOOK AGREEMENT

Illustration from W. Roberts, The Book-Hunter in London, *1895 (actual size)*
(see p. 89)

1. Early History

The later history of the book trade, after bookselling and publishing had crystallised into separate branches, is largely a prolonged wrangle about terms, culminating in the Net Book Agreement of 1899. The limiting of discount first became a burning question at the turn of the eighteenth century when Lackington and later Tegg (see under 'Histories of Individual Bookshops and Memoirs of Booksellers', pp. 62 and 64) were undercutting the rest of the trade by buying in bulk and selling for smaller profits. The dispute over terms culminated in the formation of the first Booksellers' Association in 1845. Those booksellers who joined the Association believed (and later ages have confirmed their belief), that the interests of the public were best served by fixing discount so that books could be sold by bookselling specialists. These, however, were the days of passionate belief in free trade, so that what might have been a minor trade dispute was, supported by Gladstone, blown up into a major political issue. The Booksellers' Association tried to boycott those who did not restrict discount and at one point were fairly effective in cutting off their supplies until one of the renegade booksellers, John Chapman, held a protest meeting in his Strand shop to which he invited the major authors of the day. Charles Dickens was in the chair and Carlyle pledged his support of the meeting *in absentia*: 'My answer to this question, for my own interests, and for those of the world, so far as I can see them, is decidedly "No" . . . and, indeed, I can see no issue of any permanency to this controversy that has now arisen, but absolute free trade in all branches of bookselling and book publishing.' The Booksellers' Association, led by William Longman, suggested that the matter be submitted to arbitration. The arbitrating board found for the renegades, the Booksellers' Association was thereupon dissolved, and undercutting was rife in the trade until the end of the century.

James J. Barnes, FREE TRADE IN BOOKS, *A Study of the London Book Trade since 1800,* O.U.P., 1964.

This is a study of book trade organisation and resale price maintenance since 1800, with special emphasis on the London booksellers' committee of 1829, the bookselling dispute of 1852, the first Booksellers' Association (1845–52), the public and cheap literature. A final chapter investigates the bookselling question and the Net Book Agreement (1852–1962).

John Chapman, CHEAP BOOKS AND HOW TO GET THEM: *Being a Reprint from the Westminster Review for April, 1852, or the Article on the Commerce of Literature together with a Brief Account of the Origin and Progress of the Recent Agitation for Free Trade in Books,* 2nd edition, 1852.

This contains a list of books and documents referred to during the preparation of the article. The author complains: 'Three months ago an Association of London Booksellers and Publishers attempted to restrain me from selling books as cheaply as I had determined to do. The book merchants and publishers closed their accounts with me, and refused to supply me with books, even for cash . . . in order, either to ruin me, or to compel me to conduct my business according to their prescribed formula, which, in effect, would have been to raise again my prices.'

Paul Hollister, THE AUTHOR'S WALLET: *Narrative of the Messrs. James Lackington 1745–1815 and John Chapman 1822–1894, both of London: Their Exploration and Di;overies Concerning the Price Fixing of Books; with the Testimony of Messrs. Charles Dickens, Mr John Stuart Mill, Mr Thomas Carlyle, Mr William Ewart Gladstone, Lord Macaulay, Lord Campbell and Other Distinguished Men of Letters on the Rights of Authors and Their Readers, and the Fallacies of Price Fixing,* R. H. Macy, New York, 1934.

This compilation gives the whole evidence for the case.

By the end of the century the climate of opinion regarding price-fixing had changed and Sir Frederick MacMillan, together with the Associated Booksellers of Great Britain and Ireland, and the Publishers Association, both formed 1895, were able to establish the practice of selling books at net prices with fixed discounts and in 1899, the Net Book Agreement became law.

2. *The Times* Book War and the Net Book Agreement

At the beginning of this century *The Times* was in financial straits and, with the help of the American, Horace E. Hooper, who bought the *Encyclopaedia Britannica,* sought to improve its position by starting a book club. It hoped to get exceptional terms from the publishers since it would take very large quantities of stock. *The Times* did not at first disclose that it intended to break the Net Book Agreement by offering books, bought as lending library stock, for sale to its members at less than the net price and under the limit of time (six months after publication) set down in the Agreement. When the publishers discovered this, they refused to supply and *The Times* attempted to justify its actions in a press campaign implying that the publishers were conducting a monopoly against the public interest. But *The Times* went too far in its allegations and the matter went to the High Court, who, in 1908, found for the publishers.

Sir Frederick Macmillan, THE NET BOOK AGREEMENT 1899 AND THE BOOK WAR 1906–08; *Two Chapters in the History of the Book Trade, Including a Narrative of the Dispute between the Times Book Club and the Publishers' Association by Edward Bell, M.A., President of the Association 1906–1908,* University Press, Glasgow, 1924.

This is a full, if biased, account of the affair containing a passage that was suppressed in the reissue as being libellous. This is the description of Moberly Bell with dark hints as to his origins which, in these days of racial consciousness, would never have got into print even once: 'Mr Moberly Bell, who holds the position of business manager of *The Times*, is a large and powerful-looking man with a singular face – dark-complexioned, colourless and smooth-shaven, with a prominent nose and upper jaw. His features are decidedly oriental, and though he is described in books of reference (presumably on his own authority) as the son of "Mr Henry Bell of Egypt", his real name is variously given. Mr Wilfred Blunt, who was brought into contact with him at the time of Arabi's military rebellion and is not a friendly critic, has recorded that he was "commission agent" on the Alexandrian Stock Exchange (his real name being Benjamin Moss), who acted first as Scott's assistant. . . . A well-known author who knows him told me, however, that his name was Moses Abel . . .' (p. 40).

THE PUBLISHERS' ATTEMPT TO RESTRICT THE PRIVILEGES OF SUBSCRIBERS TO THE TIMES. *A Statement of the Questions at Issue. The Times to its Subscribers,* reprinted from *The Times*, 1906.

In thundering tones that no newspaper would dare use today, the old *Times* declares: 'Fifty-four years ago the publishers attempted, by restriction on trade, to maintain the high prices then charged for books . . . today the publishers are making a similar attempt, by imposing even harsher restrictions . . . In 1852 the Times could do no more than say that it was desirable that books should be sold as freely as were other commodities. Today the Times can point to its Book Club to prove that there is at any rate one place in England at which the public can buy books without yielding to the exorbitant demands of the publishers . . .'

THE TIMES AND THE PUBLISHERS, privately printed for the Publishers Association, Stationers' Hall, 1906.

This was the reply: 'The Times has declared war upon the publishers . . .

a monopoly of the well-known American kind is what the Times Book Club, under its American controllers, is now bent on establishing . . . The origin of the Times Book Club is an open secret. It had become necessary in recent years for our great newspaper to discover some means of increasing its circulation and advertising revenue.' The origin of the Times Book Club is then investigated, its promises and performance are analysed together with the position of the bookseller, the author's interests, prices of books now and formerly, the New Book System, original proposals of the Times Book Club and misunderstandings.

Henry J. Glaisher, editor, THE TIMES, THE BOOKSELLERS, THE PUBLIC AND THE PUBLISHERS, *Being the History of the Times on the Warpath,* reprinted from *Truth,* October 3, 1906.

This attacks *The Times* and explains succinctly what the war was about. 'The scheme of running the "Club" as a second-hand bookshop as well as a circulating library threatened a serious complication in the Trade which could easily be foreseen. By offering alluring inducements to the most profitable class of customers first to read a book under the "free" library privilege, and then to purchase it at a handsome discount, if they found it to their taste, the scheme struck straight at the heart of the bookselling trade. . . .'

THE HISTORY OF THE BOOK WAR, *Fair Book Prices Versus Publishers' Trust Prices, The Times,* 1906.

This is the counter-attack by *The Times*: 'The system of today is practically that of two hundred years ago, consolidated and fortified by the organisation of the publishers into a close ring or trust. Although cost of materials has fallen very greatly, and ingenious machinery turns out cheaply what formerly had to be produced expensively by hand labour, the general range of prices . . . is higher than ever. . . . The publishers had professed not only ready but eager to supply new books in any desired quantity, and upon exceptionally favourable terms. . . . The publishers, however, changed their minds . . .'

Long after the Book War was ended, the Publishers' Association issued:

REGULATIONS FOR THE CONDUCT OF BOOK CLUBS, *Adopted by the Publishers' Association and the Associated Booksellers of Great Britain and Ireland and Brought into Force on June, 1939,* Publishers' Association, 1939.
This listed recognised political and religious book clubs, and issued regulations on the restriction of resale within twelve months, on discount, on membership of clubs and on registration.

3. The Net Book Agreement since 1956

(See also R. J. L. Kingsford, *The Publishers' Association 1896–1946*, under XIII. PUBLISHING, p. 332.)

'The net book agreement is a contract between the producer (the publisher) and the distributor (the bookseller). Under its terms the bookseller obtains supplies at trade rates upon the definite undertaking that he sells only at the full net prices fixed by the publisher and in default his supplies will be charged to him at the full published price, that is to say, he loses his trade recognition' (Kingsford). The agreement was not questioned until the passing of the *Restrictive Practices Act*, 1956. Even then, the courts, on investigation, found that the practice of fixing the price of net books was in the public interest and there the matter rested until the abolition of *Resale Price Maintenance* in 1962. The publishers and booksellers, after taking counsel's advice, decided to fight the matter on the grounds that books are different from other consumer goods and, in 1964, they won their case.

R. E. Barker and G. R. Davies, BOOKS ARE DIFFERENT, *An Account of the Defence of the Net Book Agreement before the Restrictive Practices Court in 1962* . . . a Commentary on the Economic Aspects by P. W. S. Andrews and Elizabeth Brunner and Commentaries on the Legal and Accountancy Considerations, Macmillan, London, and St Martin's Press, New York, 1966.

Part 1, in a lengthy introduction, sets the trade background. Part 2 consists of the hearing printed in its entirety. Part 3 consists of the pleadings, and other documents, including extracts from the *Bookseller* analysing trading facts and figures.

PAPER FOR BOOKWORK AND PRINTING INK

A. PAPER FOR BOOKWORK

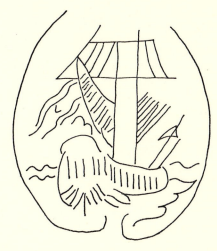

Seventeenth-century ship watermark, from Bagford's Collection, British Museum (actual size)

1. Introduction

Paper, apart from its many other uses, is above all a substance which forms a ready and cheap means of recording events, and it has had many and varied predecessors (R. H. Clapperton, *Paper and Its Relationship to Books*, see below).

Invented in China about A.D. 150, paper did not reach Europe until the mid-fifteenth century and England until 1492. It was almost as though its invention waited upon that of movable type. Yet today, bookwork is only one of the many uses, from wallpaper to Kleenex, to which paper is put.

The invention of the Fourdrinier paper-making machine about 1800, changed the paper trade from a craft to an industry and the use of raw materials other than wood pulp, esparto grass and other fibrous substances enabled the production of more and more different types of paper. 'Good papermaking depends on a very deep knowledge of the values and properties of widely differing raw materials, and their blending to give the many different papers required' (R. H. Clapperton). The old kind of craft papermaking hardly exists now. Only one firm in England, T. H. Saunders of Wookey Hole, still makes handmade paper, while a mere four others continue to produce rag papers whose high quality depends on the slow running of the Fourdrinier machine.

In the eighteenth and nineteenth centuries there was considerable state interference with the paper industry. The motive was partly the exercise of a kind of hidden censorship: high paper costs raised the price of publication and thus restricted the output of periodical literature which might be seditious (see also under VIII. LAW RELATING TO THE BOOK TRADE, pp. 211 ff.). These 'taxes on knowledge', as the very high paper customs came to be called, held back the mass production of cheap books until the repeal in the Free Trade era of the 1840s.

The traditional book format nomenclature, now being gradually excluded in favour of inches and centimetres, derives from the old names of the paper on which the books were printed: some names indicate size, such as demy, some the number of foldings of the printed sheet, such as 4to and 8vo, while the most picturesque are those of the early watermarks, such as foolscap (folio), crown or post.

2. General Histories and Studies of Papermaking

André Blum, ON THE ORIGIN OF PAPER, translated by H. M. Lydenberg, Barker, New York, 1934 (illustrated, notes on sources).

The author describes the influence of paper on printing and engraving, its invention in China and its origin in Spain, France and Germany, with a description of the oldest European mills. He suggests causes for the slow growth of the paper industry and discusses means of dating paper by watermarks and other methods.

R. H. Clapperton, PAPER, *An H.storical Account of Its Making by Hand from the Earliest T mes down to the Present Day,* Shakespeare Head, 1934 (extensively illustrated, bibliography).

This describes the beginnings and spread of paper, with numerous quotations from old sources.

R. H. Clapperton, PAPER AND ITS RELATIONSHIP TO BOOKS, J. M. Dent, 1934.

This, the fourth of the Dent Memorial Lectures (see p. 154 f.), has a fore-word by Hugh R. Dent.

R. H. Clapperton, THE PAPER-MAKING MACHINE, *Its Invention, Evolution and Development,* Pergamon Press, Oxford 1968 (extensively illustrated).

The definitive work on the Fourdrinier machine, concludes with a final chapter of biographical detail on fourteen papermakers including Henry Fourdrinier, Bryan Donkyn, John Dickinson and Johann Voith.

R. H. Clapperton and William Henderson, MODERN PAPERMAKING, Blackwell, Oxford, 1st edition, 1929, 3rd edition, 1952 (illustrated).

This describes the processes of papermaking, with a section on paper trade customs.

D. C. Coleman, THE BRITISH PAPER INDUSTRY 1495–1860, *A Study in Industrial Growth,* Clarendon Press, Oxford, 1958 (illustrated).

This is an economic history of the paper industry.

C. F. Cross and E. J. Bevan, A TEXT-BOOK OF PAPER-MAKING, 1888 (illustrated).

ESPARTO PAPERS, *Presented by the Association of Makers of Esparto Paper*, Newman Neame, 1956.

This is a pictorial account of the processes of turning esparto grass into paper, with illustrations of machinery, samples of different esparto papers, type specimens and some of the modern developments from old typefaces. It is a sad reflection on the economics of papermaking today that many of the mills which participated in the book no longer exist.

S. Carter Gilmour, editor, PAPER, ITS MAKING, MERCHANTING AND USAGE, *The Paper Merchants Textbook*, National Association of Paper Merchants and Longmans, Green, 1st edition, 1955, 2nd edition, 1965 (illustrated).

This textbook contains articles by prominent members of the trade on papermaking, raw materials, machinery, the qualities and usage of paper for different purposes, etc. Appendixes give the British paper customs, standard paper and board sizes and a glossary of terms.

R. Heering, A PRACTICAL GUIDE TO THE VARIETIES AND RELATIVE VALUES OF PAPER, *Illustrated with Samples of Nearly Every Description, and Specially Adapted to the Use of Merchants*, 1860.

Robert Higham, A HANDBOOK OF PAPERMAKING, O.U.P., 1963 (illustrated, glossary).

'The sections covered include both the science and technique of papermaking, as well as papermaking practice. The layout has been influenced largely by the changes which have taken place in the *City and Guilds* syllabuses.'

Dard Hunter, PAPERMAKING, *The History and Technique of an Ancient Craft*, Alfred Knopf, New York, 1st edition, 1943, 2nd edition revised, 1947 (illustrated, bibliography).

This, the fruit of forty years' research by the doyen of American paper scholars, incorporates most of the material to be found in the author's other books, which are therefore not listed below.

E. J. Labarre, A DICTIONARY OF PAPER AND PAPERMAKING TERMS, *With Equivalents in French, German, Dutch and Italian*, N. V. Swets & Zeitlinger, Amsterdam, 1937, O.U.P., 1952 (bibliography, 45 specimens of papers and card bound in at the end).

This 'experiment in technical lexicography' is introduced by an historical study of paper. 'The origin and historical proof of the meaning of technical

Processes of hand papermaking, from Papetrie, *1780*

words have always aroused my curiosity', the author explains, 'and as I could rarely obtain the same answer from any two members of the profession, I started to find out for myself. The result is a work far beyond my intention.' It is probably the most useful single work on the subject of paper and papermaking.

James Mason, PAPERMAKING AS AN ARTISTIC CRAFT, *With a Note on Nylon Paper,* Faber & Faber, 1959 (illustrated by Rigby Graham, introduction by Dard Hunter).

The author describes the making of handmade papers by primitive methods (at first in the kitchen) from wild plants round Leicester. Two examples of rag-made paper from the author's own mill, *The Twelve by Eight,* are appended.

John Murray, PRACTICAL REMARKS ON MODERN PAPER, *with an Introductory Account of Its Former Substitutes; also Observations on Writing Inks, the Restoration of Illegible Manuscripts, and the Preservation of Important Deeds from the Destructive Effects of Damp,* Blackwood & Cadell, 1829.

This is an interesting historical document on papermaking and paper preservation with a dedication to Sir Robert Peel whose legislation in the 1880s removed paper and rag duties.

F. H. Norris, PAPER AND PAPERMAKING, O.U.P., 1952.

This describes processes, fibres, methods of assessing the quality and properties of paper, with a glossary of trade terms, a list of books and stationery sizes, useful calculations and paper trade customs.

Papermakers' Association, PAPERMAKING, *A General Account of Its History, Processes, and Applications,* Papermakers' Association, Kenley, Surrey, 1949 (illustrated, glossary, bibliography).

This is mainly concerned with the processes, rather than history or applications.

A. H. Shorter, PAPERMILLS AND PAPERMAKERS IN ENGLAND, 1495–1800, The Paper Publications Society, Hilversum, 1957.

See under 'Watermarks and the Historic European Paper-Mills', pp. 235 ff. below, for other works in this learned series.

A. D. Spicer, THE PAPER TRADE; *A Description and Historical Survey of the Paper Trade from the Commencement of the 19th Century,* Methuen, 1907 (illustrated, classified bibliography).

This is still a key work.

Alexander Watt, THE ART OF PAPERMAKING, *A Practical Handbook of the Manufacture from Rags, Esparto, Straw, and Other Fibrous Materials . . . with a Description of the Machinery and Appliances Used . . .* Crosby Lockwood, 1890 (illustrated).

A brief history is followed by a manual for students.

3. Histories of Individual Firms and Biographies of Paper-Makers

JOHN DICKINSON (established 1804)

Joan Evans, THE ENDLESS WEB, *John Dickinson & Co. Ltd, 1804–1854,* Jonathan Cape, 1955 (illustrated).

This is an entertaining piece of industrial history by the great-niece of the founder. Illustrations include the first paper napkin, used at the firm's annual dinner in 1887.

DARD HUNTER (b. 1883)

Dard Hunter, MY LIFE WITH PAPER, *An Autobiography,* Alfred Knopf, New York, 1958 (illustrated, bibliography).

Reveals the person behind the world authority who was the son of a Virginia papermaking family and founder of the Dard Hunter Paper Museum, Massachusetts Institute of Technology. Each copy includes a piece of handmade (Dard-made) paper and a piece of Chinese *soirit* paper collected by himself.

JAMES WHATMAN (1741–98)

Thomas Balston, WILLIAM BALSTON PAPERMAKER 1759–1847, Methuen, 1954 (illustrated).

The life of James Whatman's chief assistant throws light on eighteenth-century hand papermaking at Hollingworth's Turkey Mill, which still continues to make high quality rag papers on a slow running Fourdrinier machine for security printing and the like.

Thomas Balston, JAMES WHATMAN FATHER AND SON, Methuen, 1957 (illustrated).

This gives personal and economic detail of the firm and its founders.

Appendixes review countermarks and watermarks used by the Whatmans as well as the 'contrivance' for making 'antiquarian' paper invented by James Whatman II.

WOLVERCOTE MILL (first used as a papermill 1674)

Harry Carter, WOLVERCOTE MILL, *A Study in Papermaking at Oxford,* Clarendon Press for the Oxford Bibliographical Society, New Series Extra Publication, 1957 (illustrated).

Mr Carter traces the mill's history from its beginnings in 1541, describes its extensive use by the Clarendon Press in the eighteenth and nineteenth centuries until it was bought by them, 1880. Appendixes include a note on paper mills near Oxford in 1816, and notes on drawback of duties on paper allowed to the University.

4. Watermarks and the Historic European Paper-Mills

C. M. Briquet, LES FILIGRANES, *Dictionaire Historique des Marques du Papier,* Geneva, 1907, and Leipzig, 1932.

This fundamental work on watermarks is based on more than 40,000 tracings of watermarks drawn from 250 European archives from the thirteenth to sixteenth centuries, omitting Russia, Great Britain, Spain and Portugal.

W. A. Churchill, WATER MARKS IN PAPER *in Holland, England, France etc. in the XVII and XVIII Centuries and Their Interconnection,* Menno Hertzberger, Amsterdam, 1935, reprinted 1967 (illustrated with 600 watermarks reproduced in their natural sizes).

A pioneer work in filigranology by the then British Consul at Amsterdam.

E. J. Labarre, general editor, MONUMENTA CHARTAE PAPYREAE HISTORIAM ILLUSTRANTIA, *Or a Collection of Work and Documents Illustrating the History of Paper,* 14 vols., The Paper Publications Society, Hilversum, 1950–65.

Details of the English editions (all illustrated) are given below in order of publication:

Edward Heawood, WATERMARKS, *Mainly of the Seventeenth and Eighteenth Centuries,* being vol. 1 of the *Monumenta Chartae* (see above), 1950 (list of sources).

An article on Edward Heawood, formerly librarian of the Royal Geographical Society, is followed by sections on types of watermarks, names of makers found in the watermarks, a list of works containing two or more watermarks, and plates reproducing 4,078 watermarks.

THE BRIQUET ALBUM, *A Miscellany on Watermarks, Supplementing Dr. Briquet's Les Filigranes* by various paper scholars, 1952.

ZONGHI'S WATERMARKS, 1953.

BRIQUET'S OPUSCULA, *The Collected Works of C. M. Briquet with the Exception of Les Filigranes*, with an introduction by A. H. Stevenson, 1955.

This reprint of twenty-two articles and smaller works with two unpublished manuscripts includes reproductions of 724 watermarks in their natural size.

THE NOSTITZ PAPERS, *Watermarks in the German Imperial Archives of the Seventeenth and Eighteenth Centuries, and Essays Showing the Evolution of a Number of Watermarks,* 1956.

A. H. Shorter, PAPERMILLS AND PAPERMAKERS IN ENGLAND, 1495–1800, 1957 (see under 'General Histories and Studies of Papermaking', p. 233 above).

W. F. Tschudin, THE ANCIENT PAPER MILLS OF BASLE AND THEIR MARKS, 1958.

G. Eineder, THE ANCIENT PAPER MILLS OF THE FORMER AUSTRO-HUNGARIAN EMPIRE AND THEIR WATERMARKS, 1959.

Don Francisco de Bofarull y Sans, ANIMALS IN WATERMARKS, 1959.

Z. V. Vchastkina, A HISTORY OF THE RUSSIAN HAND PAPER MILLS AND THEIR WATERMARKS, 1962.

Johann Lindt, THE PAPER MILLS OF BERNE AND THEIR WATERMARKS, 1465–1859, 1964.

S. A. Klepikov, TROMININ'S WATER MARK ALBUM – *A Facsimile of the Moscow 1844 edition,* 1965.

Don Francisco de Bofarull y Sans, HERALDIC WATERMARKS, 1966.

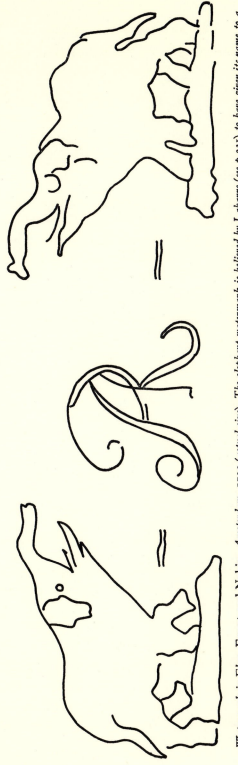

Watermark in Elwe, Egypt and Nubia, Amsterdam, 1792 (actual size). The elephant watermark is believed by Labarre (see p.231) to have given its name to a size of paper varying between 22"—23" and 34"—38". Reproduced in Edward Heawood, Watermarks, Hilversum, 1950 (see p. 231)

Henk Voorn, THE PAPER MILLS OF DENMARK AND NORWAY AND THEIR WATERMARKS, 1969.

Walter Herdeg, editor, ART IN THE WATERMARK, Amstutz & Herdeg, Graphis, Zurich, 1952.

In effect a concise *Briquet* (see above) this is presented as an inspiration to artists. The 1,600 watermarks illustrated have legends beneath them in English, German and French.

A SHORT GUIDE TO BOOKS ON WATERMARKS, The Paper Publications Society, Hilversum, 1955 (bibliography).

There are eighty-four items in English, French, Italian, Dutch, German, Spanish and Polish and sepia reproductions of watermarks in the margins.

5. Specimen Books

I exclude the specimen books put out by the various commercial firms and select:

MASON'S BOOK PAPERS, 1970, *A Book of Specimen Papers made by Paper Mills and Available through Paper Merchants in Great Britain*, Mason, 1970.

Specimens of papers from twenty mills and paper-merchants are classified under *Book Papers, Cartridge*, etc.

Society of Industrial Artists, PAPER FOR BOOKS, *A Comprehensive Survey of the Various Types of Paper Used in Book Production*, Robert Horn, 2nd edition enlarged, 1961.

This consists of illustrations by members of the S.I.A. on seventy-five specimens of book papers, with a description of their substance, bulk, stock sizes and weight details. It was unique in its day, but is now no more than a monument of the papers available during the fifteen years following the end of the war.

6. Reference Works, Glossaries and Bibliographies

Aslib, GUIDE TO SOURCES OF INFORMATION IN GREAT BRITAIN, I. *The Paper Industry*, Aslib, 1948.

B.F.M.P., INTERNATIONAL PAPER SIZES, revised edition, 1961.

This production aid for the printing industry gives the dimensions, advantages and applications of the A and B paper sizes.

British Standards, SPECIFICATION FOR PAGE SIZES FOR BOOKS, B.S. 1413, 1966.

This gives the officially recognised sizes, trimmed and untrimmed. As it omits those many sizes that the trade actually uses, it is of limited usefulness.

British Standards, GLOSSARY OF PAPER/INK TERMS FOR LETTERPRESS PRINTING, B.S. 4149, 1967.

Labarre, A DICTIONARY OF PAPER (see p. 231, above).

John Overton, PAPER FOR BOOK PRODUCTION (The Book no. 3) C.U.P. for the N.B.L., 1955.

An introduction on the history of papermaking, its raw materials, manufacture, printability, bindability, and watermarks is followed by an annotated bibliography, alphabetical by author.

Phillips, PAPER TRADE DIRECTORY OF THE WORLD, Phillips, 1971.

This is an annual volume that incorporates Phillips's *Directory of Paper Makers of Great Britain and Ireland.* The 1971 edition includes more than 200 new forms, the new metric paper sizes and conversion tables, British watermarks, and a glossary of trade terms in six languages.

Spalding & Hodge, PAPER TERMINOLOGY, *A Glossary of Technical Terms,* Spalding & Hodge, revised edition 1954.

Witherby, DIRECTORY OF PAPERMAKERS OF GREAT BRITAIN AND IRELAND, Witherby & Co., annual since 1877.

7. Paper Trade Journals

PAPER (1972–   )

Combines *The Paper-Maker* and *World's Paper Trade Review* (see p. 240).

PAPER BULLETIN (1955–   )

A quarterly review of production, markets, etc.

PAPER FACTS AND FIGURES, Corinthian Press (1961–   ), fortnightly.

THE PAPER-MAKER (formerly the PAPER-MAKER AND BRITISH PAPER TRADE JOURNAL) (1891–1972).

A monthly journal with summaries in French and German.

WORLD'S PAPER TRADE REVIEW (1879–1972).

A weekly journal for the pulp, paper, and associated engineering industries.

8. Trade Associations (of relevance to the Book Trade)

THE BRITISH PAPER AND BOARD MAKERS' ASSOCIATION

Plough Place, Fetter Lane, London, E.C.4.

THE BRITISH PAPER STOCK MERCHANTS' ASSOCIATION

21 Devonshire Street, London, W.1.

NATIONAL ASSOCIATION OF PAPER MERCHANTS

27 Chancery Lane, London, W.C.2.

P.A.T.R.A. (see under XI. THE PRINTING OF BOOKS, p. 302)

B. PRINTING INK

1. General Works

F. Askew, editor, PRINTING INK MANUAL, Society of British Printing Ink Manufacturers, Heffer, 1st edition, 1961, 2nd edition revised, 1969 (illustrated).

A team of experts, under the auspices of the Technical Training Board of the Society of British Printing Ink Manufacturers, has produced a comprehensive volume on the history, theory and practice of ink manufacture. The second edition incorporates new material that takes account of the changes which have taken place in printing and printing ink techniques in the intervening years.

C. H. Bloy, A HISTORY OF PRINTING INK BALLS AND ROLLERS, 1440–1850, Adams & Mackay, 1967 (illustrated, bibliography, ink recipes).

This describes old methods of making inks and varnishes, printing in gold, implements and 'inks of today and tomorrow'.

F. W. Wiborg, PRINTING INK, *A History with a Treatise on Modern Methods of Manufacture and Use,* Harper & Bros, New York and London, 1926 (extensive bibliography, illustrated).

This is still a definitive history of printing ink throughout the world. The bibliography is followed by reviews of some of the more important early works on the history and methods of preparing printing inks.

2. Early Printing Manuals and Encyclopaedias Containing Recipes for Printing Ink
(All approved by William Savage, see below.)

Le Breton, ENCYCLOPÉDIE METHODIQUE, Paris, 1751 – article on *Printing Ink.*

ENCYCLOPAEDIA BRITANNICA, 1788–97 – article on *Ink.*

M. D. Fertel, LA SCIENCE PRATIQUE DE L'IMPRIMERIE, St. Omer, 1723 – article on *Ink.*

T. C. Hansard, TYPOGRAPHIA, 1825 – gives Baskerville's method of making printing ink.

J. Lewis, PHILOSOPHICAL COMMERCE OF ARTS, 1763 – article on *Printing Ink.*

Joseph Moxon, MECHANICK EXERCISES, 1677–83 (see also under XI. THE PRINTING OF BOOKS, p. 255).

W. Nicholson, DICTIONARY OF CHEMISTRY, 1795 – notes on the *Preparation of Printing Ink.*

J. B. Papillon, TRAITÉ HISTORIQUE ET PRATIQUE DE LA GRAVURE EN BOIS, Paris, 1766 – article on *Printing Ink.*

A. Rees, CYCLOPAEDIA, 1819–20 – methods of preparing ink.

William Savage, ON THE PREPARATION OF PRINTING INKS: *Both Black and Coloured*, Longman, Rees, etc., 1832.

The author gives recipes of earlier ink makers as listed above, comments on their qualities and defects and then gives his own recipes. In his introduction he says: 'I can truly assert, that every statement I have made is the result of my own practice, and that there is not a direction for preparing an ink but what I have prepared and used myself to a great extent, and found them answer in the most satisfactory manner.'

THE PRINTING OF BOOKS

Wood-cut of an eighteenth-century printing office, probably Samuel Palmer's in which Benjamin Franklin (as he relates in his Autobiography) *set the 1824 First authorised edition of Wollaston,* The Religion of Nature Delineated, *from which this is reproduced (actual size) (see p. 276)*

1. Introduction

The history of printing has been told too well and too often to be repeated here. Throughout a period of some four hundred years, printing techniques and processes remained virtually unchanged. The wooden press, with types individually cast, and illustrations reproduced from wood blocks, sufficed for a limited, though gradually expanding, reading public. One small edition was all that was then wanted so that there was no need for methods that could produce long runs, or for processes of reprinting.

The eighteenth century was the prologomenon to great change and a new society welcomed and could accommodate the mechanical inventions of the Industrial Revolution which could not previously have been put to use. The new literary form, the novel, now had a market among women readers; the skilled craftsmen, the aristocracy of workers, wanted books and newspapers, while broad-sheets and chapbooks catered for the tastes of the semi-literate masses.

During the nineteenth century schemes for mass education called for printing processes that would bring down the price of books and newspapers as well as speeding up production and it does not seem a coincidence that the wooden hand press now gave way to the iron Stanhope, while, at the turn of the century, the first printing machines were invented. The cylinder-printing machine built by Koenig and Bauer for John Walter II of *The Times* in 1814 was capable of producing 1,100 impressions an hour. Colour printing was developed during this century too, enabling gaily coloured children's books, to be brought within reach of the multitude.

The two major developments of the late decades have been in the area of photographic techniques, and, in the use of computers for typesetting. It seems as though a new invention is no sooner in full production than it is superseded by another, and books on them are therefore excluded from the present Guide.

The present section, though longer than any other, has been kept within far more rigid limits. There is more literature on printing history and techniques than on other aspects of book trade history or practice so that I have been obliged to be more selective and to keep closer to my terms of reference, namely British book printing, in order to keep the proportions of this Guide. I have omitted all technical works, which are, in any case, well documented elsewhere (as indicated in the subsections on 'Directories and Trade Reference Works' and on 'Periodicals and Journals Relating to Printing'); I have also excluded books on ephemeral and jobbing printing, on printing machinery, except for one work, and with few exceptions, on printing on the Continent and in the United States, though I am well aware that Gutenberg, Plantin, Fournier and many others are key figures in the study of printing history.

2. General Works, Essays and Surveys of Printing, Encyclopaedias and Bibliographies

H. G. Aldis, A LIST OF BOOKS PRINTED IN SCOTLAND BEFORE 1700, *Including those Printed South of the Realm for Scottish Booksellers, with Brief Notes on the Printers and Stationers,* Edinburgh Bibliographical Society, 1904.

Joseph Ames, TYPOGRAPHICAL ANTIQUITIES: *Or An Historical Account of the Origins and Progress of Printing in Great Britain and Ireland, Containing Memoirs of the Ancient Printers and a Register of Books Printed by Them from the Year 1471 to the Year 1600. . . . Augmented by William Herbert . . .,* 3 vols., 1785–90, enlarged edition by T. F. Dibdin, 4 vols., 1810–19.

'The great storehouse for the history of English printers' (Bigmore and Wyman, below).

W. Turner Berry and H. Edmund Poole, THE ANNALS OF PRINTING, *A Chronological Encyclopaedia,* Blandford Press, 1966 (illustrated, classified bibliography).

A selection of salient information in a compact volume.

E. C. Bigmore and C. W. H. Wyman, A BIBLIOGRAPHY OF PRINTING, Quaritch, 3 vols., 1880–86, Holland Press Reprint, 1969 (illustrated).

This is the classic bibliography of printing, and none can fail to consult it notwithstanding later developments and modern scholarship.

Colin Clair, A CHRONOLOGY OF PRINTING, Cassell, 1969.

It is less far-ranging than *The Annals of Printing,* but easier to use.

Colin Clair, A HISTORY OF PRINTING IN BRITAIN, Cassell, 1965 (illustrated).

A useful outline history that is, nevertheless, not quite elementary enough for the non-specialist, and is also rather disjointed. It purposely omits the economic aspects of printing as having been adequately covered by Dr Plant and Cyprian Blagden (see pp. 157 and 161).

Kenneth Day, editor, BOOK TYPOGRAPHY 1860–1965, *In Europe and the United States of America,* Ernest Benn, 1966 (illustrated).

This symposium by leading printing historians in England and America describes aspects of printing and book design in England, the United States and the continent of Europe.

E. Gordon Duff, EARLY PRINTED BOOKS, C.U.P., 1893 (illustrated).

This is still a standard short work on the introduction of printing into the principal countries and towns of Europe. It includes a study of book-binding in the period, and advice on the collecting and describing of early printed books, followed by an index of printers and places.

E. Gordon Duff, FIFTEENTH-CENTURY ENGLISH BOOKS, *A Bibliography of Books and Documents Printed in England and of Books for the English Market Printed Abroad,* O.U.P. for the Bibliographical Society, Illustrated Monograph no. 18, 1917.

There are 431 entries and full-page facsimile illustrations of early books.

E. Gordon Duff, W. W. Greg, R. B. McKerrow, H. R. Plomer, A. W. Pollard and R. Proctor, HANDLIST OF BOOKS PRINTED BY LONDON PRINTERS, 1501–1556, Bibliographical Society, 1st issued 3 parts, 1895, 1896, 1905, 1st edition in 1 vol., 1913 (illustrated).

This pioneer bibliography is still indispensable.

Percy Freer, BIBLIOGRAPHY AND MODERN BOOK PRODUCTION, 1954 (see under VI. HISTORY OF THE BOOK TRADE, p. 155).

Part 2 reviews works on printing typefaces, illustration processes, facsimiles and fine printing.

P. M. Handover, PRINTING IN LONDON *From Caxton to Modern Times,* George Allen & Unwin, 1960 (illustrated, annotated bibliography).

The text of lectures given at the St Bride Institute deals with the bible patent, the periodical press, the decline of book printing in London, and the hold of the Stationers' Company over the book trade up to 1695.

James Harrison, editor, PRINTING PATENTS (see under 'Woodcroft', below).

Walter L. Heilbronner, PRINTING AND THE BOOK IN FIFTEENTH CENTURY ENGLAND, *A Bibliographical Survey,* Bibliographical Society of the University of Virginia, Charlottesville, 1967.

An introduction is followed by a list of catalogues, checklists of the period, and by a bibliographical survey of works dealing with fifteenth-century English printing.

Wytze Gerbens Hellinga, COPY AND PRINT IN THE NETHERLANDS, *An Atlas of Historical Bibliography,* with introductory essays by H. de la Fontaine Verwey and G. W. Ovink, North Holland Publishing Company, Amsterdam, 1962 (extensively illustrated, bibliography).

This describes and illustrates the layout, make-up, type, composition and presswork of the copy from which printers have had to work from the fifteenth century up to the present day. It is an invaluable record of the printer's methods of translating copy into print which the studies of Greg and Percy Simpson (qq.v.) only recorded for the early printing period.

Henry Noel Humphreys, A HISTORY OF THE ART OF PRINTING *From Its Invention to Its Widespread Development in the Middle of the Sixteenth Century* ..., Quaritch, 1867 (100 illustrations produced under the direction of the author, misleadingly annotated bibliography).

The text of this imposing volume is of little worth.

I.P.E.X., PRINTING AND THE MIND OF MAN, British Museum, 1963.

This is the catalogue of the exhibition of printing mechanisms and printed material held at Earls Court July 16–27, 1963. It illustrated the history of western civilization and the means of multiplying literary texts since the fifteenth century. The preface and the invaluable annotations to each entry are by Sir Frank Francis, Stanley Morison and John Carter. A precursor to the I.P.E.X. exhibition was held at the Fitzwilliam Museum, Cambridge, in 1940, which, because of the war lacked items that were available to I.P.E.X. twenty-three years later.

PRINTING AND THE MIND OF MAN, *A Descriptive Catalogue Illustrating the Impact of Print on the Evolution of Western Civilization during Five Centuries,* compiled and edited by John Carter and Percy H. Muir, Cassell, 1966.

This is a greatly enlarged hardback edition of the above. The descriptions of the books exhibited have been heavily revised and expanded, but the technical section is entirely omitted, so that the catalogue remains, for printing historians, the more useful document of the two.

Seán Jennet, THE MAKING OF BOOKS, Faber & Faber, 1st edition, 1951, 4th edition revised, 1967 (bibliography, polyglot glossary of technical terms).

Part I describes printing and binding, part 2 design. This book designed for the lay bookman, describes all the processes of bookmaking in detail, in non-technical language.

A. F. Johnson, SELECTED ESSAYS ON BOOKS AND PRINTING, edited by Percy H. Muir, Van Gendt, Amsterdam, and Routledge & Kegan Paul, London, 1971 (illustrated, bibliography).

This handsome volume which collects many of A. F. Johnson's key essays, many long out of print, is designed by Giovanni Mardersteig and printed at his Stamperia Valdonega in Verona.

John Johnson, THE PRINTER: HIS CUSTOMERS AND HIS MEN, J. M. Dent, 1933.

The author, Printer to the Oxford University Press, describes the relationship between the printer, those who work for him, and those he sells to, in this most celebrated of the Dent Memorial lectures.

Douglas C. McMurtrie, editor, THE INVENTION OF PRINTING: *A Bibliography*, Chicago Club of Printing House Craftsmen, Chicago, Ill., 1942.

Classified on historical principles, this work complements Bigmore and Wyman's alphabetical work—more recent though less monumental.

Francis Meynell, ENGLISH PRINTED BOOKS, Collins, 1946 (illustrated).

Intended for the general reader, yet a sound, concise account of its subject.

James Moran, THE COMPOSITION OF READING MATTER, *A History from Case to Computer*, Wace, 1965 (illustrated, bibliography).

The traditional techniques are briefly described but not the newest developments such as computer setting, since they 'are changing as the writer puts pen to paper'.

James Moran, PRINTING PRESSES: *History and Development from the 15th Century to Modern Times*, Faber & Faber, and the University of California Press, Berkeley, Cal., 1972 (illustrated, bibliography).

This is a comprehensive survey of the history of the relief printing press and machine from its inception as an adaptation of a domestic screw press in the mid-fifteenth century to the giant, fast rotary presses of today.

James Moran, TWENTIETH CENTURY PRINTING THROUGH THE EYES OF PENROSE ANNUAL, Lund Humphries, 1972.

Penrose Annual arose out of the photo-mechanical developments in printing at the end of the nineteenth century. The Annual has continued to record technical and aesthetic changes in printing for three-quarters of a century. This volume reprints some of the most percipient articles, with a running text that provides the neccessary historical background.

Stanley Morison, MODERN FINE PRINTING, *An Exhibition of Printing Issued . . . during the Twentieth Century, and with Few Exceptions Since the Outbreak of the War*, Ernest Benn, 1925.

There is an introduction, a catalogue of exhibits and an index of the types used.

Stanley Morison, FOUR CENTURIES OF FINE PRINTING, 1st edition, Ernest Benn, 1924, Students' edition, 1960 (270 illustrations, appendix of printers and craftsm en).

A long introduction precedes plates illustrating fine printing in Europe and the United States, century by century.

Stanley Morison and Kenneth Day, THE TYPOGRAPHIC BOOK 1450–1935, *A Study of Fine Typography through Five Centuries . . .*, Ernest Benn, 1963 (illustrated).

Designed 'to supersede the forty-year old *Four Centuries* incorporating the text of the earlier book and that from *Modern Fine Printing*', this has an introductory essay by Morison and supplementary material by Kenneth Day.

N.B.L., BOOKS ABOUT BOOKS, *A Catalogue of the Library of the National Book League* (see under VI. HISTORY OF THE BOOK TRADE, p. 157).

Henry R. Plomer, A SHORT HISTORY OF ENGLISH PRINTING 1476–1898, English Bookmen's Library, 1900 (illustrated).

This is still useful for the study of early printers, but the title is misleading, since the seventeenth and eighteenth centuries are almost entirely overlooked.

St Bride Institute (see under VI. HISTORY OF THE BOOK TRADE, p. 159, for the catalogue of this collection).

Oliver Simon and Julius Rodenberg, PRINTING TODAY, *An Illustrated Survey of Postwar Typography in Europe and the United States*, Peter Davies, London, and Harper, New York, 1928 (illustrated, general introduction by Aldous Huxley).

Oliver Simon writes on printing in England, Paul Beaujon (i.e. Beatrice Warde) on printing in the United States, and Julius Rodenberg on continental printing. There is an index of illustrations and typefaces.

S. H. Steinberg, FIVE HUNDRED YEARS OF PRINTING, Penguin Books, 1955, Faber & Faber, 1959 (illuminating foreword by Beatrice Warde).

This is an historian's rather than a typographer's account of the development of printing and is as much concerned with the effects of the spread as with the techniques of printing. It is a work of first importance, with no major gaps.

The Times, THE TIMES PRINTING SUPPLEMENT, 1912 (illustrated).

This survey of printing is still of first importance; it was, incidentally, the immediate cause of Stanley Morison's leaving his job as a bank clerk to work on *The Imprint* (see p. 301).

The Times, PRINTING IN THE TWENTIETH CENTURY, *A Survey Reprinted from the Special Number of the Times, October 29, 1929,* 1930 (illustrated).

This, though less celebrated than its 1912 predecessor, makes a valuable contribution to the study of twentieth-century printing.

Michael Twyman, PRINTING 1770–1970: *An Illustrated History of Its Development and Uses in England*, Eyre & Spottiswoode, 1970 (illustrated, bibliography).

This volume issued on the occasion of the publisher's bicentenary, is reminiscent of John Lewis's *Printed Ephemera*, to whom the author owns himself indebted. The development of printing is traced through two centuries, in relation to periodical and jobbing, rather than to book printing. The narrative part of the work gives a brief background of the industry, and describes the growth of techniques and of printing technology and design, interspersed with illustrations. The second part consists of illustration, largely drawn from the John Johnson Collection of Printed Ephemera (see p. 308), concentrated on the themes of ceremony, rural life, transport, wars and exhibitions.

James Watson, THE HISTORY OF THE ART OF PRINTING, *Containing an Account of Its Invention and Progress in Europe with the Names of Famous Printers* . . ., Edinburgh, 1713, Gregg reprint, Farnborough, 1965 (illustrated).

An historical curiosity, in effect a type specimen of Watson's own stock, the work is interesting today for the remarks on trade conditions of the time.

Hugh Williamson, BOOK TYPOGRAPHY, *A Handlist for Book Designers* (The Book, no. 1), C.U.P. for the N.B.L., 1955.

This provides a useful short bibliography preceded by a survey of the subject.

Wing, SHORT TITLE CATALOGUE . . . 1641–1700 (see under IIIC. ANTIQUARIAN BOOKSELLING, AUCTIONEERING AND COLLECTING, p. 102).

B. Woodcroft, PRINTING PATENTS, *Abridgements of Patent Specifications Relating to Printing 1617–1857*, 1st published, 1859, reprinted with a new preparatory note by James Harrison, Printing Historical Society, 1969.

James Harrison's foreword to the new edition describes the official encouragement of the introduction of new skills by the granting of monopolies and patents. The work is an invaluable record of the history of printing machinery, with an alphabetical list under inventor and a classified index of inventions.

3. Early Printers' Manuals (chronological)

The first work written in English expressly for the use of the trade, was Smith's *Printers' Grammar*, 1755, which consequently laid the foundation for all his successors; Luckombe's *History and Art of Printing*, 1770; Stower's *Printers' Grammar*, 1808; Johnson's *Typographia or, The Printers' Instructor*, 1824; and Hansard's *Typographia*, 1825. Stower says that Smith's was the foundation of his work; Luckombe compiled his work from three sources, namely Ames's *Typographical Antiquities* for the historical part, Smith's *Printers' Grammar* for the practical part of the composing department, and Moxon's *Mechanick Exercises* for the presswork. It is very clear that Luckombe made free use of his predecessor as far as he went; for, upon a close comparison, much of Luckombe will be found to be plagiarised from Smith, altered a little in arrangement and phraseology; and that, in his turn, Stower copied from Luckombe . . . thus it plainly appears, that each writer of a printers' grammar has not hesitated to take from his predecessor all that he thought requisite to form his own (Bigmore and Wyman, see p. 248 above).

All the early manuals have been reprinted by the Gregg Press within the last few years.

Philip Gaskell, Giles Barber and Georgina Warrilow, *An Annotated List of Printers' Manuals to 1850,* article in JOURNAL OF THE PRINTING HISTORICAL SOCIETY, no. 4, 1968, pp. 11–33.

Joseph Moxon, MECHANICK EXERCISES ON THE WHOLE ART OF PRINTING, 1677–83, edited by Herbert Davis and Harry Carter, O.U.P., 1958, 2nd edition revised, 1962 (illustrated, bibliography, full notes, index, biographical introduction).

'For most things' [relating to printing] 'it is perhaps even now the easiest and pleasantest guide to the essentials of printing. The *Meckanick Exercises* were intended to describe all the chief trades, a number to be issued every month; but the author not meeting with the encouragement he expected only published two volumes. The first volume included the trades of a smith, a joiner, a house carpenter, etc. The second volume, 1683, which on account of its extent was divided into two parts, was devoted entirely to printing. . . . Part 1 describes all the tools of a compositor and a press man with the whole art of type founding . . . Part 2 describes the work of a compositor, a press man, a warehouseman concluding with the customs of the "chappell" and a dictionary of abstruse words' (the editors).

John Smith, THE PRINTERS' GRAMMAR; *Wherein Are Exhibited, Examined and Explained, the Superfices, Graduation, and Properties of the Different Sorts and Sizes of Metal Types Cast by Letter Founders; Sundry Alphabets of Oriental and Some Other Languages; Together with the Chinese Characters; the Figures of Mathematical, Astronomical, and Physical Signs; Jointly with Abbreviations, Contractions, and Ligatures; the Construction of Metal Flowers – Various Tables and Calculations – Models of Different Letter Cases; Schemes for Casting Off Copy and Imposing; and Many Other Requisites for Obtaining a More Perfect Knowledge Both in the Theory and Practice of the Art of Printing. With Directions to Authors, Compilers, etc., How to Prepare Copy and to Correct Their Own Proofs. The Whole Calculated for the Service of All Who Have Any Concern in the Letterpress,* 1755, Gregg reprint, Farnborough, 1965.

'A good practical work on types and composition which has formed the basis for many subsequent grammars. The presswork of a printer's business is entirely omitted, the author having died before the completion of the work' (Bigmore and Wyman, see p. 248 above). It is one of the few manuals that is independent of Moxon.

Simon Pierre Fournier, MANUAL TYPOGRAPHIQUE, 1764–1766, translated and edited by Harry Carter, Soncino Press, 1930 (illustrated, bibliography, notes).

This edition of Fournier's classic manual is preceded by an illuminating introduction, and followed by a table of body-sizes, a specimen of extant types and a list of the principal letter foundries in Europe.

Philip Luckombe, A CONCISE HISTORY OF THE ORIGIN AND PROGRESS OF PRINTING, *With Practical Instructions to the Trade in General, Compiled from Those Who Have Wrote on this Curious Art,* 1770, Gregg reprint, Farnborough, 1965.

This was the first (and anonymous) edition of what is better known as *The History and Art of Printing. In Two Parts,* 1771. As Timperley (see below) points out, it is, like all the later manuals, built on the work of predecessors. Bigmore and Wyman (see above) consider the practical instructions, 'the united opinions of the most experienced of the trade', to be the best part of the work. There is a specimen of Caslon printing types and twenty-three pages of flowers including 'a number of fantastic and elegant designs made out of them; and forty-one pages of type specimens, including music type and foreign alphabets'.

Caleb Stower, THE PRINTERS' GRAMMAR, *Or Introduction to the Art of Printing: Containing a Concise History of the Art, With the Improvements in the Practice of Printing for the Last Fifty Years,* 1808, Gregg reprint, Farnborough, 1965.

'Stower's works are well written, full of practical information, and valuable in many respects, notwithstanding that some portions, such as those referring to press work, are superseded by modern machinery' (Bigmore and Wyman, see above). *The Printers' Grammar* is Stower's chief work.

Alois Senefelder, A COMPLETE COURSE OF LITHOGRAPHY, *Containing Clear and Explicit Instructions in All the Different Branches and Manners of that Art: Accompanied by Illustrative Specimens of Drawings, to which is prefixed a History of Lithography from Its Origin to the Present Time ...* translated from the original German, Ackermann, 1819.

Ackermann was quick to realise the importance of Senefelder's invention; in his advertisement he says: 'by means of it the Painter, the Sculptor, and the Architect, are enabled to hand down to posterity as many facsimiles of their original sketches as they please. . . . In short there is scarcely any department of art or business, in which lithography will not be found of the most extensive utility.' The work is in two parts: the first gives an autobiographical account of the invention leading up to the publication of the present work; the second describes the qualities of stones, the preparations to be made, the necessary instruments and utensils, different sorts of paper, presses and so forth.

J. Johnson, TYPOGRAPHIA, *Or the Printer's Instructor; Including an Account of the Origin of Printing, with Biographical Notices of the Printers of England, From Caxton to the Close of the Sixteenth Century; A Series of Ancient and Modern Alphabets and Domesday Characters Together with an Elucidation of Every Subject Connected with the Art,* Longman, 2 vols., 1824, Gregg reprint, Farnborough, 1966.

'It was written singularly enough, almost simultaneously with the only practical book to which it bears a likeness, Hansard's, and both bear the same chief title . . . both treatises were among the results of the biblio-mania which prevailed a few years earlier, but which was then on its wane as Johnson soon discovered to his cost . . . the second volume may be described as practical in contra-distinction to the first which is historical . . . very few copies of this interesting and almost unique piece of com-position now exist' (Bigmore and Wyman, see p. 248 above).

T. C. Hansard, TYPOGRAPHIA, *An Historical Sketch of the Origin and Process of the Art of Printing; With Practical Directions for Conducting Every Depart-ment in an Office; With a Description of Stereotype and Lithography,* Baldwin, Cradock & Joy, 1825, Gregg reprint, Farnborough, 1967 (illustrated by engravings, biographical notices and portraits).

The work is partly based on Stower and Mores (see above and p. 260) and its intention was 'to inform the young practitioner, and to make his work acceptable generally to men of letters and essentially so to members of the art'. Bigmore and Wyman are eulogistic: 'In the annals of biblio-graphy Mr Hansard's reputation will rest on his work cited above, . . . Mr Hansard's mechanical abilities were considerable and were assiduously applied to the improvement of his art . . . He was the first to adopt the cylinder machine into his establishment and he studied and adopted all improvements in every branch of printing' (see also under Hansard, p. 279 below).

Charles H. Timperley, THE PRINTERS' MANUAL, *Containing Instructions to Learners with Scales of Imposition and Numerous Calculations, Recipes, and Scales of Prices in the Principal Towns of Great Britain; together with Practical*

Directions for Conducting Every Department of a Printing Office, 1838, Gregg reprint, Farnborough, 1965.

This does not claim to be more than a compilation. 'It begins with an essay on punctuation, and proceeds to composing, imposing, correcting in metal, typographical marks, the readers' vocabulary and scales of prices, describing by the way all the chief implements of the art. It then gives directions to the pressmen with a description and views of the Stanhope. . . the Columbian, the Albion, and the Imperial presses, with short notes concerning other presses. He treats of presswork in a thoroughly practical manner, and gives various recipes for ink and roller making etc. . . . the work ends with a list of the technical terms used by printers, which is, by the way, very incomplete' (Bigmore and Wyman).

William Savage, A DICTIONARY OF THE ART OF PRINTING, 1841, Gregg reprint, Farnborough, 1966.

'One of the standard English works on printing. Among the principal contents are; a valuable article on records by Mr Fehon . . . specimens of Murray's improvements in electrotyping . . . specimens from the principal letter foundries; a synopsis of the statutes at large, so far as they affect printers and publishers and foreign alphabets . . . Many of the definitions are taken from Moxon, from whose book indeed, a large amount of varied matter had been extracted' (Bigmore and Wyman, see above).

4. Typography (i.e. Letter Forms and Typefoundries)
(See also under Section 10, pp. 268 ff.)

I use typography to mean the history and design of printed letter forms, ignoring, as far as possible, the wider meanings of the word, on the one hand, the craft of printing including composition, imposition and press-work; and on the other, the planning of a printed work, to which I have given a whole section, IV. BOOK DESIGN AND PRODUCTION. I also exclude works on calligraphy, as being outside my terms of reference.

Joseph Ames, TYPOGRAPHICAL ANTIQUITIES (see p. 248).

Donald M. Anderson, THE ART OF WRITTEN FORMS; *The Theory and Practice of Calligraphy*, Holt, Rinehart & Winston, New York, 1969 (illustrated, bibliography).

The title is slightly misleading in that the author describes the modern use of types in graphic design, with annotations of the modern types illustrated. The work forms a useful counterbalance to Updike (see p. 261), and to Stanley Morison's writings, which largely ignored the design trends of the 'sixties.

Harry Carter, A VIEW OF EARLY TYPOGRAPHY, *Up to About 1600,* Clarendon Press, Oxford, 1969 (illustrated).

This, the text of the Lyell Lectures for 1968, covers the problems of identifying, describing and classifying typefaces, the shaping and progress of the roman alphabet in print and the history of type founding and punch-cutting.

Geoffrey Dowding, AN INTRODUCTION TO THE HISTORY OF PRINTING TYPES, *An Illustrated Summary of the Main Stages in the Development of Type Design from 1440 up to the Present Day, An Aid to Type Identification,* Wace, 1961 (illustrated, bibliography).

A clear but colourless description of the evolution of type design.

Geoffrey Dowding, FACTORS IN THE CHOICE OF TYPEFACES (see p. 114).

Oldrich Hlavsa for the Publishers of Technical Literature, A BOOK OF TYPE AND DESIGN, Peter Nevill, Prague, 1960 (illustrated).

An introductory brief history of typefaces is followed by specimen romans, venetians, old faces, transitional, modern, and such display cases as fats, sanserifs, square serifs, decorated types, script types and finally Czech typefaces. The work is well set out and easy to use.

R. S. Hutchings, *Trends in Typography,* 16 articles published in the BRITISH PRINTER during 1965.

This examination of current typographical fashions and forecasts for the future, is sound on the typography of the 1930s, less so on modern trends.

A. F. Johnson, TYPE DESIGNS, *Their History and Development,* André Deutsch, Grafton, 1934, 3rd revised edition, 1966 (illustrated, bibliography).

This classic work covers gothic, roman, venetians, and old face, the evolution of modern face, old face in the Victorian age, italic in the eighteenth century, script types, and early advertising types.

Edward Rowe Mores, A DISSERTATION ON ENGLISH TYPOGRAPHICAL FOUNDERS AND FOUNDERIES, 1778, *With a Catalogue and Specimen of the Type Foundery of John James,* 1772, edited with an introduction and notes by Harry Carter and Christopher Ricks, Oxford Bibliographical Society, 1961 (illustrated).

This edition of Mores includes books on printing in Mores's library, a foreword to *The Dissertation,* an appendix from John Nichols, *Literary Anecdotes* (see p. 270) and a list of the equipment of his press.

Talbot Baines Reed (see below), owns himself indebted to 'the learned Edward Rowe Mores. . . . It is in fact the only work in the language purporting to treat of Letter Founding as distinct from the art it fosters. This quaint and crabbed sketch, full of valuable but half digested information was intended to accompany a specimen of the type of John James, whose foundry had gradually absorbed all the minor English foundries, and, on the death of its owner, had become the property of Mores himself. The enthusiasm of the Oxford antiquary infused new life into the dry bones of this decayed collection. Working backwards, he restored in imagination the old foundries of the seventeenth and eighteenth centuries as they had been before they became absorbed in his own. He tracked back a few famous historical types to their fountain head . . .'.

Bigmore and Wyman (see p. 248 above) concur that 'its importance to typographical history can hardly be over-rated. The literary style and punctuation are quite in keeping with the quaintness of the narrative which, nevertheless, abounds in manly strength of thought and observation'.

Talbot Baines Reed, A HISTORY OF THE OLD ENGLISH LETTER FOUNDRIES, *With Notes Historical and Bibliographical on the Rise and Progress of English Typography,* 1887, new edition revised and enlarged by A. F. Johnson, Faber & Faber, 1952 (illustrated, bibliography).

In the preface to the original edition Talbot Baines Reed explains that 'the present work represents the labour of several years in what may be considered some of the untrodden by-paths of English typographical history'. The new edition takes the story from 1830, which was Reed's limit, to 1890. It covers English typebodies and faces, learned foreign and peculiar characters, the letter founders from Caxton to today, letter founding as an English mechanical trade, and its state control. There are many chapters on individual founders, such as William Caslon, John Baskerville, Joseph and Edmund Fry, Vincent Figgins, and foundries like the Oxford University Foundry.

Oliver Simon, INTRODUCTION TO TYPOGRAPHY, Faber & Faber, 1945 (illustrated, bibliography, glossary).

This has never been and probably will never be surpassed as a lucid exposition of rules for composition, choosing typefaces, setting, prelims, illustration, paper, press work, binding, jackets, swash letters, brackets and swelled rules, printers' flowers and numerals.

Herbert Spencer, PIONEERS OF MODERN TYPOGRAPHY, Lund Humphries, 1969 (illustrated, bibliography).

'That revolution in typography paid scant regard to the traditions of the printing industry' is the theme. An introduction is followed by illustrated examples of pioneer typography with biographical notes on the designers.

Daniel Berkeley Updike, PRINTING TYPES, THEIR HISTORY, FORMS AND USE, *A Study in Survivals*, 2 vols., Harvard University Press, Cambridge, Mass., and O.U.P., London, 1st edition, 1922, 3rd edition, 1962, (illustrated).

This was long considered the definitive study of the history of letter forms. The author, owner of the Merrymount Press, expanded what had been lectures into a two-volume work, laying open to the layman the mysteries of letter-design, type-founding, and composition. 'Fashion in design and type of composition . . . is explained in terms of art and of the social, economic and industrial conditions of the period.' The author is, at times, prejudiced, and even inaccurate in the light of later scholarship, but his work has not yet been replaced.

Theodore Low de Vinne, PLAIN PRINTING TYPES, *A Treatise on the Process of Type Making, the Point System, the Name Sizes, and Styles of Type*, Oswald, New York, 1899 (illustrated, bibliography).

This is a useful technical guide to how types are made, being volume 1 of *The Practice of Typography* (see pp. 267, 295 and 299).

5. Legibility

Sir Cyril Burt, A PSYCHOLOGICAL STUDY OF TYPOGRAPHY, O.U.P., 1959 (specimens of typefaces, glossary, bibliography, introduction by Stanley Morison).

Legibility is here qualified as: ease of reading, accuracy, and speed, in a study of the influence on legibility of different faces, boldness, size, interlinear spacing, length of line and width of margin as well as aesthetic merits. Sir Cyril Burt reaches the conclusion, after numerous tests, that: 'Almost everyone reads most easily matter set up in the style and size to which he has become accustomed.'

G. W. Ovink, LEGIBILITY, ATMOSPHERE-VALUE AND FORMS OF PRINTING TYPES, Sijthoff's Uitgeversmaat-Schappj, Leiden, 1938 (illustrated, appendix of *The most important modern printing types*).

This, the foundation stone of all later studies on legibility, 'propounds the theoretical foundations of the legibility of isolated letters', preceded by a short introduction on typefounding and typesetting for the unitiated.

Alison Shaw, PRINT FOR PARTIAL SIGHT, *A Report of the Library Association Sub-Committee on Books for Readers with Defective Sight*, Library Association, 1969 (extensive bibliography, glossary, tables of statistics, specimen settings).

This account of a Nuffield research project in which over 400 partially sighted children and adults were tested with reading matter in different styles and arrangements of print, concludes that type size and weight affects legibility for the partially sighted far more than typeface and typespacing.

Herbert Spencer, THE VISIBLE WORD, *Problems of Legibility*, Lund Humphries, 1st edition, 1968, 2nd edition revised, 1969 (illustrated, bibliography).

The relationship between content and form is considered, capitals versus lower case – 'all capital reading retards the speed of reading to a greater extent than any other single typographic factor' – bold face types, italics, numerals, type size, line length and leading, unjustified setting, paragraphs, margins, paper size, non-horizontal alignment, paper and ink, all with relevance to their legibility. 'It would be nice if *The Visible Word* could be made required reading for everybody who has to do with making words visible' (*British Printer*).

6. Printers' Ornaments

H. R. Plomer defines printers' ornaments as the decoration of books apart from book illustrations, used to heighten the attraction of the letterpress.

H. R. Plomer, ENGLISH PRINTERS' ORNAMENTS, Grafton, 1924.

This describes the genesis of printers' ornaments, English printers and their ornaments, borders, head and tail pieces, miscellaneous initial letters and 'modern work'.

John Ryder, A SUITE OF FLEURONS, *Or a Preliminary Enquiry into the History and Combinable Natures of Certain Printers' Flowers*, Phoenix, 1956 (illustrated).

This little book gives the origin of and illustrates such flowers as the vine leaf, the venetian arabesque, Granjon's arabesque, the acorn and Fournier's flowers.

Frederic Warde, PRINTERS' ORNAMENTS, *Applied to the Composition of Decorative Borders, Panels, and Patterns*, Monotype, 1928.

An illustrated catalogue of Monotype ornaments is followed by specimen papers using ornamental patterns skilfully arranged by Frederic Warde.

Henry T. Wyse, MODERN TYPE DISPLAY, *And the Use of Ornament*, Henry T. Wyse, Edinburgh, 1911 (extensively illustrated, bibliography).

The design and combination of type ornaments are described; the history of the alphabet, early printers and British typefounders is traced and an analysis of typefaces is given.

7. Specimen Books and Encyclopaedias of Typefaces

A. J. Bastien, ENCYCLOPAEDIA TYPOGRAPHICA, 2 parts, Bastien, 1953 (illustrated).

A. J. Bastien, ALPHABET IN TYPE, *A Survey of Typographic Letter Design*, Bastien, 1958 (illustrated).

250 alphabets are shown in large point sizes, 48 to 72, to provide, 'a bench tool for lettering artist, designer, architect, and sign artist'.

W. Turner Berry and A. F. Johnson, ENCYCLOPAEDIA OF TYPEFACES, Blandford Press, 1st edition, 1953, 4th edition revised and enlarged by W. Pincus Jaspert, W. Turner Berry and A. F. Johnson, 1970.

This is the most useful and comprehensive of the type encyclopaedias, despite some deficiencies. The latest edition adds 400 new specimens, lists of typefounders' addresses and an index to designers.

W. Turner Berry and A. F. Johnson, A CATALOGUE OF SPECIMENS OF PRINTING TYPES, *By English and Scottish Printers and Founders,* 1665–1830, O.U.P., 1935 (introduction by Stanley Morison).

An invaluable *catalogue raisonné* of thirty-five founders is preceded by an essay on bibliography and typography by Stanley Morison.

Stephenson Blake, CASLON LETTER FOUNDRY, SPECIMENS OF PRINTING TYPES FROM STEPHENSON BLAKE, Stephenson Blake, 1953.

A history of the firm (somewhat apocryphal as to beginnings), a reference work on type qualities, and a specimen book.

W. S. Cowell, A BOOK OF TYPEFACES, *With Some Illustrated Examples of Text and Display Setting,* W. S. Cowell, 1952, supplements 1959 and 1960.

More or less comprehensive and easy to use.

W. S. Cowell, A HANDBOOK OF PRINTING TYPES, Cowell, 1947.

Complements *A Book of Typefaces* (see above).

R. S. Hutchings, THE WESTERN HERITAGE OF TYPE DESIGN, *A Treasury of Currently Available Typefaces Demonstrating the Historical Development and Diversification of Form of Printed Letters, Selected and Arranged with an Introduction, Commentaries and Appendices,* Hastings House, New York, and Cory, Adams & Mackay, London, 1963 (illustrated, bibliography).

R. S. Hutchings, A MANUAL OF SCRIPT TYPEFACES, *A Definitive Guide to Series in Current Use, Selected and Arranged with an Introduction, Commentaries and Appendices,* Hastings House, New York, and Cory, Adams & Mackay, London, 1965 (illustrated, bibliography).

Mackays of Chatham, TYPE FOR BOOKS, *A Beginners Manual,* Mackay, Chatham, 1959, revised edition, 1965 (illustrated, specimen tables, character and word count tables).

J. Sutton and A. Bartram, AN ATLAS OF TYPE FORMS, Lund Humphries, 1968 (illustrated).

Though disappointing as a type specimen book, a delight to leaf through.

Western, THE WESTERN TYPE BOOK, *Analysed Specimens of Monotype, Linotype and Intertype Faces Suitable for Bookwork and Available at Western*

Printing Services, Bristol, Hamish Hamilton, 1st edition, 1960, revised edition, 1962 (illustrated, foreword by Hans Schmoller).

Particularly useful for the book designer are specimen pages set in 191 typefaces in current use for bookwork in England, presented in a variety of sizes and leadings, each page being provided with a mask so that Crown 8vo, Large Crown and Demy 8vo type areas can be viewed. Simple casting-off information is given on each page.

8. Printers' Marks

This corner of printing history is of interest to collectors and relevant to publishing history and trade history in general. H. W. Davies (see below) explains the origin: 'the sign then, is a picture or symbol to enable a person readily to distinguish a house from afar and goes back to the days when the populace was illiterate and long before the plan of numbering houses was thought of'.

McKerrow (see below) explains further, 'so far as the English printing trade is concerned the origin of the practice is clear enough; it came from the Continent, where devices have been employed by many printers since the first appearance of the Fust-Schoeffer mark in the Bible of 1462'.

W. Roberts (see below) considers that: 'This subject is in many respects one of the most interesting in connection with the early printers, who, using devices at first purely as trademarks for the protection of their wares against pirates, soon began to discern their ornamental value, and, consequently, employed the best available artists to design them.'

J. P. Berjeau, EARLY DUTCH, GERMAN AND ENGLISH PRINTERS' MARKS, E. Rascal, 1866.

These facsimiles of printers' marks, first issued in six parts, have no accompanying text, but there is a list of printers, towns, emblems used by printers on their devices, books with notices of printers, and also mottoes of printers.

Hugh William Davies, DEVICES OF THE EARLY PRINTERS 1457–1560, *Their History and Development with a Chapter on Portrait Figures of Printers,* Grafton, 1935 (annotated illustrations, bibliography).

This includes chapters not only on printers' devices and the dating of colophons, but also on bale marks and other merchants' symbols and on marks and emblems in general.

R. B. McKerrow, PRINTERS' AND PUBLISHERS' DEVICES IN ENGLAND AND SCOTLAND 1485–1640, Chiswick Press for the Bibliographical Society, 1913 (illustrations of 485 mottoes and devices, bibliography).

The introduction to this definitive work classifies the devices as: signs indicating where the printer worked, puns upon the owner's name, monograms, portraits, heraldic devices or emblems. There are lists of devices, notes on their transfer from one printer to another, also indexes of the devices used by booksellers and printers, of mottoes, of initials of artists or engravers, and of devices according to subject.

W. Roberts, PRINTERS' MARKS, *A Chapter in the History of Typography*, Bell, 1893 (illustrated, bibliography).

This pioneer study deals with printers' marks in England, France, Germany, Switzerland, the Netherlands, and some late nineteenth-century examples.

Victoria and Albert Museum, EARLY PRINTERS' MARKS, H.M.S.O., 1962 (illustrated, bibliography).

A two-page introduction is followed by illustrations of twenty-eight marks, 1481–1595.

9. Title Pages

The history of the title page is a feature in the development of the printed book. Manuscripts, bound as soon as completed, did not need the protection that a title page gives to an unbound text, nor did incunabula, modelled as they were on manuscript books. Title pages first appeared in the early sixteenth century and, as printed books were delivered to the bookseller in sheets and only bound up as sold, the first pages of the text called for some protection, and we may surmise that this was the chief motive for the introduction of the title page.

Edward Rowe Mores, in *A Dissertation upon English Typographical Founders*, says:

Mr Stevens was a gentleman of a typographical turn, but no great adept . . . he devised and printed *title-pages* of strange and ludicrous books *speedily to be published* which were never to be published, nor indeed had any existence; and these title pages he dabbed up in the cool of the evening at the corners of the public streets to stir up the expectation of those who stopped there – this was *his* amusement, and harmless enough.

Less harmless was the amusement of the book-vandal, a customer of G. Orioli (see p. 88), who collected

nothing but title-pages of which he told me, he had already got together 2,000; in other words he had already ruined 2,000 good books. With the help of these title pages, he declared, he was going to write a history of the art of printing. He was quite annoyed when I told him that he had started a century too late; and when I showed him some incunabula he would not look at them; where were the title pages? I said that incunabula were born without title pages and that his history of printing would be valueless unless it began with them. He shook his head. Perhaps he was thinking; a book without a title page isn't a book at all. . . . He invited me to a flat he had bought on the Lungarno, a fine place, in order to show me this collection. There they were, several thousand title pages of all sizes and periods, beautifully bound in many volumes by Ortic, a French bookbinder.

This eccentric did not write his history of title pages but several have been written since.

Alexander Nesbitt, TWO HUNDRED TITLE PAGES, Dover Publications, New York, 1965 (illustrated, bibliography indicating sources of illustrations used).

The illustrations, each bearing an informative caption, are grouped into three sections, each preceded by a short essay; the first, the period of the wood-cut title, 1478–1620; the second, the etched and engraved title, 1545–1795; and then finally, the nineteenth century and up to 1929.

A. W. Pollard, LAST WORDS ON THE HISTORY OF THE TITLE PAGE, *With Notes on Some Colophons and 27 Facsimiles of Title Pages*, Nimmo, 1891.

Theodore Low de Vinne, A TREATISE ON TITLE PAGES, limited edition, Grolier Club, New York, 1901; popular edition, Century, New York, 1902 (vol. 3 of *The Practice of Typography*, see pp. 261, 295, and 299), (illustrated).

The author, writing as a printer rather than a bibliographer, prefers to concentrate on 'the title page of type'. The first part of the work is historical, the second practical and the third critical. The illustrations are grouped into sections on: the colophon, styles with engraved borders, borders of flowers or rules, the chapbook, French title pages, Kelmscott typography, etc.

Hermann Zapf, TYPOGRAPHIC VARIATIONS DESIGNED BY HERMANN ZAPF ON THEMES IN CONTEMPORARY BOOK DESIGN AND TYPOGRAPHY IN 78 BOOK AND TITLE PAGES, Museum Books, New York, 1964 (illustrated).

There are prefaces by Paul Standard, G. K. Schauer and Charles Peignot, and commentary and notes in English, French and German, on the work of this book designer.

10. House Histories, Memoirs and Biographies of Printers, Typefounders and Type Designers

STEPHEN AUSTIN & SONS (established 1768)

James Moran, STEPHEN AUSTIN'S OF HERTFORD, *A Bi-Centenary History*, Austin, 1968 (illustrated).

THE BALLANTYNE PRESS (established 1796)

W. T. Dobson, compiler, THE BALLANTYNE PRESS AND ITS FOUNDERS 1796–1908, Ballantyne Hanson, Edinburgh, 1909 (illustrated, bibliography of works published by the press in its early years).

This describes the origins, the removal to Edinburgh, the association with Scott and the printing of the Waverley novels, the controversy with Lockhart and the demise of the works at Old Paul's.

See also **Eric Quayle,** THE RUIN OF SIR WALTER SCOTT under XIII. PUBLISHING, p. 354.

JOHN BASKERVILLE (1706–75)

'At the age of 20 Baskerville became a writing-master in Birmingham. This occupation he appears to have supplemented by, or exchanged for, that of engraving inscriptions on tombstones and memorials, a profession in which he is said to have shown much talent. . . . His artistic tastes led him afterwards to enter into the japanning business in which he prospered. . . . About the year 1750 his inclination for letters induced him to turn his attention to typography, and to add to his business of a japanner that of a printer. . . . Once more it was left to an outsider to initiate the new departure; and as in 1720 the art of letter-founding had been roused from its lethargy by the genius of a gunsmith's apprentice, so in 1750 the art of printing was destined to find its deliverer in the person of an eccentric Birmingham japanner' (T. B. Reed, *A History of the Old English Letter Foundries*).

Philip Gaskell, JOHN BASKERVILLE, *A Bibliography*, C.U.P., 1959 (illustrated).

An introduction is followed by a table showing the correspondence of this bibliography with that of Straus and Dent (see below). Each entry provides a transcription of the title page, contents, cancels, plates, paper, type, etc. A pocket at the end contains a facsimile of Baskerville's last type specimen.

Talbot Baines Reed, A HISTORY OF THE OLD ENGLISH LETTER FOUNDRIES (see p. 260 above); chapter 13, pp. 267–89, *John Baskerville*.

Ralph Straus and Robert K. Dent, JOHN BASKERVILLE, *A Memoir*, C.U.P. for Chatto & Windus, 1907 (illustrated).

A twenty-six-page memoir is followed by a bibliography in two parts, the first consisting of works, authentic and suppositious, printed by Baskerville and the second including letters, agreements and a copy of Baskerville's will (see also 'Cambridge University Press', p. 309 below.)

JOHN BELL (1745–1831).

Stanley Morison, JOHN BELL, 1745–1831, *Bookseller, Printer, Publisher, Type Founder, Journalist*, C.U.P. for the author, 1930 (illustrated).

This critical biography of the founder and part proprietor of the *Morning Post, The World, The Oracle* or *Bell's New World, Bell's Weekly Messenger, La Belle Assemblée*, original proprietor of *The British Library, Bell's British Letter Foundry, Bell's British Theatre, Bell's Poets of Great Britain* and *Bell's Edition of Shakespeare* is an elegant production. There are appendixes on Bell's book and newspaper typography, the story of his types in the United States, and his type specimens.

THE HOUSE OF BEMROSE (established 1826)

H. H. Bemrose, THE HOUSE OF BEMROSE 1826–1926, Bemrose Press, Derby, 1926 (illustrated).

This centenary volume describes the beginning of railway printing, the firm's formation and expansion, the effect of the First World War on its growth, social activities and technical advances, with brief biographies of fourteen members of the family. The further expansion of Bemrose into one of the giants of the printing industry, calls for a sequel. (For the connection with Allen & Unwin see p. 333 below.)

WILLIAM BLADES (1842–90)

There is still no biography of Blades, printer, partner in the firm of Blades, East & Blades, Caxton scholar and collector of a typographical library that is the foundation of the St Bride Printing Library, (see p. 309 etc.).

CATALOGUE OF AN EXHIBITION IN COMMEMORATION OF THE CENTENARY OF WILLIAM BLADES, December, 1924.

Pages 5–11 contain a list of Blades's writings.

James Moran, *William Blades,* in THE LIBRARY, December, 1961, pp. 251–66.

This is the text of a paper read before the Bibliographical Society.

WILLIAM BOWYER II (1699–1777)

The son of Caslon's patron, William Bowyer I, was printer to the Royal Society and known as 'the learned printer'.

William Bowyer, ANECDOTES, BIOGRAPHICAL AND LITERARY, *of the Late Mr. William Bowyer, Printer, Compiled for Private Use,* 1778.

John Nichols, BIOGRAPHICAL AND LITERARY ANECDOTES OF WILLIAM BOWYER, PRINTER, F.S.A. *And of Many of his Learned Friends . . . from the Beginning of the Present Century to the End of the Year 1777,* 1782, reprinted, Centaur Press, 1967, as LITERARY ANECDOTES OF THE EIGHTEENTH-CENTURY.

These have proved the sources of many later writings on the eighteenth-century book trade, many cribbing Nichols's very words.

CAMBRIDGE UNIVERSITY PRESS (1520? – this was the year in which John Sieberch set up the first press outside London)

I select the following:

Brooke Crutchley, TWO MEN, 1968 (a privately printed Christmas volume, see also under 'Stanley Morison', below).

'In 1922 Stanley Morison was formally engaged by the then Lanston Monotype Corporation in London as its typographical adviser; in the following year Walter Lewis became University Printer at Cambridge.

The effect these two appointments were to have upon each other, en-hanced shortly afterwards by Morison's further attachment to the Cam-bridge Press . . . "resulted" on the one hand in the fulfilment of a vigorous and enlightened programme of new type-cutting for the Monotype machine, and on the other the building up at Cambridge of a wealth of typographical material such as no printing house had ever before been able to offer its customers' (from the Preface to *A Tally of Types*, see below).

E. P. Goldschmidt, THE FIRST CAMBRIDGE PRESS IN ITS EUROPEAN SETTING, C.U.P., 1955 (illustrated).

This, the text of the Sandars Lectures for 1953, also includes a type fac-simile of John Sieberch, the first Cambridge printer.

D. F. Mackenzie, THE CAMBRIDGE UNIVERSITY PRESS 1696–1712, 2 vols., C.U.P., 1966 (illustrated, bibliography).

'It is a study in depth, the terminal dates of which have been dictated entirely by the nature of the records that happen to have survived' (Pre-face).
The first volume of detail of printing house design, staff ratios and turn-over, output of compositors and pressmen, shared work, prices, edition sizes and the like, is followed by a volume of facsimile documents.

Stanley Morison, A TALLY OF TYPES, 1953 (a privately printed Christmas volume, see also under 'Stanley Morison' below).

S. C. Roberts, A HISTORY OF THE CAMBRIDGE UNIVERSITY PRESS, 1521–1921, C.U.P., 1921 (illustrated, bibliography).

The fullest of the histories put out by the Press during the interwar years, has appendixes of the University Printers 1521–1750, and of the books printed at the Press during those years (see also under XIIIA, THE HISTORY OF PUBLISHING, p. 336 for Sir Sydney's autobiography).

THE UNIVERSITY PRINTING HOUSES AT CAMBRIDGE, *From the Sixteenth to the Twentieth Century*, privately printed, C.U.P., 1962 (illustrated), (a Christmas number to celebrate the move to Fitzwilliam Road).

The above-mentioned privately printed volumes dealing with the Press's history, are selected from the annual Christmas presents that are printed for friends (see under 'Collections of Printed Material and Equipment', p. 309, below).

WILLIAM CASLON (1692–1777)
The first great English typefounder 'served his apprenticeship to an

engraver of gun-locks and barrels ... the ability he displayed in his art was conspicuous ... the chasing of silver and the designing of tools for bookbinders [also] occupying his attention. While thus engaged, some of his bookbinding punches were noticed for their neatness and accuracy by John Watts, the eminent printer, who, fully alive to the present degenerate state of the typographical art in this country, was quick to recognize the possibility of raising it once more to its proper position. He accordingly encouraged Caslon to persevere in letter-cutting ... about the same time, it is recorded that another greater printer, the elder Bowyer, accidentally saw in the shop of Mr Daniel Browne, bookseller, near Temple Bar, the lettering of a book, uncommonly neat; and enquiring who the artist was by whom the letters were made, Mr Caslon was introduced to his acquaintance, and was taken by him to Mr James's foundery in Bartholomew Close' (Talbot Baines Reed, *A History of the Old English Letter Foundries*, see below).

Caslon started his own foundry in 1720, was succeeded by his son, grandsons and great-grandsons until, in 1937, the firm was taken over by Stephenson Blake & Co.

James Mosley, *The Early Career of William Caslon*, article in the JOURNAL OF THE PRINTING HISTORICAL SOCIETY, no. 3, 1967.

This contains new material on Caslon's work for the S.P.C.K. and lists his early type specimens, the first use of his types, and the documents relating to his dealings with the Board of Ordnance.

Talbot Baines Reed, A HISTORY OF THE OLD ENGLISH LETTER FOUNDRIES, revised edition A. F. Johnson, Faber & Faber, 1952.

Chapter 11, pp. 229–7, gives, with the editor's notes, a full and reliable account of Caslon's career.

THE CATNACH PRESS (established 1790) (see also 'Chapbooks' under VII. CHILDREN'S BOOKS, pp. 181 ff.).

Charles Hindley, THE HISTORY OF THE CATNACH PRESS, *At Berwick-on-Tweed, Alnwick, and Newcastle-upon-Tyne, in Northumberland, and Seven Dials,* Charles Hindley, 1886 (illustrated).

'There can be little doubt that Jemmy Catnach, the printer, [son of John Catnach, printer in Northumberland, and who founded the press] justly earned the distinction of being one of the great pioneers in the cause of promoting cheap literature. . . . We do not pretend to say that the productions that emanated from his establishment contained much that was likely to enlighten the intellect...but to a great extent they serve well in creating an impetus in the minds of many to soar after things of a higher and more ennobling character. He could cater for the taste and fancies of all...so paving the way for that bright day in the annals of British history, when every child in the land should be educated.'

Percy Muir, CATNACHERY, Book Club of California, 1955 (illustrated, bibliography).

The life and works of James Catnach, the printer of street ballads at Seven Dials, son of John Catnach the failed printer of Berwick, Alnwick, Newcastle and London.

WILLIAM CAXTON (1422–91)

William Blades, THE BIOGRAPHY AND TYPOGRAPHY OF WILLIAM CAXTON, *England's First Printer,* Trübner, 1st edition, 2 vols, 1861–3, 2nd edition, 1 vol., 1882 (illustrated, bibliography), reprinted Frederick Muller, 1971.

'A reprint of the author's former work in two volumes, this traces Caxton's history and the influence which surrounded him in youth and manhood. It shows why he became a printer and of whom he learnt the art. There is a minute account of Caxton's printing office and the typographic habits of his workmen. His types are classified and their chronological sequence shown, and the great advantage, bibliographically speaking, to be derived from their systematic study. All the books at present known to have been issued from his press are described, and remarks made upon them, various minor matters being also treated.' (Bigmore and Wyman, see p. 248 above). This is still a key work. The new reprint, with a foreword by James Moran, corrects Blades's misconceptions in the light of modern scholarship.

Charles Knight, WILLIAM CAXTON, *The First English Printer, A Biography,* 1877 (illustrated, bibliography of books consulted and of books printed by Caxton).

Despite Knight's limitations as a scholar, he remains a readable historian of the trade.

H. R. Plomer, WILLIAM CAXTON 1424–1491, Leonard Parsons, 1925 (bibliography, list of principal dates).

The author assesses Caxton's importance as printer, translator, editor and author.

K

William Caxton, THE GAME AND PLAYE OF THE CHESSE, 1474, *A Verbatim Reprint of the First Edition,* with an introduction by William E. A. Axon, Elliot Stock, 1883.

An assessment of the various editions of *The Game and Playe of the Chesse,* a list of bibliographical references and extracts from the translations in French, Spanish, Catalan, Italian, German, Dutch, and other versions of the work, are preceded by a scholarly introduction.

JOHN CHENEY (*c.* 1732–1808)

JOHN CHENEY AND HIS DESCENDENTS, *Printers in Banbury since 1767,* privately printed Banbury, 1936 (70 plates, family tree, plan of works).

This detailed history of an old-established firm of country printers, includes an inventory of chapbooks and broadsides printed at Cheney's *Unicorn Press,* with details of costing in the early years.

CLOWES & SONS (established 1803)

A DESCRIPTION OF THEIR PRINTING OFFICE, *With a Memoir of the Late William Clowes, The Founder of the Establishment,* privately printed, 1840. (A reprint of articles in the *Quarterly Review.*)

W. B. Clowes, FAMILY BUSINESS 1803–1953, Clowes, 1953 (illustrated).

This house history of five generations unfortunately lacks an index.

THE CURWEN PRESS (established 1863)

The Curwen Press played a leading part in the revival of fine printing between the wars.

Holbrook Jackson, CATALOGUE RAISONNÉ OF BOOKS PRINTED AT THE CURWEN PRESS 1920–1923, Medici Society, 1924 (illustrated).

An introduction describes the Press's beginnings and assesses the work done in the first years.

Oliver Simon, PRINTER AND PLAYGROUND, *An Autobiography,* Faber & Faber, 1961 (illustrated).

The first part covers the author's early years, the founding of the *Fleuron* and the Double Crown Club (qq.v.). The second part deals with the printing of books and periodicals during the 1930s. An appendix provides an index to *Signature, 1935–1940* (see p. 303).

EYRE & SPOTTISWOODE (see under 'Strahan' below)

JOHN FELL (see under 'Oxford University Press' and 'Stanley Morison' below)

VINCENT FIGGINS (established his own foundry *c.* 1792)

Vincent Figgins I (1776–1844) was apprenticed to a punch cutter and later started a foundry of his own, which was carried on by his son, Vincent Figgins II (d. 1860), and subsequently by his grandsons James and Vincent, when the firm became V. & J. Figgins.

Talbot Baines Reed, A HISTORY OF THE OLD ENGLISH LETTER FOUNDRIES (see p. 260), Chapter 18, pp. 328–37, *Vincent Figgins.*

Berthold Wolpe, VINCENT FIGGINS, *Type Specimens 1801 and 1815,* Printing Historical Society, 1967 (illustrated, appendixes of a comparative table of type sizes, and extracts relating to the Figgins foundry from *The Penny Magazine,* 1833).

An introduction describes the state of typography in the time of Figgins and assesses his importance as a type founder. Illustrations include facsimiles of the 1801 and the 1815 broadside specimens, a wood-engraving of a casting mould, and a view of the Figgins' foundry.

THE FOULIS PRESS (Glasgow University Press) (established 1743). (See also under 'Scottish Publishers and Publishing', p. 355).

The University Press of Glasgow, founded by Robert and Andrew Foulis in 1743, 'issued some of the finest books ever printed', some believe with James Maclehose, rivalling the work of Baskerville. The press has always been private property, yet the university has never failed to encourage its printers. The Foulis brothers lived at a time when 'increases of wealth, the growth of culture, the development of taste, reflected themselves in printing and book production. When Robert Foulis was born, there was no public in Scotland to support a printer whose object was not only to furnish some literature, but to produce well printed and handsome books; at the lapse of fifty years, there was a large and increasing demand for such books' (David Murray, see below). The modern bookbinding firm of Hunter and Foulis is an offshoot.

Philip Gaskell, A BIBLIOGRAPHY OF THE FOULIS PRESS, Rupert Hart-Davis, 1964 (illustrated).

The introduction describes the extent and character of the output of the

Foulis Press, the paper and type used, and the operation of the Foulis brothers as publishers and booksellers, all illustrated with tables and diagrams. The bibliography, which is in three sections, is followed by appendixes of *The Proposal for Plato*, 1751, and the correspondence between Robert Foulis and James Boswell, 1767–68.

James Maclehose, THE GLASGOW UNIVERSITY PRESS 1638–1931, *With Some Notes on Scottish Printing in the Last 300 Years*, Glasgow University Press, 1931 (illustrated, bibliography including a list of manuscript and printed authorities).

This describes the beginnings, the heyday of Scottish printing, the connection between Blackie's and the university printers, the work that Macmillan's gave to the Glasgow University Press because of the friendship between the Macmillan brothers and James Maclehose as fellow apprentices, and the foundation of Robert Maclehose & Co. There is a list of university printers and dates.

David Murray, ROBERT AND ANDREW FOULIS, *and the Glasgow Press With Some Account of the Glasgow Academy of the Fine Arts*, James Maclehose & Sons, Glasgow, 1913 (illustrated).

Part 1 is concerned with the Glasgow Press, its influence on local printing and the activities of Robert Foulis as printer, publisher and bookseller. Part 2 relates his interest in the Glasgow Academy of Fine Arts.

BENJAMIN FRANKLIN (1706–90)

Benjamin Franklin, distinguished alike as printer, inventor and philosopher, introduced copperplate printing into America, and established a type foundry in Philadelphia in 1785. A platen press was called the Franklin Press after him. He also worked in London as a printer in the office of Samuel Palmer (see illustration, p. 245).

There are many editions of his autobiography; I select two early original editions and a recent one:

Benjamin Franklin, MEMOIRS OF THE LIFE AND WRITINGS OF BENJAMIN FRANKLIN ... *Continued to the Time of his Death by his Grandson, William Temple*, 3 vols, 1818.

Benjamin Franklin, AUTOBIOGRAPHY, edited from the manuscript by John Bigelow, Philadelphia, Pa., 1868.

Benjamin Franklin, AUTOBIOGRAPHY, in *Collected Works*, edited by L. W. Labaree, Yale University Press, New Haven, Conn., 1964; also separately published in paperback.

THOMAS GENT (1693–1778)

THE LIFE OF THOMAS GENT, PRINTER, OF YORK, *Written by Himself*, Thomas Thorpe, 1832 (illustrated).

This autobiography, amusing in itself, revealing in a number of details of printing history in the second half of the eighteenth century, is to be re-edited for the Printing Historical Society, from the original manuscript, inserting the passages that Thorpe bowdlerised.

ERIC GILL (1882–1940) (See also St. Dominic Press under XII. PRIVATE PRESSES, p. 324.)

Eric Gill, AN ESSAY ON TYPOGRAPHY, Sheed & Ward, 1931, revised edition, J. M. Dent, 1941 (illustrated).

A philosophical discourse on the reconciliation between industrialism and craftsmanship is followed by chapters on lettering and the evolution of letter forms, typography, paper and ink, etc.

Eric Gill, AUTOBIOGRAPHY, Jonathan Cape, 1940.

Chapter 6 describes the author's work as a typographer and gives his views on type design.

Evan Gill, A BIBLIOGRAPHY OF ERIC GILL, Cassell, 1953 (foreword by Walter Shewring).

The definitive bibliography.

Robert Speaight, THE LIFE OF ERIC GILL, Methuen, 1966 (illustrated, bibliography, index of life and works).

Written with the authority of one who knew him well, this biography describes Gill's importance as a stone-carver, typographer, wood-engraver and polemicist. Speaight regards Gill finally as a 'Catholic D. H. Lawrence'.

Joseph Thorp, ERIC GILL, Jonathan Cape, 1929 (with a critical monograph by Charles Marriott).

Mainly about his work as a sculptor.

A true Representation of a Printing House *with the Men at Work.*

Engraved for the New Universal Magazine.1752.

An eighteenth-century printing office, engraved for the New Universal Magazine, *1752*

GLASGOW UNIVERSITY PRESS (see under 'Foulis Press' above)

FREDERIC GOUDY (1865–1947)

One of the foremost American typographers, designer of more than 100 typefaces, including Kennerly and old-face Goudy, was the founder of the journal, *Ars Typographica*.

Frederic Goudy, A HALF CENTURY OF TYPE DESIGN AND TYPOGRAPHY, 1895–1945, 2 vols., The Typophiles, New York, 1946 (illustrations of types cut by Goudy, bibliography by G. L. Mackay, index of Goudy types and dates of their design).

This typographical autobiography is followed by a note on *The Book and its Author* by G. L. Mackay.

THE GRESHAM PRESS (see under 'T. Fisher Unwin' below)

JOHN GUTENBERG (*c.* 1394–1468)

Mention cannot be omitted of the inventor of printing.

Victor Scholderer, JOHANN GUTENBERG, *Inventor of Printing,* British Museum, 1963 (illustrated, select bibliography).

This provides a scholarly introduction to the life, invention and importance of the father of printing. Illustrations include a facsimile of the thirty-line indulgence of 1454, the earliest piece of printed matter, other Gutenberg specimens, reconstructions of his hand-mould for casting type, and of his press.

HANSARD (Luke Hansard was printer to the House of Commons 1744–1828)

Luke's eldest son, Thomas Curson Hansard was the author of *Typographia*, 1825 (see p. 257), and other members of the family wrote on printing, and were connected with the printing of the proceedings of the House of Commons.

BIOGRAPHICAL MEMOIR OF LUKE HANSARD ESQ. *Many Years Printer to the House of Commons,* 1829 (portrait).

J. C. Trewin and E. M. King, PRINTER TO THE HOUSE, *The Story of Hansard,* Methuen, 1952 (illustrated, bibliography).

HARRISON & SONS (established 1733)

The nephew of Thomas Harrison the founder, was Government confidential printer and his son and grandson continued in that office.

THE HOUSE OF HARRISON, *Being an Account of the Family and Firm of Harrison and Sons Printers to the King*, Harrison, 1914 (illustrated, bibliography).

HAZELL, WATSON & VINEY (established 1839)

H. J. Keefe, A CENTURY IN PRINT, *The Story of Hazell's 1839–1939*, Hazell, Watson & Viney, 1939 (illustrated).

This includes appendixes of chronological events in the firm's history, selected imprints, a list of subsidiaries and associated firms.

HAZELL'S IN AYLESBURY 1867–1967, *A Scrap-book to Commemorate the First 100 Years at the Printing Works, Aylesbury*, Hazell, 1968 (illustrated).

JAN VAN KRIMPEN (1892–1958)

For many years, chief type designer at the Enschedé type foundry at Haarlem, van Krimpen had a direct influence on British book production through his designs for the Soncino Press, the Fleuron, and the Nonesuch Press edition of *The Iliad*. His Lutetia, Romulus and Cancelleresca Bastarda types were cut by the Monotype Corporation.

John Dreyfus, THE WORK OF JAN VAN KRIMPEN, *A Record in Honour of His Sixtieth Birthday*, Sylvan Press, 1952 (foreword by Stanley Morison, 83 pages of illustrations of type specimens, lettering and book work, bindings and book jackets, etc.).

This critical biography assesses Van Krimpen's place in modern book design and calligraphy.

Jan van Krimpen, DESIGNING AND DEVISING TYPE, Typophiles, New York, and Sylvan Press, London, 1957 (illustrated, biographical postscript on *The Author and His Book* by Paul Bennett).

This is a typographical autobiography.

J. H. MASON (1875–1951)

The compositor for the Doves Press (see p. 318), was later instructor in printing classes at the Central School of Arts and Crafts, where he had considerable influence in the printing revival inspired by William Morris.

John Mason, J. H. MASON, R.D.I., *A Selection from the Notebooks of a Scholar-Printer Made by his Son,* Twelve by Eight Press, 1961 (illustrations by Rigby Graham).

MONOTYPE CORPORATION (established as the Lanston Monotype Corporation 1897)

The American, Tolbert Lanston (1844–1913) was the inventor of the type-setting and casting machine, an improved version being marketed in Britain from 1897.

THE MONOTYPE RECORDER (1902–   ).

Vol. 39, no. 1., Autumn 1949, is a history of the Corporation.
This intermittent review issued by the Monotype Corporation, publishes special numbers, the result of research by the Corporation's staff. Many important articles on typefaces came from the pens of Stanley Morison and Beatrice Warde, the latter its editor from 1926 until her retirement in 1962 (see also under 'Stanley Morison', below, and 'Beatrice Warde', p. 289).

STANLEY MORISON (1889–1967)

Nicolas Barker, STANLEY MORISON, Macmillan, 1972 (illustrated).

The definitive biography.

John Carter, A HANDLIST OF THE WRITINGS OF STANLEY MORISON, C.U.P., privately printed, 1950, (notes by Morison, indexes by Graham Pollard).

This was undertaken as a sixtieth birthday tribute.

Brooke Crutchley, TWO MEN, *Walter Lewis and Stanley Morison at Cambridge,* C.U.P., privately printed, 1968 (illustrated with photographs and specimen title pages designed by Morison).

P. M. Handover, *A Handlist of the Writings of Stanley Morison, 1950–59,* in MOTIF, no. 3, September 1959.

James Moran, *Stanley Morison 1889–1967,* article in the MONOTYPE RECORDER, 1968, vol. 43, no. 3, Monotype Corporation (illustrated).

This sketches the typographic background, the influence of calligraphy on Morison's attitude to typography, the far-reaching effect on him of the 1912 *Times Printing Supplement,* his work at Burns & Oates, and at the Pelican and Cloister Presses, as adviser to Monotype, the *Fleuron* and

Penrose Annual; it describes the many types redesigned for the Monotype Corporation under his guidance, his relations with the Cambridge University Press, the Fanfare Press, the history of Perpetua and Gill Sans, the Gollancz yellow jackets, the connection with *The Times* and the design of Times New roman, other work on newspaper design, the John Fell book and *Printing and the Mind of Man* (see p. 250).

James Moran, STANLEY MORISON; *His Typographical Achievement*, Lund Humphries, 1971 (illustrated, bibliography).

A critical reassessment of Morison's contribution to the art of typography which goes into greater detail than the issue of the *Monotype Recorder* (see above).

I select the following key writings (chronologically arranged) in which Morison either set out his views on typography for the first time, or where they find their most complete expression:

FOUR CENTURIES OF FINE PRINTING, 1924 (see under 'General Works', p. 252 above).

TYPE DESIGNS OF THE PAST AND PRESENT, Fleuron, 1926, new edition, Benn, 1962 (illustrated).

This, Morison's first exposition of the influence of calligraphy on modern type design, traces letter forms through history from the Carolingian to the contemporary period.

FIRST PRINCIPLES OF TYPOGRAPHY, Fleuron, vol. 7, 1929, and many times reprinted as one of the Cambridge University Press Authors' and Printers Guides, and elsewhere.

This could be called Morison's typographic *credo*, stating his view of the principles governing choice in type design, composition and proportion.

A TALLY OF TYPES, *Cut for Composition and Introduced at the University Press Cambridge*, 1922–32, C.U.P., privately printed, 1953 (illustrated preface and postscript by Brooke Crutchley).

Stanley Morison tells how, 'The Corporation, after long years of poverty, had begun to prosper. It should make a contribution to the invention rendered beautiful, as well as useful, by Gutenberg, Fust and Schoeffer . . . and other illustrious masters.' Morison describes the collection of types cut under his direction at Monotype between 1922–32, and adopted by the Cambridge Press. Certain inaccuracies will be corrected in a later edition.

Classification of Typographical Varieties, introduction to TYPE SPECIMEN FACSIMILES, 1963.

This provides a survey of the literature on the subject, an evaluation of Dutch roman and Modern faces, a description of the rise of English typefounding, the importance of the Private Press movement, and an analysis of the script faces of the nineteenth century.

Some Italian Scripts of the XV and XVI Centuries, introduction to Carla Marzoli, CALLIGRAPHY, 1535–1885, Milan, 1962.

These two essays were reissued as:

LETTER FORMS, *Typographic and Scriptorial, Two Essays on Their Classification, History and Bibliography*, Typophiles, New York, and Nattali and Maurice, London, 1968 (illustrated).

JOHN FELL, THE UNIVERSITY PRESS AND THE 'FELL' TYPES, 1967 (see also under 'Oxford University Press' below).

Morison's *magnum opus* was begun in 1925, the third centenary of Fell's birth. But it suffered a setback when Morison's notes were bombed in 1941 and he started work for the second time in 1947. Then Harry Carter collaborated with a thorough investigation of the punches, matrixes, account books and inventories at the Plantin-Moretus Museum, he and J. S. G Simmons subsequently sorting and examining the punches for the larger types and the exotics that were at Oxford. Morison started writing in 1956, delivered the manuscript to the Press in 1960 and, after expert criticism and considerable rewriting, the work was ready to go to the printer in 1964. It took a further two and a half years until publication, which coincided with the author's death. There was a sad irony that the T.L.S. review outlining Morison's plans for the new work appeared on the very morning of his death, when *The Times* carried his obituary notice. The production of the book was itself a piece of printing history. 'In Feil's honour it had been decided to set the entire book in type cast in the typefoundry at the Press with the matrixes that he had bought and bequeathed. That meant setting by hand, using and re-using a fount of type. The fount was enough for 40 pages; so, as soon as the proofs were passed, the formes for five sheets of the book were sent to machine' (*Introduction* to the Catalogue of an exhibition on John Fell, held October–December 1967).

JOHN NICHOLS (see under 'William Bowyer' above)

OXFORD UNIVERSITY PRESS (established 1585? when Joseph Barnes set up as self-styled Printer to the University)

Oxford was given a charter to print bibles and other 'privileged' books, 1632. Printing was carried on in the Sheldonian Theatre, and later the Clarendon Building, during the eighteenth century. The Press moved to the present Clarendon Press building in Walton Street, 1830. Later the publishing house expanded to London, to Amen House, Warwick Square, and in 1968, it moved to Ely House, Dover Street.

I select the following:

Horace Hart, NOTES ON A CENTURY OF TYPOGRAPHY AT THE UNIVERSITY PRESS, OXFORD 1693–1794, *A Photographic Reprint of the Edition of 1900 with An Introduction and Additional Notes by Harry Carter*, Clarendon Press, Oxford, 1970 (illustrated).

Horace Hart, the first author of the much reprinted *Hart's Rules* (see p. 300), was University Printer (1883–1915). Stanley Morison's major work on the Fell types (see above) with its many references to Hart's work, suggested a reprint of this book.
'The record of old typographical material that Hart provided in his notes is most painstaking, and there are only a few places where it has become apparent since he wrote that he had made mistakes' (Harry Carter's introduction to the latest edition.)

Horace Hart, CHARLES EARL STANHOPE AND THE OXFORD UNIVERSITY PRESS, edited with notes by James Mosley and reprinted from the Oxford Historical Society Journal *Collectanea*, no. 3, 1896, Printing Historical Society, 1966.

John Johnson and Strickland Gibson, PRINT AND PRIVILEGE AT OXFORD TO THE YEAR 1700, O.U.P., 1946 (illustrated, appendix of 7 documents).

This scholarly work describes the establishment of privilege in Oxford, the freeing of the Stationers' Company's hold over Oxford printing, and the work of John Fell in setting the Press's house in order.

Falconer Madan, THE EARLY OXFORD PRESS, *A Bibliography of Printing and Publishing at Oxford 1468–1640*, Clarendon Press, Oxford, 1895 (with notes, appendixes, and illustrations).

An appendix on the fifteenth- and early sixteenth-century Press gives a detailed account of books, type and copies known. There is a chronological list of persons and proceedings connected with book production at Oxford,

1180–1640, wood-cut and metal ornaments, lists of imprints, and tables of Oxford printers and publishers 1585–1640.

Falconer Madan, A BRIEF ACCOUNT OF THE UNIVERSITY PRESS AT OXFORD, Clarendon Press, Oxford, 1908 (illustrations, together with a chart of Oxford printing).

This includes descriptions and illustrations of curiosities of the Press, Civil War counterfeits, Dean Fell's New Year books, 1661–1709, Oxford almanacs from 1674 and the Caxton Memorial Bible, 1877.

Stanley Morison, with the assistance of **Harry Carter,** JOHN FELL, THE UNIVERSITY PRESS AND THE 'FELL' TYPES, *The Punches and Matrices Designed for Printing in the Greek, Latin, English and Oriental Languages Bequeathed in 1688 to the University of Oxford by John Fell D.D., Delegate of the Press, Dean of Christchurch, Vice Chancellor of the University and Bishop of Oxford,* Clarendon Press, Oxford, 1967 (illustrated, bibliographies of Fell's works and of authorities cited).

The first part gives the historical background to Fell's enterprise in learned printing, a biography and an account of the acquisition of the type equipment; the second describes the types with detail of their history. John Fell, as Dean of Christchurch and Bishop of Oxford, set up a 'public academic printing-house' at Oxford together with three other eminent men in 1672. Hiring the University's privilege of printing 'all manner of books', they conducted a press in the Sheldonian Theatre until Fell's death in 1686. He bequeathed the equipment of the press to the University thus enabling the printing and selling of learned, religious and educational books to be carried out under the direct control of the University.

JOHN FELL 1625–1686, *Bishop, Printer and Typefounder,* Clarendon Press, Oxford, 1967.

This is the catalogue of the exhibition held at Ely House, Dover Street, October 12–December 28, 1967, to celebrate the publication of *John Fell, The University Press and the 'Fell' Types* (see above). The exhibition comprised 113 items, including loan material from the Plantin-Moretus Museum, the Monotype Corporation, and other bodies, and distinguished collectors.

SOME ACCOUNT OF THE OXFORD UNIVERSITY PRESS 1468–1921, Clarendon Press, Oxford, 1922 (illustrated).

The history of the Press in Oxford and London, and the Wolvercote Paper Mill (see also under X. PAPER FOR BOOKWORK, p. 235) is traced, and descriptions of Oxford imprints and books, and of the Press abroad, with reproductions of old engravings.

JOHN PITTS (see under 'Chapbooks' in VII. CHILDREN'S BOOKS, p. 183 ff.)

THE RAMPANT LIONS PRESS (established 1949)

Will Carter, engraver, typographer and printer started the Rampant Lions in 1949, and now runs it with his son Sebastian. They now undertake book printing as well as jobbing, and have so far issued many fine editions, several published by the Chilmark Press, New York.

Will Carter, THE FIRST TEN, *Some Ground Covered at the Rampant Lions Press 1949–58*, Rampant Lions, 1959 (includes specimens).

James Moran, *Will Carter, Printer*, article in BOOK DESIGN AND PRODUCTION, vol.2, no. 2, 1959, pp. 28–37 (illustrated).

Alan Tarling, WILL CARTER, PRINTER, *An Illustrated Study*, Galahad Press, 1968.

This is not very good but contains some information not available elsewhere.

TALBOT BAINES REED (1842–93)

The son of Sir Charles Reed, proprietor of the Fann Street Letter Foundry which absorbed Fry's foundry was the author of *A History of the Old English Letter Foundries* (see p. 260) and equally famous in another sphere as the author of *The Fifth Form at St Dominic's* and other boys' stories.

Stanley Morison, TALBOT BAINES REED, *Author, Bibliographer, Typefounder*, privately printed C.U.P., 1960 (illustrated).

Illustrations include the signatures of members present at the inaugural meeting of the Bibliographical Society of which Talbot Baines Reed was the first honorary secretary.

SAMUEL RICHARDSON (1689–1761)

The author of *Pamela*, 1740, the first English novel, has a place as a printer.

William M. Sale, SAMUEL RICHARDSON MASTER PRINTER, Cornell University Press, New York, 1950 (bibliography).

This includes a list of books printed by Richardson, arranged alphabetically by author, and chronologically by short title, of the ornaments used by him, booksellers for whom he printed and a list of law patents.

OLIVER SIMON (see under 'Curwen Press' above)

CHARLES MANBY SMITH (1804–80)

Charles Manby Smith, THE WORKING MAN'S WAY IN THE WORLD, 1st published 1853, reprinted with a preface and notes by Ellic Howe, Printing Historical Society, 1967 (appendix of notes on the text, chronological checklist of Smith's known publications).

Reminiscences of a journeyman printer from 1818 to about 1840. He describes conditions in printing offices in Bristol, London and Paris, and life as a personal printer to a country gentleman who, desiring to print some volumes of his own sermons, hired a printer for a year to live in his house and set up his types there; he subsequently married the old gentleman's ward. In his preface, Ellic Howe says 'as an observer of the contemporary social scene, Smith was hardly inferior to Mayhew . . .'

Simon Nowell Smith, *Charles Manby Smith, His Family and Friends, His Fantasies and Fabrications*, article in JOURNAL OF THE PRINTING HISTORICAL SOCIETY, no. 7, 1971, pp. 1–28.

This exposes Manby Smith—not all he describes, though authentic enough, is written from personal experience as he would have us believe.

CHARLES EARL STANHOPE (see 'Oxford University Press' above)

STEPHENSON BLAKE (see under 'Caslon' above)

WILLIAM STRAHAN (1715–85), (now *Eyre & Spottiswoode*)

Richard Austen-Leigh, THE STORY OF A PRINTING HOUSE, *Being a Short Account of the Strahans and the Spottiswoodes*, Spottiswoode, 1911 (illustrated).

The author, grandson of Archbishop Chevenix-Trench gives the dates on which the various premises were first occupied, and the genealogy of the family (see also F. A. Mumby, *The House of Routledge*, p. 347 below).

J. A. Cochrane, DOCTOR JOHNSON'S PRINTER, *The Life of William Strahan,* Routledge & Kegan Paul, 1964.

Strahan's biographer describes trade practices of the day as well as discussing his printing of Johnson's *Dictionary* and Hume's works, and his position as King's Printer.

C. H. TIMPERLEY (1794–1846)

C. H. Timperley, A DICTIONARY OF PRINTERS AND PRINTING, *With the Progress of Literature Ancient and Modern,* 1839 (illustrated, bibliography).

'One of the most interesting works a printer can possess; while laying no claim to originality, it is full of anecdote and historical facts' (Bigmore and Wyman, see p. 248 above). It is, in effect, one of the numerous cribs from Nichols's *Bowyer* (see p. 270), but more easily accessible than the original.

C. H. Timperley, AN ENCYCLOPAEDIA OF LITERARY AND TYPOGRAPHICAL ANECDOTES . . . *Compiled and Condensed from Nichols's Literary Anecdotes and Numerous Other Authorities* . . . 1842.

'This is in reality the *Dictionary of Printers and Printing* with another title, the quire-stock or remainder having been bought by Mr H. G. Bohn' (Bigmore and Wyman, see p. 248 above).

JAN TSCHICHOLD (b. 1902)

This German typographer has influenced British book production at many points, most directly through his work at Penguin Books where he was engaged by Sir Allen Lane in 1947 'to overhaul the entire Penguin typography when war economy standards could be relaxed' (Ruari McLean, see below).

Jan Tschichold, ASYMMETRIC TYPOGRAPHY, translated with a foreword by Ruari McLean, Faber & Faber, 1967 (illustrated, bibliography of Tschichold books in print).

In its day this was the most revolutionary work on book design. W. E. Trevett, in his introduction calls Tschichold 'the Rosetta stone of our field. Without his experiments in both symmetric and asymmetric design we would all be back, fiddling around with the Private Press Movement and artistic rule bending'.

Ruari McLean who worked under Tschichold as a young designer at Penguin, is therefore peculiarly fitted to translate and edit this key work.

Ruari McLean's article on Tschichold in *Penrose Annual,* 1970, shows how Tschichold has gone beyond asymmetric typography in his own later designs, and analyses his 'fundamental contribution to typography in the twentieth century'.

T. FISHER UNWIN (established 1826) (see under XIII. PUBLISHING, pp. 333 f., for the connection with *Allen & Unwin*).

UNWINS, A CENTURY OF PROGRESS, *Being a Record of the Rise and Present Position of the Gresham Press, 1826–1926*, Unwins, 1926 (illustrated).

JAN VAN KRIMPEN (see above, p. 280)

BEATRICE WARDE (NEÉ LAMBERTON BECKER) ('Paul Beaujon') (1900–69)

'Paul Beaujon', *The Garamond Types, Sixteenth and Seventeenth Century Sources Considered*, article in FLEURON, no. 5, 1926.

This article on the real source of the so-called Garamond types first brought 'Paul Beaujon' acclaim as a typographer, scholar and printing historian.

John Dreyfus, *Beatrice Warde. The First Lady of Typography*, article in PENROSE ANNUAL, 1970.

'I am a Communicator', *A Selection of Writings and Talks by Beatrice Warde/ Paul Beaujon*, MONOTYPE RECORDER, vol. 44, no. 1, Autumn, 1970 (illustrated, bibliography of Mrs Warde's published work).

This issue of the *Recorder*, devoted to its former editor, gives extracts, autobiographical, critical and educational from her most important writing.

Beatrice Warde, THE CRYSTAL GOBLET, *16 Essays on Typography Selected and Edited by Henry Jacob*, Sylvan Press, 1955 (select bibliography of 'Paul Beaujon's' Writings).

This contains much of Beatrice Warde's most important writing, first published in *Penrose Annual*, the *Monotype Recorder*, and elsewhere. It includes: 'The Crystal Goblet, or Printing should be Invisible', an address before the British Typographer's Guild at St Bride's Institute 1932; 'Artists and Craftsmen'; Section 1 appeared as 'Typographic Transformations', in a special number of the *Monotype Recorder*, Summer, 1952; Section 2 appeared as 'The Pencil Draws a Vicious Circle', *Penrose Annual*,

1953; 'Improving the Compulsory Book', *Penrose Annual*, 1950; 'Thirty-Two Outstanding Dates in the History of Printing', a paper read at the Guildford School of Arts and Crafts, 1947. These articles are here arranged under the subject headings of *An Approach to Typography*, *Typography as a Vocation* and *Tradition and Progress*.

BERTHOLD WOLPE (b. 1906)

Charles Mozley, WOLPERIANA, Merrion Press, 1960 (frontispiece portrait taken outside Fabers).

A kindly caricature of one graphic artist by another.

WYNKYN DE WORDE (*c.* 1477–1534)

Wynkyn de Worde set up his press in Fleet Street after the death of his master, Caxton, and was the first English printer to use roman type.

James Moran, WYNKYN DE WORDE, *Father of Fleet Street*, Wynkyn de Worde Society, 1960 (illustrated, bibliography).

H. R. Plomer, WYNKYN DE WORDE AND HIS CONTEMPORARIES, *From the Death of Caxton to 1535, a Chapter in English Printing*, Grafton, 1925 (illustrated).

This includes such contemporaries as Richard Pynson, Julian Notary, J. & W. Rastell and there are chapters on provincial and Scottish presses.

YELF (established 1816)

A. N. Daish, PRINTERS' PRIDE, *The House of Yelf at Newport, Isle of Wight, 1916–1866*, Yelf, Newport, 1967 (illustrated, bibliography).

HERMANN ZAPF (b. 1918)

This outstanding modern typographer is more known on the continent and in the United States than in this country.

Hermann Zapf, ABOUT ALPHABETS: *Some Marginal Notes on Type Design*, Typophiles, New York, 1960 (illustrated).

This is a typographical autobiography.

Hermann Zapf and Jack Werner Stauffacher, HUNT ROMAN: *The Birth of a Type*, Pittsburgh Bibliophiles, Pittsburgh, Pa., 1965 (annotated illustrations).

George N. M. Lawrence's descriptive foreword is enforced by illustrations which also show how a design is made and a punch cut.

11. Studies of Regional Printing

Most of the important studies of individual printers outside London are to be found in the Proceedings of the various Bibliographical Societies and in the *Journal of the Printing Historical Society*. The following are separately published studies of printing in the Midlands and North.

BIRMINGHAM (for individual studies of Baskerville and Caslon see above, pp. 268 f. and 271 f.)

Joseph Hill, THE BOOK MAKERS OF OLD BIRMINGHAM; *Authors, Printers and Book Sellers*, Shakespeare Press for Cornish Brothers, Birmingham, 1907 (illustrated).

The author opens with an apology for his study: 'Should justification for the following pages be needed, it may be found in the fact that in past times the interest in the book trade centred in the productions of the London Press. . . . This was of course the direct and natural result of the great monopolies and privileges vested in the London Stationers' Company.

But whilst the general interest in books was thus drawn to the London press, every provincial town had its unwritten literary history in its books, its pamphlets and its newspapers.'

CHESTER

D. Nuttall, A HISTORY OF PRINTING IN CHESTER FROM 1688 TO 1965, privately printed, Chester, 1969.

CUMBERLAND

K. Smith, LIST OF BOOKSELLERS, BOOKBINDERS, PUBLISHERS, PAPER MANUFACTURERS, ENGRAVERS, ETC. *Operating in Cumberland up to the Year 1861*, Carlisle Public Libraries, 1966.

NEWCASTLE

Newcastle Central Reference Library, HISTORY OF THE BOOK TRADE IN THE NORTH EAST, Newcastle, 1966.

SHEFFIELD

E. C. Gilberthorpe, BOOK PRINTING AT SHEFFIELD IN THE EIGHTEENTH CENTURY, Sheffield Public Libraries, 1967.

WALES

Ifano Jones, A HISTORY OF PRINTING AND PRINTERS IN WALES TO 1810, *And of Successive and Related Printers to 1923; Also a History of Printing and Printers in Monmouthshire to 1923,* Lewis, Cardiff, 1925 (bibliography).

WARWICKSHIRE

Paul Morgan, editor, WARWICKSHIRE PRINTERS' NOTICES 1799–1866, Clarendon Press for the Dugdale Society, Oxford, 1970 (illustrated).

An appendix gives a list of unregistered printers.

12. Practical Printing
(See also under IV. BOOK DESIGN, pp. 112 ff. and V. BOOK ILLUSTRATION, pp. 142 ff.)

I select the following works explaining the simpler techniques, processes and printing office procedures:

GENERAL WORKS

William Atkins, general editor, THE ART AND PRACTICE OF PRINTING, 6 vols., Pitman, 1932–33, originally issued in 24 monthly parts (illustrated).

The series was designed to explain all the processes of the day, and describe the running of a print shop. It has been superseded by Victor Strauss's much more detailed modern work (see p. 294 below).

Vol. 1: **A. G. Sayers and Joseph Stuart,** THE COMPOSING DEPARTMENT.

The author describes the compositor's work, how type is made, the point system and gives rules for setting.

Vol. 2: LETTERPRESS BOOKBINDING (see under II. BOOKBINDING, p. 51).

Vol. 3: LITHOGRAPHY: (see below, p. 298).

Vol. 4: PHOTO-ENGRAVING: (see below, p. 295).

Vol. 5: BOOKBINDING AND RULING (see under II. BOOKBINDING, p. 51).

Vol. 6: PRINTING OFFICE MANAGEMENT INCLUDING COSTING AND ESTIMATING.

Experts in their field describe the work of the order clerks, paper and the paper warehouse, printers' accountancy, salesmanship and so forth.

R. F. Brand, PRINTING TECHNIQUES, Printing and Allied Trades Association of South Australia, 1956 (illustrated, glossary, historical index).

This handbook is based on a series of lectures given to Australian students of printing administration with no printing training who needed help in keeping abreast of modern production methods. A brief history of printing is followed by a description of letterpress, lithographic and intaglio processes, binding, papermaking and workshop efficiency.

John Brinkley, DESIGN FOR PRINT, *A Handbook of Design and Reproduction Processes*, Sylvan Press, 1949 (illustrated, bibliography, glossary).

The first part describes the work of an advertising agency, the designer and his tools. The second is more relevant to our purpose in that it describes the various printing processes, with an emphasis on letterpress.

British Federation of Master Printers, PRINTING OFFICE PROCEDURE, *A Special Course for Order Clerks and Others Employed in Printing Offices*, 6 vols., B.F.M.P., 1969 (illustrated, classified bibliography in vol. 1).

Vol. 1 describes the structure of the printing industry and the organisation of a printing establishment, with specimen forms used in the office and works; the order clerks' work is outlined, the terms used to describe different printed items listed and explained, and legal considerations reviewed.
Vol. 2 is devoted to advice on copy preparations and considerations of design and format.
Vol. 3 concerns production control and methods of working, such as how paper is printed, deciding on the paper to be used, and working to standard specifications.
Vol. 4 describes composition, blockmaking, binding, account book rulings.
Vol. 5 gives the principles guiding the choice of printing process, with clear notes on the visual characteristics of the main processes, preparation of copy for offset and a description of such finishing processes as varnishing, lacquering and lamination.
Vol. 6 gives questions based on the first five books, on how to handle complaints, gives details of postal regulations and other useful information.

This is a most excellent series of handbooks.

William Clowes, A GUIDE TO PRINTING, *An Introduction to Print Buyers,* William Heinemann, 1963 (illustrated, bibliography, glossary).

This is intended as an introductory handbook to the various printing processes and to the structure of the industry, designed for those who have dealings with printers but lack expert knowledge.

Alan Delgado, PRINTING (Modern Industries Series), Wheaton, Exeter, 1969 (illustrated, glossary).

This is comparable to Clowes's *Guide* (see above).

Dorothy Harrop, MODERN BOOK PRODUCTION, Clive Bingley, 1968 (illustrated, bibliography).

This useful introduction to the major modern processes is intended for the use of librarians and library students, and technicalities and trade jargon are kept to a minimum.

Ernest A. B. Hutchings, A SURVEY OF PRINTING PROCESSES, William Heinemann, 1970 (illustrated, bibliography).

This survey of modern developments in printing and binding is arranged in the categories demanded in examinations on general printing knowledge, but is also a practical working guide for non-specialists.

F. Pateman and L. C. Young, PRINTING SCIENCE, Pitman, 1st edition, 1963, 2nd edition, 1969.

A straightforward account, intelligible to the layman, of the techniques of printing.

Victor Strauss, THE PRINTING INDUSTRY, *An Introduction to Its Many Branches, Processes and Products,* Printing Industries of America Inc., and Bowker, New York and London, 1967 (illustrated, bibliography).

Though designed for the American trade, this compendium is equally useful to expert or amateur on this side of the Atlantic. Arranged in encyclopaedia form, there are brief articles on all the printing processes and methods, on composition, colour printing, photography, machines, presswork, paper, printing inks, binding, and copy preparation.

Call Swann, THE TECHNIQUES OF TYPOGRAPHY, Lund Humphries, 1969 (illustrated, foreword by Herbert Spencer).

A concise essay on modern typographical methods precedes an illustrated guide to printing processes, including computer typesetting and photo-setting.

John C. Tarr, PRINTING TODAY, O.U.P., 1st edition, 1944, revised edition, 1958 (illustrated, glossary, bibliography, introduction by Sir Francis Meynell, note on modern typography by Bertram Evans).

This survey of printing history, the development of type design, type casting, modern printing processes, machining, paper, ink and design, was written for intending printers and designers.

John C. Tarr, PRINTING, Muller, 1960 (illustrated, glossary).

More elementary and covering a wider field than the preceding work (it includes sections on bookbinding machinery and machines for illustration processes), this handbook is part of a series on the mechanical age.

Theodore Low de Vinne, THE PRACTICE OF TYPOGRAPHY, 4 vols., Century Co., New York, 1899–1904 (see pp. 261, 267 and 299).

Wynkyn de Worde Society, PRINT, *A Handbook for Entrants to the Printing Industry and Its Services*, privately printed, Wynkyn de Worde Society, trade edition, Ernest Benn, 1966 (bibliography, type specimens).

Based on original contributions by members of the society, the transition of printing from a craft to a modern engineering industry is described, as are the various processes and the structure of the industry. Beatrice Warde's *Thirty-two Outstanding Dates in Printing History* is used as an appendix, and there is information on the signing of indentures.

PROCESSES: INTAGLIO

T. S. Barber, PHOTO-ENGRAVING, ELECTROTYPING AND STEREO-TYPING, Pitman, vol. 4 of *The Art and Practice of Printing* (see p. 292) (illustrated).

Though now largely superseded, this is still a simple introduction for the uninitiated to the principles of photography and photographic printing processes.

S. W. Hayter, NEW WAYS FOR GRAVURE, 1st edition, Routledge & Kegan Paul, 1949, 2nd edition revised, O.U.P., 1966 (extensively illustrated, bibliography by Bernard Karpel, preface by Herbert Read).

This surveys the history and techniques of etching, and colour engraving from the fifteenth century to the present day with a final chapter on the future of gravure. There is, unfortunately, no index.

Otto M. Lilien, EARLY HISTORY OF INDUSTRIAL GRAVURE PRINTING TO 1900, *A Paper Read to the Eighth International Congress for the History of Science Held in Florence, September 1956,* Berkshire College of Art, Reading, 1963.

Otto M. Lilien, THE DAILY TELEGRAPH MAGAZINE GUIDE TO GRAVURE PRINTING, Daily Telegraph, 1968 (illustrated).

The gravure process is described and illustrated, and the technical differences between gravure, letterpress and offset explained. 'It must surely become the work which will impress more informed laymen than any of the advanced technical books available in the gravure field' (*British Printer*).

PROCESSES: LETTERPRESS

Peter Gibson, MODERN TRENDS IN LETTERPRESS PRINTING (Facts of Print Series), Studio Vista, 1966 (illustrated).

'The number of innovations is so extensive that no one printer is likely to be able to keep abreast of them, let alone acquire them for his own use. . . . The Monotype, Linotype and Ludlow machines set in hot metal, while the new machines set in no type at all. They merely take a picture of the letters and words to be printed on film or photographic paper.'

The author describes the wide variety of plates now available and tries to indicate where the letterpress industry will go in the years ahead.

Charles Holtzapffel, PRINTING APPARATUS *For the Use of Amateurs,* 1st edition, 1839, 3rd edition enlarged, 1846, facsimile reprint edited by James Mosley and David Chambers, Private Libraries Association, 1971 (illustrated).

This work has a valuable scholarly and diverting introduction and notes.

Lucien Alphonse Legros and John Cameron Grant, TYPOGRAPHICAL PRINTING SURFACES, *The Technology and Mechanism of Their Production,* Longmans, Green, 1916 (illustrated, glossary of technical terms, bibliography).

This monumental work on type design, punch-cutting and printing machinery, describes the operation and features of almost all the casting, composing, justifying, and distributing machines of the day, with a few final chapters on intaglio and planographic methods, then in their infancy as industrial processes for printing books. Appendixes include a list of British and American patents.

John Ryder, PRINTING FOR PLEASURE, *A Practical Guide for Amateurs,* Phoenix, 1955 (illustrated, glossary, foreword by Sir Francis Meynell).

'*Printing for Pleasure* . . . justifies its name . . . but physically also it is practical as you may judge from the early consideration that it gives to the question, "how much space shall I need?". . . . Materials, equipment, cost are examined. History is invoked, experiment is demonstrated' (Sir Francis Meynell). It is an unpretentious, yet admirable, work.

Herbert Simon, INTRODUCTION TO PRINTING, *The Craft of Letterpress,* Faber & Faber, 1968 (illustrated, bibliography, glossary, list of suppliers' names and addresses).

Although this book is concerned with jobbing rather than with book printing, it cannot be omitted as it explains in simple terms, the process of letterpress printing, proof reading, design and choice of paper.

'Herbert Simon has done for handsetting and machining much the same as Oliver Simon did for typography in his famous *Introduction to Typography*' (*British Printer*).

Herbert Simon and Harry Carter, PRINTING EXPLAINED, *An Elementary Practical Handbook for Schools and Amateurs,* Dryad, Leicester, 1931 (illustrated, bibliography, glossary, specimen settings, foreword by Sir Francis Meynell).

This small classic is praised by Sir Francis as being, 'a book about a process – not a product'.

John Southward, PRACTICAL PRINTING, Printers Register Office, 1st edition, 1882, last edition, 1911.

Has a good deal on hand printing that *Modern Printing* (see below) lacks.

John Southward, MODERN PRINTING, *The Practice and Principles of Typography and the Auxiliary Arts,* 2 vols., 1st edition, de Monfort Press, Leicester, 1900; 7th edition, Odhams, edited through many editions by Harry Whetton, and fully revised by specialist authors, 1965 (illustrated).

This compendium of (mainly letterpress) printing outlines the structural requirements of a printing office, equipment, the processes of printing, describes the variety of machines in use and the manufacture of paper and humidity control. This long standard work has been kept up to date by constant revision.

PROCESSES: PLANOGRAPHIC (see also under V. BOOK ILLUSTRATION, pp. 143 ff for further works on *Lithography*, long thought of as almost exclusively an illustration process)

W. Turner Berry and M. C. Thomson, COLLOTYPE PRINTING PROCESSES, *A Special Subject List,* Library Association, 1958.

Francis Carr, A GUIDE TO SCREEN PROCESS PRINTING, (Facts of Print Series), Studio Vista, 1961 (illustrated, bibliography, conversion tables, list of suppliers and institutions teaching screen printing).

An introductory history of stencilling and screen printing is followed by descriptions of equipment and processes, with the manufacturer's instructions where appropriate.

Eric Chambers, PHOTOLITHO-OFFSET, (Handbooks to Printing), Ernest Benn, 1967 (illustrated, bibliography, glossary).

The basic process is described with instructions on preparation of copy for reproduction and platemaking methods. Appendixes cover chromo-lithography, poster work, autolithography.

Henry Cliffe, LITHOGRAPHY, Studio Handbook, 1965 (illustrated, brief bibliography, list of suppliers).

This describes, in detail, the making of a lithograph with advice on the care of prints. An appendix defines an original print.

Helmut and Alison Gernsheim, THE HISTORY OF PHOTOGRAPHY, Thames & Hudson, 1st edition, 1955, 2nd edition, revised, 1969 (extensively illustrated, bibliography).

Not all is relevant, but there are chapters on photography and the printed page, on photo-engraving, photolithography, collotype and other planographic processes.

L. E. Lawson, OFFSET LITHOGRAPHY, (Facts of Print Series), Studio Vista, 1963 (illustrated).

This describes, step by step, in non-technical terms, the modern process that has developed from lithography, and reviews recent equipment and the application of 'small' offset which has developed yet further since 1963.

N. Montague, LITHOGRAPHY, Pitman, vol. 3 of *The Art and Practice of Printing* (see p. 292).

Now only of historic interest.

Peter Weaver, THE TECHNIQUE OF LITHOGRAPHY, Batsford, 1964 (illustrated, bibliography, glossary, list of suppliers, private galleries specialising in the sale of prints in England and the U.S.A.).

This describes techniques old and new, and outlines some of the aspects of the law affecting the lithographer.

13. Proof Correction and Printing Style
(See also under 1. AUTHORSHIP, pp. 12 f.)

The printing office concerns itself with house style and with mistakes of literals, leaving textual changes to the author and the publisher's editor. I omit guides to house style issued by particular printers and publishers and select the following general official works:

British Standard 1219, RECOMMENDATIONS FOR PROOF CORRECTION AND COPY PREPARATION, B.S.I., 1958.

British Standard 1749, ALPHABETICAL ARRANGEMENT, B.S.I., 1951.

CAMBRIDGE AUTHORS' AND PRINTERS' GUIDES (see under 1. AUTHORSHIP, p. 13).

T. W. Chaundy, P. R. Barrett and Charles Batey, THE PRINTING OF MATHEMATICS, *Aids for Authors and Editors, and Rules for Compositors and Readers at the University Press*, Clarendon Press, Oxford, 1954 (illustrated).

T. Howard Collins, AUTHORS' AND PRINTERS' DICTIONARY, *A Guide for Authors, Editors, Printers, Correctors of the Press, Compositors and Typists*, Clarendon Press, Oxford, 1st edition, 1905, 10th edition revised, 1956.

Theodore Low de Vinne, CORRECT COMPOSITION, *A Treatise on Spelling, Abbreviations, the Compounding and Division of Words, the Proper Use of Figures and Numerals, Italic and Capital Letters, Notes, etc, with Observations on Punctuation and Proof Reading*, New York, 1901 (vol. 2 of *The Practice of Typography*, 4 vols., see pp. 261, 267 and 295).

James Garrett, PRINTING STYLE *For Authors, Compositors and Readers*, George Allen & Unwin, 1960.

This book is based on a series of articles on matters affecting the work of the Reader, contributed to the *British and Colonial Printer* (now *Printing*

World). It is therefore of more use to periodical than to book printers, with its chapters on 'NU Spelling', slang and the form of titles.

Horace Hart, RULES FOR COMPOSITORS AND READERS AT THE UNIVERSITY PRESS, Clarendon Press, Oxford, 1st edition, 1903, 37th edition revised, 1967.

This, besides being a guide to the house style of the Oxford University Press, serves as every proof corrector's authoritative reference.

Herbert Rees, RULES OF PRINTED ENGLISH, Darton Longman & Todd, 1970 (bibliography, proof correction marks).

This gives advice on where to find the answer to some points, and gives rules for others. It is less reliable but also less daunting than Hart's *Rules* (see above) being much more selective.

14. Periodicals and Journals Relating to Printing

I select the following trade periodicals and historic or current journals or annuals devoted to printing history and typography. Most are British, but I include a few scholarly American journals.

ALPHABET: *International Annual of Letter Forms*, edited by **R. S. Hutchings** and published by James Moran for the Kynoch Press, 1963, all published.

ALPHABET AND IMAGE, edited by **Robert Harling,** Shenval Press, 8 nos., monthly, 1946–48 (succeeded by *Typography*, see below).

Contributors included Stanley Morison, Ruari McLean, Sir Francis Meynell and Percy Muir.

THE BLACK ART, edited and published by **James Moran,** 1962–64, quarterly, 3 vols., all published.

This may be considered the precursor of the *Journal of the Printing Historical Society* which Mr Moran founded in 1964 and of *The Printing Art*, 1973 (see below).

BOOK DESIGN AND PRODUCTION, edited by **James Moran,** various publishers, quarterly, 1958–64.

THE BRITISH PRINTER, McLean-Hunter, now edited by **Roy Brewer,** monthly, 1888–   .

This contains articles on current developments and labour relations, techniques of interest to the printing industry, as well as book reviews and articles of historic interest.

THE FLEURON, *A Journal of Typography*, 3 nos. edited by **Oliver Simon;** 4 nos. edited by **Stanley Morison**, annual, 7 issues, 1923–30.

Many of the key articles by Stanley Morison, 'Paul Beaujon' and Sir Francis Meynell first appeared in this historic journal.

GRAPHIS, *International Journal for Graphic and Applied Art*, edited by **Walter Herdeg**, fortnightly, 1944–   .

GRAPHIS ANNUAL (see under IV. BOOK DESIGN, p. 117).

GUTENBERG JAHRBUCH, edited by **Aloys Ruppel,** annual, 1957–   .

Contributions on aspects of historical bibliography and book production are in English, German, French, Italian and Spanish.

IMAGE, edited by **Robert Harling**, 8 nos., 1949–52 (see *Alphabet and Image* above).

THE IMPRINT, edited by **Gerard Meynell, Ernest Jackson, J. H. Mason and Edward Johnston,** 9 nos., 1913.

The aim was to raise the standard of printing, and inspiration was drawn from the Private Press Movement, with a new typeface, *Imprint*, designed for the journal, which is still popular today.

JOURNAL OF THE PRINTING HISTORICAL SOCIETY, edited by **James Mosley,** annual 1964–   (see under 'Professional Associations', p. 304 below).

LITHOPRINTER, Haymarket Press, monthly, 1958–   .

MONOTYPE RECORDER, *Journal of the Monotype Corporation* (see p. 281 above), intermittent since 1902.

MOTIF, *A Journal of the Visual Arts*, edited by **Ruari McLean,** Shenval Press, 13 nos., 1958–67.

This contained articles, reviews and checklists by P. M. Handover, James Mosley, Hans Schmoller, Hermann Zapf and others.

P.A.G.A. (PRINTING AND GRAPHIC ARTS), edited by **Ray Nash and Roderick D. Stinehour,** Stinehour Press, Vermont, quarterly, 1953–65.

Aspects of typography and historical bibliography are discussed, and books on the subjects reviewed by scholars and typographers on both sides of the Atlantic, who include Fredson Bowers, Harry Carter, E. P. Goldschmidt and Merald Wrolstad.

PAPER AND PRINT, quarterly, 1928–66.

P.A.T.R.A. (see P.I.R.A. below).

PENROSE ANNUAL, *A Review of the Graphic Arts,* edited since 1963 by **Herbert Spencer,** Lund Humphries, 1895– .

This important review was founded by William Gamble as *The Process Work Year Book,* and edited by him.

P.I.R.A. PRINTING ABSTRACTS, monthly, 1945–   .

Summarises articles from the 350 journals in the P.I.R.A. library.

PRINT, *A Quarterly Journal of the Graphic Arts,* William Rudge, Newhaven, Conn., quarterly, 1941– .

Articles by leading American authorities.

PRINT (Formerly *Graphical Journal*) edited by **J. M. Bonfield,** National Graphical Association, monthly 1964– .

PRINT IN BRITAIN, edited by **Andrew Bluhm,** monthly, 1953–68.

PRINTING ABSTRACTS (see P.I.R.A. PRINTING ABSTRACTS above).

THE PRINTING ART, edited by **James Moran,** Stellar Press, quarterly, 1973–   .

PRINTING TRADES JOURNAL AND SALE AND WANTS ADVERTISER, now edited by **Derek Muggleton,** Benn Bros., monthly, 1887–   .

PRINTING WORLD, now edited by **F. Colley,** weekly, 1878–   (formerly *The British and Colonial Printer*).

THE PRIVATE LIBRARY (see pp. 104, 106 etc.).

SIGNATURE: *A Quadrimestrial of Typography and the Graphic Arts*, edited by **Oliver Simon,** Curwen Press, 1st series, 1935–40, 15 nos., new series, 1946–54, 18 nos.

Leading typographers, graphic artists and printing historians contributed to this journal, which was, in itself, a fine example of design and production.

SMALL PRINTER, British Printing Society, monthly 1965–   (see 'British Printing Society, p. 305).

TYPOGRAPHICA, *A Review of Typography and the Graphic Arts,* edited by **Herbert Spencer,** Lund Humphries, 1st series, 1949–59, 19 nos., new series, 1960–68, 16 nos.

An important series to which leading authorities contributed.

TYPOGRAPHY, edited by **Robert Harling,** Shenval Press, 8 nos., 1936–39 (succeeded by *Alphabet and Image,* see above).

VISIBLE LANGUAGE (originally JOURNAL OF TYPOGRAPHIC RESEARCH, then JOURNAL OF LETTERFORM RESEARCH) edited by **Merald E. Wrolstad,** Cleveland Museum of Art, Cleveland, Ohio, quarterly, 1966–   (summaries in French and German).

15. Directories and Trade Reference Works
(See also 'Proof Correction and Printing Style', p. 299 f., above.)

British Federation of Master Printers, GUIDE TO BOOK PRODUCTION PRACTICE, B.F.M.P., 1st edition, 1955, revised edition, 1964 (bibliography of Federation publications).

A guide to what seemed to be the most general procedure in printing houses, standard conditions of the printing industry and suggestions for economies.

Rudolf Hostettler, TECHNICAL TERMS OF THE PRINTING INDUSTRY, Hostettler, St Gallen, and Redman, London, 1st edition, 1949, 3rd edition, revised, 1959.

An illustrated dictionary in English, French, German, Italian and Dutch of the fundamentals of type design, British and continental sizes, composing materials, case layouts, proof marking, blocks and engraving is followed by a glossary of printing and allied trade terms in English, Dutch and the other three languages. Beatrice Warde called it 'definitely a must book for the reference shelf of every printer and user of print'.

THE MASTER PRINTER'S ANNUAL, B.F.M.P., 1920– .

This contains much information not easily found elsewhere – a directory of trade unions, a list of agreements including a model indenture form, education and training, a directory of kindred associations, printers' charities, law for printers, and who's who in the printing trade.

PRINTING AND ALLIED TRADES DIRECTORY, annual since 1963, Ernest Benn.

This includes an alphabetical and geographical index to printers in the United Kingdom, a guide to printers' specialities, agents and distributors for overseas printing machinery, etc., trade names and trade marks of printers' suppliers, trade organisations and schools of printing and the graphic arts.

F. J. M. Vijnekus, DICTIONARY OF THE PRINTING AND ALLIED INDUSTRIES, in 4 Languages, English, French, German, Dutch, Elsevier, Amsterdam, 1967.

No technical dictionary is ever entirely satisfactory, but this is a very useful one.

16. Professional Associations and Printing Societies
(See also under 'Histories of Printing Unions and Associations', pp. 306 ff. below.)

BRITISH FEDERATION OF MASTER PRINTERS (founded 1900)

This is an association of employers whose members, at present numbering around 4,000, must be owners of a printing plant. It publishes THE MASTER PRINTER'S ANNUAL (see above), A MEMBERS' CIRCULAR and also books on costing, estimating, method study and other subjects of interest to members. Activities include labour negotiations and management, legal, costing and technical services to employers.

BRITISH PRINTING SOCIETY (founded 1944)

The last honorary Vice-President was Mrs Beatrice Warde. The Society was founded to bring together small printers of every description to exchange views and experiences and foster the spirit of friendship and printing craftsmanship. It is non-profit making and open to anyone, professional or amateur who is interested in printing. It publishes a monthly, the SMALL PRINTER (see p. 303 above).

INSTITUTE OF PRINTING (founded 1961)

This independent professional body was created for those directly engaged in the development of printing, bookbinding and associated techniques. It aims to promote the advancement of the science and art of printing and bookbinding. It offers scholarships, grants and prizes and encourages the foundation of faculties of printing technology and university chairs.

P.I.R.A. – PRINTING INDUSTRY RESEARCH ASSOCIATION (founded as P.A.T.R.A., [Packaging and Allied Trades Research Association] 1930)

The aims of the organisation are to research into problems submitted by members. It circulates abstracts of technical information selected from some 350 journals from all over the world. The library includes an information service which prepares monthly PRINTING ABSTRACTS (see under 'Periodicals and Journals relating to Printing', p. 302 above).

PRINTING AND KINDRED TRADES FEDERATION (founded 1901)

This is a federation of printing unions whose membership of more than 360,000 comprises printing employees (the British Federation of Master Printers is the employers' association). The aims of the Printing and Kindred Trades Federation are to co-ordinate the activities of the various printing unions involved and to uphold their rights and privileges.

PRINTING HISTORICAL SOCIETY (founded 1964)

This society aims to encourage the study of the history of printing, the preservation of printing machinery, records, and equipment of historical value. It holds winter meetings and issues an annual journal. Its other publications so far include an edited reprint by James Mosley of Horace Hart, CHARLES EARL STANHOPE AND THE OXFORD UNIVERSITY PRESS; Charles Manby Smith, THE WORKING MAN'S WAY IN THE WORLD, edited by Ellic Howe; Vincent Figgins, TYPE SPECIMENS 1801 AND 1815, edited by Berthold Wolpe. A DICTIONARY OF LONDON PRINTERS 1800–1840 is in process of preparation.

THE WYNKYN DE WORDE SOCIETY (founded 1957)

This is a group of people associated with printing who meet socially to exchange and disseminate information on printing and allied subjects. Its publications include James Moran, WYNKYN DE WORDE, FATHER OF FLEET STREET, 1960, and PRINT, A HANDBOOK FOR ENTRANTS TO THE PRINTING INDUSTRY, 1966.

17. Histories of Printing Unions and Associations (alphabetical under associations)

(See also under 'Professional Associations and Printing Societies', p. 304 above.)

Printing was organised into unions of workmen much earlier than other crafts or trades. Whether it was that the printer, because he could read, had an ascendancy over other craftsmen, the fact is that printing associations were powerful two centuries ago, and have kept their power, as well as many of their archaic rituals and jargon, ever since.

A number of unions have amalgamated since the publications of the histories listed below.

THE ASSOCIATION OF CORRECTORS OF THE PRESS (founded 1855)

T. N. Shane, PASSED FOR PRESS, *A Centenary History of the Association of Correctors of the Press*, A.C.P., 1955 (illustrated).

BRITISH FEDERATION OF MASTER PRINTERS (founded 1900)

Ellic Howe, THE BRITISH FEDERATION OF MASTER PRINTERS 1900–1950, C.U.P. for the B.F.M.P., 1950.

This concentrates on the later history of the Federation.

Mary Sessions, THE FEDERATION OF MASTER PRINTERS: *How it Began Together with a History of Some of the Associations and Groups of Master Printers Who Helped to Form and Build up the Federations*, William Sessions, 1950 (sources at the beginning of each chapter).

Much attention is given to local branch associations.

THE LONDON SOCIETY OF COMPOSITORS (re-established 1848)

Ellic Howe and Harold E. Waite, THE LONDON SOCIETY OF COMPOSITORS, *A Centenary History*, Cassell, 1948 (foreword by Sir Francis Meynell).

The authors describe aspects of the London printing trade 1476–1810, the precursors of the London Society 1801–48, as well as the story of the Society's first century which is also a history of technical developments and working conditions.

THE NATIONAL UNION OF PRINTING BOOKBINDING AND PAPER WORKERS (amalgamated 1921)

Clement J. Bundock, THE STORY OF THE NATIONAL UNION OF PRINTING BOOKBINDING AND PAPER WORKERS, O.U.P., 1959 (illustrated).

A family tree makes for easier assimilation of the various permutations and combinations of the eleven societies that finally amalgamated to form the National Union, whose story is told from their initiation in the nineteenth century.

NATSOPA (founded 1889)

James Moran, NATSOPA, *Seventy-Five Years, The National Society of Operative Printers and Assistants 1889-1964*, William Heinemann, 1964 (illustrated).

The author throws light on the conflicts of the various printing unions as well as describing the gradual amelioration of working conditions and wages.

THE PRINTERS' PENSION CORPORATION (founded 1827)

Geoffrey Bensusan, THE BENEVOLENT YEARS, *Some Notes on the Printers' Pension and Its Background in the Trade*, Printers Pension Corporation, 1955 (illustrated).

This confines itself chiefly to the Society's activities in the Victorian period.

THE SCOTTISH TYPOGRAPHICAL ASSOCIATION (founded 1853)

S. C. Gillespie, A HUNDRED YEARS OF PROGRESS, *The Record of the Scottish Typographical Association 1853-1952*, Glasgow, 1953.

THE TYPOGRAPHICAL ASSOCIATION (founded 1849)

A. E. Musson, THE TYPOGRAPHICAL ASSOCIATION, *Origins and History up to 1949*, O.U.P., 1954.

The author traces the progress of trade unions in the provincial printing industry before the founding of the Association in 1849, the growth and policy of the Typographical Association as a union of provincial printers, its relations with employers, wages and hours, apprentices, and working conditions generally.

18. Collections of Printed Material and Equipment and Permanent Exhibitions

Derek Nuttall describes a number of printing collections in England and on the Continent in a series of five articles in *Atpas Bulletin*, 1964–66. These purport to form a comprehensive survey of all the major and minor collections, but, in fact, they do not. Some of those collections reviewed by Derek Nuttall are listed below, together with others excluded from his survey.

BODLEIAN LIBRARY, OXFORD

The John Johnson Collection of Printed Ephemera was formed by the late Printer to the University between the 1930s and 1950s, and consisted of many thousands of items from 1500–1939. It was housed in the Clarendon Press until 1968, when it was moved to the Bodleian Library, where additional material is being acquired. It was known also as the Constance Meade Collection in honour of the benefactrice who paid for much of the equipment at the Clarendon.

Bodleian Library, THE JOHN JOHNSON COLLECTION, *The Catalogue of an Exhibition*, Bodleian Library, 1971 (illustrated).

An introduction by Michael Turner is an expanded version of the lecture given to the Printing Historical Society in November 1969. 259 exhibits are annotated and there is a full index.

BRITISH MUSEUM, LONDON

The King's Library of the British Museum has a permanent display of early printed books which includes a copy of the 36-line and 42-line bibles, early Caxtons and other monuments of the incunable period, nowhere else assembled in one collection, and here permanently on view.

CAMBRIDGE UNIVERSITY PRESS

The Printing House of the Cambridge University Press, Fitzwilliam Road, Cambridge, has a unique collection of Baskerville punches and printed material, including the Golden Types. This is not a formal museum, and viewing is by appointment only.

THE CASTLE MUSEUM, YORK

The museum contains a section showing reconstructions of workshops of early crafts and trades, among which is an early nineteenth-century printing office.

PLANTIN-MORETUS MUSEUM, ANTWERP

Jan Moretus succeeded to the press of Christopher Plantin in 1589, and his press remained with the Moretus family until 1876 when the City of Antwerp acquired it for use as a museum. Here we see, perfectly preserved, a printing office as it would have been in the time of Shakespeare; it must, however, be borne in mind that Plantin's press, being that of a continental printer of great prestige in his own day, is far grander than any English printing office of the period would have been.

This is one among several important collections of printing on the continent, which include the Museo Bodoniano at Parma, and the Musée d'Imprimerie at Lyons.

THE PRINTER'S DEVIL, FETTER LANE, LONDON

This is a public house, not a formal museum, possessing an outstanding collection of printing specimens on permanent display, which can be seen for the price of a drink.

ST BRIDE PRINTING LIBRARY, BRIDE LANE, LONDON

The reference library of more than 30,000 books and pamphlets and files of over 700 periodicals on the technique, design and history of printing and related subjects originated with the purchase of William Blades's library in 1891. Also acquired about the same time were the libraries of Talbot Baines Reed (see p. 286), John Southward (see under 'Practical Printing', p. 297 above), and the London Society of Compositors (see p. 307).

St Bride's contains important collections of technical manuals, type-founders' specimens, documents relating to the early printing unions, chapbooks and broadsides. From 1894–1921, the St Bride Institute conducted a printing school which then became the London School of Printing. The technical library stayed at St Bride's. In 1970 an exhibition and lecture room was opened so that historical material and selected examples of historical printing equipment could be on permanent display.

THE SCIENCE MUSEUM, LONDON

A section on *Printing Machinery* shows early presses, and later printing machines, the latter at work, though there is no related display of the material they print.

VICTORIA AND ALBERT MUSEUM, LONDON

This shows two permanent exhibitions relating to printing. *The Art of the Book* contains examples of fine printing, from time to time, removed to make way for temporary exhibitions that cannot be shown elsewhere. Even more worth while, because unique, is the display of illustration processes, attached to the Library of Prints and Drawings, which shows equipment and specimens of British and International illustrations and makes the processes of printmaking clear to the least mechanical and visual-mind of spectators.

PRIVATE PRESSES

(See also under IIIC. ANTIQUARIAN BOOKSELLING, AUCTIONEERING AND
COLLECTING, IV. BOOK DESIGN AND PRODUCTION and V. BOOK
ILLUSTRATION)

The inside of the Printing office at Strawberry Hill (see p. 325)

1. Introduction

Private printing has an ancient origin. Certainly by the eighteenth century it was not unusual for a gentleman to employ a printer as part of his household staff. Colt Hoare, the Wiltshire historian, employed the printer Adolphus Brightley who had worked for Sir Thomas Phillipps at the Middle Hill Press (see p. 324). The printer, Charles Manby Smith (see under XI. THE PRINTING OF BOOKS, p. 287) purported to work for a benign clergyman and marry his ward. The owners of these presses were not particularly concerned to produce the Book Beautiful so much as to print their own works. Nor were many concerned with the therapy of craft work themselves, employing professionals to do it for them. However, there was some 'conscious endeavour towards fine printing' (Franklin) in the case of Sir Egerton Brydge's Lee Priory Press, and a certain amount, though less, in Horace Walpole's Strawberry Hill Press.

A private press may now generally be defined as a handpress operated for pleasure and not for profit. The owner himself prints what he wants to see in print, the way he wants to print it. Runs are small, often below the copyright number of 500. Motives vary: 'Authors have set out to give form and substance to their own writings; designers have been impelled to record their ingenuity in the use of type and decoration; artists have used books as vehicles for their drawings and engravings' (Will Ransom, *Private Presses and Their Books*, see p. 316 below).

The Daniel Press, in the mid-nineteenth century, was perhaps the first attempt to use old types in order to produce finely designed and executed books worthy of their literary content, and also to print as a family affair – Dr Daniel's wife did much of the binding. The importance of the whole book as a single construction was a principle of the Arts and Crafts Movement which owed its being to Morris, whose influence on book design is seen even today. Speaking of his aims in founding the Kelmscott Press, he wrote: '... it was the essence of my undertaking to produce books which it would be a pleasure to look upon as pieces of printing and arrangement of type'. The work of the Kelmscott, Doves, Ashendene and other presses of the Private Press Movement at the turn of the century have been an inspiration to printers and designers and have helped to improve the quality of work in present-day commercial presses, combining the innovation of new types and designs with the revival of old types.

Sometimes what began as a hobby grew into a profitable enterprise. Such was the case both with the Kelmscott and the Golden Cockerel

Presses which became publishing houses as well as printers. Other handpress owner-printers hope to make a living by what they love doing, maintaining high standards of craftsmanship and design.

Today the collecting of 'Press' books is coming increasingly into vogue. Such books are sought not only for their beauty but, sadly, for their value as capital investments. A Kelmscott Chaucer fetches a higher price than most of the sixteenth-century editions and only Caxton's first printing of the *Canterbury Tales* is more prized.

In the post-war years another kind of private publisher, the little press, allowed 'authors to give form and substance to their own writings'. The little press owner often despises the Book Beautiful and is chiefly concerned to make public new kinds of poetry or underground literature. Editions are limited to as few as fifty copies. After the war, when production costs rose steeply, the trade publishers found that to publish poetry for prestige alone was altogether too costly. They therefore tended to issue only the most established and traditional kinds of poetry where there was least financial risk and most prestige. The invention of Concrete and other new poetry which the commercial publisher dared not risk capital on, called the little presses into being to print it. An Association of Little Presses was formed in 1966. In 1968 an exhibition was held at the American Embassy of the Little Press Movement of England and America; and in February 1970 the National Book League held an exhibition of the work of the Association, in which eighty-six presses exhibited, and an annotated catalogue of sixty-five of these attempted to 'provide definitive information about the little presses and their work'.

2. General Works, Bibliographies and Catalogues

Association of Little Presses, CATALOGUES OF LITTLE BOOKS IN PRINT 1970, *Published in the United Kingdom*, A.L.P., 1970.

F. C. Avis, EDWARD PHILIP PRINCE, *Type Punchcutter*, Avis, 1967.

A profile that gives details and specimens of this great punchcutter's work for the Kelmscott, Vale, Eragny, Doves, Ashendene, Cranach and Zilverdistel Presses, with photographs and smoke proofs of rejected punches for the Doves Roman.

Norman E. Binns, editor, UNION LIST OF PRIVATE PRESS MATERIAL IN THE EAST MIDLANDS, East Midland Division of the A.A.L., 1955: a stencilled list.

Roderick Cave, THE PRIVATE PRESS, Faber & Faber, 1971 (illustrated).

The author describes representative presses from the earliest period to the present day, and he examines the equipment they used and the books they produced.

Desmond Flower, *Private Presses,* an excellent article in Cassell's EN-CYCLOPAEDIA OF LITERATURE, 2 vols., 1953.

Colin Franklin, THE PRIVATE PRESS, Studio Vista, 1969 (illustrated, select bibliography of private press books).

It was over forty years since the publication of a major work on the Press Movement. This work assesses the influence of the Kelmscott, Ashendene, Essex House, Vale, Eragny, Doves, Gregynog and Golden Cockerel Presses. There is a chapter on the collecting of press books, an aspect ignored by earlier books on the movement.

Johannesburg Public Library, MODERN PRIVATE PRESSES, *A Catalogue of Books in the Johannesburg Public Library from Some Modern Private and Other Similar Presses,* Johannesburg, 1955: a stencilled list.

The National Book League's copy is annotated with details of presses not included.

LITTLE PRESSES, Birmingham, 1968 (the catalogue of an exhibition).

Edward Lucie-Smith, editor, THE LITTLE PRESS MOVEMENT IN ENGLAND AND AMERICA, Turret Books, 1968.

The catalogue of an exhibition held in the American Embassy, with an introduction by Edward Lucie-Smith.

Manchester Public Libraries, PRIVATE PRESS BOOKS, Reference Library Subject Catalogue, edited by Sydney Horrocks, Manchester Libraries Committee, 2 vols., 1959–60.

This is classified alphabetically by press, each entry preceded by a note on date, origin, ownership and special features of the press.

James Moran, *Private Presses and the Printing Industry,* BRITISH PRINTER, April 1962.

This assesses the importance of the private presses in raising trade standards of production and design.

Percy Muir, PRIVATE PRESSES, Amsterdam, 1966: a paper read at the opening of the exhibition of *Books from British Private Presses.*

Private Libraries Association, THE PRIVATE LIBRARY, the journal of the P.L.A., quarterly since 1957.

Contains articles on various aspects of collecting and preserving press books as well as checklists on particular presses.

Private Libraries Association, PRIVATE PRESS BOOKS, compiled by Roderick Cave, David Chambers, Peter Hoy and Thomas Rae, P.L.A., annual since 1959 (illustrated, bibliography on the literature of private printing).

The first issue compiled by Thomas Rae and Roderick Cave was preceded by the Signet Press's *The Book of the Private Press,* Greenock, 1958. It lists presses in this country and elsewhere with their publications during the year. Early issues contained an article on private press design.

Will Ransom, PRIVATE PRESSES AND THEIR BOOKS, Bowker, New York, 1929, reprinted Philip C. Duschnes, 1963 (illustrated, bibliography).

Though selective, and out of date, this is still very useful.

Will Ransom, SELECTIVE CHECK LISTS OF PRESS BOOKS, *A Compilation of All Important and Significant Private Presses, or Press Books which Are Collected,* C. Duschnes and Duschnes Crawford 1945–50, reprinted Philip C. Duschnes, 1963.

Invaluable checklists of fifty-six presses, supplementing those in *Private Presses and Their Books* (see above).

William Ridler, BRITISH MODERN PRESS BOOKS, *A Descriptive Checklist of Unrecorded Items,* Covent Garden Press, 1971.

Listed alphabetically under press, with details of foundation date, address and so forth, this gives items that are not covered by Ransom, Tomkinson and *Private Press Books* (see above and below), based on the author's own extensive collection of books.

Juliet Standing, THE PRIVATE PRESS TODAY, Kings Lynn Festival, Brewhouse Press, 1967.

An illustrated and annotated catalogue of an exhibition of the work of forty current presses. It is a useful supplement to the bibliographies of private press books issued by the Private Libraries Association (see above).

Times Literary Supplement, PRINTING SUPPLEMENT, 1912.

This has an excellent article on the rise and importance of the Private Press Movement.

G. S. Tomkinson, A SELECT BIBLIOGRAPHY OF THE PRINCIPAL MODERN PRESSES, PUBLIC AND PRIVATE, IN GREAT BRITAIN AND IRELAND, with an introduction by B. H. Newdigate, First Edition Club, 1928 (illustrated).

This is still a useful work despite its early date.

Gilbert Turner, THE PRIVATE PRESS, *Its Achievement and Influence*, A.A.L. Midland Division, 1954.

Discusses the aims and achievements of the Kelmscott, Doves, Essex House, Ashendene, Golden Cockerel, Gregynog and Nonesuch Presses, and their influence on the productions of the Victoria and Albert Museum, Penguin Books, Gollancz and other commercial publishers.

3. Individual Private Presses and Their Owners

THE ASHENDENE PRESS (1895–1935)

This was founded by C. H. St John Hornby, a director of W. H. Smith, who was inspired by a visit paid to William Morris at the Kelmscott Press in 1893, to start printing in his own house.

A DESCRIPTIVE BIBLIOGRAPHY OF THE BOOKS PRINTED AT THE ASHENDENE PRESS 1895–1935, Ashendene Press, 1935.

The complete list; neither St Bride nor the N.B.L. has a copy.

A HANDLIST OF THE BOOKS PRINTED AT THE ASHENDENE PRESS 1895–1925, Shelley House, 1925.

C. H. ST. JOHN HORNBY 1867–1946, *An Anthology of Appreciations*, privately printed by W. H. Smith, 1946.

THE CUALA PRESS (1908–25) and THE DUN EMER PRESS (1903–07)

This was founded by Elizabeth Corbet Yeats and Lily Yeats, W. B. Yeats's sisters, in order to stimulate Irish industries. The name of the Dun Emer Press was taken from Lady Emer, famous in Irish history as an embroideress. The presses were worked entirely by women. Many of W. B. Yeats's poems were first printed by them.

William Maxwell, THE DUN EMER PRESS 1903–1907 AND THE CUALA PRESS 1908–1925, *A Complete List of the Books, Pamphlets, Leaflets and Broadsides Printed by Miss Yeats with Some Notes by the Compiler,* privately printed, 1932.

THE DANIEL PRESS (1845–1919)

This was the first of the Victorian private presses which (outside the Arts and Crafts Movement) attempted to improve the quality of typography by producing finely designed and executed books worthy of their content. C. H. O. Daniel, an Oxford scholar, selected books that were admirably suited to the use of the Fell types (see under XI. THE PRINTING OF BOOKS, p. 285) which he re-discovered. The Daniel Press is also renowned for its connection with Robert Bridges; nine of his books issued from the press.

Falconer Madan, MEMORIALS OF C.H.O. DANIEL *With a Bibliography of the Press 1845–1919,* Daniel Press, 1921 (frontispiece portrait and plates).

Colin Franklin calls it 'a flawless bibliography'. There are memorial pieces by seven contributors including two poems (one in Spanish by don F. de Artega y Pereira). The bibliography by Falconer Madan, the renowned librarian of Bodley, is preceded by an introduction on the Press, which quotes from the article on private presses in the 1912 *Times Printing Supplement.* The bibliography is in two parts, one listing those books printed at Frome 1845–63, the other those printed at Oxford 1863–1919. There are appendixes on the Fell types which Dr Daniel used for most of the books printed in Oxford, and on other Oxford private presses; the fifteen pages of plates include a photograph of the press as it now stands in the Bodleian Library.

DOVES PRESS (1900–16)

The name was taken from Doves Place, a part of Upper Mall, Hammersmith, where T. J. Cobden-Sanderson started the Doves Bindery. The

Press was founded by himself and Emery Walker, on the suggestion of William Morris and his wife. The type, a version of Jenson's roman, was designed by Emery Walker, and cut by E. P. Prince. The partnership was dissolved in 1909 and when the Press was closed in 1916, after having issued fifty-one titles, the types and matrices were consigned to the Thames. The Doves is the most renowned of all the private presses except Kelmscott from which it took its inspiration, and the Doves Bible the most renowned of all Press books except for the Kelmscott Chaucer. Its purpose was to carry out the ideal of the Book Beautiful, and titles were selected 'partly for the sake of particular typographical problems presented by them, and partly also in view of the second object of the Press, viz. to print in a suitable form, some of the literary achievements of man's creative or constructive genius' (G. S. Tomkinson, see p. 317).

Colin Franklin (see p. 315) devotes a chapter of his book to 'The Doves Press and High Idealism'. Bibliographies and critical notes appear in the following:

Manchester Public Libraries, PRIVATE PRESS BOOKS (see p. 315).

Will Ransom, PRIVATE PRESSES AND THEIR BOOKS (see p. 316).

G. S. Tomkinson, A SELECT BIBLIOGRAPHY OF THE PRINCIPAL MODERN PRESSES (see p. 317).

T. J. Cobden-Sanderson, CATALOGUE RAISONNÉ OF BOOKS PRINTED AT THE DOVES PRESS, 1900–1916 (with a portrait of the founder).

THE JOURNALS OF THOMAS JAMES COBDEN-SANDERSON 1879–1922, 2 vols., Richard Cobden-Sanderson, 1926.

All references to Emery Walker are deleted by the editor, Cobden-Sanderson's son, yet the journals remain a valuable source of information about the Doves Press.

C. Volmer Nordlunde, THOMAS JAMES COBDEN-SANDERSON, *Bookbinder and Printer*, Bogtrikkeri, Stockholm, 1957.

THE ERAGNY PRESS (1894–1914)

This Press was founded and run by Lucien Pissaro, son of the French artist Camille Pissaro, and his wife Esther as 'a conscious attempt to carry on the traditions of the Vale Press'. The first fifteen items were in fact printed with the Vale types. E. P. Prince, who cut the types for the Vale and the Kelmscott, then cut the Brook types to Lucien Pissaro's own design; these were first used in 1903. The name was taken from the Brook, Chiswick, where the Eragny Press was later housed and the owners lived. Thirty-one items were issued from this Press.

Thomas Sturge Moore, A BRIEF ACCOUNT OF THE ORIGIN OF THE ERAGNY PRESS, & *a Note on the Relation of the Printed Book as a Work of Art, To Life. A Bibliographical List of the Eragny books Printed in the Vale Type by Esther & Lucien Pissaro on Their Press at Epping, Bedford Park, and the Brook, Chiswick, In the Order in Which They Were Issued,* Eragny Press, 1903 (wood-cut illustrations).

'It is no longer necessary', Moore says, 'to defend the beautiful printed book, because its price is established, and the collector appreciates its rarity. . . . The small edition is as essential to this art as the high price. . . .'

Lucien Pissaro, NOTES ON THE ERAGNY PRESS, AND A LETTER TO J. B. MANSON, edited with a supplement by Alan Fern, privately printed at the C.U.P., 1957 (illustrated with reproductions from Eragny books).

There is a preface by Brooke Crutchley, and a bibliographical and critical supplement. The notes explain how the Press came into being and the letter provides fuller discussion of the technical problems involved.

ESSEX HOUSE PRESS (1898–1910)

This was founded by C. R. Ashbee who purchased the Kelmscott plant (but not the types and blocks), in an attempt to keep alive that Press's traditions of guild life and fine craftsmanship. Ashbee's Endeavour type was cut by E. P. Prince. A. K. Coomaraswamy took over the direction in 1907. The first ten years were the important ones and ninety books were issued in all.

C. R. Ashbee, A BIBLIOGRAPHY OF THE ESSEX HOUSE PRESS, *With Notes on the Designs, Blocks, Cuts, Bindings, etc., from the Year 1898 to 1904,* Essex House Press, Campden, Glos., 1904.

C. R. Ashbee, THE PRIVATE PRESS: A STUDY IN IDEALISM. *To Which is Added a Bibliography of the Essex House Press,* 1909 (illustrated, list of artists and craftsmen who have worked for the Essex House Press).

FANFROLICO PRESS (founded 1926)

FANFROLICANA, *Being a Statement of the Aims of the Fanfrolico Press, Both*

Typographical and Aesthetic With a Complete Bibliography and Specimen Passages and Illustrations from the Books, Fanfrolico Press, 1928.

Jack Lindsay, FANFROLICO AND AFTER, The Bodley Head, 1962 (illustrated, bibliography of Jack Lindsay's works).

This, the third volume of Jack Lindsay's autobiography describes the Australian author's arrival in London and the founding by Jack and Norman Lindsay and P. R. Stephenson of the Fanfrolico Press. There is much about the connection of D. H. Lawrence with the Press.

GOLDEN COCKEREL PRESS (founded 1920, first book issued 1921)

The aim was to print and publish new works of literary significance by young authors. The founder, Harold Taylor, retired in 1924 and the Press was bought by Robert Gibbings (q.v.). It is important for its connection with Eric Gill and the revival of wood-engraving. From 1933 it was directed by Christopher Sandford, Francis Newbery and Owen Rutter. It was then no longer strictly a private press.

CHANTICLEER, *A Bibliography of the Golden Cockerel Press April 1921–August 1936*, with an introduction by Humbert Wolfe and wood-engravings reproduced from the books, Golden Cockerel, 1936.

PERTELOTE, *A Sequel to Chanticleer . . . 1936–1943*, Golden Cockerel, 1943.

COCKALORUM, *A Sequel to Chanticleer and Pertelote . . . 1943–1948*, foreword and notes by Christopher Sandford, Golden Cockerel, 1950.

GREGYNOG PRESS (founded 1922)

This was founded at Gregynog, Montgomeryshire, to introduce and encourage fine printing in Wales, to print literature both in English and Welsh relating to Wales which was not available except in rare editions, to print editions of the English classics, to give great attention to decoration and illustration, and to bind all its own work.

J. Michael Davies, THE PRIVATE PRESS AT GREGYNOG, Leicester College of Art, 1959 (illustrated by Rigby Graham).

A history of the Press.

Thomas Jones, THE GREGYNOG PRESS, *A Paper Read to the Double Crown Club, 7 April 1954*, O.U.P., 1954 (illustrated, bibliography).

This, an informal, informative paper on this remarkable Press was reprinted as spoken, with illustrations from the original blocks with an annotated bibliography of the forty-two books it produced.

THE KELMSCOTT PRESS (1891–98) and WILLIAM MORRIS (1834–96)

This immensely influential press was founded by William Morris and continued working for another eighteen months after Morris's death (1896) under the direction of F. S. Ellis and Sydney Cockerell. The presses used by the Kelmscott were afterwards used by the Essex House Press. The Kelmscott books were bound by J. & J. Leighton. The name was taken from the village of Kelmscott in the Thames Valley where Morris lived in the manor house.

There is an immense amount of literature on William Morris and on the Kelmscott Press. I select the following:

A NOTE BY WILLIAM MORRIS ON HIS AIMS IN FOUNDING THE KELMSCOTT PRESS, Kelmscott Press, 1898, reprinted Irish University Press, 1969.

In his often-quoted words Morris explains: 'I began printing books with the hope of producing some which would have a definite claim to beauty, while at the same time they should be easy to read and should not dazzle the eye, or trouble the intellect of the reader by eccentricity of form in the letters. I have always been a great admirer of the calligraphy of the Middle Ages, and of the earlier printing which took its place . . . And it was the essence of my undertaking to produce books which it would be a pleasure to look upon as pieces of printing and arrangement of type. Looking at my adventure from this point of view then, I found I had to consider chiefly the following things: the paper, the form of the type, the relative spacing of the letters, the words and the lines; and lastly the position of the printed matter on the page. It was a matter of course that I should consider it necessary that the paper should be hand-made both for the sake of durability and appearance. It would be very false economy to stint in the quality of the paper as to price: so I had only to think about the kind of hand-made paper. . . .'

A CHRONOLOGICAL LIST OF THE BOOKS PRINTED AT THE KELMSCOTT PRESS, *With Illustrative Material from a Collection Made by William Morris and Henry C. Marillier* now in the Library of Marsden J. Perry of Providence Rhode Island, Merrymount Press, 1928.

H. Buxton Forman, THE BOOKS OF WILLIAM MORRIS, *Described with Some Account of His Doings in Literature and the Allied Crafts,* Frank

Hollings, 1897 (illustrated, bibliographical appendix of contributions to periodicals, lectures and addresses, and Kelmscott publications).

The work includes chapters on the Kelmscott Press and the *editiones principes* issued from it with bibliographical detail and background notes.

H. Halliday Sparling, THE KELMSCOTT PRESS AND WILLIAM MORRIS MASTERCRAFTSMAN, Macmillan, 1924 (illustrated, bibliography).

The standard work on the Kelmscott Press by Morris's son-in-law, describes Morris's apprenticeship, his work at Kelmscott and assesses his achievement. Appendixes give the note on William Morris's aims, quoted from above, a short description of the Press by Sydney Cockerell and an annotated list, also by Sydney Cockerell, of the books printed at the Press, as well as lists, leaflets and announcements printed at the Press.

Philip Henderson, WILLIAM MORRIS, *His Life, Work and Friends,* Thames & Hudson, 1967 (illustrated, bibliography).

This, and J. W. Mackail's *Life of Morris*, are the two most important critical biographies of Morris. There is a chapter on the Kelmscott Press.

Holbrook Jackson, WILLIAM MORRIS, Jonathan Cape, 1st edition, 1908, revised edition, 1936 (bibliography).

This is mainly concerned with Morris's art.

William Morris, COLLECTED WOKKS, edited by May Morris, 24 vols., Longmans, 1910–24.

This is the definitive edition of his works.

Bibliographies and critical notes appear in the following:

Manchester Public Libraries, PRIVATE PRESS BOOKS (see p. 315).

Will Ransom, PRIVATE PRESSES AND THEIR BOOKS (see p. 316).

G. S. Tomkinson, A SELECT BIBLIOGRAPHY OF THE PRINCIPAL MODERN PRESSES (see p. 317).

Wilfrid Blunt, COCKERELL. *Sydney Carlyle Cockerell, Friend of Ruskin and William Morris and Director of the Fitzwilliam Museum, Cambridge,* Hamish Hamilton, 1964 (illustrated).

Sydney Cockerell was connected with the Kelmscott Press first as librarian to William Morris and later as secretary of the Kelmscott Press. This story is told in chapter 6 (pp. 58–67), and the background to the Cockerell handmade papers (since 1972 the only hand-marbled papers made in England), is told in chapter 8: *Walker and Cockerell Progress Engravers* (pp. 76–85).

Ray Watkinson, WILLIAM MORRIS AS DESIGNER, Studio Vista, 1967 (illustrated, classified bibliography).

There is an index of presses as well as a general index, and ninety plates appended to the text. Chapter 6, pp. 57–67, is on Morris's printing.

LEE PRIORY PRESS (1814–23)

This may be considered to be the first attempt at a private press making a 'conscious endeavour towards fine printing' (Colin Franklin, see p. 315). The owner, Sir Egerton Brydges, employed printers at his son's house of Lee Priory in Kent. One of these was John Johnson, author of the printer's manual *Typographia* (see p. 257).

WOODCUTS AND VERSES, Lee Priory, 1820.

Colin Franklin considers this in effect a kind of bibliography of the engravings used at Lee Priory.

MIDDLE HILL PRESS (1822–72)

The owner, Sir Thomas Phillipps, called his Press after his Worcestershire home. He used it for the practical purpose of issuing copies of some of his early manuscripts, for anti-popish pamphlets and domestic ephemera. The story is told by A. N. L. Mumby in *Phillipps Studies* (see pp. 88 f. above).

THE NONESUCH PRESS (see under XIII. PUBLISHING, pp. 344 f.)

ST DOMINIC PRESS (founded 1916)

This was founded at Ditchling by Hilary Pepler and was dedicated to St Dominic.

Hilary Pepler, THE HAND PRESS, *An Essay by H. D. C. Pepler, Written for the Society of Typographic Arts*, Chicago, 1934, and reprinted with facsimile reproductions from the original, St Dominic Press, Sussex, [1953].

Brocard Sewell, MY DEAR TIME'S WASTE, St Alberts Press, 1966 (illustrated).

In chapter 4 of his autobiography Brother Sewell describes (pp. 65–85) his work with Hilary Pepler at the St Dominic Press, Ditchling.

The Press continues as a commercial concern now called the Ditchling Press.

THE SCHOLARTIS PRESS (founded 1926)

This was founded by the lexicographer Eric Partridge. The name, 'combining Scholarship and Art, crisply and definitely indicates the intention' (Will Ransom, see above).

Eric Partridge, THE FIRST THREE YEARS, *An Account of the Bibliography of the Scholartis Press*, Scholartis Press, 1930.

THE SEIZIN PRESS (1928–39)

James Moran, *The Seizin Press of Laura Riding and Robert Graves*, article in THE BLACK ART, vol. 2, 1963.

STRAWBERRY HILL PRESS (1757–89)

This, the best known of the private gentlemen's presses was founded by Horace Walpole in his mock-gothic castle at Strawberry Hill (see also 'Lee Priory' and 'Middle Hill' Presses above).

A. T. Hazen, A BIBLIOGRAPHY OF THE STRAWBERRY HILL PRESS, *With a Record of the Prices at which Copies Have Been Sold together with a Bibliography and Census of the Detached Pieces*, Yale University Press, New Haven, and O.U.P., London, 1942 (illustrated).

This, besides giving the information described in the sub-title, gives the number of copies printed of each edition.

JOURNAL OF THE PRINTING OFFICE AT STRAWBERRY HILL, *Now First Printed from the Manuscript of Horace Walpole*, with notes by Paget Toynbee, Chiswick Press, 1923 (illustrated).

This fascinating work includes accounts and indentures of apprenticeship, and a chronological list of books and detached pieces printed at Strawberry Hill. (By detached pieces may be understood letters, lines of poetry, catalogues, etc.)

VALE PRESS (1896–1904)

So called after Charles Rickett's house in the Vale, Chelsea, where he and

Charles Shannon published the first number of the *Dial* in 1889. The Vale Press books were printed at the Ballantyne Press, where Ricketts supervised the work and had a press set aside for his use.

C. Ricketts, BIBLIOGRAPHY OF THE VALE PRESS 1896–1904, *Bibliography of the Books Published by Hacon and Ricketts, Printed in Three Founts 'The Vale', 'The Avon', and 'The Kings.' Engraved Frontispiece by C. Ricketts After the Signboard Painted by C. H. Shannon for The Old Vale Premises*, 1904.

This is a complete list of the Vale Press books with the exception of *Daphnis and Chloe, Hero and Leander*, and the *Dial* magazine because these were not printed in the Vale type. The bibliography was published after the demise of the Press and the consigning of the punches and matrices to the Thames; as 'it is undesirable that those founts should drift into other hands than their designer's and become stale by unthinking use, it has been decided to destroy the punches, matrices and type.' Cobden-Sanderson followed this example with the punches, matrices and types of the Doves Press which were also consigned to the bed of the Thames in 1917. An introduction by Ricketts gives this information and thoughts on the reason for decoration of certain books. At the end there are several specimen pages set in the Avon, Kings and Vale types which were designed by Ricketts.

4. Private Press Associations

ASSOCIATION OF LITTLE PRESSES (A.L.P.) (founded 1966) (see 'Introduction', p. 314).

This describes itself as 'a loosely knit association of individuals running little presses who have grouped together for mutual self help, while retaining their right to operate autonomously'. It is intended to produce a yearly catalogue.

PRIVATE LIBRARIES ASSOCIATION (founded 1957) (see also under 'General Works, Bibliographies and Catalogues', p. 316 above).

This is a voluntary international society of book collectors and those interested in private presses. Publications include a quarterly journal, THE PRIVATE LIBRARY, an Exchange List, and an annual bibliography, PRIVATE PRESS BOOKS.

SECTION XIII

PUBLISHING

A. THE HISTORY OF PUBLISHING

LONGMAN AND COMPANY.

'*Longman and Company,*' *from* Punch, *1842 (actual size)*
(see p. 342)

1. Introduction

The distinction between publishing and bookselling, selling to the trade as opposed to selling direct to the public, is relatively modern. The word publisher, when it came into vogue at the end of the seventeenth century, was a synonym for bookseller. By then the printer did not always sell his books to the public. The publisher (as we would now call him), or bookseller, who negotiated with the author and financed the production of a book, also did a retail trade with his wares and, in order to display a more varied stock, he would exchange copies of his own publications with those of other booksellers. This dual function of producer and retailer gradually disappeared as a regular system of discounts developed during the nineteenth century. So completely separate are publishing and bookselling today that under the Industrial Training Act, publishing (with printing) is placed under one board while bookselling is counted as one of the distributive trades.

The trend in publishing as in other spheres of industry and commerce, is today towards amalgamation into bigger and bigger units. The very small firm can still flourish, but the medium-sized publisher is often forced out of business by rising costs unless he merges or allows himself to be taken over by a larger British, or an American, company. Sometimes the resulting subsidiary keeps its own identity and imprint and the general public does not even know that financial control has passed to a parent company.

The history of mid-twentieth-century publishing, when it comes to be written, will be the story of takeovers and mergers and of the Americanisation of British publishing.

Certain major aspects of publishing history do not feature in the sections below; serial publication is only documented for the years before 1750 (see R. M. Wiles, p. 330 below); the stories of sponsored publishing and the paperback explosion remain to be written though there are articles in periodicals on the latter.

2. General Histories of Publishing

In effect there are none that do not include other branches of the trade, bookselling, printing and the like. Moreover, important aspects of publishing history, such as sponsored, part and paperback publishing have been little documented.

Michael Alexander, *Publishers' Colophons*, article in TYPOGRAPHICA, vol. 9, 1954, pp. 4–11.

A short article on the history of publishers' devices is followed by illustrations of the devices used by some twenty-eight current publishers.

Cassell's ENCYCLOPEDIA, Cassell, 1963: article on publishing by Clifford Simmons.

Richard de la Mare, A PUBLISHER ON BOOK PRODUCTION, Dent, 1936 (see also p. 155).

ENCYCLOPAEDIA BRITANNICA: article on publishing by Ernest Rhys, editor of the Everyman Library, in the 14th edition, 1930.

This describes the publishing scene in the inter-war period. The latest edition will carry a new article by Philip Unwin.

F. A. Mumby, PUBLISHING AND BOOKSELLING, new edition, Jonathan Cape, 1954 (see under VI. HISTORY OF THE BOOK TRADE, p. 157).

Marjorie Plant, THE ENGLISH BOOK TRADE, 2nd edition, George Allen & Unwin, 1965 (see under VI. HISTORY OF THE BOOK TRADE, p. 157).

Philip Unwin, PUBLISHING FROM MANUSCRIPT TO BOOKSHOP (The Book no. 5), C.U.P. for the N.B.L., 1955.

An introductory outline is followed by a checklist of house histories, biographies of publishers, books on publishers' advertising and on the book trade in general.

R. M. Wiles, SERIAL PUBLICATION IN ENGLAND BEFORE 1750, C.U.P., 1957 (illustrated, bibliography).

This traces the history of books in parts during the later seventeenth and eighteenth centuries, describes legal aspects, production, promotion and distribution. Appendixes give the text of the Queen Anne copyright act, a short-title list of books published in fascicules before 1750, and the names and addresses of booksellers, printers and others who had some share in the production and distribution of books issued in parts before 1750. These include Camden's *Britannia,* Foxe's *Book of Martyrs,* and Moxon's *Mechanick Exercises* (see p. 255).

'The Publisher', *from the* Poetical Works of Alexander Pope, *edited by R. Carruthers, 1853*

See also: **R. J. L. Kingsford,** THE PUBLISHERS' ASSOCIATION 1896–1946, C.U.P., 1970 (bibliography).

This, as well as tracing the history of the P.A., describes fully and lucidly the history of the Net Book Agreement, copyright and novel prices, the control of printing and warehouse charges, and paper economy in the Second World War. Indeed it constitutes a history of publishing in the last seventy-five years.

[Publishers Association], F. D. Sanders, BRITISH BOOK TRADE ORGANISATION: *A Report on the Work of the Joint Committee*, George Allen & Unwin, 1939 (introduction by Stanley Unwin, reports and recommendations of the Joint Committee of Booksellers and Publishers).

This is the Publishers Association report on getting orders, distribution, trade organisation and practices, with a description of actual procedures and a long list of appendixes of historical interest including a short history of the Society of Bookmen, the Society's memorandum on the possibilities of a trade advertising campaign, report of the Commercial Circulating Libraries' subcommittee, library and book agents' licences, exhibitions and coupon advertising.

3. Popular Publishing

(See also 'Charles Knight', p. 341 below, and 'Chapbooks' under VII. CHILDREN'S BOOKS, pp. 181 ff.)

There are few studies of English bestsellers or of the production of cheap educational books for the masses, despite the vogue in readership surveys and studies of children's reading. Moreover most of what there is consists of literary criticism or social comment, not book trade history. I select the following, mostly American:

Margaret Dalziel, POPULAR FICTION 100 YEARS AGO, *An Unexplored Tract of Literary History*, Cohen & West, 1957 (illustrated, list of cheap periodicals of the mid-nineteenth century).

Desmond Flower, A CENTURY OF BEST SELLERS 1830–1930, National Book Council, 1934.

An introduction is followed by a list of British bestsellers compiled by Desmond Flower, now out of date, but there is nothing to put in its place.

Alice Payne Hackett, 60 YEARS OF BEST SELLERS 1895–1955, 1st edition, Bowker, New York, 1956; 70 YEARS OF BEST SELLERS 1895–1965, revised edition, Bowker, New York, 1968 (bibliography).

This gives the publication figures of bestsellers, analyses the subjects of those published in America, and lists the titles year by year.

James Hart, THE POPULAR BOOK, *A History of America's Literary Taste,* O.U.P., New York, 1950 (illustrated, bibliography).

Louis James, FICTION FOR THE WORKING MAN 1830–1850; *A Study of the Literature Produced for the Working Classes in Early Victorian Urban England,* O.U.P., 1963.

Frank Luther Mott, GOLDEN MULTITUDES, *The Story of Best Sellers in the United States,* Macmillan, New York, 1947 (appendixes listing over-all bestsellers in the U.S.A. etc.).

4. English Publishers and Publishing

GEORGE ALLEN & UNWIN (established 1914)

F. A. Mumby and Frances H. S. Stallybrass (daughter of W. S. Sonnenschein), FROM SWAN SONNENSCHEIN TO GEORGE ALLEN & UNWIN LTD., George Allen & Unwin, 1955.

Sir John Murray, in his introduction, explains that the firm's 'foundations were laid in the seventies of the nineteenth century when John Ruskin, on the one hand, started his Arcadian business in Kent, with George Allen, the engraver, as his publisher, and William Swan Sonnenschein, on the other, turned from medicine to publishing in the heart of London. ... William Swan Sonnenschein, known in later life, when he adopted his mother's maiden name, as William Swan Stallybrass, was born in 1855, son of a native of Moravia, Austria, who came to England in 1848, opened a school in Highbury, and wrote textbooks and other works that had a widespread influence in his adopted land'. Mumby describes the connection between Bemrose, the Liverpool printers and George Allen & Unwin (see also under 'Routledge & Kegan Paul', below and 'Bemrose' under XI. THE PRINTING OF BOOKS, p. 269).

Philip Unwin, THE PUBLISHING UNWINS, William Heinemann, 1971.

This can be considered as an unofficial sequel to Sir Stanley's auto-biography, written in a more modest vein, and giving all credit for publishing success to the author's august uncles.

Sir Stanley Unwin, THE TRUTH ABOUT A PUBLISHER, George Allen & Unwin, 1960 (illustrated).

Sir Stanley's autobiography traces the history of T. Fisher Unwin from 1848–1955. In 1883 there was a merger with Benn brothers, from which the firm of Sir Ernest Benn developed. Sir Stanley took an active part in the Publishers Association, the International Publishers Association and the British Council and he concludes his autobiography with appendixes on these organisations. 'A success story unself-consciously told', his book is packed with stories about authors and publishers of the last sixty years, of the author's own family and background, illustrated by photographs of the author from Victorian babyhood to old age.

JOHN BAKER (see under 'Practical Publishing', p. 365 below).

BATSFORD (established under this name 1843)

A BATSFORD CENTURY, *The Record of a Hundred Years of Publishing and Bookselling 1843–1943*, Batsford, 1943 (illustrated).

This describes how the firm developed out of Isaac Taylor's eighteenth-century engraving business, on the one hand, and the sale of Weale's Technical Series on the other. There is also much concerning Victorian London, with quotations from letters and anecdotes of publishing characters of old Bloomsbury.

Batsford is still an independent house without subsidiaries, architectural books still being quite a feature of its list.

GEORGE BELL & SONS (established 1838)

Edward Bell, GEORGE BELL, PUBLISHER, *A Brief Memoir*, Chiswick Press, 1924.

The founder's son describes the connection between Bell and Bohn's libraries, the purchase of the Chiswick Press, the association with Whitaker's, and early Bell authors such as Mrs Gatty, G. O. Trevelyan and Mrs Ewing.

George Bell was for some years proprietor of Deighton, Bell, the Cambridge bookseller currently owned by Messrs Dawson of Pall Mall.

BENTLEY, COLBURN (established in partnership 1829–97) (see also under 'Cambridge University Press' and 'Macmillan' below)

Royal A. Gettman, A VICTORIAN PUBLISHER, *A Study of the Bentley Papers*, C.U.P., 1960 (illustrated).

'This is a study of the rise and activity of the London publishing house which started in 1829 as Bentley & Colburn and was absorbed by Macmillan in 1898. . . . It discusses movements of taste and cycles of popular reading from the cheap edition series to the decline of the three decker novel . . . it illustrates the relationship between author and publisher . . . the success of the early best seller, *The Ingoldsby Legends* . . . deals with author's contracts and rewards, advertising, the influence of the circulating library, the work of the publisher's reader and editor.'

A. & C. BLACK, BLACKIE & SON, WILLIAM BLACKWOOD (see under 'Scottish Publishers and Publishing', pp. 351 ff. below)

THE BODLEY HEAD (established 1894)

J. Lewis May, JOHN LANE AND THE NINETIES, John Lane, The Bodley Head, 1936 (illustrated).

This describes John Lane's early partnership with Elkin Mathews (see also under III. BOOKSELLING, pp. 87 f.). John Lane came to publishing and bookselling from being a railway clerk. He was more ambitious and enterprising than his elder partner, Mathews, and parted from him in 1894 to found the Bodley Head and publish *avant-garde* poets (see also under 'Penguin Books', below, p. 345, for the story of his nephew, Allen Lane's, pioneering venture). In 1937 The Bodley Head was taken over as a co-operative venture by George Allen & Unwin, Jonathan Cape and J. M. Dent. Today it is part of the group comprising Max Reinhardt, the Nonesuch Press, Hollis & Carter, and Bowes & Bowes.

CADELL & DAVIES (see under 'Scottish Publishers and Publishing', p. 352 below)

CAMBRIDGE UNIVERSITY PRESS (John Sieberch printed the first Cambridge Book, 1521) (see also under XI. THE PRINTING OF BOOKS, pp. 270 f.)

S. C. Roberts, THE EVOLUTION OF CAMBRIDGE PUBLISHING, C.U.P., 1956 (illustrated).

The text of the Sandars Lectures for 1954 deals with aspects of eighteenth-nineteenth- and twentieth-century Cambridge publishing, including the Bentley revival (see also under 'Bentley, Colburn' above), the development of the London publishing house and the controversy surrounding the publication by the Press of the 11th edition of the *Encyclopedia Britannica* (see also under 'A. & C. Black', p. 351 below).

S. C. Roberts, ADVENTURES WITH AUTHORS, C.U.P., 1966.

The late Secretary to the Syndics devotes several chapters of his autobiography to his work at the Press, with anecdotes of Press authors and staff.

JONATHAN CAPE (established 1921)

Michael S. Howard, JONATHAN CAPE, PUBLISHER, Jonathan Cape, 1971 (illustrated).

The former chairman, son of G. Wren Howard, joint founder with Jonathan Cape, traces the firm's history and that of its directors and authors from the beginning to the present. Extracts from letters and anecdotes of authors and publishing personalities of the period are interspersed in the narrative to give insight into publishing during the last fifty years.

CASSELL (began publishing *The Teetotal Times* 1848)

Cassell's history is well documented, despite the destruction of most of the archives during the bombing of London in 1941.

Sir Newman Flower, JUST AS IT HAPPENED, Cassell, 1958 (illustrated).

Reminiscences about a Dorsetshire boyhood, literary apprenticeship at a penny a week, and rise to chairman. Sir Newman retired in 1958. His son was the last chairman of the firm as an independent house.

E. Golden Pike, JOHN CASSELL, Cassell, 1894.

Members of the staff give their recollections of the founder.

Simon Nowell-Smith, THE HOUSE OF CASSELL, Cassell, 1958 (illustrated).

The founder was a Manchester carpenter turned tea and coffee merchant, a temperance reformer who started *The Teetotal Times* (1848). He was a pioneer in the publication of magazines and popular books of knowledge such as the National Library. The book concludes with the publication of Churchill's *History of the English-Speaking Peoples*. The book does not mention the subsidiary firms of Baillière & Tindall and G. Blunt & Sons, bookbinders (see also A. E. Stevens, RECOLLECTIONS OF A BOOKMAN, 1933 for the author's reminiscences of working at Cassell's).

CATNACH PRESS (see under XI. THE PRINTING OF BOOKS, p. 272)

W. & R. CHAMBERS (see under 'Scottish Publishers and Publishing', pp. 352 f. below)

CHAPMAN & HALL (established 1830)

Arthur Waugh, A HUNDRED YEARS OF PUBLISHING, *Being the Story of Chapman, Hall Ltd.*, 1930 (illustrated).

This is a full history of Dickens's publishers.

Arthur Waugh, ONE MAN'S ROAD, *Being a Picture of Life in a Passing Generation*, Chapman & Hall, 1931 (illustrated).

The autobiography of a past managing director of the firm, father of the novelists Alec and Evelyn Waugh, contains much about his life in publishing.

The firm is now owned by the Associated Book Publishers (together with Methuen, Eyre & Spottiswoode, Sweet & Maxwell and Tavistock Publications) but continues to publish under its own imprint.

CHATTO & WINDUS (established in partnership 1873) (see also 'William Pickering', below)

A CENTURY OF WRITERS 1855–1955, Chatto & Windus, 1955.

This anthology of Chatto authors chosen by D. M. Low and others is preceded by a brief history of the first hundred years by Oliver Warner.

Subsidiary companies owned by the firm include the 'Hogarth Press' (see p. 341).

COLLINS and A. CONSTABLE (see under 'Scottish Publishers and Publishing', pp. 353 and 354 below)

EDMUND CURLL (1675–1747)

Ralph Straus, THE UNSPEAKABLE CURLL: *Being Some Account of Edmund Curll, Bookseller,* Chapman & Hall, 1927 (illustrated, bibliography, hand-list of Curll's publications).

This is the definitive biography of one of the most diverting rogues of the eighteenth-century book trade.

J. M. DENT (established 1888)

THE HOUSE OF DENT 1888–1938, J. M. Dent, 1938.

This is a reissue of *The Memoirs of J. M. Dent,* privately printed at Letchworth, 1921, adding four chapters to cover the years 1926–38.

James Thornton, A TOUR OF THE TEMPLE PRESS, *An Account of Printing and Binding Books at the Works of J. M. Dent & Sons Ltd. at Letchworth Garden City in Hertfordshire,* J. M. Dent, 1935 (illustrated).

'At the time of the first successes of "Everyman's Library" another ideal in a different direction was being realized – that of the garden city. First Garden City Limited had been formed in 1903, and the town of Letchworth was beginning to grow. The late J. M. Dent was in sympathy with the ideals of the garden city, and in 1906 five acres of land were leased as the site for a new factory.' This gesture on J. M. Dent's part to promote the movement prospered and this book gives an account of the processes going forward in the printing department and bindery.

Ernest Rhys, EVERYMAN REMEMBERS, J. M. Dent, London and Toronto, 1931 (illustrated).

The editor of Dent's Everyman series combines publishing history with reminiscences of authors in his autobiography.

LOVAT DICKSON (publishing independently ?–1938)

Lovat Dickson, THE ANTE-ROOM: *Early Stages in a Literary Life,* Macmillan' 1959.

Lovat Dickson, THE HOUSE OF WORDS, 2 vols., Macmillan, 1963.

These two volumes of autobiography tell much of the publishing life of the author, an Australian, who started his own publishing house in Canada, was editor of the *Review of Reviews* and of the *Fortnightly Review,* sold his publishing interest to Macmillan's in 1938, and subsequently became a director of Macmillan's. He was also connected with Cape for some years which is recounted in *Jonathan Cape, Publisher* (see p. 336).

ROBERT DODSLEY (1704–64)

Robert Dodsley was probably the most important publisher of the mid-eighteenth century. A footman with literary ambitions, he was an author of poor quality, but became an exceptionally successful bookseller and publisher, one who, moreover, unlike most of his rivals, enjoyed friendly and pleasant relations with his authors, who included most of the literary figures of the day. These congregated at his shop in Pall Mall, The Tully's Head.

Ralph Straus, ROBERT DODSLEY, *Poet, Publisher and Playwright*, John Lane, The Bodley Head, 1910 (illustrated, bibliography of Dodsley's own writings and list of publications, transcript of his will and other appendices).

This is still the definitive work on Dodsley, and written with Straus's customary wit and scholarship.

JAMES DUCKETT (d. 1601)

M. M. Merrick, JAMES DUCKETT; *A Study of His Life and Times*, Douglas Organ, 1947 (illustrated, bibliography).

Three chapters are devoted to describing the state of the book trade in the sixteenth century, and Duckett's life in bookselling. They are: book 2, chapter 2, *Books and Bookselling*; book 2, chapter 3, *James Duckett, Apprentice*; book 4, chapter 1, *Printers and Booksellers*.

The biographer explains that: 'James Duckett was never an author . . . but he came from Westmoreland into the world of book-reading, book-binding, book-selling that he was never afterwards to leave.'

JOHN DUNTON (1659–1733)

John Dunton, THE LIFE AND ERRORS OF JOHN DUNTON, *Citizen of London, Written by Himself in Solitude*; . . . *Intermixed with the New Discoveries the Author Has Made in his Travels Abroad, and in His Private Conversation at Home*, 1818.

'An interesting work, containing many curious particulars of this heterogeneous character' (Lowndes, *Bibliographer's Manual*, see p. 101). A pioneer book-auctioneer, publisher, he is mentioned by Nichols in his *Literary Anecdotes* (see p. 270) and is one of the gallery of portraits by Knight and Marston (see under III. BOOKSELLING, p. 59).

EYRE & SPOTTISWOODE (see under 'Strahan' in XI. PRINTING, p. 287)

FOULIS PRESS (GLASGOW UNIVERSITY PRESS) (see under XI. PRINTING, pp. 275 ff.)

GOLLANCZ (established 1927)

John Lewis, THE HISTORY OF THE LEFT BOOK CLUB, Gollancz, 1970 (preface by Dame Margaret Cole).

This includes a great deal about Victor Gollancz and the pre-war history of the publishing house that bears his name: much more than his two volumes of autobiography, which are more concerned with his spiritual development and early life than with book trade history (see also James Moran, *Stanley Morison*, p. 281 above) for the story of Morison's designing of the Gollancz distinctive yellow bookjackets, an innovation, in their day, in book promotion).

GEORGE G. HARRAP (established 1901)

George G. Harrap, SOME MEMORIES 1901–1935, *A Publisher's Contribution to the History of Publishing*, Harrap, 1935 (illustrated).

This is a slight memoir of the firm's founder.

PARTNERS IN PROGRESS, *Some Recollections of the Past Quarter Century at 182 High Holborn*, privately printed, 1962.

This commemorative volume contains extracts from Harrap authors and staff.

WILLIAM HEINEMANN (established 1890)

During the 1920s and 30s, Heinemann were the leading publishers of fiction. On the death of the founder in 1928, the firm became a subsidiary of the American Doubleday. Now it forms part of the Thomas Tilling group of companies, which also include the publishing houses of Peter Davies, and Secker & Warburg (see p. 348).

William Heinemann, THE HARDSHIPS OF PUBLISHING, privately printed, 1893.

This is 'an exchange of correspondence between William Heinemann and others emphasising the growing difficulties of publishing including increased overheads, the intervention of literary agents, underselling by booksellers'.

The author expresses pleasure at the establishment of a publishers' union out of which developed the Publishers Association (see also I. AUTHORSHIP, p. 8, and Kingsford, *The Publishers' Association*, p. 332 above).

A. E. Stevens, THE RECOLLECTIONS OF A BOOKMAN, Witherby, 1933 (illustrated).

Chapter 5 gives a portrait of the founder and describes the author's association with the firm.

Frederic Whyte, WILLIAM HEINEMANN, *A Memoir*, Jonathan Cape, 1928.

This narrates the firm's story up to the move to Great Russell Street on the death of the founder.

HOGARTH PRESS (first publication issued 1918)

Publication started on a handpress in the dining-room of Virginia and Leonard Woolf's house in Richmond at the end of the First World War. The story is told in:

Leonard Woolf, BEGINNING AGAIN: *An Autobiography of the Years 1911–1918*, Hogarth Press, 1964.

The firm is now a subsidiary of Chatto & Windus, but continues publishing under its own imprint.

CHARLES KNIGHT (1791–1873)

Charles Knight was the son of a bookseller, a chronicler of the book trade (see under III. BOOKSELLING, p. 59), and a pioneer in the production of cheap literature for the education of the masses (see also under 'Popular Publishing', pp. 332 f. above).

Alice B. Clowes, CHARLES KNIGHT, *A Sketch*, Bentley, 1892 (bibliographies of books written by, and edited by Knight).

The author was Knight's granddaughter.

Charles Knight, PASSAGES OF A WORKING LIFE, *During Half a Century with a Prelude of Early Reminiscences*, 3 vols., Bradbury & Evans, 1864.

This is a mine of information about the book trade of the late eighteenth and early nineteenth centuries.

LONGMAN (until 1968, Longmans, Green: established as Longman, 1724)

There is no full history of the oldest continuing British publishing house. In 1890 Longmans bought Rivington's (see below). In 1968 they took over Constable Young Books to become Longman Young Books. Then Longmans, Green merged with the Financial and Provincial Publishing Company and now use the imprint of Longman. The last member of the family to be its chairman, Mark Longman, died in 1972.

Cyprian Blagden, FIRE MORE THAN WATER, *Notes for the Story of a Ship,* Longmans, Green, 1949 (illustrations of some of Longmans' colophons and a family tree showing the date of entry of each partner since 1724).

This was produced to mark the firm's 225th anniversary.

Harold Cox and John E. Chandler, THE HOUSE OF LONGMAN, *With a Record of Their Bi-Centenary Celebrations, 1724–1924,* privately printed, Longmans, Green, 1925 (illustrated).

This is a reprint of Harold Cox's article in the *Edinburgh Review,* 1924, with a list of the firm's succession, 1724–1918.

Indiaman, THREE ADDRESSES, *An Essay in Publishing Ecology, 1939–47,* Longmans, Green, 1947.

The bombing of Paternoster Row in 1941 is described, as well as the move to Ambleside during the war and subsequent return to a London office in Clifford Street.

C. J. Longman, THE HOUSE OF LONGMAN 1724–1800, *A Bibliographical History with a List of Signs Used by Booksellers of that Period,* Longmans, Green, 1936.

There is an introduction by the editor, John E. Chandler, and a list of the works that Longmans took part in publishing up to 1800, with details of price, and other information.

MACMILLAN (established 1843) (see 'Lovat Dickson' above and also under III. BOOKSELLING, p. 61, for the firm's connection with 'Bowes & Bowes', and under IX. NET BOOK AGREEMENT, p. 223).

Thomas Hughes, MEMOIR OF DANIEL MACMILLAN, Macmillan, 1882.

This gives the story of the two Scottish brothers who founded the firm, from their youth through their Cambridge bookselling days, to the zenith of their publishing career.

Macmillan & Co., BIBLIOGRAPHICAL CATALOGUE OF MACMILLAN AND CO'S PUBLICATIONS, 1843–89, Macmillan, 1891.

LETTERS OF ALEXANDER MACMILLAN, privately printed, 1908 (illustrated).

These are preceded by an introduction by George Macmillan, and reminiscences of Alexander Macmillan by Professor William Jack.

LIFE AND LETTERS OF ALEXANDER MACMILLAN, edited by C. L. Graves, Macmillan, 1912.

This contains material not included in the privately printed edition.

Charles Morgan, THE HOUSE OF MACMILLAN 1843–1943, Macmillan, 1943 (illustrated).

Charles Morgan, himself a Macmillan author, draws on the works listed above as well as archive material. He continues the firm's story up to the war.

Simon Nowell-Smith, editor, LETTERS TO MACMILLAN, Macmillan, London and New York, 1967.

'. . . not a history, though it contains a number of footnotes to history. It is in the nature of a scrapbook drawn from the firm's correspondence files . . .'

MINERVA PRESS (1790–1820)

William Lane who founded the Minerva Press, though no booklover, was an interesting figure in book trade history on account of his circulating libraries and his early, if disguised and disreputable, entry into the reprint business. He fostered the taste for the Gothic novel at the end of the eighteenth century by establishing circulating libraries in the most fashionable towns. His Minerva Press revived old favourites by reprinting forgotten books with fresh titles which he issued as the latest thing and thereby made himself a fortune.

Dorothy Blakey, THE MINERVA PRESS, 1790–1820, O.U.P. for the Bibliographical Society, 1939 (illustrated, bibliography of the Press publications).

MUDIE'S

Guinevere L. Griest, MUDIE'S CIRCULATING LIBRARY AND THE VICTORIAN

NOVEL, Indiana University Press, Indiana, and David & Charles, Newton Abbott, 1971.

This first full-scale study of the most famous of the circulating libraries fills an important gap in book trade history.

JOHN MURRAY (established 1768) (see also 'Smith, Elder', below)

John Murray IV, JOHN MURRAY III 1808–1892, *A Brief Memoir*, Murray, 1919 (illustrated).

George Paston, AT JOHN MURRAY'S, 1843–1892, Murray, 1932 (illustrated).

This covers the reign of John Murray III.

Samuel Smiles, A PUBLISHER AND HIS FRIENDS, *Memoir and Correspondence of the Late John Murray with an Account of the Origin and Progress of the House 1768–1843*, 2 vols., Murray, 1891 (illustrated).

This concentrates on the life of John Murray II (John Murray I dies at the end of chapter 1). It is concerned with that period of British publishing when the great Scottish houses were forming an alliance with the London firms. The publisher of Byron, Scott, Lockhart and the *Quarterly Review*, narrowly escaped ruin in the financial panic of 1825 which finally pulled down Scott, Constable and the Ballantynes (see under 'Scottish Publishers and Publishing', below).

THOMAS NELSON (see under 'Scottish Publishers and Publishing', p. 355 below)

JOHN NEWBERY (1713–67) (see also under VII. CHILDREN'S BOOKS, p. 179)

Charles Welsh, A BOOKSELLER OF THE LAST CENTURY, *Being Some Account of the Life of John Newbery, and of the Books He Published, with a Notice of the Later Newberys*, Griffith, Farran, Okeden & Welsh, 1885 (illustrated).

This account of the eighteenth-century pioneer of children's publishing, bookseller and newspaper publisher, has not been superseded. It contains a transcript of Newbery's will, a catalogue of the books the Newberys published, a list of John Newbery publications and some of the newspapers that he was connected with.

NONESUCH PRESS (established 1923) (now part of the Bodley Head–Reinhardt Group)

Founded by Vera Mendel, Francis Meynell and David Garnett to produce worthwhile books in a beautiful format and at a moderate price.

Sir Francis Meynell, MY LIVES, The Bodley Head, 1971 (illustrated).

The autobiography of the founder of the Pelican Press, and later of the Nonesuch Press.

A. J. A. Symons, Desmond Flower and Francis Meynell, THE NONE-SUCH CENTURY, *An Appraisal, A Personal Note, and a Bibliography of the First Hundred Books Issued by the Press 1932–1934*, Nonesuch Press, 1936.

The Appraisal by A. J. A. Symons, the Personal Element by Francis Meynell and the Bibliography by Desmond Flower.

ODHAMS PRESS

R. J. Minney, VISCOUNT SOUTHWOOD, Odhams Press, 1954 (illustrated).

OSGOOD, MCILVAINE & CO. (1891) (see p. 359 below).

OXFORD UNIVERSITY PRESS (see XI. THE PRINTING OF BOOKS, pp. 284–6)

PENGUIN BOOKS (established 1935) (see also under 'The Bodley Head' above and under 'Paperback Publishing', p. 369, below)

BOXWOOD AND GRAVER: *A Miscellany of Blocks from a Score of Books Published Since 1949*, Penguin, Harmondsworth, 1958.

One of the delicious Christmas cards Sir Allen Lane used to send to his colleagues.

THE PENGUIN STORY 1935–1956, Penguin, Harmondsworth, 1956 (illustrated, complete catalogue, list of all colophons used up to 1956).

PENGUIN'S PROGRESS, 14 issues, Penguin, Harmondsworth, 1935–60.

These describe how Sir Allen Lane started what is now called the Paperback Revolution with the publication of ten sixpenny pocket books.

PENGUIN'S PROGRESS 1935–60, *Published on the Occasion of the Silver Jubilee of Penguin Books*, Penguin, Harmondsworth, 1960.

Short articles by Compton Mackenzie, Michael Grant, Reuben Heffer and others.

WILLIAM PICKERING (1796–1854)

William Pickering was both a rare book dealer (the firm continues as Pickering & Chatto) and publisher of the elegant Aldine Poet series, and the Diamond Classics, early miniature books. He was boycotted by the first Booksellers' Association for suspected undercutting (see pp. 221 ff.).

Geoffrey Keynes, WILLIAM PICKERING, PUBLISHER, *A Memoir and a Handlist of His Editions*, 1st edition, Fleuron, 1924, enlarged and revised edition, Galahad Press, 1969 (illustrated).

The second edition includes descriptions of the devices used by Pickering.

SIR ISAAC PITMAN (first work, on *Phonography*, published 1840)

Alfred Baker, THE LIFE OF SIR ISAAC PITMAN, Pitman, 1908 (illustrated)

This is more concerned with Pitman's work on spelling reform and phonography than with his life in publishing.

THE HOUSE OF PITMAN, Pitman, 1930 (illustrated).

GRANT RICHARDS (later THE RICHARDS PRESS) (published under his own imprint 1897–1948)

Grant Richards was the founder of the World's Classics (now published by O.U.P.) and the one-time publisher of George Bernard Shaw and A. E. Housman's *Shropshire Lad*, and assistant editor of the *Review of Reviews* under W. T. Stead. He died in 1948.

Grant Richards, MEMORIES OF A MISSPENT YOUTH 1872–1896, *With an Introduction by Max Beerbohm*, William Heinemann, 1932 (illustrated).

Describes his beginnings in journalism and his entry into publishing.

Grant Richards, AUTHOR HUNTING *by an Old Literary Sportsman, Memories of Years Spent Mainly in Publishing 1897–1925*, Hamish Hamilton, 1934, 2nd edition with an introduction by Alec Waugh, Unicorn Press, 1960 (illustrated).

Continues the story of a highly individual publishing personality.

RIVINGTON (1711–1890)

This old-established firm, publisher of the S.P.C.K., was bought by Longmans in 1890 and is now owned by Evans Brothers.

SELF AND PARTNERS (*Mostly Self*) *Being the Reminiscences of C. J. Holmes*, Constable, London, and Macmillan, Toronto, 1936 (illustrated).

Holmes describes life in and out of publishing.

Septimus Rivington, THE PUBLISHING FAMILY OF RIVINGTON, Rivington, 1919 (illustrated).

The narrator gives details of the early members of the family and also much about publishing in the eighteenth and nineteenth centuries, including aspects of copyright and the publishing congers.

THE PUBLISHING HOUSE OF RIVINGTON, Rivington, 1894 (illustrated).

This is less substantial than the above, but useful for the extracts from Charles Rivington's journal 1778–81.

ROUTLEDGE & KEGAN PAUL (established 1834)

F. A. Mumby, THE HOUSE OF ROUTLEDGE, 1834–1934, *with a History of Kegan Paul, Trench, Trübner and Other Associated Firms*, 1934 (see also 'George Allen & Unwin' above, 'Secker & Warburg', below, and 'William Strahan', p. 287 above).

C. Kegan Paul, MEMORIES, Routledge & Kegan Paul, 1st edition, 1899, new edition, with a foreword by Colin Franklin, 1971.

'He was a publisher only at the end of an attractive intellectual life, and it would be hard to recall another book so filled with entertaining stories of country and parish life, school and nursery in the high Victorian years' (foreword). Chapter 9 tells of Kegan Paul's publishing activities.

SAMPSON LOW MARSTON & CO. (formerly publishers of the *Publisher's Circular* and the *English Catalogue of Books*)

Edward Marston, AFTER WORK, *Fragments from the Workshop of an Old Publisher*, William Heinemann, London, and Charles Scribner's Sons, New York, 1904.

This contains much detail about the partnership with Sampson Low and the authors they published including Wilkie Collins, R. D. Blackmore, Jules Verne, Froude and Carlyle. A list of booksellers and publishers in 1846 is appended.

SECKER & WARBURG (founded as a joint imprint, 1936)

Frederic Warburg, AN OCCUPATION FOR GENTLEMEN, Hutchinson, 1959 (illustrated).

The author tells his life story from his entry into publishing after the First World War with Stallybrass of Swan Sonnenschein (see also under 'George Allen & Unwin' and 'Routledge & Kegan Paul', above).

SMITH, ELDER (1816–1916)

The first George Smith, a Scot who came to find his fortune in London, worked for John Murray II in 1814; a century later the firm, already bound to Murray's by marriage ties, was taken over by Murray on the death of Reginald Smith (son-in-law of George Smith II) in 1916. Alexander Elder, also a young Scot, found the money for the original partnership. Smith, Elder published *The Cornhill* (now published by John Murray) under the editorship of Thackeray. In 1882 George Smith II launched the *Dictionary of National Biography* under Sir Sidney Lee's editorship. This was taken over by the O.U.P. on Reginald Smith's death.

ELLIOT STOCK (1838–1911)

Sybille Pantazzi, *Elliot Stock,* article in THE BOOK COLLECTOR, vol. 20, no. 1, pp. 25–46, 1971 (illustrated).

This article traces the career of Elliot Stock with the aid of hitherto unpublished letters, and assesses his importance as a publisher of bibliography, including *Book Prices Current,* and his popularising series of periodicals, *The Bibliographer, Book-Lore* and *The Book Worm* (qq. v.).

TAYLOR & HESSEY (1806–25)

Edmund Blunden, KEATS'S PUBLISHER: *A Memoir of John Taylor 1781–1864,* Jonathan Cape, 1936 (illustrated and appended by a list of Taylor's writings).

'A memorial to the publisher in which there will be found some emphasis on his value in our literature. The long vanished firm of Taylor & Hessey never became one of the dynasties. Its career was comparatively brief – one of less than twenty years. . . . Yet within a few years their imprint was associated with the works of Keats, Clare, Hood, Lamb, Hazlitt, Coleridge, De Quincey and Carlyle.' Written with Edmund Blunden's customary charm, it is informative on early nineteenth-century publishing. Taylor met his partner Hessey when they were both apprentices of Lackington (see p. 62).

The Literary Laboratory

'The Literary Laboratory', from *West*, Fifty Years Recollections of An Old Bookseller,
1835 (see p. 65)

Tim Chilcott, A PUBLISHER AND HIS CIRCLE *The Life and Work of John Taylor, Keats' Publishers,* Routledge & Kegan Paul, 1972 (bibliography).

This new study lacks Blunden's elegance of writing and is also a less elegant piece of book production. On the other hand, being the result, as the writer tells us, of years of research, it contains much new material inaccessible to Blunden, and gives a full picture of the early nineteenth-century publishing scene.

JACOB TONSON (1656–1736)

Harry M. Geduld, PRINCE OF PUBLISHERS: *A Study of the Work, and Career of Jacob Tonson,* Indiana University Press, Bloomington, Ind., 1970 (illustrated).

WARD LOCK (established 1854)

Edward Liveing, ADVENTURE IN PUBLISHING, *The House of Ward Lock, 1854–1954,* Ward Lock, 1954 (illustrated).

This tells of the firm's early struggles and rivalries, the association with the Beetons, Rider Haggard, Conan Doyle, Browning and Tennyson as well as the historic sites which the firm occupied in the City.

WARNE (established 1865)

Arthur King and A. F. Stuart, THE HOUSE OF WARNE, *100 Years of Publishing,* Warne, London and New York, 1965 (illustrated).

The impression given is that Warne's reputation rests solely on the publication of Kate Greenaway and Beatrix Potter.

5. Scottish Publishers and Publishing

'Scotland's day of reputation in printing and publishing arrived with the Foulises, who set a standard not only for Scotland but for Europe.... With the beginning of the nineteenth century we enter a magnificent period when Edinburgh took the limelight from London, ... and some of the greatest publishing firms in Britain today had their beginnings in Edinburgh and Glasgow at this time, and a number still stand' (R. D. McLeod, see below).

Not all publishers of Scottish nationality form part of the history of

Scottish publishing. Macmillan, for example (see above, pp. 342 f.), has never had a Scottish office. Others, namely Thomas Nelson, Constable and A. & C. Black, have lost their Scots connections, yet figure below because they started in Scotland. Only Chambers and Blackwood (who today publish little besides their *Magazine*) operate from a main Scottish office.

R. D. McLeod, THE SCOTTISH PUBLISHING HOUSES, W. & R. Holmes, 1953 (bibliography).

This is an expanded version of a paper read before the Glasgow Bibliographical Society.

The *Proceedings* of the Edinburgh and Glasgow Bibliographical Societies contain articles on individual members and aspects of the Scottish book trade.

Publishing in Edinburgh

A. & C. BLACK (established 1807)

ADAM AND CHARLES BLACK, 1807–1957, A. & C. Black, 1957.

This commemorative house history draws on Nicolson's *Memoirs* (see below) and on surviving records. It describes the purchase and subsequent sale through *The Times* of the *Encyclopedia Britannica* (see under 'Cambridge University Press', p. 336 above, and also under IX. THE NET BOOK AGREEMENT, p. 222). It also describes the firm's publication of *Who's Who* and the *Writers' and Artists' Yearbook*.

Alexander Nicolson, editor, MEMOIRS OF ADAM BLACK, A. & C. Black, 1885.

This is a biography of the founder, who was a political figure as well as a publisher.

BLACKWOOD'S (established 1804)

Blackwood's history is more fully documented than many bigger houses.

WILLIAM BLACKWOOD AND HIS SONS, *Their Magazine and Friends, Annals of a Publishing House*, 3 vols., vols. 1 and 2 by Mrs Oliphant, 1847 and vol. 3 by Mrs Gerald Porter (William Blackwood's daughter), Blackwood, Edinburgh, 1848.

Mrs Oliphant was one of the publisher's more prolific and faithful authors, 'for forty years worked incessantly for the Magazine', was intimate with its history, thoroughly imbued with all its traditions, and very loyal to its past. Her work is invaluable as a chronicle of Edinburgh publishing of the period although it was somewhat partisan in its description of the wars between Blackwood's and the *London Magazine* and other feuds of the then publishing scene. Each of the forty-eight chapters is summarised in the contents.

A SELECTION OF THE OBITUARY NOTICES OF THE LATE JOHN BLACKWOOD, *Editor of Blackwood's Magazine*, privately printed, Edinburgh, 1880.

Elegantly produced in the manner of the period, its mourning character is emphasised by black borders to the pages.

F. D. Tredrey, THE HOUSE OF BLACKWOOD 1804–1954, *The History of a Publishing Firm*, Blackwood, Edinburgh and London, 1954 (extensively illustrated, bibliography and appendixes).

This centenary volume, by a director of Blackwood's, contains much information not to be found elsewhere, particularly on the more recent history. The earlier part, though drawing on *William Blackwood and His Sons* (see above) also contains much from other sources on old and new Edinburgh, mid-nineteenth-century literary London, the navy and army, etc., to fill in the social and political background of the firm's publishing activities.

CADELL & DAVIES (Cadell set up as publisher and bookseller 1739–1836)

Theodore Besterman, THE PUBLISHING FIRM OF CADELL AND DAVIES, *Select Correspondence and Accounts 1793–1836*, edited with introduction and notes, O.U.P., 1938.

This makes available valuable material on Edinburgh publishing of the period, and the firm's relations with the Constables, and Blackwoods. An introduction gives the background to the firm's activities and status, and relations with other publishers and with distinguished authors such as Hazlitt, Leigh Hunt, Coleridge, Jane Austen and Burns. The letters are grouped in sections.

W. & R. CHAMBERS (established 1832)

William Chambers, MEMOIR OF ROBERT CHAMBERS, *With Autobiographic Reminiscences of William Chambers*, W. & R. Chambers, London and Edinburgh, 1872.

Running titles to the fifteen chapters make for easy reference. The second half of the book tells of the movement in cheap literature and of the progress of *Chambers Journal* founded 1832.

William Chambers, STORY OF A LONG AND BUSY LIFE, W. & R. Chambers, London and Edinburgh, 1882.

This is a slighter version of the former. The Chambers brothers, coming comparatively late to the Edinburgh scene, escaped the turmoil and financial tangles that dogged the fortunes of those printers and publishers who surrounded Scott.

William Chambers, MEMORIES OF THE CHAMBERS BROTHERS, *An Account by William Chambers of the Struggles of Himself, and His Brother Robert in Edinburgh 1813-22*, Galahad Press, 1967 (illustrated, with an introduction by Derek Maggs).

This is an abbreviated edition of the above.

CONSTABLE (present firm established 1890)

The first Archibald Constable 'was the first publisher to break in upon the monopoly of the London trade. A man of rare sagacity and enterprise, Constable gauged the public taste to a nicety, and paid generously for his books. Gradually collecting the best authors about him, he raised the prestige of the publishing trade throughout Scotland, and made Edinburgh a centre of scholarship and literature' (*Archibald Constable and His Literary Correspondents*, see below).

Constable, together with Ballantyne, foundered in the 1820s because both 'were in their later days so entangled financially, through Sir Walter Scott's engagements, that when one went down in bankruptcy, the other inevitably followed' (R. D. McLeod, see p. 351 above). The founder's grandson re-started the firm in London, and in 1968 it was taken over by the Hutchinson group, except for Constable Young Books, which was bought by Longman to become Longman Young Books.

ARCHIBALD CONSTABLE AND HIS LITERARY CORRESPONDENTS, *A Memorial by His Son Thomas Constable*, 3 vols., Edmonston & Douglas, Edinburgh, 1873.

This is a very full biography of the first founder.

Ralph Arnold, ORANGE STREET AND BRICKHOLE LANE, Rupert Hart-Davis, 1963 (illustrated).

The Orange Street chapters of this autobiography by Constable's last chairman give insight into the work of a medium-sized publisher between the wars and up to the end of the 1950s. Relations with authors and literary agents are described and there is a picture of Michael Sadleir (see under III. BOOKSELLING, p. 90) who was Mr Arnold's predecessor as chairman.

Eric Quayle, THE RUIN OF SIR WALTER SCOTT, Rupert Hart-Davis, 1968 (illustrated, bibliography).

This tells the story of the Ballantyne/Constable/Scott crash.

Publishing in Glasgow

BLACKIE & SON (established 1809)

Agnes A. C. Blackie, BLACKIE AND SON 1809–1959, *A Short History of the Firm*, Blackie, Glasgow, 1959 (illustrated).

This is a slight, but readable and useful house history (see also 'Glasgow University Press' below, from whom John Blackie purchased type owned by the Duncan Brothers).

150 YEARS OF PUBLISHING: *Catalogue of an Exhibition to Celebrate the 150th Anniversary of the Foundation of the Firm on 20 November, 1959.*

A general introduction is followed by introductions to each section of the exhibition, and full notes on each exhibit which give information about the firm and its history.

Walter W. Blackie, A SCOTTISH STUDENT IN LEIPZIG, *Being Letters of W. G. Blackie, His Father and His Brothers in the Years 1839–40, With Introduction and Sundry Notes*, Blackie, 1932 (illustrated).

These letters by the founder, John Blackie, and his three sons, John, Walter and Robert give more information about the printing than the publishing side of the business.

COLLINS (established 1819)

The Glasgow firm of Collins, now owning Geoffrey Bles, the Harvill Press and others, started during the golden age of Scottish publishing, at the turn of the eighteenth century. William Collins I and Dr Chalmers opened in Wilson Street, Glasgow in 1819, and the firm gradually expanded in London and Glasgow until its shares were floated on the market in 1949.

David Keir, THE HOUSE OF COLLINS, *The Story of a Scottish Family of Publishers from 1789 to the Present Day*, Collins, 1952.

GLASGOW UNIVERSITY PRESS and FOULIS PRESS (see under XI. THE PRINTING OF BOOKS, p. 275)

THOMAS NELSON & SONS (established 1798)

Daniel Wilson, WILLIAM NELSON 1816–87, *A Memoir*, privately printed, 1889.

The founder, a native of Stirlingshire, after gaining useful experience in bookselling in London, set up an Edinburgh bookshop and began to issue popular religious works in cheap monthly parts. He was the first publisher to engage a travelling representative.

6. American Publishers and Publishing

General Histories

Henry W. Boynton, ANNALS OF AMERICAN BOOKSELLING 1638–1850, Boynton-Wiley, New York, 1932.

E. L. Bradsher, BOOK PUBLISHERS AND PUBLISHING, Cambridge History of American Literature, vol. 3, 1921.

W. Charvat, LITERARY PUBLISHING IN AMERICA, 1790–1850, Pennsylvania University Press, University Park, Pa., and O.U.P., London, 1959. (The Rosenbach lectures for 1957–58.)

Chandler B. Grannis, editor, WHAT HAPPENS IN BOOK PUBLISHING (see under 'Practical Publishing', p. 366 below).

Adolph Growoll, BOOK TRADE BIBLIOGRAPHY IN THE UNITED STATES IN THE NINETEENTH CENTURY, 1898, reprinted, Brick Row bookshops, 1939.

W. Jovanovitch, NOW BARABBAS, Harper & Row, New York, 1964, and Longmans, London, 1965.

D. Kaser, BOOKS IN AMERICA'S PAST, University Press of Virginia, Charlottesville, Va., 1966.

H. Lehmann-Haupt, THE BOOK IN AMERICA, 2nd edition, Bowker, New York, 1951.

C. A. Madison, BOOK PUBLISHING IN AMERICA, McGraw-Hill, New York, 1966.

W. Miller, THE BOOK INDUSTRY, Columbia University Press, New York, and O.U.P., London, 1949.

D. H. Sheehan, THIS WAS PUBLISHING, Indiana University Press, Bloomington, Ind., 1952, and George Allen & Unwin, London, 1954.

M. B. Stern, IMPRINTS ON HISTORY, *Book Publishers and American Frontiers,* Indiana University Press, Bloomington, Ind., 1956.

This consists of biographies of American publishers and concludes with full notes of United States book publishing firms surviving before 1900, and a chronological list of American publishers.

Walter Sutton, THE WESTERN BOOK TRADE, *Cincinnati as a 19th Century Publishing and Book Trade Center,* Ohio State University Press, Columbus, Ohio, 1961.

G. Thomas Tanselle, THE HISTORIOGRAPHY OF AMERICAN LITERARY PUBLISHING, in STUDIES IN BIBLIOGRAPHY, vol. 18, University Press of Virginia, Charlottesville, Va., 1965, pp. 3–39.

Contains an extensive bibliography of American book publishing, history, practice and copyright.

Histories of Individual American Publishing Houses and Biographies of Publishers

APPLETON (established 1825)

G. Overton, PORTRAIT OF A PUBLISHER: *And the First 100 Years of the House of Appleton 1825–1925,* Appleton, New York, 1925.

THE HOUSE OF APPLETON-CENTURY, Appleton-Century, New York, 1936 (illustrated).

A. S. BARNES (established 1838)

J. B. Pratt, A CENTURY OF BOOK PUBLISHING 1838–1938, *Historical and Personal,* A. S. Barnes, New York, 1938.

THEODORE BLISS

Arthur Ames Bliss, THEODORE BLISS, PUBLISHER AND BOOKSELLER, *A Study of Character and Life in the Middle Period of the XIX Century,* Northampton Historical Society, 1941 (illustrated).

CAREY & LEA

D. Kaser, MESSRS CAREY AND LEA OF PHILADELPHIA: *A Study in the History of the Book Trade*, Pennsylvania University Press, University Park, Pa., and O.U.P., London, 1957 (illustrated, bibliography).

G. H. DORAN

G. H. Doran, CHRONICLES OF BARABBAS 1884–1934, Methuen, 1935.

This autobiography tells of the founding of the firm of Doran and its eventual merger with Doubleday.

DANA ESTES & CO (1898–1914)

R. L. Kilgour, ESTES AND LAURIAT: *A History 1872–1898*, Michigan University Press, East Lansing, Mich., and O.U.P., London, 1957 (illustrated, preface by Frederic Melcher).

EXPOSITION PRESS

Edward Uhlman, THE ROGUE OF PUBLISHERS' ROW, *Confessions of a Publisher*, Exposition Press, New York, 1956 (bibliography).

This autobiography of the founder of Banner Books and the Exposition Press is both informative and amusing.

GINN (established 1867)

Thomas Bonaventure Lawler, SEVENTY YEARS OF TEXT BOOK PUBLISHING: *A History of Ginn and Co., 1867–1937*, Ginn, 1938 (illustrations include a list of the Ginn colophons).

FERRIS GREENSLET

Ferris Greenslet, UNDER THE BRIDGE, *The Autobiography of a Publisher*, Collins, 1944.

HARPER & ROW (established 1817) (for Harper's connection with Osgood see below, p. 359).

Eugene Exman, THE HOUSE OF HARPER: *150 Years of Publishing*, Harper & Row, New York, 1948 (illustrated).

Eugene Exman, THE BROTHERS HARPER, *A Unique Publishing Partnership and Its Impact on the Cultural Life of America from 1817–1853*, Harper & Row, New York, 1965 (bibliography, introduction by Allan Nevins).

J. H. Harper, THE HOUSE OF HARPER: *A Century of Publishing in Franklin Square*, Harper, New York, 1911 (illustrated).

THE HARPER ESTABLISHMENT: *or, How the Story Books are Made*, Harper Bros, New York, 1855 (illustrated).

This period piece of advertising describes the Harper building, and printing and binding processes.

HOLT, RINEHART & WINSTON (established 1866)

Henry Holt, SIXTY YEARS A PUBLISHER, George Allen & Unwin, 1923.

C. A. Madison, AN OWL AMONG THE COLOPHONS: *Henry Holt as Publisher and Editor*, Holt, Rinehart & Winston, New York, 1966 (lists of Holt's own books and of outstanding Holt publications).

HOUGHTON MIFFLIN (established 1852)

FIFTY YEARS OF PUBLISHING: *A History of the Educational Department of the Houghton Mifflin Co.*, Houghton Mifflin, Boston, Mass., 1930.

ALFRED A. KNOPF

C. Fadiman, FIFTY YEARS: *Borzoi Books 1915–65*, Knopf, New York, 1965.

The introduction gives the history of Borzoi Books.

H. S. LATHAM

H. S. Latham, MY LIFE IN PUBLISHING, Dutton, New York, 1965, and Sidgwick & Jackson, London, 1966.

LITTLE, BROWN (established 1837)

ONE HUNDRED AND TWENTY-FIVE YEARS OF PUBLISHING, Little, Brown, New York, 1962.

FIELDING LUCAS

J. W. Foster, FIELDING LUCAS, JR.: *Early 19th Century Publisher of Fine Books and Maps,* American Antiquarian Society, New York, 1956.

FREDERIC G. MELCHER

Frederic G. Melcher, FRIENDLY REMINISCENCES OF A HALF CENTURY AMONG BOOKS AND BOOKMEN, Book Publishers Bureau, New York, 1945 (illustrated).

This consists of biographical essays by Melcher and others.

OSGOOD, MCILVAINE & CO. (established 1891)

C. J. Weber, THE RISE AND FALL OF JAMES RIPLEY OSGOOD: *A Biography,* Colby College Press, Waterville, Maine, 1959 (illustrated).

Started in Albemarle Street, London, when J. R. Osgood became the English representative of Harper and Brothers (see p. 357).

PUTNAM (established 1838)

George Haven Putnam, MEMORIES OF MY YOUTH, 1844–65, Putnam, New York, 1914 (illustrated).

George Haven Putnam, MEMORIES OF A PUBLISHER 1865–1915, Putnam, New York, 1915 (illustrated).

George Haven Putnam, GEORGE PALMER PUTNAM, A MEMOIR, *Together with a Record of the Earlier Years of the Publishing House Founded by Him,* 1st edition, privately printed, 1903, Putnam, London and New York, 1912.

The earlier, privately printed, edition is fuller.

George P. Putnam, WIDE MARGINS; *A Publisher's Autobiography,* Harcourt Brace, New York, 1942.

The author is the grandson of the firm's founder.

ROBERTS BROTHERS (1837–98)

R. L. Kilgour, MESSRS ROBERTS BROTHERS, PUBLISHERS, Michigan University Press, East Lansing, Mich., and O.U.P., London, 1952.

Roberts Brothers's list was taken over by Little, Brown, 1898.

CHARLES SCRIBNER'S SONS (established 1846)

R. Burlinghame, OF MAKING MANY BOOKS, *100 Years of Reading, Writing and Publishing,* Charles Scribner's Sons, New York, 1946.

Maxwell E. Perkins, EDITOR TO AUTHOR, *Letters Selected and Edited,* with a commentary and introduction by John Hall Wheelock, Charles Scribner's Sons, New York, 1950.

Maxwell Perkins was associated with Scribner's for thirty-seven years.

STOKES (established 1881)

THE HOUSE OF STOKES 1881–1926, *A Record,* Stokes, New York, 1926. Lippincott's acquired this firm in 1941.

J. A. THAYER

J. A. Thayer, GETTING ON: *The Confessions of a Publisher,* Werner Laurie, New York, 1911.

TICKNOR & FIELDS (established 1832)

James T. Fields, YESTERDAYS WITH AUTHORS, Osgood, New York, 1871.

James T. Fields, BIOGRAPHICAL NOTES AND PERSONAL SKETCHES, Houghton Mifflin, Boston, 1881.

Warren Tryon, PARNASSUS CORNER: *A Life of James T. Fields, Publisher to the Victorians,* Houghton Mifflin, Boston, 1963.

Warren Tryon and William Charvat, THE COST BOOKS OF TICKNOR AND FIELDS ... 1832–1858, Bibliographical Society of America, New York, 1949.

UNITED STATES GOVERNMENT PUBLICATIONS

J. H. Powell, THE BOOKS OF A NEW NATION, *U.S. Government Publications 1774–1814,* Pennsylvania University Press, University Park, Pa., and O.U.P., London, 1957 (illustrated, notes on source material).

This is the text of the Rosenbach Lectures in Bibliography for 1956.

VAN NOSTRAND (established 1848)

A CENTURY OF BOOK PUBLISHING, 1848–1948, Van Nostrand, New York, 1948 (illustrated).

VICTOR WEYBRIGHT

Victor Weybright, THE MAKING OF A PUBLISHER, *A Life in the 20th Century Book Revolution*, Weidenfeld & Nicolson, 1968.

The founder of Signet and Mentor Books and the New American Library which is part of the history of the paperback revolution, writes his autobiography.

H. W. WILSON COMPANY (established 1900)

J. L. Lawler, H. W. WILSON COMPANY, University of Minnesota, Minneapolis, Minn., and O.U.P., London, 1950 (chronological list of general publishers 1900–49, and notes on sources).

This is the story of the *Cumulative Book Index* and other Wilson reference works.

WILEY (established 1807)

THE FIRST ONE HUNDRED AND FIFTY YEARS: *A History of John Wiley & Sons 1807–1957*, Wiley, New York, and Chapman & Hall, London, 1957.

7. Periodicals containing Articles on the History of Publishing

(See also under III. BOOKSELLING, pp. 103 ff. and XI. THE PRINTING OF BOOKS, pp. 300 ff.)

THE PROCEEDINGS of the Bibliographical Societies of: America, Cambridge, Edinburgh, London, Oxford, the University of Virginia (see under III. BOOKSELLING, pp. 103 ff.)

THE BOOK COLLECTOR (see under III. BOOKSELLING, p. 104).

THE BOOKSELLER contains articles on current aspects of publishing, memoirs and obituary notices of notable publishers, etc.

THE PUBLISHERS' WEEKLY, Bowker, New York, 1872– .

The organ of the American book trade useful for articles, obituary notices, etc., of American publishers.

B. PRACTICAL PUBLISHING

1. Introduction

There are no manuals of instruction for apprentice publishers and, until the passing of the Industrial Training Act, there were no training courses for publishing personnel. A few evening and short courses have been arranged since then, mostly on aspects of book production, open only to those already working in publishing, and there is one degree course for aspirants, at the Oxford Polytechnic. Many are still as much confused as Israel Sieff was, when he asked Frederic Warburg at a cocktail party: 'Tell me, since you seem to know something about it, is publishing an occupation for gentlemen or is it a real business?'

2. The Practice of Publishing

John Baker, THE BOOK BUSINESS, John Baker, 1971.

A modest, methodical, sober version of 'the truth about' today's publishing scene (compare it with Anthony Blond, *The Publishing Game*, see below), with an appendix in the shape of a production budget of a book published in July 1970. The author reflects that: 'A middle-aged man, casting backwards and forwards, might be forgiven for regarding the future of the Trade with misgiving. It seems a great distance away when John Murray gave his dinners to the assembled booksellers and, having filled them with unaccustomed food and drink, invited them to take up his edition of Livingstone's *Travels*. He is bemused, on television, by the sight of publishers looking like disc jockeys and pop stars calling themselves publishers; he looks uncomprehendingly at interviews with teen-age girls explaining, in lisping accents, how they have spent a few days "writing" a best-seller, perhaps as far away from real life as the fabrications of Charlotte Yonge and Mrs Henry Wood. He has seen the Trade, solid, respectable, an occupation for gentlemen, change into a very lively business indeed, and fully in the market place.'

Clive Bingley, BOOK PUBLISHING PRACTICE, Crosby Lockwood, 1966 (bibliography).

In a hundred pages the editorial, production, sales and rights sides of publishing are described and there are tables of profit margins, paper sizes, typefaces and a cost sheet.

Clive Bingley, THE BUSINESS OF BOOK PUBLISHING, Pergamon Press, Oxford, 1972.

A manual of practice for experienced and would-be publishers.

Anthony Blond, THE PUBLISHING GAME, Jonathan Cape, 1971 (bibliography, glossary of terms).

A highly individual, even idiosyncratic view of the trade by one of its practitioners, the appendixes on some London publishers and literary agents are particularly revealing, giving a personal view of the type of establishment and personalities to be found there.

BOWKER LECTURES ON PUBLISHING, Bowker, New York, 1957.

This has informative articles on such aspects of publishing practice as textbooks, subscription books, book clubs, copyright and the paperbound book in America.

Andrew Dakers, PUBLISHING, Hale, 1961.

This is intended for school leavers; the chapter on training is now out of date, since it was written before provisions for training had been made under the Industrial Training Act. It appends a list of members of the Publishers' Association.

Robert Escarpit, THE BOOK REVOLUTION, Harrap, London, and UNESCO, Paris, English edition, 1966 (tables and diagrams).

This chronicles and assesses the important changes in the publishing world in the last few decades, as newspapers, radio, films and television increasingly compete with books as mass information media.

Chandler B. Grannis, editor, WHAT HAPPENS IN BOOK PUBLISHING, *With Contributions by Twenty-one Leaders in the Book Industry*, Columbia University Press, New York, and O.U.P., London, 1957 (bibliographies at chapter ends).

This survey of operations in American book publishing is, in many respects, equally relevant for the young English publisher. It covers steps in book trade publishing, rights, business management, distribution of (American) books abroad, special publishing such as children's, religious, technical, university presses, paperbacks and book clubs.

Gerald Gross, editor, PUBLISHERS ON PUBLISHING, Grosset & Bowker and Dunlap, New York, 1961, and Secker & Warburg, London, 1962.

This consists of thirty-six articles by well-known publishers on both sides of the Atlantic, many drawn from material published elsewhere in book form.

Sydney Hyde, SALES ON A SHOESTRING, *How to Advertise Books*, André Deutsch, 1956 (illustrated, prologue by Sir Allen Lane, epilogue by William Foyle, chapter on selling books in the United States by Tom W. Boardman, Jr.).

This is the only book on book advertising, now somewhat out of date in view of the expansion of world markets since 1956, rising costs, and the changing pattern of hard and paperback publishing.

Michael Joseph, THE ADVENTURE OF PUBLISHING, Wingate, 1949.

This is, like Sir Stanley Unwin's *The Truth About Publishing* (see below), the fruit of long experience. It covers many aspects of publishing including the publisher's relations with literary agents and with the B.B.C.

William Jovanovich, NOW, BARABBAS, Longmans, 1957.

There are essays on the relations between publisher, author and reader.

Walter H. Page, A PUBLISHER'S CONFESSION, *With an Introduction by F. N. Doubleday*, William Heinemann, 1924 (articles first published in the *Boston Transcript*, 1905).

The sum of Walter Page's experience is the quizzical thought: 'The wonder is (and in my mind it grows every year) how the publishers of books make enough money to keep their shops going. . . . See what a long series of processes, or adventures, if you will, a book must go through between the writer and the reader; every step costs money; and the utmost possible profit is small.' This work has long been superseded in America as here, but has a personal charm that warrants its inclusion.

Datus C. Smith, A GUIDE TO BOOK PUBLISHING, Bowker, New York and London, 1966 (bibliography).

This contains sections on the economics of publishing, editing the manuscript, production, promotion, kinds of book publishing, etc. It cites American book publishing practice, but is equally useful to the young English publisher or reader seeking information on what goes on in publishing.

Sir Stanley Unwin, THE TRUTH ABOUT PUBLISHING, George Allen & Unwin, 1st edition, 1926, 7th edition revised, 1960.

This has been translated into many languages (the N.B.L. library possesses twelve foreign-language versions ranging from French to Japanese). There are chapters on: the arrival of manuscripts, 'casting off' and estimating, the price of books, agreements, production, selling, book distribution on the Continent, publicity, copyright and rights, 'other aspects' which include stock-taking, titles, series, censorship, valuation for probate, and 'publishing as a profession'. There are appendixes on organisations connected with the book world, a copy of the Net Book Agreement, proof reader's marks, and the schedule of a book publisher's working expenses. Although out of date on financial and even organisational details, ignoring the new trend towards large groupings, it has not been superseded, perhaps because it incorporates the lifelong experience of one of the great figures in twentieth-century publishing.

3. Technical and Educational Publishing

TEXTBOOKS IN EDUCATION, *A Report from the American Textbook Publishers Institute to Its Membership, Its Friends, and Others whose Interest in the Development of the Educational System in the United States Goes Beyond a Mere Passing Fancy*, American Publishers Institute, New York, 1949.

This is the only book on the subject, out of date and American.

Whitaker, TECHNICAL BOOKS IN PRINT, annual.

This lists the latest publications by category.

4. University Publishing
(See also individual houses listed under 'The History of Publishing' above.)

Again, the books on the subject are American or Canadian:

Eleanor Harman, editor, THE UNIVERSITY AS PUBLISHER, University of Toronto Press, Toronto, 1961.

This is a collection of articles by members of the Press's staff on aspects of university publishing such as scholarly journals, editorial function, selling, printing of mathematics, 'a bookstore on the campus'. Although the articles all relate to the Toronto Press, much of the information is of general interest.

Rush Welter, PROBLEMS OF SCHOLARLY PUBLICATION IN THE HUMANI-TIES AND SOCIAL SCIENCES, *A Report for the Committee on Scholarly Publication*, American Council of Learned Societies, New York, 1959.

This small book deals with the publication of scholarly books with small potential sale and scholarly journals. There are appendixes on university presses.

5. Paperback Publishing
(See also 'Penguin Books', p. 345 and 'Victor Weybright', p. 361 under XIIIA. THE HISTORY OF PUBLISHING.)

Some consider that the paperback revolution, or explosion, as it is variously called, had its roots in the cheap railway literature and popular books for the education of the masses, of the nineteenth century. Others go even farther back in time to the small books for the saddle bag that Aldus Manutius issued in sixteenth-century Venice. Most would agree that the revolution really began in 1935 when Sir Allen Lane thought of producing books 'that would be bought as easily and casually as a packet of cigarettes', and the first ten Penguin titles were published (see also under 'Penguin Books', p. 345 above). Paperback publishing has become very important since then (over 33,000 titles were in print in this country in 1971) and yet there are few books on the subject, and few detailed statistics.

Desmond Flower, THE PAPERBACK, *Its Past, Present and Future*, Arbor-field, 1959.

This paper read to the Double Crown Club is useful, readable but naturally somewhat out of date.

J. E. Morpurgo, PAPERBACK ACROSS FRONTIERS, Bowater, 1960.

This pamphlet, by the former Director of the National Book League, defines terms and discusses the origins of the paperback.

F. L. Schick, THE PAPER BOUND BOOK IN AMERICA, Bowker, New York, 1958.

This American book is the only full-sized work on paperbacks. Some of it is relevant to British publishing, but British authors are still nearly always published in hardback first whereas many good selling American authors never achieve the dignity of hardcovers.

6. Directories and Reference Books

Book Centre, BOOK CENTRE LTD. *Services for the Book Trade, Parcels Clearing, Book Deliveries (London), Packing and Dispatch, Orders Clearing, Overseas Booksellers Clearing House (OBCH), Publishers' Accounts Clearing House (PACH),* 1965.

BOOKSELLERS' ASSOCIATION DIRECTORY OF BRITISH PUBLISHERS, 1st edition, 1900, 3rd edition, 1967.

THE BOWKER ANNUAL *of Library and Book Trade Information,* edited by **Phyllis B. Steckler,** Bowker, New York and London.

This is a mine of information on libraries and publishers in the United States, trade statistics, law, important people and much besides.

CASSELL'S DIRECTORY OF PUBLISHING, *in Great Britain, the Commonwealth, Ireland and South Africa,* Cassell, 1st edition, 1963, 7th edition, 1970.

This is divided into two parts, the first, on the publishing and promotion of books, lists book publishers, overseas representatives, British publishers classified by field of activity, societies and associations of interest to publishers, prizes, a calendar of trade events, a bibliography of periodicals and reference books concerning the book trade, etc. Part 2, *Representatives and Services,* has sections on agents, photographic agencies, translators, editorial and research services, indexing services, press cutting services and many others.

CLEGG'S DIRECTORY OF THE WORLD'S BOOK TRADE, Clarke, annual, 1950.

This has sections on British book publishers, overseas booksellers and publishers, and trade associations throughout the world.

LITERARY MARKET PLACE 1971–72, Bowker, New York, 1971.

This annual directory of American book publishers includes agents, book clubs, courses for the book trade, literary awards, paper mills, translators, writers' conferences and much else as well as publishers' names and addresses.

MASON'S PUBLISHERS, *An Annotated Directory of the Publishing Trade*, 3rd edition revised, Mason, 1971.

This covers some of the same ground as the above, indicates number of titles published by each publisher, subsidiary or associated companies, or parent or holding company of those many firms now linked together.

Publishers Association, BOOK DISTRIBUTION, *A Handbook*, P.A., 1961.

This gives details of reference works, the work of the N.B.L., ways and means of ordering books, information on invoicing delivery, and methods of settling accounts. Now somewhat out of date, since the imposition by most publishers of handling charges which rise steeply on single copy orders.

PUBLISHERS' INTERNATIONAL YEAR BOOK, *World Directory of Book Publishers*, 4th edition, Wales, 1966.

Taubert, Sigfred, editor, THE BOOK TRADE OF THE WORLD, Vol. 1: Europe and International Section, André Deutsch, 1972.

Whitaker, PUBLISHERS IN THE UNITED KINGDOM AND THEIR ADDRESSES, Whitaker, annual.

This now gives the standard book numbers of each publisher as well as address and telephone number.

Whitaker, BRITISH BOOKS IN PRINT, *The Reference Catalogue of Current Literature*, Whitaker, annual.

This is preceded by a comprehensive list of British publishers and their addresses (see also under III. BOOKSELLING, p. 71).

7. Trade Associations

ASSOCIATION OF MAIL ORDER PUBLISHERS (founded 1970)

This has been founded to establish a code of practice (see *Bookseller* October 24, 1970, pp. 2158–60)

THE BOOK DEVELOPMENT COUNCIL (B.D.C.) (founded 1965)

This aims to foster the spread of British books overseas. It became part of the Publishers Association, July 1969, taking over such matters as assistance to students and teachers in the developing countries through the English Language Society Low-priced Book Scheme, assistance to overseas book trades by training schemes, research into overseas markets for books, the organising of exhibitions and of a computerised mailing service.

THE BOOK PUBLISHERS' REPRESENTATIVES ASSOCIATION (B.P.R.A.) (founded 1924)

THE INDEPENDENT PUBLISHERS' GUILD (I.P.G.) (founded 1963)

This seeks the means of reducing production costs for the smaller publisher and improving distribution through collaboration in bulk paper buying and the like. A MONTHLY BULLETIN is issued to members

THE PUBLISHERS ASSOCIATION (founded 1896)

This was the result of the struggle for fixed discounts to booksellers (see IX. 'NET BOOK AGREEMENT'. pp. 219 ff. above). It regulates conditions of employment in the trade and gives the means for publishers to deal collectively. Its training department helps publishers to fulfil their obligations under the Industrial Training Act. Its publications include A GUIDE TO ROYALTY AGREEMENTS, PHOTOCOPYING AND THE LAW, and GETTING INTO PUBLISHING. It now incorporates the *Book Development Council* (see above).

THE PUBLISHERS PUBLICITY CIRCLE

This is a club confined to members of the Publishers Association which meets at irregular intervals for discussion of topics of interest to members.

SOCIETY OF INDEXERS

Aims to raise the standard of indexing and the status of indexers by maintaining a panel of indexers on which authors, editors and publishers can draw, and by advising on remuneration. The Society publishes a journal, the INDEXER.

THE SOCIETY OF YOUNG PUBLISHERS (founded 1949)

Younger members of the trade (those under thirty-five on joining) meet to discuss trade matters and hear papers from distinguished book trade figures. Members must have had at least one year's book trade experience and belong to a firm that is a member of the Publishers Association.

ABBREVIATIONS USED IN TEXT

A.A.L.	Association of Assistant Librarians
A.B.A.	Antiquarian Booksellers' Association
A.L.P.	Association of Little Presses
B.A.R.	BOOK AUCTION RECORDS
B.D.C.	Book Development Council
B.F.M.P.	British Federation of Master Printers
B.N.B.	British National Bibliography
B.R.P.A.	Book Publishers' Representatives Association
B.S.I.	British Standards Institute
C.B.I.	Cumulative Book Index
C.B.L.	Cumulative Book List
C.U.P.	Cambridge University Press
E.U.P.	English Universities Press
G.K.D.W./G.K.W.	GESAMTKATALOG DER WIEGENDRUCKE
H.M.S.O.	Her Majesty's Stationary Office
I.B.B.Y.	International Board on Books for Young People
I.P.E.X.	International Printing Machinery and Allied Trades Exhibition
I.P.G.	Independent Publishers' Guild
I.Y.L.	International Youth Library
N.B.L.	National Book League
O.C.E.L.	OXFORD COMPANION TO ENGLISH LITERATURE
O.U.P.	Oxford University Press
P.A.	Publishers Association
P.A.G.A.	PRINTING AND GRAPHIC ARTS
P.A.T.R.A.	Packaging and Allied Trades Association
P.I.R.A.	Printing Industry Research Association
P.L.A.	Private Libraries Association
P.L.R.	Public Lending Right
S.o.A.	Society of Authors
S.P.C.K.	Society for the Promotion of Christian Knowledge
S.T.C.	A SHORT TITLE CATALOGUE OF BOOKS PRINTED IN ENGLAND, SCOTLAND AND IRELAND (Pollard and Redgrave)
T.L.S.	TIMES LITERARY SUPPLEMENT
Wing	A SHORT TITLE CATALOGUE OF BOOKS PRINTED IN ENGLAND, SCOTLAND, IRELAND, WALES AND BRITISH AMERICA . . .

ANALYTICAL INDEX OF NAMES AND TITLES

(Titles of books and periodicals in italics)

History of the Book Trade in the North East, 291
History of the Book War, 224
History of the Cambridge University Press, 271
History of the Catnach Press, 272
History of the English-Speaking Peoples, 337
History of the Horn-Book (Folmsbee), 176
History of the Horn Books (Tuer), 178
History of the Left Book Club, 340
History of the Legal Deposit of Books, 207
History of the Newbery and Caldecott Medals, 192
History of the Old English Letter Founders, 260,
    272, 275
History of Printing Ink Balls and Rollers, 1440–
    1850, 243
History of the Russian Hand Paper Mills and Their
    Watermarks, 236
History of Wood-Engraving (Bliss), 123
History of Wood-Engraving (Woodberry), 125
Hitchcock, Frederick H., 5, 8, 59, 81
Hlavsa, Oldrich, 259
Hoare, Colt, 313
Hobbs, Anne, 180
Hobson, A. R. A., 25, 27, 31, 81
Hobson, G. D., 25, 27, 28, 32, 33, 37
Hodgson and Co., 78, 81
Hodgson, Sidney, 57
Hodnett, Edward, 124
Hodson, James Shirley, 146
Hodson, T., 142
Hodson, W. H., 165, 166
Hoe, Robert, 28
Hofer, Philip, 138
Hogarth, Grace, xi
Hogarth Press, 337, 341
Hogarth, William, 134
Hold Your Tongue!, 217
Hollis and Carter, 335
Hollister, Paul, 62, 222
Holme, Geoffrey, 137
Holmes, C. J., 347
Holmes, R. R., 36
Holt, Henry, 358
Holt Rinehart and Winston, 358
Holtzapffel, Charles, 296
Hood, Thomas, 201, 208, 348
Hooper, Horace E., 222
Hopkins, Gerard, 133
Horn Book Magazine, 187
Hornby, C. H. St. John, 317
Horne, Herbert P., 28
Horne, T. H., 99
Horrocks, Sydney, 315
Horton, Carolyn, 51
Hostettler, Rudolf, 303
Houghton, Arthur Boyd, 134
Houghton Mifflin Co., 358
House of Appleton-Century, 356

House of Bemrose, 269
House of Blackwood, 352
House of Cassell, 336
House of Collins, 354
House of Dent 1888–1938, 338
House of Harper (Exman), 357
House of Harper (Harper), 358
House of Harrison, 280
House of Kitcat, 34
House of Longman 1724–1800, 342
House of Longman 1724–1924, 342
House of Macmillan, 343
House of Menzies, 62
House of Pitman, 346
House of Routledge, 14, 347
House of Stokes 1881–1926, 360
House of Warne, 350
House of Words, 338–9
Housman, A. E., 346
Housman, Laurence, 134
Howard, G. Wren, 336
Howard, Michael S., 336
Howe, Ellic, 33, 34, 287, 305, 306, 307
How To Become An Author, 6
How To Find Out about Children's Literature,
    174, 177, 188
How To Obtain British Books, 72
How To Plan Print, 115
Hoy, Peter, 316
Hughes, Thomas, 342
Hugo, Thomas, 125, 126
Hullmandel, C., 142
Hume, David, 288
Humphreys, Charles, 61
Humphreys, Henry Noel, 250
Hundred and Fifty Years of Publishing, 354
Hundred Years of Progress, 307
Hundred Years of Publishing, 337
Hunt, Leigh, 352
Hunter, Dard, 231, 233, 234
Hunt Roman: the Birth of a Type, 290
Hurlimann, Bettina, 177, 184
Hutchings, Ernest A. B., 294
Hutchings, R. S., 259, 264, 300
Hutchins, Michael, 114
Hutchinson Group, 353
Huth, Henry, 84
Hulton, William, 61
Huxley, Aldous, 253
Hyams, John, 70
Hyde, H. Montgomery, 215
Hyde, Sydney, 367

I Am a Communicator, 289
Iconography of Stephen Gooden, 134
I Could a Tale Unfold, 177
IFLA News, 187